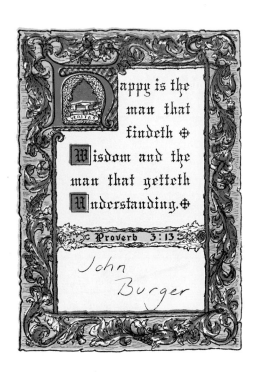

TELL EL-HESI

The Site and the Expedition

Dedicated to the Memory of
Harry Thomas Frank
1933-1980

AMERICAN SCHOOLS OF ORIENTAL RESEARCH
EXCAVATION REPORTS

edited by
Eric M. Meyers

The Joint Archaeological Expedition
to Tell el-Hesi

Volume Four

Tell el-Hesi

The Site and the Expedition

edited by

Bruce T. Dahlberg and Kevin G. O'Connell, S.J.

with contributions by
John W. Betlyon — Jeffrey A. Blakely
Michael D. Coogon — †H. Thomas Frank
Fred L. Horton, Jr. — Frank L. Koucky
†John M. Matthers — Kevin G. O'Connell, S.J.
†D. Glenn Rose — Robert B. Stewart
Lawrence E. Toombs — John E. Worrell

Eisenbrauns
Winona Lake, Indiana

Publications of
The Joint Archaeological Expedition
to Tell el-Hesi

Vol. 1 *The Tell el-Hesi Field Manual*, by Jeffrey A. Blakely and Lawrence E. Toombs. American Schools of Oriental Research, 1980.

Vol. 2. *Tell el-Hesi: Modern Military Trenching and Muslim Cemetery in Field I. Strata I-II*, by Lawrence E. Toombs. Wilfrid Laurier University Press, 1985.

Vol. 3. *Tell el-Hesi: The Persian Period (Stratum V)*, by W. J. Bennett, Jr., and Jeffrey A. Blakely. Eisenbrauns, 1989.

Vol. 4. *Tell el-Hesi: The Site and the Expedition*, edited by Bruce T. Dahlberg and Kevin G. O'Connell, S.J., Eisenbrauns, 1989.

Library of Congress Cataloging-in-Publication Data

(Revised for vol. 4)

Blakely, Jeffrey A., 1953–
    The Joint Archaeological Expedition to Tell el-Hesi.

    (Excavation reports)
    Vol. 4   has imprint: Winona Lake, Ind.: Eisenbrauns.
    Includes bibliographical references.
    Contents: v. 1. The Tell el-Hesi field manual   v. 2. Tell el-Hesi: modern military trenching and Muslim cemetery in field I, strata I-II   v. 4. Tell el-Hesi: the site and the expedition / edited by Bruce T. Dahhberg and Kevin G. O'Connell, S.J., with contributions by John W. Betlyon. . . [et al.].
    1. Hasi Site (Israel). 2. Excavations (Archaeology)   Middle East. 3. Archaeology Methodology. I. Toombs, Lawrence E., joint author. II. O'Connell, S.J., Kevin G. III. Title. IV. Series.

DS110.T4B58   930.1'028   80-21724
ISBN 0-89757-203-3 (v. 1. : pbk.)

ISBN 0-931464-54-4 (v. 3)
ISBN 0-931464-57-9 (v. 4)

CONTENTS

Part I: The Site

Part IV: Particular Reports

TABLES

FIGURES

ABBREVIATIONS

A	articulated (skeleton)	MB	Middle Bronze
Aeg	Aegean	MB 1	Middle Bronze 1
Ar.	artifacts, objects	MB 2	Middle Bronze 2
Arab	Arabic	MB 2A	Middle Bronze 2A
Ass	Assyrian	MB 2B	Middle Bronze 2B
Bot.	botanical (remains)	MC	material culture
BP	before the present	MCR	material culture registry
bs	body sherd	mm.	millimeter(s)
Byz	Byzantine	mort.	mortaria
C	to be coded	mos.	months
ca.	circa, about	Myc	Mycenaean
Chal	Chalcolithic	N	North
cm.	centimeter(s)	na	not available
Cyp	Cypriot	NA	neutron activation
D	(1) disarticulated (bones)	NE	Northeast
	(2) to be drawn	no(s).	number(s)
Dispo.	disposition	nr	not recorded
E	East	NR	not registered
EB	Early Bronze	ns	not saved
EB 1	Early Bronze 1	NS	North-South
EB 2	Early Bronze 2	NW	Northwest
EB 3	Early Bronze 3	OR	object registry
EB 3A	Early Bronze 3A	Osteo.	osteological (samples), human and animal
EB 3B	Early Bronze 3B		bones
EB 4	Early Bronze 4	Ot	other
e.g.	for example	PA	articulated partial (skeleton)
EW	East-West	Pers	Persian
ext	exterior	Phil	Philistine
fig(s).	figure(s)	pl(s).	plate(s)
freq	frequency	PR	pottery registry
Geol.	geological (samples), stone	R	to be registered
Hell	Hellenistic	Rom	Roman
H 70 (etc.)	Hesi 1970 (etc.)	rt	right
i.d.	insufficient data	S	South
i.e.	that is	SE	Southeast
imp	import	Spec	specialist ('s/s/s')
int	interior	SW	Southwest
I1, I2	Iron 1, Iron 2 (field forms only)	ua	unassigned
km.	kilometer(s)	ud, UD	undetermined
LB	Late Bronze	UK	unknown
LB 1	Late Bronze 1	ur	unregistered
LB 2	Late Bronze 2	UR	unreported
LB 2A	Late Bronze 2A	us	unstratified
LB 2B	Late Bronze 2B	viz.	namely
lt	left	Vt	vertical
m.	meter(s)	W	West
m²	square meter(s)	yrs.	years
Mal.	malacological (samples), shell		
	(including snails)		

EDITORS' PREFACE

Tell el-Hesi is an ancient site about an hour's drive southwest of Jerusalem, 23 km. from the Mediterranean, 26 km. northeast of Gaza, and only 7 km. southwest of the modern city of Qiryat Gat. Situated on a low plateau on the west bank of the Wadi Hesi (Nahal Shiqma), the tell includes a twenty-five-acre walled city dating from the mid-third millennium BCE (Early Bronze III Period) with a small acropolis in its northeast corner. The acropolis and some sections of the EB III city wall are on higher ground formed by ancient sand dunes. There had been some occupation prior to the EB III city, but the precise extent and duration are still unclear (see Chapter IX for a report on Chalcolithic remains found in Field III). The EB III city itself came to an end after a century or two of life, and the site lay abandoned for eight hundred to a thousand years. The beginnings of reoccupation in the second half of the second millennium BCE (Late Bronze and Iron I Periods) are still only scantily known, but by the ninth century BCE (Iron II Period) the small acropolis had become the object of major reconstruction. Altogether, it was used and reused more or less continuously for close to a thousand years, until the Hellenistic Period brought a wider political and cultural continuity that made it unnecessary to maintain a border post or garrison at the Hesi site. It was abandoned once again, except for traces of Arabic agricultural activity, until the higher ground served as a cemetery for a Muslim village or tribe, probably during the seventeenth and eighteenth centuries of modern times. After yet another abandonment, the site was partially excavated in the late nineteenth century (see Chapter II) and subsequently fortified by the Israeli army in the mid-twentieth century.

After a brief survey of the site in 1969, the Joint Archaeological Expedition to Tell el-Hesi, sponsored by the American Schools of Oriental Research and a consortium of educational institutions, had its first field season in June 1970 and returned to the site for further excavation in the summers of odd-numbered years. The first four seasons (1970–75) have been designated Phase One, and the next four seasons (1977–83) Phase Two. The first phase was largely limited to the later occupation levels on the summit and southern slope of the site's northeast hill or acropolis, although there were also probes and limited exploration of the larger Early Bronze city. In Phase Two, work continued in the Iron Age levels of the acropolis, and extensive excavation began in the southern EB city wall and associated domestic structures. At the conclusion of Phase Two in 1983, the expedition staff had largely completed the preparation of Phase One results for final publication and was ready to begin the final publication of Phase Two's Iron II and Early Bronze remains (together with remains from later strata that were uncovered in the new fields of Phase Two).

TELL EL-HESI: The Site and the Expedition is one of several volumes primarily devoted to Phase One in the expedition's series of final publications. However, several chapters look beyond the 1975 season and include additional information gained during Phase Two, and the small article reprinted as Chapter XII deals with a lone epigraphic find from the 1977 season.

Although the various volumes in this series have different publishers, every effort is being made to preserve a unified format and external appearance. The volumes currently completed or in final stages of composition have been accepted by the American Schools of Oriental Research (ASOR) as a special group within its series of Excavation Reports, and we hope that subsequent volumes will also be permitted to bear that designation. The editors wish to express the gratitude of the Hesi staff to ASOR Presidents G. Ernest Wright (the originator and guiding mentor of the Hesi project until his untimely death in 1974), Frank M. Cross, Philip J. King, and James A. Sauer; to ASOR Vice Presidents David Noel Freedman, William G. Dever, Eric M. Meyers, and Edward F. Campbell, Jr.; and to all other members of the ASOR staff.

In a particular way we wish to single out Mrs. Helen D. Estey, whose devoted service in the Cambridge office of ASOR until her retirement in 1982 was deeply appreciated by all who had the good fortune to deal with her.

The work of the Joint Expedition would not be possible without generous contributions of time, energy, and financial resources from many individuals and institutions. First and most important, although they cannot be listed individually here, are the many dedicated archaeologists, scientific specialists, and others who have served for varying periods of time on the Hesi staff, and the hundreds of students and others who have come to join us in the field as members of the volunteer program. Staff and volunteers for all four seasons of Phase One are mentioned or listed in Chapter VI and Chapter V, respectively. Both staff and volunteers have served at Hesi at great personal expense, and their shared spirit of generosity and dedication to a common task has done much to make a difficult and often tedious operation exciting and attractive. The countless hours of contributed services in and out of the field, the travel costs paid by so many participants, and the hefty volunteer fees since 1973 together constitute the largest contribution to the total Hesi budget. Without that contribution, neither this volume nor the Hesi operation itself would have been possible.

A second major source of support for the Hesi expedition has been the financial contributions from the academic institutions comprising the Hesi consortium for one or more seasons. In addition to Oberlin College, which has been a member of the consortium from the first season to the present, the following institutions were members of the consortium for the seasons indicated: Ashland Theological Seminary (1973), Central State University in Oklahoma (1981), CHERS: Consortium for Higher Education—Religious Studies (1975), College of the Holy Cross (1975, 1977), General Theological Seminary (1973), Golden Gate Baptist Theological Seminary (1983), Hartford Seminary Foundation (1970, 1971), John Carroll University (1981, 1983), Oklahoma State University (1979, 1981), Phillips University (1981), Seabury-Western Theological Seminary (1973, 1975, 1977), Smith College (1975, 1977, 1979, 1981, 1983), The Protestant Episcopal Theological Seminary in Virginia (1975, 1977, 1979, 1981, 1983), The University of Oklahoma (1981), Trinity Lutheran Seminary (1975, 1977, 1979, 1981, 1983), Wake

Forest University (1977, 1979, 1981, 1983), Wartburg Theological Seminary (1979, 1981, 1983), and Wilfrid Laurier University (1973, 1975, 1977, 1979, 1981, 1983). Many of these institutions also made financial and other contributions to the work of the Joint Expedition either in addition to their consortium payments or for seasons during which they were not consortium members.

In particular, Wilfrid Laurier University has generously provided staff time, equipment, and archival facilities for the expedition's photographic work and has made its computers available for analysis of data and for manuscript preparation. Golden Gate Baptist Theological Seminary has provided full funding for the expedition's newsletter, *Trowel and Patish*. Smith College and John Carroll University have given reductions in teaching load and considerable computer time to the two editors for final preparation of the manuscripts in the present volume. Wake Forest University has provided the valuable services of University Editors Martha W. Lentz and Jeanne P. Whitman, Editorial Assistant Adele LaBrecque, Supervisor of Publications Teresa B. Grogan, as well as considerable financial subsidy for the volume's publication as a memorial tribute to the University's distinguished alumnus, Dr. Harry Thomas Frank, who had served as director of the expedition's educational and volunteer program from its inception until his untimely death in 1980.

Other institutions also providing support to the Joint Expedition for one or more seasons include Christian Theological Seminary, EARTHWATCH: The Center for Field Research, Harvard Divinity School's Research Team for Religion and Culture in the Aegean in New Testament Times, Harvard Semitic Museum, and Weston School of Theology. Much of the initial editing for manuscripts in the present volume was done by Kevin O'Connell from 1977 through 1980, while he was on the faculty at Weston and could draw extensively on the school's resources to support the work.

Further major support was received by way of grants from The Smithsonian Institution (1970–73), The National Endowment for the Humanities (1973–76), and the Canada Council (1971). In addition, a number of contributions were received from private donors each season. For all of this important financial support and the encouragement which it has brought with it, the Joint Expedition once again expresses public thanks.

It is appropriate to thank here the successive Directors of the Department of Antiquities for the

State of Israel, Avraham Biran and Avi Eitan, and their staffs for their constant encouragement and ready assistance over the past eight seasons. The directors of the Albright Institute of Archaeological Research (AIAR) in Jerusalem (David Noel Freedman, Robert J. Bull, William G. Dever, Eric M. Meyers, Albert E. Glock, and Seymour Gitin) and the AIAR staff have always provided a warm welcome and much-appreciated work space during the summers in the field. In recent years the Pontifical Biblical Institute has made crucial storage space available to the Joint Expedition between seasons, and its hospitable superiors (Fr. Francis Furlong, S.J., and Fr. William Dalton, S.J.) have made many of the Hesi staff feel welcome within the walls. Our technical men from Balata, Nasser Diab Mansur (Abu 'Issa) and Jabber Muhammad Hasan (Abu 'Abid) have made notable contributions in the field and have been our most valuable instructors. Samir Khayo of Beit Hanina has helped in many ways with the successful operation of the tent city at the site. Many other residents of Jerusalem, the West Bank, and the Qiryat Gat region have served in support positions in the field or have provided us with advice and assistance in other ways. Even though we cannot list all their names here, each is remembered with gratitude and respect by Hesi personnel.

Among those at Smith College who helped in the preparation of the final manuscript, special thanks are due to Louise Zimmer (who typed the text of several chapters onto the computer's word-processing program) and to the staff of the College's Academic Computer Center. Most especially do we express our deep appreciation for the active support of Dr. Jill Conway during her tenure as President of Smith College, and for that of Dean Frances Volkmann. Their many practical encouragements, including generous provision for a faculty member's temporary part-time release from teaching duties, contributed significantly to the completion of this project.

At John Carroll University, special thanks are due to Fr. Emmanuel Carreira, S.J. (who rephotographed several difficult illustrations and made them publishable), Donald Grazko and John Bell of the Computer Center staff, and President Thomas P. O'Malley, S.J., and other members of the University administration.

Many members of the Hesi staff reviewed and commented upon one or more manuscripts that are included in the volume. Particular thanks are due to past and present members of the expedition's editorial committee: W. J. Bennett, Jr.; Valerie M. Fargo; Frank L. Koucky; D. Glenn Rose; Lawrence E. Toombs; and John E. Worrell. Those whose suggestions have been accepted will easily recognize that fact, but all should know that their comments were taken very seriously by the individual authors and by the editors. Except where otherwise noted, all figures are the work of the authors. Any deficiencies that remain are the sole responsibility of the respective authors or of the editors.

Thanks are due to Melanie Robbins for the cover drawing for this volume.

It is with deep gratitude to the academic community at Wake Forest University (and especially President Thomas K. Hearn, Jr.; Provost Edwin G. Wilson; Professor E. Willard Hamrick; and Professor Fred L. Horton) for their generous support of this memorial volume, that the authors and editors join in dedicating *TELL EL-HESI: The Site and the Expedition* to the memory of our beloved friend and colleague, Harry Thomas Frank. May his work and his vision continue to bear fruit in the Hesi program and in the lives of all whom he influenced. We are happy and grateful to count ourselves among those who knew and loved him.

Bruce T. Dahlberg, Smith College
Kevin G. O'Connell, S.J., Le Moyne College
1 July 1988

INTRODUCTION

by
Kevin G. O'Connell, S.J.
Le Moyne College

Although its ancient name remains unknown, the site of Tell el-Hesi has a secure place in the history of archaeology. It was there, in 1890, that Sir William Flinders Petrie conducted the first truly scientific excavation in Palestine, followed by the complete examination of all occupation levels in the northeast quadrant of the site's acropolis from 1891 through 1892 by Frederick Jones Bliss, both under the sponsorship of the Palestine Exploration Fund, based in London. Petrie's initial identification of the site with biblical Lachish proved unfounded, but no alternate identification has won full acceptance. Petrie and Bliss published final reports on their findings in 1891 and 1894, respectively, and the site returned to an obscurity that was punctuated by army fortification in 1948 and perhaps during World War I.

Archaeologists often referred to the importance of the work done by Petrie and Bliss, and their pottery chronology and stratigraphic analyses continued to be influential, but it was only in 1969 that serious consideration was given to renewed excavation at the site. From 1970 through 1983, the Joint Archaeological Expedition to Tell el-Hesi has conducted a total of eight seasons of excavation at the site, in two four-season phases (1970–75 and 1977–83). The present volume is one of several devoted to Phase One (1970–75) in the expedition's publication series.

The initial volume in the Hesi series was *The Tell el-Hesi Field Manual* (Blakely and Toombs 1980), which provided both an introduction to the procedures in use in the field and an exposition of the rationale underlying those procedures. The second volume in the series (Toombs 1985) is a detailed study of the Muslim cemetery (Stratum II) and the later Israeli military trenching (Stratum I) in Field I (directly south of "Bliss's Cut" on the acropolis), as these latest levels were known at the conclusion of Phase One in 1975.

The next volume of Phase One in the Hesi series (Bennett and Blakely 1989) analyzes the Persian remains (Stratum V) on the acropolis and deals in detail with the stratigraphy, pottery, and material-culture remains of the five Persian substrata that have been identified at the site (VA, Vb_1, Vb_2, Vc, Vd).

Fragmentary remains from an Arabic agricultural phase antecedent to the Muslim cemetery and from the Hellenistic Period were also discovered during Phase One. They have been reported in the expedition's various preliminary publications, but they are too limited and fragmentary to receive final publication at this time. As research continues on the remains from all periods at the site, the staff anticipates arriving at conclusions about the Hellenistic materials that will warrant further publication as part of a later volume in the series. It is not clear that it will ever be possible to say much more about the late Arabic agricultural remains in Stratum III.

The present volume, *TELL EL-HESI: The Site and the Expedition*, was conceived as a place where background studies and briefer analyses of particular finds could conveniently be drawn together under one cover. While the scope of the final product is somewhat broader than originally planned, the initial purpose has been retained.

The articles in this volume have all been written by members of the Hesi staff. They have held a variety of positions within the expedition's organizational chart, and some have had primary responsibility for the organization and operation of the entire project. While three are deceased (H. Thomas Frank, John M. Matthers, and D. Glenn Rose) and one retains no active involvement in the project (John E. Worrell), the others all continue to have staff and/or publication responsibilities with the expedition.

The chapters that follow are grouped under four

1

headings. Part I, "The Site," includes contributions by the expedition's geologist, Dr. Frank L. Koucky of the College of Wooster, on the present and past physical environment that shaped the region and conditioned the different periods of settlement at Hesi, and by the late Fr. John M. Matthers, who served as a field supervisor at Hesi in 1973 and 1975 and was subsequently Honorary Secretary of the Palestine Exploration Fund. Matthers was able to draw on previously unpublished correspondence by Petrie and Bliss to provide a fresh account of their late-19th-century excavations at Hesi and a correlation between their results and current investigations by the Joint Expedition.

Part II, "Formative Influences on the Expedition," treats three factors that combined to shape the present expedition. Dr. John E. Worrell of Sturbridge Village Foundation, the project director at Hesi during most of Phase One, recounts the initial goals and plans of the founding staff, traces their developing insights into the task, and describes their revised assessments by the 1975 season. His account makes clear the debt of the Hesi project to its immediate predecessors at Shechem and Gezer, in particular, while also drawing attention to what was innovative or experimental about the Hesi expedition. The late Dr. D. Glenn Rose of Phillips University, the expedition's second project director, who died suddenly in Jerusalem only days after successfully completing the 1981 field season at Hesi, had prepared a careful assessment of the methods developed in North American archaeology, largely for the investigation of prehistoric remains, and had analyzed their influence on the expedition's work at Hesi. His chapter continues his gentle presence among us and exemplifies one of his own most important contributions to the quality of our expedition. The final chapter in Part II is by the late Dr. H. Thomas Frank of Oberlin College, the director of the volunteer and educational program at Hesi from the first season in 1970 until his untimely death in the Fall of 1980. His chapter had been completed in first draft, but he had not been able to make final revisions, so Dr. Fred L. Horton of Wake Forest University, a member of the Hesi staff since the 1977 season, graciously agreed to review the chapter and make whatever changes proved necessary. The result is a crisp account of the evolving program for participation by students and other volunteers in the context of an organized field school accredited by the project's sponsoring institutions. Members of the Hesi staff recognize

the complications and difficulties consequent on the commitment to a highly organized educational program, but they are convinced that this program is one of the Hesi project's strengths and a significant contribution to the future of archaeology in the region. The inclusion of Tom Frank's chapter and the dedication of this volume to his memory acknowledge our debt to him for all that he did to plant and nurture the volunteer and educational program among us. We continue to draw on his inspiration and rely on his example.

Part III contains two extensive chapters that complement each other. The first was largely prepared by John Worrell as a narrative of each season's work, with the developments that took place between field seasons, from the beginnings of the project through the completion of the 1975 season. Since John had not been in the field in 1975, Glenn Rose had agreed to bring the narrative up through that final season of Phase One. Unfortunately, his death meant that the task remained undone, and Dr. John W. Betlyon of Smith College, a volunteer at Hesi in 1973 and subsequently a member of the Hesi staff, agreed to take up the task. By judicious consultation, he was able to conclude the narrative and see to the revision of the entire chapter. It serves as a valuable record of the expedition's history to the conclusion of Phase One. The other chapter in Part III is an analysis of the stratigraphy at Hesi as it was understood at the end of Phase One, with careful attention to the methodology that undergirds our stratigraphic conclusions. Its author is Dr. Lawrence E. Toombs of Wilfred Laurier University, who served from the start of the current excavations through the 1981 season as Senior Archaeologist (later called the Archaeological Director) for the expedition. While ours is a cooperative venture drawing on the investigations, analyses, and insights of many staff, it is also true to say that the unifying vision and the decisive articulation of conclusions has been particularly the gift of Larry Toombs, and so his discussion of the stratigraphy of the site is an important contribution to this volume.

The remaining five chapters are grouped together in Part IV, "Particular Reports." They include two final reports by Dr. Michael D. Coogan of Stonehill College, a member of the Hesi staff throughout Phase One, on the limited excavations in Field II (a first attempt to find well-preserved remains of the Early Bronze city) and on the Chalcolithic structures uncovered in the course of extensive excavation of the Iron II wall at the base of the acropolis in Field III. The other three chapters reprint articles that had been published earlier in journals, which the editors judged appropriate to the present volume. One is Michael Coogan's final publication of the group of burials from the Persian Period that had been cut into the remains of the Iron II wall in Field III. It was originally published in *Bulletin of the American Schools of Oriental Research* 220 (December 1975), 37–46. The second reprint is by Dr. Robert B. Stewart of Sam Houston State University, the expedition's staff paleoethnobotanist for several seasons, and discusses various aspects of his work at the Hesi site. It first appeared in *Economic Botany* 32 (1978), 379–86. The last reprint in Part IV is by Dr. Kevin G. O'Connell, S.J., formerly of John Carroll University and now President of Le Moyne College, a member of the Hesi staff since he came as a volunteer in 1971, currently chairman of the Board of Directors of the Expedition, and the author of this Introduction. It is a detailed presentation of the only piece of legible writing found at the site since the start of Phase One, a two-line seal impression from the seventh or sixth century BCE whose survival is due to the very fire that destroyed the document it was securing. The article was initially printed in *Israel Exploration Journal* 27 (1977), 197–99 and pl. 26. The editors wish to express their gratitude to the editors of those three journals for their kind permission to republish the respective articles.

After a brief conclusion to the series of twelve chapters, the volume includes a complete bibliography of publications on Tell el-Hesi through 1982 plus selected later items. It lists both primary and secondary publications and is not limited to Phase One or even to the work of the current expedition. This research tool was prepared by Mr. Jeffrey A. Blakely of the University of Pennsylvania, who has been associated with Hesi since 1971 and has served as a field supervisor since 1979.

Since the Editors' Preface has already acknowledged the many contributions made to the Hesi Project by funding agencies, sponsoring institutions, dedicated staff, generous volunteers, indispensable support personnel, and all who offered encouragement and criticism over the years, it remains only to invite you to join or rejoin our venture by plunging into the various chapters that follow. I hope you will find as much enjoyment and profit in the reading as we did in the work and in the writing.

BIBLIOGRAPHY

Bennett, W. J., Jr., and Blakely, J. A.
   1989   *Tell el-Hesi: The Persian Period (Stratum V)*. Edited by K. G. O'Connell, S.J., with F. L. Horton, Jr. Excavation Reports of the American Schools of Oriental Research: Tell el-Hesi 3. Winona Lake, IN: Eisenbrauns.
Blakely, J. A., and Toombs, L. E.
   1980   *The Tell el-Hesi Field Manual*. Edited by K. G. O'Connell, S.J. Excavation Reports of the American Schools of Oriental Research: Tell el-Hesi 1. Cambridge, MA; 2nd ed. (1983), Philadelphia, PA: American Schools of Oriental Research.
Toombs, L. E.
   1985   *Tell el-Hesi: Modern Military Trenching and Muslim Cemetery in Field I, Strata I–II*. Edited by K. G. O'Connell, S.J. Excavation Reports of the American Schools of Oriental Research: Tell el-Hesi 2. Waterloo, Ontario: Wilfrid Laurier University Press.

Chapter I

THE PRESENT AND PAST PHYSICAL ENVIRONMENT OF TELL EL-HESI, ISRAEL

by
Frank L. Koucky
College of Wooster

At present no ancient name is known for the site that is Tell el-Hesi. The earliest reference to the name Hesi is from the Third Crusade. Beha ed-Din reports that Richard Coeur de Lion rested his troops along the Wadi Hesi on his return (in June 1192) from the capture of ed-Darun (Beha ed-Din 1897: 337). Richard later used the Hesi region as a staging area for his attack on a caravan advancing against him from Egypt (Beha ed-Din 1897: 343).

In the eighteenth century C. F. Volney wrote of a village named Hesi, one that he apparently had not personally visited, but a description of which impressed him enough to record it:

> . . . Seven hours journey from [Beit Jibrin] toward the south-west, is another village of Bedouins, called the Hesi [*sic*], which has in its neighbourhood an artificial square hill, above seventy feet high, one hundred and fifty wide, and two hundred long. The whole ascent to it has been paved, and on its summit we still find the remains of a very strong citadel.
>
> (Volney 1787: II, 337)

If this description corresponds with any site in the region at all, it may be of nearby Tell Sheqef, since Volney's account does not match the condition of Tell el-Hesi as reported by Sir Flinders Petrie when he first visited it a little over a hundred years later.

The following report aims to provide a reliable description of Tell el-Hesi and its region. Beginning with discussions of its geographical location and the general characteristics of regional climate, geological history, paleoclimate, and soil composition, we shall go on to investigate the geomorphic history of the site and provide a descriptive analysis of the various topographical features of Hesi and its immediate environs.

PART I: GENERAL CHARACTERISTICS OF THE HESI REGION

Location of Tell el-Hesi

Tell el-Hesi is not on a major road or near a major city, so its location is difficult to describe. The different types of description that can be used to show various aspects of Hesi's relationship to its surroundings are summarized in table 1.

Site locations are commonly designated in terms of coordinates located on a grid system. Thus Tell el-Hesi can be located on an earth grid system at 34°43′50″ east longitude and 31°32′45″ north latitude. Since longitude lines converge at the North and South Poles and thus are not parallel, the grid established by this system is not truly rectangular. For practical use, therefore, rectangular grids for particular local or regional areas are also established. For the Palestine region the British military kilometric grid system was constructed and appears on modern Israeli maps. In this system Tell el-Hesi is located at 12451063 (read 124.5 east and 106.3 north on the grid; figs. 1 and 2 use this grid). Though both systems give accurate locations, either set of

---

Table 1. The location of Tell el-Hesi according to various conventions.

I. GRID SYSTEMS

A. Latitude and longitude: 31°32′45″N, 34°43′50″E

B. British Military Grid: 10631245

II. GEOGRAPHICAL REFERENCE

A. Relation to major cities: Tell el-Hesi is 17 km. (10.5 English miles; 11 Roman miles) SW of ancient Eleutheropolis (modern Bet Guvrin) and 26 km. (16.5 English miles; 17.5 Roman miles) NE of Gaza.

B. Relation to topographic features: Tell el-Hesi is on the south bank of Nahal Shiqma (also called Wadi Hesi, Wadi Hesy, Wadi Hasy, Wadi Al Hissi, Wadi Simsim, or Wadi el-Jizair) about 23 km. (14.5 mi.) from the Mediterranean Sea, in the valley of el-Jizair.

III. PHYSIOGRAPHIC REGION

Tell el-Hesi is in the SE margin of the coastal plain of Israel (in the Pleshet, or "Plain of the Philistines") near the meeting-line between the Shephelah and the Negev.

IV. POLITICAL REGION IN VARIOUS HISTORICAL PERIODS

A. Late Turkish Period (until 1918): in the Nahit el-Majdel district in the region of Arab el-Jubarat.

B. Crusader Period (1099-1291 CE): in the Kingdom of Jerusalem, near the boundary of the fiefs of St. Abraham and Ascalon.

C. Byzantine Period (324-640 CE): in Palaestina Prima in the Eleutheropolis district.

D. Roman Period (63 BCE - 324 CE): near the boundary of Idumea and Judea.

E. Persian Period (539 - 332 BCE): the fifth Persian satrapy, in Idumea near the boundary with Ashdod and Judea.

F. From the division of the Monarchy to the Babylonian exile (ca. 922 - 586 BCE): in a western hill province of the kingdom of Judah, with the cities of Eglon and Lachish, near the Philistine border.

G. Period of the Judges (ca. 1200 - 1020 BCE): In the territory of the tribe of Judah, near the tribe of Simeon in the land of Canaan.

---

data is useful only to one who has access to the corresponding type of grid map.

Figs. 1 and 2 are maps showing the same general region around Tell el-Hesi. Fig. 1 is a map (1959) that shows the present road system and the Israeli names of cities, villages, and the main wadis. Fig. 2 is a pre-1947 map of the Hesi region showing the Arab names and a somewhat older road network. In this discussion the wadi that flows past Tell el-Hesi will be referred to by its older name, Wadi Hesi (as in fig. 2), rather than by its newer but less well-known name, Nahal Shiqma (as in fig. 1).

A second common method for locating a site is by reference to a well-known geographical feature, such as a city, mountain, lake, or river. Eusebius's *Onomasticon* of biblical place names (Klostermann 1904) uses such a system. There, localities in the region of southwest Palestine are described in terms of their distances from the contemporary Roman capital city, Eleutheropolis ("city of free men"). This

is why Robinson was so delighted to identify the modern Arab town of Beit Jibrin (Bet Guvrin) with the ancient Eleutheropolis (Robinson 1841: II, 404-8; 1856: II, 24-29). In the *Onomasticon* the unit of distance is the Roman mile—1670 yds. or 1.527 km. (the modern English mile is 1760 yds. or 1.609 km.). Examples of Tell el-Hesi's location by this method are presented in section II.a of table 1. The Bible often used a similar reference system, locating cities of the plains or low hills in relation to prominent rivers or streams. Major battles were also described in this way; thus, according to tradition, David battled Goliath in the valley of Elah ("Terebinth," 1 Sam. 17:2). The Bible makes no reference to the brooks (i.e., wadis) of the Tell el-Hesi area (see table 1, section II.b).

A third convention for fixing the location of a site is by geographical (or physiographical) region. Palestine is rather easily divided into such regions (see fig. 3):

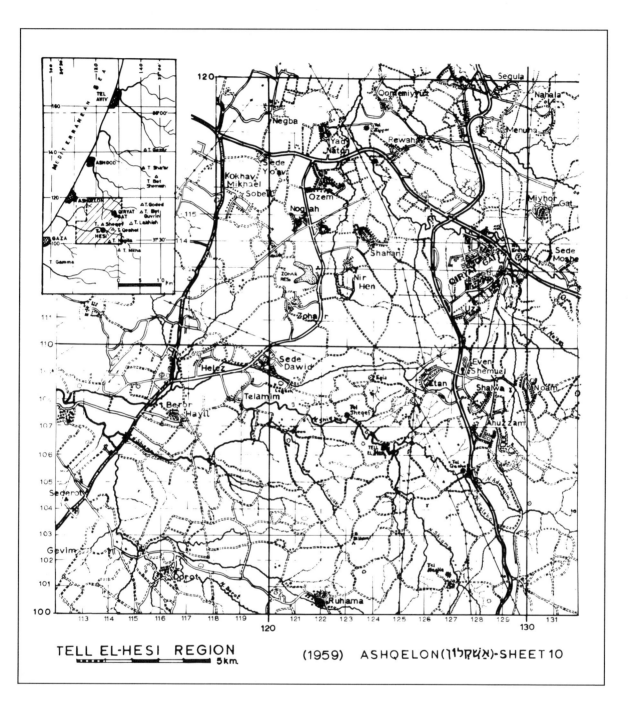

Fig. 1. Recent base map of cultural features and wadi system of the Tell el-Hesi region (Survey of Israel 1959).

a) the coastal plain
b) the western foothills (the Shephelah)
c) the western (Judean) mountains
d) the Jordan Rift valley (includes the Dead Sea)
e) the mountains and plateau east of the Jordan Rift valley
f) the southern desert (the Negev)

The geographical regions of Palestine are discussed in many books and atlases; thus, the concern here will be with only those geographical regions near Tell el-Hesi. Fig. 3 shows that the site is on the coastal plain very near its boundary with the Shephelah and the Negev. Due to differences in toponymic conventions or geographical boundary determinations, or due simply to language trans-

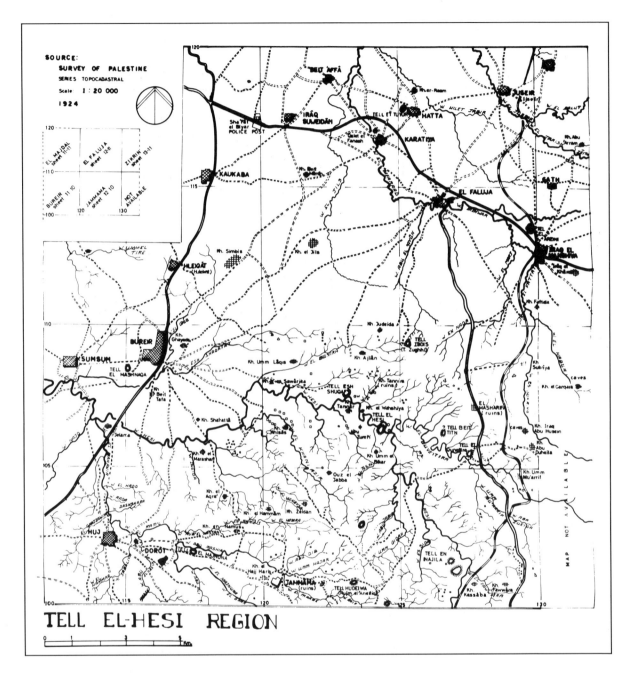

Fig. 2. Base map of the Tell el-Hesi region showing archaeological sites, towns, roads, and drainage features as they existed prior to the 1948 war. Based on several British Mandatory Government Administrative Maps of Palestine (Survey of Palestine 1924).

lation, map representations of a given region or topographic feature may differ from one publication to another. Such differences in nomenclature and in the delineation of natural regions can be puzzling to someone not aware of these variables. It should be noted that geographical (as distinct from political) boundaries are usually gradational

within a transitional zone. Such a transitional zone exists south of Tell el-Hesi between the coastal plain and the Negev. It is difficult to classify geographically because, although the topography resembles that of the chalk-formed Shephelah hills found farther east, the hills—like other hilly regions on the coastal plain—are composed of sandstone (kurkar ridges). In addition, these hills have been eroded into a badlands topography due to dissection of a thick loess cover. The thickness of loess (compacted powdery soil deposited by winds from the desert) rapidly increases on approaching the Negev. A few

scattered outlying hills of the Shephelah rock-type can be found in this region (e.g., Tell Nagila). To sum up, then: the geographical boundaries are gradational near Tell el-Hesi, and the tell is on the coastal plain near the juncture of the northern

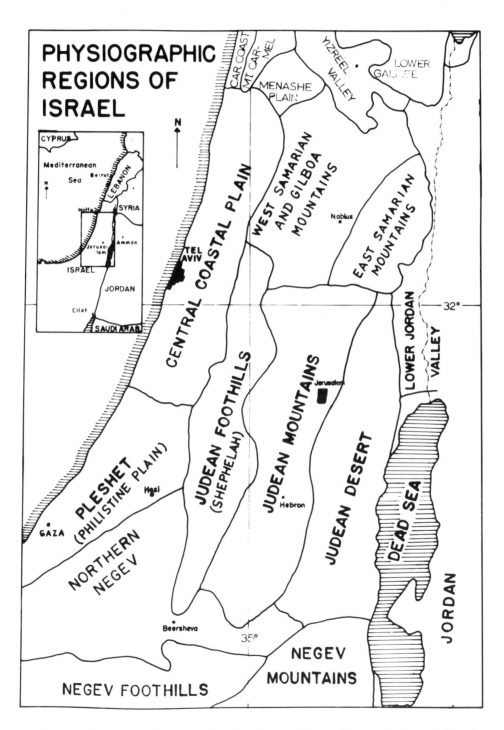

Fig. 3. Geographical or physiographical regions of Israel and part of Jordan. Drawing by Frank L. Koucky.

Negev and southern Shephelah regions.

Israel's coastal plain is a young geological feature that came into existence only after the formation of the present Nile River system that deposited the great quantity of sand necessary to build it. The sands are swept eastward from the Delta by strong longshore currents, and they accumulate in the southeastern end of the Mediterranean. Fluctuating sea levels during the last two million years have caused the growth of dune ridges on a rather flat plain that was once the sea bottom. At least three (and probably five) prominent dune ridges that are nearly parallel with the present coast can be recognized in the northern part of the coastal plain. These ridges become more obscure in the southern region where loess blown in from the southern desert has partially buried them. Because of the large supply of sand continuously available from the Nile, the coastal plain is still growing. The sand moves rapidly, filling in any irregularity along the coast of Israel and causing a straight, smooth coastline that extends from the Nile River to Mount Carmel. This abundant sand supply has blocked the mouths of wadis in the past as it does in the present and has forced the wadis to be deflected northward as they flow across the coastal plain. It is clear to anyone who looks at a map that the coastal plain is broadest in the south nearest the sand source and is thinnest toward the north.

The coastal plain can be divided into a series of regions such as the Plain of Sharon (not shown in fig. 3) and the Philistine Plain. These subdivisions reflect mainly a climate change in the amount of moisture as one moves from the steppe-like Philistine Plain in the south to moister and more tree-covered plains to the north. But as Orni and Efrat (1971: 35) point out, there is also a noticeable three-fold division of the coastal plain from west to east:

a) coastal dunes on the west
b) interior medial plains with low dune ridges
c) an eastern hilly section

Tell el-Hesi is in the third, or easternmost, of these regional sections, surrounded by sand hills (see table 1, section III).

A fourth way to locate sites is in terms of political units or subdivisions. Political subdivisions are of course clearly to be distinguished from geographical divisions—if possible, by the use of separate nomenclatures for each type. Confusingly, the same names often have been used to designate both political and geographical boundaries. Thus, "plain of the Philistines" has meant either a geographical region of the southern coastal plain or territory held during a certain historical period by the Philistines.

Although the general location of many other political regions is known, their exact boundaries cannot always be identified now. Section IV of table 1 lists a few possible politically-defined locations of Tell el-Hesi at different times in history. It is interesting to note that the site is close to political boundaries in several periods. At those times the tell probably served to guard the political frontier. The occupational history of the tell is a story that should develop from the record of its excavation; therefore it will be the subject of later chapters in this volume.

Climate

The present climate of the coastal plain varies from semi-tropical arid in the south to semi-tropical humid in the north. Tell el-Hesi is in the southern semi-arid region that receives an average of 300–400 mm. (12–14 in.) of rain per year. More important for this region than the total rainfall is the distribution of rain over the course of the year. In Israel 72 percent of the rain comes in December through February, and for agriculture it is important that it be well distributed during this period. The first rains soften the ground for working in preparation for planting; after the crops are planted a distributed rain is necessary. The number of days with rain becomes a prime factor in crop development. Normally, in the seven months of a rainy season (October through April) there are forty to sixty days with rain. Except along the coastal margin, little rain or none is expected from late April through early October. During these dry summer months a high amount of night dew develops, and the southern coastal plain will have 200 or more nights with dew per year. Melons and certain other crops grow especially well under these climatic conditions.

In the winter months the weather patterns that pass over Israel move first across northern Italy and the Aegean, bringing in Mediterranean low pressure systems and colder weather from Europe.

In the summer months the weather patterns sweep across southern Italy and the length of the Mediterranean before reaching Israel. This passage over the large expanse of water greatly modifies low pressure systems and brings extremely uniform warm summer weather.

Most important for making the coastal plain region habitable is the diurnal cycle that helps form the heavy dew. In the Tell el-Hesi region on a typical day, summer or winter, the winds are usually calm in the morning until about 11:00. During this time the temperature reaches its maximum for the day. Then, at about 11:00, the warm air rising over the coastal plain allows a sea breeze to develop which usually prevents any further increase of temperature. This breeze continues until late afternoon, with its maximum strength between noon and 2:00. The calm then returns in the early evening until the wind reverses to give an east breeze from the land. At Hesi in the summer this land breeze is often at its strongest between 9:00 and 11:00 p.m. The land breeze cools the temperature until about midnight, when the daily minimum is reached, and then a calm sets in with a constant temperature until morning. The late evening cool land breeze precipitates the heavy dew and often causes fog.

Mean coastal plain temperatures (at Tel Aviv) are 26.7°C in July and 13.9°C in January (in contrast with Jerusalem in the mountains, which has 23.2°C for July and 8.6°C in January). Record coastal plain temperature is 45°C (113°F).

A westerly wind pattern is normal, and only during transitional months (May–June or September–October) do occasional sirocco winds come in from the southern desert region. These are essentially off-track monsoon storms that normally would move on to India. Accompanying these storms comes a heat wave (khamsîn) with south and east winds loaded with dust. Generally these storms are of short duration, but they can sweep great quantities of dust from the desert into adjacent regions like that of Hesi.

When the mapping was done for their *Survey of Western Palestine*, it was noted by Conder and Kitchener (1883: 256) that the Wadi Hesi formed the southern boundary for farming and that the region south of the wadi was left mainly for grazing. This apparently had been the practice in the past, and many of the early pilgrims made comments about passing through fields of grain after crossing the Wadi Simsim (Wadi Hesi) northward. Traditional farming methods had to wait for the first rain to soften the ground before plowing. Much of the benefit of the early rains was lost. Since 1950, mechanized farming has allowed breaking of the ground before the first rain. This decreases the runoff of water and allows earlier planting. This in turn has allowed the farming to be pushed farther south, so that the Wadi Hesi is no longer the southern farming limit. Farming here takes advantage of the region of highest dew (which reaches a maximum in the northern Negev, where more

than 250 days of dew occur each year).

The geological record clearly indicates that the coastal plain had a variety of climates in Pleistocene and Holocene times. The fossil remains of hippopotami, rhinoceri, and gazelles suggest the existence of warm, humid periods when thick husma soils developed. These fauna perished when the northward encroachment of the southern desert produced periods of tropical dry conditions.

To aid in understanding changes in the paleoclimate of the coastal plain, a brief survey of the geologic history of the area is in order.

Geologic History of the Coastal Plain

The geologic history of Israel and of the southeastern Mediterranean region is closely involved with the development and destruction of the Tethys Ocean, of which the present Caspian Sea, Black Sea, and Mediterranean Sea are the only remnants.

A geologic time scale is presented in table 2, and the highlights of the geologic history for the region under discussion are presented as a series of sketches in fig. 4. The sketches are based mainly on three sources: Dewey *et al.* 1973; Gvirtzman 1973; and Ginzburg *et al.* 1975.

During late Triassic time (fig. 4, A) a long linear rift (much like the present Red Sea) developed, breaking up a supercontinent mass into the European, African, and North American continents. At this time also a broad ocean, the Tethys Sea, opened to the east.

During Jurassic and early Cretaceous times (fig. 4, B and B') the Arabian plate warped into a series of open folds trending NE-SW, and finally faulting took place along the Pelusium line. The eastern side of this fault (the Arabian block) was uplifted to form a shelf. This shelf started to receive shallow-water limestones and reef sedimentary deposits.

During Oligocene time (fig. 4, C and C') new stresses had accumulated to cause the Arabian block to break from the African plate along the Red Sea rift. At this same time the Dead Sea (Jordan Valley) rift developed, and the intervening block (called the "central block" by Neev [1975]) was crumpled into an anticlinorium and uplifted out of the sea, so that the shoreline was shifted far to the west.

During early Miocene time (fig. 4, D) downward faulting of the western part of the anticlinorium of the "central block" formed a shelf platform over which the sea was able to transgress eastward to the margin of the Judean hills. This shelf, the later

Table 2. Geologic time scale with reference to several events affecting Eastern Mediterranean geologic history.

ERA	PERIOD	EPOCH	EVENTS	YEARS BEFORE THE PRESENT
CENOZOIC	Quaternary	Holocene (recent)	(See figs. 6–7)	10,000
		Pleistocene (Glacial)	(See figs. 4G–5)	2,000,000
	Tertiary	Pliocene	(See fig. 4F)	13,000,000
		Miocene	African and European plates start converging.	24,000,000
		Oligocene	Arabian block breaks from African plate along Red Sea Rift.	36,000,000
		Eocene		58,000,000
		Paleocene	Deposition of chalks & calcareous marls of Shephelah foothills.	65,000,000
MESOZOIC	Cretaceous		Africa's counterclockwise rotation closing Tethys Sea. Deposition of thick lime-stones of Judean anticline.	
			——— (Start of ophiolite sequences) ———	136,000,000
	Jurassic		Widening Tethys Sea. In Atlantic Ocean, plate accretion of ocean crust begins.	195,000,000
	Triassic		Africa and Europe break away from North America. Late Permian & Triassic sediments deposited in a new Tethyan mobile belt that was superimposed on S. part of older Hercynian belt.	230,000,000

Shephelah, is a structural syncline that had formed on the western side of the hills.

During middle Miocene times (fig. 4, E) the African and European plates had started to move together. At this time the Tethys Sea was blocked north and east of the Arabian block, leaving the Mediterranean basin separate for the first time. In late Miocene time the continued movement of the African plate toward the European plate blocked the Gibraltar portal, and the Mediterranean became a closed basin. High evaporation caused the enclosed sea to shrink eventually to a series of hypersaline lakes with thick evaporite sediments of salt and gypsum. Rivers flowing into this deep basin caused rapid erosion and cut valleys over the

shelf area of the "central block" in the Israel region.

When the Gibraltar portal reopened in the early Pliocene (fig. 4, F), very rapid refilling of the Mediterranean Basin took place. At this time the Israel shelf, without a source for clastic sediments, formed mainly carbonate coral and algae reefs. These carbonate sediments were succeeded by calcareous marls and chalks. The Pliocene high-level seas were able to reach the Jordan rift valley through several openings.

The convergence of Africa with the European plate had crumpled the marginal zones into a series of mountain ranges during late Miocene time. This movement continued into Pliocene time, forming the Alps, the Zagros, the Himalayas, and other

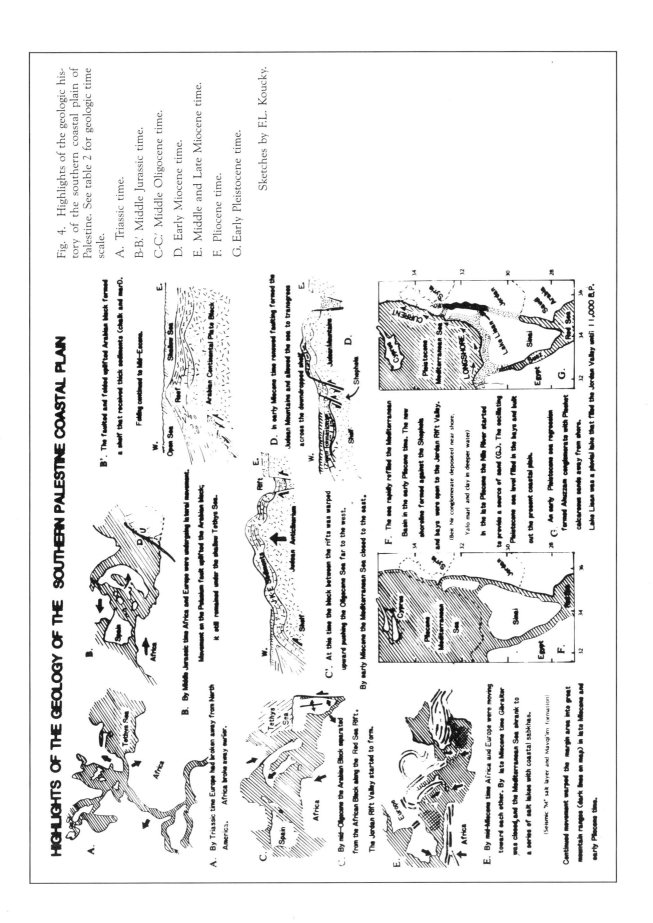

Fig. 4. Highlights of the geologic history of the southern coastal plain of Palestine. See table 2 for geologic time scale.

A. Triassic time.

B-B'. Middle Jurassic time.

C-C'. Middle Oligocene time.

D. Early Miocene time.

E. Middle and Late Miocene time.

F. Pliocene time.

G. Early Pleistocene time.

Sketches by F.L. Koucky.

mountain ranges.

By late Pliocene time (fig. 4, G), the Nile River system had started to supply sand to the Mediterranean Sea, where it was dumped to form mainly the Nile Delta. The Mediterranean currents swept eastward along the northern coast of Africa and transported the sands eastward from the Nile Delta to the Israel shelf region (which later became the Israel coastal plain). First this sand built bars and spits across stream outlets that deflected northward the drainage from the Judean hills. Then the sand filled in bays and indentations to build a straight shoreline.

During Pleistocene time the sea level oscillated greatly, with low sea levels during glacial periods, when much ocean water was tied up as glacial ice, and high sea levels during the warm interglacial periods. The high sea levels left a series of distinct shoreline marine terraces, though none of these reached as high as the late Pliocene shoreline. These terraces are especially prominent on the coastal plain, where they are paralleled by a dune ridge similar to the dune ridge now developing along the modern shoreline.

Not only were there major shoreline shifts during the Pleistocene, but the climatic zones also shifted significantly. The sea-level changes were in response to climate changes which are investigated in the next section.

Paleoclimate

The geologic record indicates that a slow and continuous climate cooling had taken place since the end of the Cretaceous period. This was probably because a large amount of land was no longer covered by the sea and because land masses were redistributed. Rapid and marked cyclic climate changes began only in the Pleistocene. The start of the Pleistocene is generally agreed to be the first time that cold-water microfaunae appeared in the Mediterranean Sea (Calabrian transgression; Horowitz 1979: 5). More recently this has been dated close enough to the Olduvai normal magnetic reversal to use the reversal for worldwide correlation of the start of the Pleistocene. With the use of magnetic reversals for dates within the Pleistocene and with the recovery of deep-sea cores of the Pleistocene period, a new understanding of paleoclimate is just beginning.

Fig. 5 presents in curves A through H paleoclimatic data derived by various different techniques for the last part of the Pleistocene. List I outlines

the correlative European glacial stages. Also shown by dashed lines are the mean datings of high-level Mediterranean shorelines (Tyrrhenian III and II) for Morocco. (A recent summary of shorelines is contained in Horowitz 1979: 7 and 95–108.)

All of the types of data presented in fig. 5 are basically consistent in indicating the broad warm and cold periods of the late Pleistocene. They suggest that the whole northern hemisphere of the earth went through long-term climatic cycles. The ocean waters appear to have cooled at nearly the same time that the land shows changes in vegetation and changes in the rate of evaporation of lakes.

The last glacial period, the Würm, is characterized by a long period of cold water in which the Mediterranean was more than 6°C cooler than at present. There is evidence of greater rainfall in the Dead Sea region, although the amount of rainfall is still open to question. Curve C of fig. 5 suggests heavy rains only at the beginning and end of the Würm glaciation. This view is supported by Fairbridge (1972: 101) and fits the various phases in glacial stadia and the effects beyond the ice front in the Mediterranean region that he has described:

a) **Anaglacial** (the transition from warm to cold): initiation of glaciation in the northern latitudes; in the Mediterranean, increased precipitation, causing a minor pluvial period

b) **Pleniglacial** (maximum northern latitude glaciation): in the Mediterranean region, reduced precipitation, long dry seasons, silting up of streams, interruption of Nile flooding, much loess deposition and dune building, and low sea level

c) **Kataglacial** (transition from cold to warm): great increase in precipitation in the Mediterranean region, causing a pluvial period; also monsoon rains, stream dissection, and the resumption of Nile flooding

d) **Interglacial** (climate like the present): in the Mediterranean region, minor cycles of drought and rain; a rising sea level (rapid at first); widespread return of forests

Both curves C and D indicate heavy rainfalls that caused the Dead Sea to expand and form the high-level Lake Lisan. The rainfall also created other pluvial lakes in the Mediterranean region within the last 20,000 years.

All of the curves of fig. 5 recognize several cold periods within the Würm glacial stadia (70,000–11,500 BP). The Würm subdivisions suggested by Horowitz (1975) are as follows:

70–65,000 to 50,000 BP Early Würm: pluvial period with climate in the southern coastal plain like that now found in the Mt. Carmel region

50,000 to 29,000 BP Late Monastirian interstadial: warm; dune migration

29,000 to 19,000 BP Main Würm: 50 percent arboreal pollen, mainly oak; hamra development; pluvial period; extra dry about 23,000 BP

19,000 to 16,000 BP Epi-Monastirian interstadial: reduction to 30 percent arboreal pollen; oak, pine, pistachio, and olive

16,000 to 11,500 BP Late Würm: 50 percent arboreal pollen, mainly oak; pluvial period

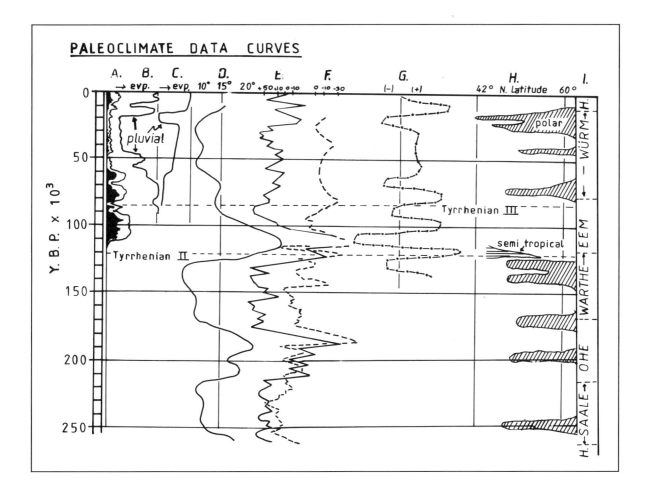

Fig. 5. Late Pleistocene paleoclimate data curves. Horizontal dash lines indicate dated strandlines (Stearns and Thurber 1965).

A. Pollen abundance for oaks (dark area) and herbs (light area) in Phillipi, Greece (Van der Hammen, Wijmstra, and Zagwin 1971).

B and C. Interpretations of the runoff/evaporation ratio for the Dead Sea (B: Neev and Emery 1967; C: Begin, Ehrlich, and Nathan 1974).

D. Ocean temperatures derived from oxygen 18/oxygen 16 ratios measured on Mediterranean core ALB-189 (Wollin, Ericson, and Wollin 1974).

E. Magnetic inclination measurements derived from Mediterranean core RC-9-181 (Wollin, Ericson, and Wollin 1974).

F. Magnetic inclination measurements derived from Mediterranean core V12-122 (Wollin, Ericson, and Wollin 1974).

G. Calculated solar radiation for the northern hemisphere: (–) indicates cooler than present temperature and (+) indicates warmer. One of a series of curves from Broeker 1968.

H. Marine fossil assemblages in ocean cores (between northern latitudes 42° and 60°) used to interpret water temperatures in the North Atlantic (Kellogg 1974: 34).

I. European glacial stages and their approximate dates.

Drawing by Melanie Robbins from an original by Frank Koucky.

More important to the interpretation of the cultural periods represented at Tell el-Hesi is the paleoclimate record of the Holocene (the time since the Würm glacial stadia; i.e., from the end of the Pleistocene to the present). Rapid melting of ice took place at northern latitudes due to a temperature rise about 15,000 BP, but the great volume of melting ice kept the climate cool. By 7000 BP ocean levels had risen close to their present stage, while the main ice sheet had retreated from Scandinavia and was nearly gone from Canada.

Horowitz (1979: 6) divides the Holocene for Israel into three main episodes (fig. 6) as follows:

The **Versilian episode** is characterized as an interpluvial climate much like the present, when warming pushed the glacial pluvial flora and fauna northward in Israel. Sea level rose rapidly from over 150 m. below present levels to 2 or 3 m. above the present level, forming the Versilian (or Flanderian) shoreline.

The **Atlantic episode** was a return to a pluvial period with some summer rains and mild brief winters. Temperatures may have risen 1–2°C over the present, and sea level dropped to a point 5 m. to 6 m. below the present level.

About 2,500 BCE, the start of Horowitz's **Recent episode,** the climate cooled to about what it is today, and the drier interpluvial conditions became prevalent.

Many other schemes of climatic episodes are described for Europe and North America, and one of these is offered also in fig. 6. The warm Atlantic episode is universally recognized; it is also referred to as the "Post-Glacial Optimum," "Hypsithermal," "Altithermal," or "Neolithic Wet" phase. At this time there was probably a poleward displacement of the subtropical anticyclonic belts allowing westerly winds over the Sahara and the Near East, for these areas became more humid, though warm. Worldwide, the mountain snow lines are recorded as having retreated at least 300 m. higher.

Many shorter climatic events have been suggested for the Recent climatic episode, as in fig. 6. One of the most complete records of climatic variation is that gained from dendrochronology, as summarized by Euler et al. (1979). In this study regional tree-growth departures (variations in ring widths) are plotted at ten-year and twenty-year intervals for the period 200 BCE to the present. The record clearly indicates long-term cyclic climatic variation with a period of about 570 years. These cycles are not great climatic changes, and in most areas of the world they would go unnoticed; however, the

changes would be seen by peoples living in marginal lands, where the limits of the desert would be affected by the advance and retreat of glaciation. Climatic changes such as these are discussed by Lamb (1966) and Ladurie (1971).

A 570-year cycle that parallels the dendrochronological data is plotted in fig. 7. Major climatic variations of the Recent climatic episode from fig. 6 fit this curve, since they were deduced from pollen data (e.g., the Little Ice Age, Medieval Warm Period, etc.). It has been supported that major cultural disruptions clearly parallel or follow these biological disruptions (Wendland and Bryson 1974: 23). The curve also fits known periods of farming and expansion into desert regions by empires followed by periods of withdrawal. It must be stressed that portions of the curve extending to dates earlier than 200 BCE have not yet been supported by dendrochronological data. If such a long-term cyclic variation in climate is occurring, it must be due to variation in the sun's energy or to the fact that the earth has had periodic volcanic eruptions. This topic has been summarized by Molnár (1981).

Historically recorded severe drought periods are of too short duration to show up on such a chart, but an *actual* drought of only one year causes serious hardship in Mediterranean countries and, if extended over two years, produces disaster. The year 1973 was a dry year over much of the northern Mediterranean region. On Cyprus in the fall of 1972 the rains came early, and the crops were planted as usual. Enough rain fell at that time to cause the plants and weeds to sprout, but then no more rain fell. The seedlings died, and even the weeds did not grow. The grapes and tree crops such as almonds and figs failed to leaf and flower properly. There was no feed for livestock, and the latter had to be marketed early. Later rains did little to save the situation. If food reserves had been used for seed the second year and the second-year crops had failed, the situation clearly would have been disastrous, and the people would have had to seek new seed and livestock elsewhere. Josephus (1958: XV.ix.1) described a two-year drought in Israel which occurred around the thirteenth year of Herod's reign (25–24 BCE), when grain had to be purchased from Egypt. Such major droughts were probably of too short duration to be seen on the type of paleoclimate curve presented, and obviously other causes of famine such as locusts, plagues, hail, or volcanic eruptions should not be expected to appear. Even in a wet regime a poor rain distribution (such as described earlier for Cyprus) might

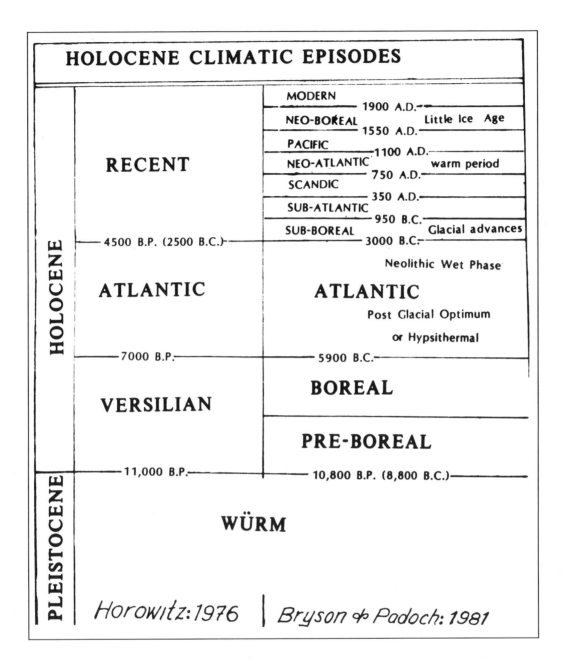

Fig. 6. Holocene climatic episodes. Following the Würm glaciation in Europe various climatic episodes have been detected and described. The warmest period was the Atlantic episode. The Boreal episodes are cooler periods (Horowitz 1976; Bryson and Padoch 1981).

cause a crop failure, and this might be interpreted as a drought.

Since *actual* droughts do not appear on the chart, only periods of potential drought can be recognized. The curve shows that droughts in the Mediterranean region would most likely have occurred in the following time periods: 2100–1950, 1550–1400, 950–800, and 400–200 BCE; and 200–350, 750–950,

and 1350–1500 CE. It is beyond the scope of this chapter to discuss the historical evidence for droughts in these periods (see Lamb 1966 or Bell 1975). It should be noted that years of ice advance and of cold in Europe and North America were years that brought summer rains to the desert margins and were good farming years around the Mediterranean, and that the warm years for Europe

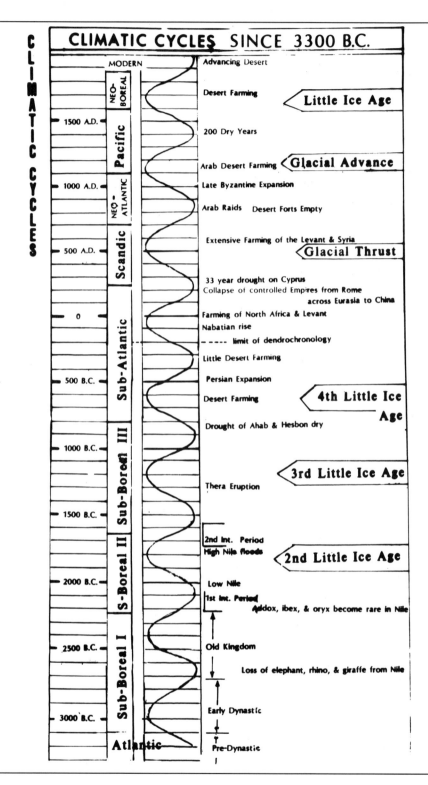

Fig. 7. Holocene climatic cycles. Cycles appear to follow a 570-year period based on dendrochronology after Euler *et al.* (1979: 1093). The climatic episodes are from fig. 6 (based on Bryson and Padoch 1981). When the cycle is to the right, the desert region tends to be dryer and warmer (Europe at these times had good growing seasons). When the cycle is to the left, the desert margins are agriculturally productive (at these times glacier advances are recorded in mountains and at northern latitudes).

were the hot, dry years for the Mediterranean region.

Tell el-Hesi is at the margin of the Negev desert, and its region would be greatly affected by small climatic disruptions. It is hoped that the Hesi excavation will contribute to a better understanding of paleoclimates.

Soils and the Southern Coastal Plain (Southern Pleshet)

The southern coastal plain of Israel is bordered on the east along the Mediterranean by an active dune field of shifting sand. Swamps once formed east of these dunes where drainage ways were blocked by this migrating sand, but they are now drained as a control against malaria.

The active dune process along the coast reflects only a part of the continuous process that built the coastal plain. The whole region is underlain by sand and near-shore deposits, and these sandy materials form the parent material for any soil-development process. To the east of the active dunes, older shoreline materials have been stabilized and are developing brown (hamra) soils in the southern Pleshet and light brown loessal soils in the northern Negev.

Soil development on these sandy parent materials was long misunderstood as soil scientists attempted to apply traditional genetic soil-development concepts to this region. Under the traditional hypothesis new material should be added continuously to the B soil horizon (the subsoil) from the C horizon (the parent or native, original material—here, silt and sand). Yet the composition of the B horizon and the A horizon (surface) of these coastal plain soils made it very unlikely that they could be related in origin to the underlying C horizon (which is the sand dune or sandy marine deposits).

Progress in understanding semi-arid regions like the one under consideration came after recognition that C horizon materials (partially decayed bedrock) are here being added at a rapid rate to the A horizon. The new material added arrives in the form of aeolian loess (wind-carried dust). Thus soil formation and aeolian accumulation have gone on simultaneously, and this has often obscured pedogenic (soil-forming) boundaries between soil horizons. The soils of the region are thus considered polymorphic, since they owe their origin to a combination of major soil-forming factors.

The important role that loess plays in this region has recently been summarized in several papers from which the following discussion has been derived (Yallon and Dan 1974; Yallon and Ganor 1973).

The general vernacular name, "hamra," has been applied to the brown, sandy clay-loam soils of the coastal plain, and this name implies a non-calcareous soil. More recent detailed mapping of soils around Tell el-Hesi has classified the upland soil as grumusolic dark brown soil, and this grades south to the light brown loessal soils of the northern Negev. Where the brown-red hamra soil has developed a strong calcic horizon (calcrete of caliche with nodules of petrocalcic crusts), the soil has been called a polygenetic husma soil. The leached hamra soil is thought to have developed during periods of subhumid to humid conditions when calcium could be flushed downward through the soil. A change to drier climate causes extensive surface evaporation, which encourages calcrete development, and the husma soils occur. Under still drier conditions the chemical breakdown is slow enough that loess accumulation predominates, and calcareous loess without concretions develops.

The occurrence of several climatic cycles in this region is indicated by paleosols buried in the stratigraphic sequences of loess exposed in wadis. The paleosols vary from thick hamra soils to thin zones of calcrete nodular development. At least four horizons of calcrete development have been recognized in this region. Much more regional work is needed before these paleosols can be used for datable stratigraphic horizons.

Loess is accumulating over the region now at the rate of 0.02 mm. to 0.08 mm. annually. The major accumulation is during the sirocco-type storms, but the actual dust is migratory and slow to settle. Its southern source is clearly shown by its tendency to build thick deposits in wind shadows on north-facing slopes, while south-facing slopes receive only thin accumulations. Studies of the loess composition and of other factors clearly indicate that the source areas are the Sahara and Sinai deserts.

Though the underlying parent sands are often 90 percent or more quartz, the overlying loess and the soil derived from it are much more variable in composition. Analyzed fractions freed of clay are 25 to 45 percent calcite, 10 to 20 percent dolomite, 30 to 50 percent quartz, and 3 to 10 percent feldspar. The clay component is predominately montmorillonite and mixed clays which expand when wet and are strong binding agents.

Loess, unlike other sediments, retains stable vertical walls when it is dissected. This allows topography characteristic of badlands to develop. The thick loess that has accumulated in the northern

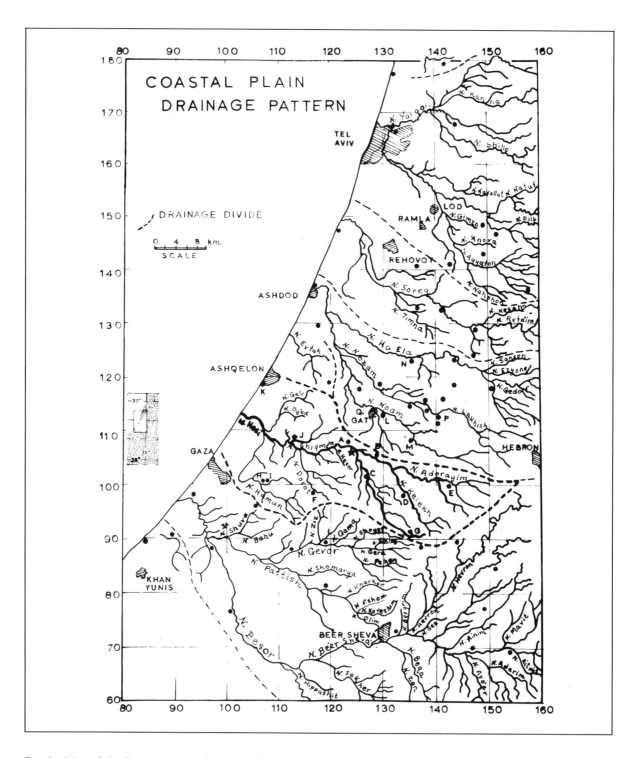

Fig. 8. Map of the drainage pattern for the southern coastal plain, showing the present pattern of streams. The drainage divisions between major streams are indicated by dash lines (following Gvirtzman 1973). The modern names are shown for streams, but Wadi Hesi stands in bold type at the mouth of that stream, now called Nahal Shiqma. Tell el-Hesi's location is indicated by a star. Heavy dots indicate other major tells of the region. Those of the Hesi drainage basin and near to Hesi are identified by letters as follows:

A. Sheqef	D. Kelekh	G. Migdalit	J. Beror	M. Lachish
B. Qeshet	E. Agra	H. Mefallesim	K. Ashqelon	N. Zafit
C. Nagila	F. Mifshah	I. Irit	L. ᶜAreini	P. Bet Guvrin

Negev and the southern coastal plain has been dissected into areas of badlands topography north of the Wadi Besor and south of the Wadi Hesi. These badlands are extremely difficult to traverse, and no easy routes from the Judean hills to the sea exist in this region. The actual flood plain of the Wadi Hesi provides a natural route to the sea, however. North of the Wadi Hesi the thinner loess accumulation has allowed a less rugged topography to develop.

PART II: THE TELL EL-HESI SITE

Geomorphic History of the Tell el-Hesi Site

The drainage basin of the Wadi Hesi is outlined in fig. 8. The streams start to coalesce after leaving the Shephelah to begin their passage across the coastal plain, and the Wadi Hesi becomes the master drainage of much of the southern coastal plain. Tell el-Hesi (marked in fig. 8 with a star) is located just beyond the junction of two main tributaries. What cannot be seen on this map is that Hesi is situated where the valley is relatively narrow, while a short distance downstream the Wadi Hesi again flows west and the valley opens to a broad flood plain.

The sharp 90° deflection in the course of the Wadi Hesi just to the north of the tell has been caused by ancient dune-building along an abandoned Pleistocene shoreline of the Mediterranean by processes similar to those that are producing the present shore dunes. The record of past events is well preserved in terrace-wall stratigraphy exposed along the Wadi Hesi and in an excavation south of Tell el-Hesi in a trench dug by Dr. David Gilard in 1972. Although the information is yet to be confirmed, it is the understanding of the present author that at the Gilard site evidence may have been found of Upper Paleolithic pebble culture and horse bones. This site represents a terrace remnant of a swamp formed behind a dune complex that marked an ancient Pleistocene shoreline. Such a swamp environment existed behind the modern shore dunes until quite recently, when the swamps were drained for malaria control.

A dune complex marking an ancient Mediterranean shoreline forms a line of hills southwest and northeast of the site. Fig. 9 attempts to show in diagrammatic form the development of this shoreline. Dissection of these ancient shoreline dunes has left a rugged topography with deeply entrenched narrow wadi valleys. These ancient dunes have long been stabilized with vegetation, and a deep husma soil has developed over them. The underlying sands that compose the dunes are cemented with calcareous and silica cement to form resistant beds (kurkar ridges). At several times in the past the vegetation cover over these ancient dunes was broken by drought or fire, and during these times the predominant westerly wind created blow-outs on the west side of the dune complex. The freed sand and soil from these blow-outs washed into the broad Wadi Hesi flood plain. During dry periods the sand was blown to the east and funneled through the wadi gap in the dune to be deposited east of the dune ridge. The blowing sand resettled behind shrubs, trees, and other obstructions and formed a series of migrating barchan dunes (see fig. 14) on the surface of what had been the ancient swamp (see fig. 9, F). The barchan dunes probably developed during the long droughts associated with maximum glaciation of the regions to the north (pleniglacial stage). With the return of the more moist conditions of the interglacial stage, vegetation was again able to stabilize the dunes and end their migration. The sketches of fig. 9 thus show how the hollow pocket now occupied by Tell el-Hesi's acropolis and the higher ridges on three sides of the site came into existence.

Fig. 10 shows the topography near the tell within the hollow pocket. A large barchan dune (South Ridge) exists just to the southwest of the tell. While the windward face of this dune has suffered much recent dissection by streams, its leeward slope still retains the steep 35° slope which represents the angle of repose for the sands of this region. Tell el-Hesi itself is founded on another small barchan dune, but its shape is now much modified by erosion on the east side by the Wadi Hesi, and by human activities on the surface. The barchan dunes, as well as having a characteristic geomorphic shape, can also be recognized by their internal composition of well-sorted yellow sand, referred to at the site by excavators since Petrie as the Hesi "golden sand."

Description of the Tell el-Hesi Site

The region around Tell el-Hesi is shown on the sketch map of fig. 10. This drawing is based on a stereographic study of aerial photographs taken of the region in 1949. On this map, general names without genetic implications have been placed on hills and small drainages to aid in subsequent

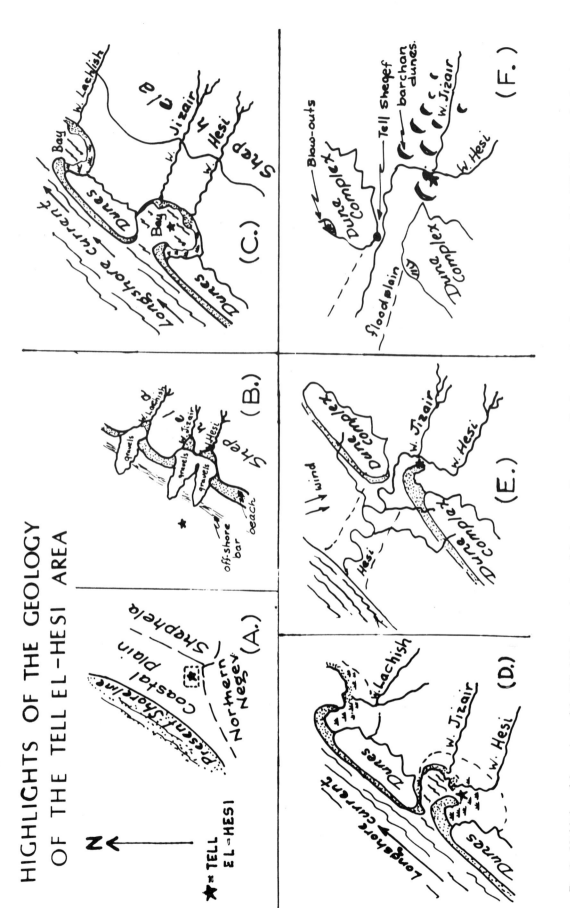

Fig. 9. Highlights of the geology of the Tell el-Hesi area. A series of sketch maps diagrammatically illustrating how the geomorphology of the Tell el-Hesi site developed.

A. Sketch map of the present physiographical relations. The dotted square area is an inset of the region shown in the following sketches. Tell el-Hesi's location is indicated by the star in each sketch, although all sketches show relationships that obtained long before the tell of Tell el-Hesi was formed.

B. The Pliocene shoreline at the present edge of the Shephelah. Jizair is historically the older name of the stream now called Nahal Adorayim (as in fig. 8).

C. A broad, wide coastal plain developed during the first period of glaciation in the northern regions, when the sea level fell because much ocean water was tied up as ice. The diagram shows the maximum readvance of the ocean with the melting of this glaciation. Note that a new shoreline developed to the west of the Pliocene shoreline.

D. Conditions several thousand years after those shown in C. The backdune swamp area is slowly being filled in, and the river-mouth bay is greatly reduced in size.

E. Conditions after the next period of glaciation in a later interglacial period as a new shoreline farther west now starts to be established.

F. During the next glaciation a period of drought (pleniglaciation) allows blow-outs to develop on the dune ridge, and the free sand forms migrating barchan dunes along the valley of Wadi Hesi (see further illustration and explanation in fig. 15).

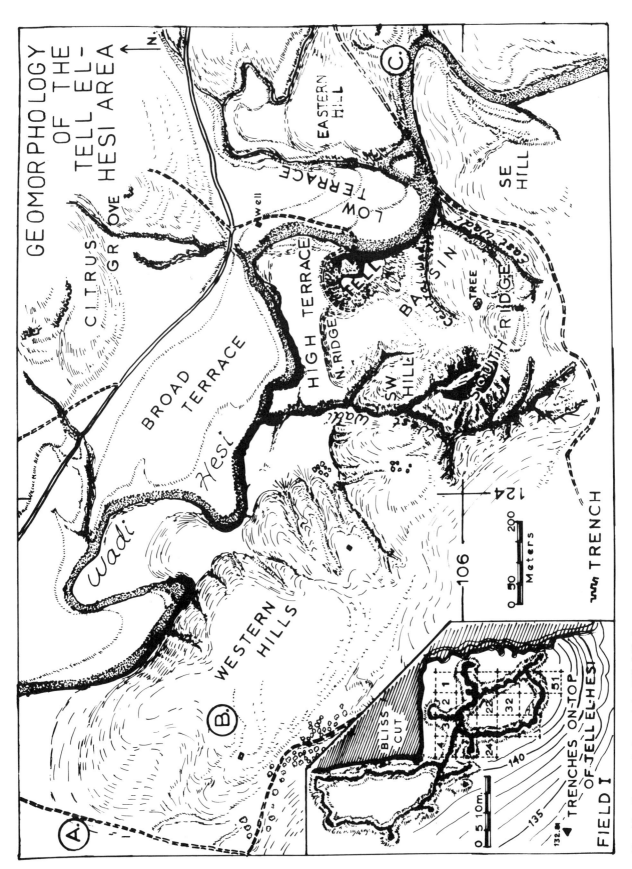

Fig. 10. Geomorphology of the Tell el-Hesi area.

discussion. The approximate location of the area on the Israeli kilometric grid system is indicated by the intersection of 106 and 124 at the lower left. Since the 1949 aerial photographs clearly show military trenches (dug during the 1947–48 War of Independence), details of the trench system on top of the tell appear in a small insert map at the lower left corner of the plate. The large circled letters indicate special areas that will be discussed later in the text.

A more detailed topographic map of the region around the tell is shown in fig. 11. The metric contours on and near the tell are taken from the Expedition's survey of the site (1970–73), while metric contours farther away from the tell, at 10-meter intervals, are taken from the British Mandate Administration 1:20,000 topographic maps of the region. The location of fields under investigation through the 1975 season is shown by Roman numerals, and "camp" indicates where the Expedition's tents were located in the 1971, 1973, and 1975 seasons.

On these maps the Wadi Hesi flows from the southeast to the northwest. Just to the west of the area shown in fig. 11 the wadi's flood plain triples in size, and the wadi abruptly changes direction to flow due west. During most of the summer months the wadi itself is dry, while water flows underground through the sand and gravel that fill the valley. Standing water appears in some deeper

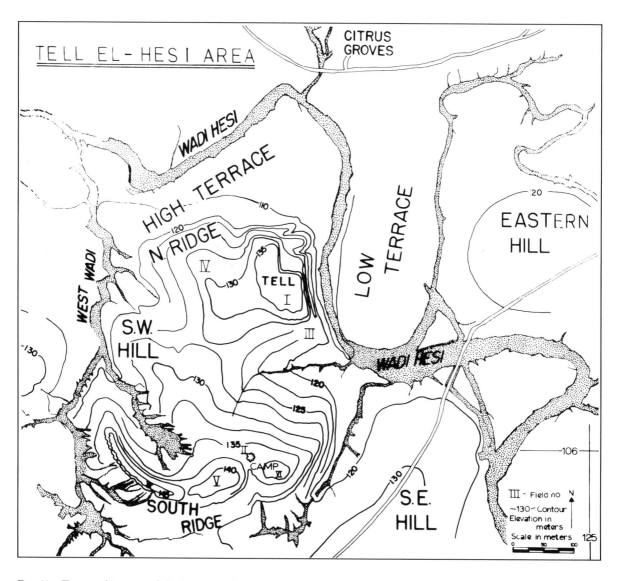

Fig. 11. Topographic map of the Tell el-Hesi area.

holes as well as downstream from springs. Around the springs, heavy cane growth has developed. The Bedouin water their flocks in the summer by digging shallow holes in the wadi floor, and they use the same holes for bathing and for washing clothes.[1] The gradient of the Wadi Hesi across the region of fig. 10 is about 3.3 m. per kilometer (17.4 ft. per mile).

Topographic features of the Tell el-Hesi site will be discussed individually using the nomenclature of fig. 10. The area enclosed within the Early Bronze city at its maximum extent is indicated in fig. 12. At that time the top of the tell probably served as an acropolis overlooking the rest of the city and the surrounding farm and grazing lands.

Tell el-Hesi.[2] Edward Robinson visited the tell in 1838 and described it as a "truncated cone with a fine plain on the top" (Robinson 1841: II, 390; 1856: II, 48). All written accounts of visits by pilgrims note the steep, high slope on the eastern side, but Petrie was the first to determine that the tell rises slightly more than 120 ft. above the Wadi Hesi floor on the east (Petrie 1891: 12). Petrie gave the dimensions of the flat, nearly square surface on top as about 200 ft. north-south and east-west. He also said that the tell rises with a more gradual slope only to about 60 ft. above the general land surface on the other sides.

From the top of the tell, according to Robinson, ". . . the summit commands a rich and pleasing prospect, over a wide extent of undulating country, low swelling hills and broad valleys, all of the finest soil; yet without a single village or ruin rising above ground, on which the eye can rest" (Robinson 1841: II, 390; 1856: II, 48).

Though this is an accurate description of the semi-arid grassy steppe that surrounds the site, actually two other tells are clearly visible: Tell Sheqef, about 1.6 km. on a line N 47° W (read "north, 47° west") to its intersection with the Hesi valley, and Tell Nagila, about 6 km. distant at a direction of S 30° E. The top of a third mound, Tell Qeshet, can be seen 1.6 km. off at S 70° E by those who know where to look; its presence is not obvious from a distance. The view described above no longer exists on the north, for in 1960 a large citrus grove was planted there when water was piped into the region. The grove is now dense and mature and surrounded by a windbreak of tall cypress trees.

The top of the tell (i.e., of the so-called acropolis; see note 2) has long lost the flat square outline noted by Robinson and Petrie, mainly due to the removal of most of the northeast quadrant of the

tell by Bliss in 1891 and 1892 (Bliss 1894; see Matthers 1989 [Chapter II below]: 51, 58). Further modifications were caused by the military trenching of 1947–48.

"Bliss's cut," as it has come to be called, can be seen in figs. 10–12 and 16. The walls of this excavation have remained remarkably vertical and well preserved; ash layers and layers rich in pebbles can still easily be traced along their faces. Bliss related that before he left the field after his last season heavy rains had washed down the dump piles, filled in the cuts, and left a flat surface over the bottom of his large excavation, yet the walls remained relatively undisturbed (Bliss 1894: 156). Brush, scrub growth, water erosion toward the wadi, and the army's use of the tell for military half-track vehicle training have contributed to modifying further the Bliss excavation.

Only the flanks of the tell were trenched by Petrie, in part because he was unwilling to meet the purchase price to buy out the barley crop on top (see Matthers 1989 [Chapter II below]: 43). The resultant scars and associated dump piles of Petrie's work are still visible, especially on the south side of the tell. Work in the present expedition's Field III, on the south flank of the tell, has carefully avoided Petrie's trenches.

In 1975, this writer examined the nature of the soil underlying the occupational phases of the tell in the sides and bottom of Bliss's cut, as well as in a stratigraphic trench cut on the east side of the tell and a long north-south trench through the wall system in Field III on the southeast side. Each of these locations yielded the fine, well-sorted, yellow-stained sand, commonly called "the golden sand" at the excavation. This slightly indurated (slightly cemented) sand had been stripped of its soil profile before any of the construction phases on the tell. On the east side of the tell the yellow sands of the upper dune overlie a weakly developed paleosol which in turn covers strongly stratified silts and sands of fluvial origin. The stratified fluvial deposits rest on well-indurated conglomerates and calcareous marine sandstones of the Pleshet Formation (Pliocene Age). The indurated Pliocene marine sediments form a series of ledges below the tell on the east side and are exposed to a height of about 6 m. above the wadi floor. These stronger, lower sediments prevent rapid undercutting of the tell by the Wadi Hesi. The upper, uniform "golden sands" are aeolian in origin, representing a small barchan dune whose form has been greatly modified.

The Basin.[3] Extending from the base of the tell to the south and west is a broad, low area which has long been used for farming, but only in the past few years has very deep plowing been done there. Abundant sherds, lithics, and rock fragments are found in the ash-rich soil over this whole expanse, and the annual plowing brings new material to the surface each year. Into this basin Petrie dug a series of probes to test the depth of any occupation debris (see fig. 12). He also traced a segment of thick mud-brick wall at the basin's northern edge, and he viewed both this and the comparatively shallow layer of occupation debris covering the basin as associated with the earliest

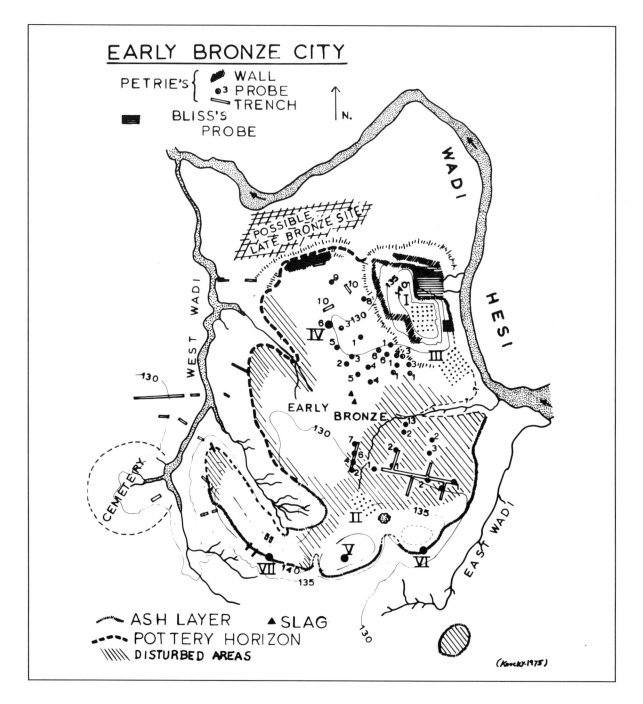

Fig. 12. The Early Bronze city, as determined from tracing ash and sherd horizons exposed in wadi cuts. The locations of Petrie's probes are indicated with depths in feet. The "disturbed" areas are those having undergone deep plowing.

Fig. 13. Tell el-Hesi viewed toward the southwest from the northeast across the Wadi Hesi (foreground). The Early Bronze strata occupy the entire area from the acropolis at the right to the dune ridge behind the tent camp at the left. Photo by R. Adams and C. Peachey.

phase of occupation on the tell (Petrie 1891: 31–32).

A year later F. J. Bliss dug about 30 more probes into the basin west of the tell, but he did not indicate their location or describe them except to state in one place that he dug over 17 ft. to reach the underlying barren soil in his deepest probe (Bliss 1894: 22). Bliss also dug a 27.5 ft. x 19.5 ft. probe to a depth of 12 ft. near the place where Petrie had found the wall on the crest of the north ridge. In this probe Bliss believed there could be as many as four phases of occupation representing the earliest occupation levels of the tell, extending "probably to the period of the great bed of ashes," which for him meant that these phases possibly included both the "Amorite" and the "Phoenician" periods, or (as this would be understood today) the Early Bronze and the Late Bronze periods, respectively (Bliss 1894: 22–27 and 130). Petrie, on the other

hand, had noted that pottery older than any found elsewhere on the site occurred in his probes of the basin. "The pottery found in the lower depths is not only Amorite in style, but more archaic than any found in the city" (Petrie 1891: 31). The present expedition's 1973 surface survey of the basin found a limited amount of Chalcolithic pottery in the area that supported Petrie's observation.

On the west side of the basin small wadis are eroding the soil, and in the banks of these wadis a zone rich in Early Bronze pottery can be traced. This appears to correlate with the Early Bronze occupational layers in the basin encountered in the probes by Petrie and Bliss, described above, as well as in the present expedition's Field IV probe (1973), described below. Since this pottery-rich zone has not been encountered on the west side of the west wadi, the latter must form the western limit to the

Early Bronze city. Fig. 13 pictures the considerable expanse of this occupation. The Early Bronze strata underlie the acropolis at the right of the picture and extend southward to the ridge beyond the tent camp at the left. In 1975 and subsequent seasons, portions of the EB mud-brick city wall have been exposed along this ridge.

The amount of cover that remains over the Early Bronze occupation levels in the basin area can be estimated fairly well. Fig. 12 indicates the areas where occupation levels have probably been disturbed by recent deep plowing. Field II was opened in 1970 to explore the Early Bronze horizons, but it was discovered that plowing had disturbed the occupational levels and only pits remained.

Late in the 1973 season another probe into the basin, Field IV, was dug west of the tell. Here the plowing had disturbed the tops of some standing mud-brick walls, but well-preserved floors were found below the plowed depth. The probe is described in detail in another chapter (see Toombs 1989 [Chapter VII below]: 155). Since the bottom of the occupation levels had not been reached at the end of the 1973 excavation season, an auger probe was drilled in the bottom of the Field IV probe to identify the underlying materials. It appeared that the mud-brick house in Field IV was founded on a deep red husma soil that had developed on stratified sandy deposits. This undisturbed soil zone suggests we were at the bottom of the occupation levels, and, since no yellow dune sand ("golden sand") was encountered in this probe above the indurated bedrock, this area is beyond the limit of the dune that underlies the acropolis of Tell el-Hesi.

In 1970, discovery of Chalcolithic sherds in the lowest stratum above virgin soil in Field III indicated that remains of a small Chalcolithic occupation may underlie part of the Early Bronze city (see Coogan 1989 [Chapter IX below]). Additionally, sherd accumulations found in surface surveys place a possible center for this occupation in the basin near the mouth of the central wadi just southeast of the tell. This is also known to be a disturbed area where later inhabitants (Iron II and Persian periods) dug clay pits to obtain brick material to build up the tell. This region along the central wadi is a natural place to locate pits to trap rain water in the winter months to make bricks, and such a disturbance of the area may have turned up the Chalcolithic sherds. The clay pits probably contributed to the dissection of the central wadi, and it now cuts deeply below all occupation levels.

Thus far there is no archaeological evidence for construction horizons in the basin area later than Early Bronze, but the high concentration of ash and later pottery over this region suggests that it was used also in subsequent periods for occupation, probably by tent dwellers. Even now, Bedouin tents occupy the area over the winter months.

The South Ridge (Barchan Dune). The South Ridge is today actually three separate hills due to stream dissection, but it may well have been one continuous ridge at the time of Early Bronze occupation. The two eastern hills are fairly low with broad tops, and the Expedition's tent camps in 1971, 1973, and 1975 were set up centering on the one lone tree—a large spreading tamarisk—that grows in the gap between these two hills (see fig. 13). Several stone-heap graves exist on the easternmost hill, and bones that have washed out of the south side of this hill indicate that a much larger Arab cemetery existed in this area in the recent past. The slope of these hills and the stones on top have prevented plowing, and their only disturbance has been the shallow Arab burials.

The westernmost of the three hills is a long, narrow, linear high ridge with an elevation greater than that of the tell, and it is now the highest point in the immediate region of the tell. Rapid stream-erosion is cutting into the west slope of this ridge, and its original shape as a barchan dune (see fig. 14) has been distorted. Probably at the time of Early Bronze occupation this hill had a broad surface gently sloping southwest, but, with the breaking of vegetation cover during periods of drier climate, blow-outs developed, and these were enlarged by water erosion at a rate too rapid for vegetation to become reestablished. The northeastern side of this ridge still retains a steep concave slope of about 35° that would be typical of the angle of repose for sand on the lee side of a barchan dune. Thus the northeast lee slope of this dune is unchanged since Early Bronze times and is far too steep to expect constructions, though caves and burials could well have been dug into it.

An ash layer containing an abundance of Early Bronze sherds can be traced along the steep south and southwest sides of these three hills that form the South Ridge. This occupation debris rests on a well-preserved soil horizon, which suggests that Early Bronze was the earliest period of occupation in this area. Since this occupation horizon is exposed, it clearly indicates that the Early Bronze city was larger, although perhaps only slightly larger, than the region outlined in fig. 12. The city's

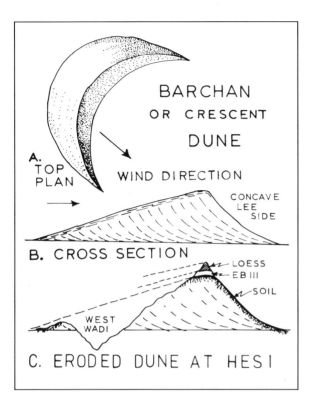

Fig. 14. Development of the South Ridge (barchan dune).
A. Top plan of a barchan-type dune. The arrow indicates
   the predominant wind direction to form this dune.
B. A dune-section through the middle of the barchan dune
   form shown in A. The windward side has a gentle slope,
   but the lee side is concave and forms at the angle of repose of the material that makes up the dune.
C. The west end of the South Ridge has been eroded by wind
   blow-out and by the west wadi. Probably this dune had
   the form shown in B during the time of Early Bronze occupation. The acropolis of Tell el-Hesi itself may well have
   been built on a smaller barchan dune.
                              Drawings by F. L. Koucky.

extent is suggested by the fact that only one small
patch of ash containing Early Bronze sherds was
found farther south. The Early Bronze ash layer
is discontinuous at two notches (near Field VII)
on the highest, westernmost hill, probably at probes
by Petric (see Matthers 1989 [Chapter II below]:
fig. 6). In Field VII about one meter of construction and loess overlies the Early Bronze ash
horizons.

In 1973 two large, dressed stones were noted
on the crest of the middle hill. Each stone had
been carefully cut in the form of a flat, circular
disk which might have been the base for a large
column (see fig. 15). The larger disk was cut from
Mishash Formation brecciated chert and had a

diameter of 102 cm. x 110 cm. (nearly round)
and a thickness of 46 cm. While small cobbles of
this brecciated chert can be found in the wadi,
such a large stone had to have been quarried in
the Judean mountains and imported into the
region. The second stone disk was nearly identical
with the larger disk (93 cm. x 80 cm. in diameter—
more elliptical than the larger stone—and 38 cm.
thick), but had been carved from the local conglomerate which is exposed along the Wadi Hesi
in several places near the tell. The stones are too
large to be moved without great difficulty and are
therefore thought to be near their original sites.[4]
In 1975, a probe was dug at the crest of the central
hill between the two stones (Field V). Excavation
proved that the stones had been moved in comparatively recent times and were not now in the
places of their original use.

Over a meter of loess had accumulated between
the stones and the Bronze Age occupation horizons. No distinct paleosols could be identified in
the loess accumulation, but a calcrete horizon had
developed at a shallow depth under the surface.
A second well-developed calcrete (caliche) zone of
concretions had developed across the Early Bronze
horizons. There may be a weak, thin intermediate
zone of calcrete development above the main Early
Bronze occupation horizons. Calcrete develops from
leaching the carbonate-rich loess during more
humid periods. The calcrete forms below the exposed surface and often fills cavities left by roots.
Thus two, possibly three, humid periods in this
region are indicated after the Early Bronze occupation. So thick an accumulation of loess on top
of a hill could have been retained by walls constructed there.

Several pits were noted in association with the
ash layer along the high west hill of the south ridge.
In the interiors of these pits there was evidence of
heat intense enough to fuse the underlying soil into
a greenish slag. The use of these pits is not yet
known. They may have been only fire pits associated with cooking, yet the temperatures generated
could easily fire pottery. In a 1973 test, pottery made
of local clays was successfully fired with local wood
in a similar open pit.

The High (North) Terrace. The north side of
the tell and the north side of the north ridge drop
off sharply to a lower, flat-surfaced, high-river terrace. This same level surface can be traced along
the Wadi Hesi west of the west wadi. Fig. 10 shows
that drainage paths developed on the western hills
suddenly end in small alluvial fans when they

Fig. 15. Larger of the two disk-shaped stones. This one is carved from the Mishash brecciated chert formation and imported from quarries in the Judean mountains. Diameter: 120 cm. × 110 cm. (nearly round); thickness: 46 cm. The exposed surface is polished. Photo by B. T. Dahlberg.

reach the high terrace, because of its great porosity. Water immediately percolates through the gravel and sand beds that compose the terrace. The high terrace is truncated on the east by the Wadi Hesi, and along the wadi are fresh vertical cuts that expose the stratigraphy of the terrace (see fig. 16). Since the Wadi Hesi flows past the areas of occupation and the tell before passing the high terrace, occupational debris will become a part of any terraces formed after occupation had begun. A careful study of the cuts into this high terrace by the wadi reveals that at the bottom of the cuts, near the level of the present wadi and a few feet above, coarse gravels are exposed. These gravels are well sorted and contain large angular fragments of Early Bronze pottery. These sherds could not have been transported far and must have been introduced into a clear, fast stream very near where they were found.

The size of the gravel decreases upward in these terrace cuts, and layers of stratified, water-laid beds of loess become more numerous and thicker. The water-laid loess is barren of sherds, but the higher, fine-gravel layers contain numerous rounded and worn fragments of Early Bronze pottery. These fragments clearly contrast with the large, angular fragments found in the lowest gravel layers. Careful searching has found no fragments other than those of Early Bronze in the gravel layers, but Late Bronze pottery is fairly abundant on the top surface of the terrace.

This evidence leads to the conclusion that the high terrace was not in existence during the Early Bronze period and that the Wadi Hesi probably flowed just below the north ridge. It is likely that broken pottery was thrown into the wadi from the north ridge and worked its way quickly between the gravels. During the Early Bronze period the wadi was as deeply or slightly more deeply incised than at present, but by the Middle Bronze period the wadi was rapidly aggrading and by the Late

Fig. 16. Vertical section through the high (north) terrace cut by erosion from the Wadi Hesi. View is west-southwest; access road crosses wadi at the right. Photo by R. Adams and C. Peachey.

Bronze period had reached the height of the high terrace. In the Late Bronze period the silting (eluviation) ended, and the wadi again began to downcut (illuviation), thus preserving the high terrace. These changes in stream regime must have been climatically induced and suggest that, while Early Bronze III was a wet humid period, the climate changed during the Middle Bronze to a much drier one with abundantly available loess. By Late Bronze time the climate had become wet enough to allow the stream to start downcutting again. The very rapid eluviation of the Wadi Hesi during the Middle Bronze period may well have been the result of the clearing and farming of lands along the wadi by the Early Bronze peoples.

Apparently the Hesi region was not occupied during the Middle Bronze period when the high terrace formed, but Middle Bronze shaft tombs were found at the base of Tell Nagila (about 6 km. to the southeast of Tell el-Hesi). When visited in the summer of 1975, these tombs showed evidence of recent robbing, and an abundance of large sherds was collected near some of the recently opened tombs. The Hesi site was reoccupied in the Late Bronze period but not on the scale of the Early Bronze occupation.

The Low Terrace (NE of Tell el-Hesi and E of the Wadi Hesi). Surprisingly, the low terrace northeast of the tell and east of the wadi has not yielded a single sherd of pottery, not even of the recent black "Gaza" ware, though it has been subjected to several reconnaissance surveys. More surprisingly, no pottery was found near the wells just across the Wadi Hesi from the tell. These facts suggest that the low terrace is of quite recent origin.

On Petrie's map of the tell region (Petrie 1891: fig. 1), the south end of this terrace is mapped as a shingle (imbricated gravel) shoal. At present the shingle material is not exposed, and the region is covered by fine, water-laid loess which is probably the result of recent flooding. The sediment source for materials building this terrace is south of the tell, and consequently no sherds are washed in. It is very likely that in Early Bronze times the Wadi Hesi flowed where the terrace now exists and was not then eroding the tell area.

The join of the Wadi Jizair (Nahal Adorayim) with the Wadi Hesi (fig. 11; see also fig. 9) is quite abnormal, since it flows in a very straight, narrow trench in a direction just opposite to that of the Wadi Hesi before they join. It is very likely that a trench was dug in the past to divert the Wadi Jizair's flow to the south and allow it to irrigate the whole lower terrace. Even today the lower terrace retains green grass long after other fields have turned brown. A short distance upstream on the Wadi Jizair is a ruined dam, built to pond water and force it into linear irrigation ditches in the surrounding fields.

As one studies the map of the Wadi Hesi to the west of Tell el-Hesi, it is clear that steep wadi scarps exist only on the south side of the wadi and that the stream now uses only the south side of the Wadi Hesi valley. Thus the abnormal join of the Wadi Jizair and the Wadi Hesi and the formation of the recent low terrace could also be due to recent tectonic activity in the region. If the region had been given a slight southern tilt, streams such as the Wadi Hesi would have been forced to "slide" slightly southward and thus cut into southern banks, forming scarps, and to develop a low, northern terrace system as the result of periodic flooding. (A broader region would need to be studied to test this last hypothesis.)

The Eastern Hill. The modern road to the tell crosses the Wadi Jizair, passes over the lower part of the Eastern Hill, and then descends into the valley of the Wadi Hesi. The high steel towers of power lines form a prominent landmark on the north side of this hill. It is from along this road that the most spectacular view of the tell can be gained, for here one can look at the steep scarp on the eastern side of the tell rising above the Wadi Hesi.

Preliminary reconnaissance of the eastern hill indicates a low amount of surface sherds (but these represent nearly all the archaeological periods from Early Bronze to the present) and a moderate amount of lithic material. The lithics are especially abundant on the crest of the hill and down the southeast side to a series of trenches cut into the banks of the Wadi Hesi in 1972 by a team from Tel Aviv University. This site is marked by a circled "C" in fig. 10. This Upper Paleolithic excavation, directed by Dr. David Gilard, was mentioned above (p. 21).

The entire hill area is now plowed yearly and planted in grain or melons, except for a small area around a pipe stem that marks the site of recent and, as yet, unsuccessful drilling for oil.

The Southeast Hill. Nearly all the southeast hill is plowed each year and used for grain cultivation. Only a low sherd and lithic density was noted in reconnaissance of this area, except on the eastern edge on a bedrock exposure above a steep cliff overlooking the Wadi Hesi, where there is an abundance of broken lithics, chips, and cores that could represent a Paleolithic work site.

The Western Hills. On the lower eastern edge of the western hills along the western wadi, an early cemetery was discovered by Petrie (see fig. 12). Here he found numerous burials of bones in jars, though most of the bones were of animals (see Chapter II, p. 43, below). The area of Petrie's cemetery has been examined each year, and sherds and bones continue to wash out there. In 1971 a small exploratory probe was dug in this region as part of the survey, and five human burials were found in the sand without associated grave stones or goods. The only pottery associated with these burials was LB II.

The western hills are part of a large, ancient, sand-dune ridge that has been described above (see fig. 9). The gently rolling upland of these hills is now plowed and planted in grain each year. A deep red husma soil has developed there. In some years the fields are burned after harvest, and in some years the chaff and straw are plowed in, so that the plowed soil looks much like decayed mud brick over the whole region. Actually, any of this soil material could be used to make mud bricks.

Relatively few sherds were found in a reconnaissance of these hills. They were mainly Byzantine or later black "Gaza" ware except for the two places marked by circled "A" and "B" in fig. 10. At "B" on the crest of the hill is a *weli* (tomb of a Muslim holy man). Surrounding the *weli* is a dark grayish, ash-rich soil that is in marked contrast to the reddish soil over the rest of the hill. A moderate amount of sherd material has been found in this ashy soil. If the recent sherds among them are disregarded, all the pottery sherds here are from the Iron II or Persian Period. It is very likely that this is but a small exposure of a much larger Iron II and Persian occupation that has been buried under the loess that covers this region. As illustrated in fig. 17, this thick loess makes it difficult to find sites by simple surface surveys. There is no evidence that the basin area surrounding the tell was used as a permanent living site by the peoples who modified

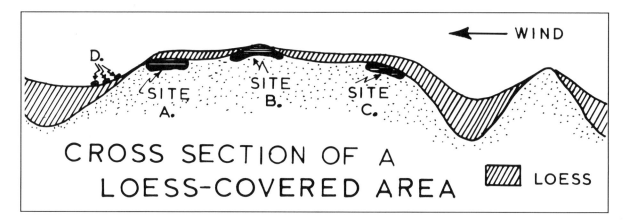

Fig. 17. Generalized section of the region to illustrate the variable thickness of the loess cover. In general, the crest of hills has the thinnest loess cover and has the greatest tendency to become exposed. Site B illustrates this. Sites A and C on the lower lands have received thicker loess covers. Note that site A at the edge of a wadi is now being eroded and that sherds are washing down on top of the loess at D. This creates a situation in which the site might be mislocated in a surface survey. It could also cause problems in interpreting the stratigraphy of the region. (Sites A-C in this sketch are illustrative only and are not related to sites A-C in fig. 10.) Drawing by F. L. Koucky.

the tell's acropolis after the Early Bronze Age. It is likely that the Iron II and Persian Period villages related to the tell were built west of it on this upland overlooking the broad Hesi valley.

At "A" in fig. 10 is a very large site that still contains outlines of building foundations and some stone walls. When Robinson described his travels through this region, he mentioned passing the stone ruins of a former village called Tunnur (Robinson 1841: II, 390; 1856: II, 48). This could well be the site of the Bedouin village mentioned by Volney (1787: II, 337, see p. 5, above), since there are abundant Late Arab pottery sherds scattered over the region. Most of the pottery collected was Byzantine, but there were also moderate amounts of Late Roman to Umayyad and Mameluke. It is not unlikely that this village was occupied from Late Roman times until the Crusades and then reoccupied and rebuilt in the late 1700s as an Arab village called Hesi. This village was built on the western flank of the western hills and on the broad upper terraces of the wide valley of the Wadi Hesi. Tell Sheqef is but a short distance to the northwest of this site. As with site B, here also the deep plowing is encroaching on the site more each year. In 1975 several whole Byzantine cooking pots were found crushed and cut in the new plow furrows.

In Avi-Yonah's "Map of Roman Palestine" (1936) it is suggested that the main Roman road through this region passed a Roman villa described by Petrie at Umm Lakis (Petrie 1891: 9–10) and that it ex-

tended up the valley of Wadi Hesi to site A (see fig. 10). Petrie thought Tell Sheqef (Tell Abu Shukf; see Petrie 1890: 221; 1891: 53) was a late construction, since it contained Roman buildings on top. Visits to that tell in 1973 and 1975 by members of the Hesi Expedition have noted the high concentration of Roman and later sherds, but some that were characteristic of Philistine and Late Bronze pottery were also collected, and a large Chalcolithic site is SW of the tell. It is not unlikely that the Wadi Hesi formed an early political boundary between territories, and that Tell el-Hesi and Tell Sheqef represent two lookout posts that were used to watch a road along this boundary and guard it against violation.

The Citrus Grove. The region to the north of the tell and north of the Wadi Hesi was much like the area of the western hills until the early 1960s, when water was brought into the region and a large citrus grove was established. Because there has been much leveling and filling there since then, and because the area now has a dense tree growth and is under continuous cultivation, it is almost impossible to survey that region. A sparse to moderate scatter of sherds has been found in various traverses over it. They represent all of the periods found at the tell, but no real evaluation has been attempted. A study of aerial photographs taken before the citrus grove was planted did not reveal any occupational sites, but it must be remembered that the ground surface in this region is rapidly covered by wind-blown loess; thus sites do not necessarily disclose themselves to aerial photography.

Clearly the most-traveled route from Gaza to Jerusalem would take the military or the traveler close to Tell el-Hesi. In contrast to the more southerly routes (which are longer), this one would have well-spaced wells and grazing land even through the summer. Trade with the migrant Bedouin to the south and the farmers on the north would be expected at stations along this route, yet guards would be needed to prevent the Bedouin from driving their herds into the cultivated areas.

In a proposed study on the geology of the region in this series of reports on Hesi, other areas farther from the tell will be discussed. This should help elucidate the economy prevailing among those who once occupied the site.

NOTES

1. Following his visit to the site in 1838, Edward Robinson argued from the geographical allusions in Acts 8:26-40 that it "might not improbably" have been the Wadi Hesi, where it nears the tell, in which Philip the Evangelist baptized the Ethiopian (Robinson 1841: II, 640-42; 1856: II, 514-15). —Editor.
2. "Tell el-Hesi" as an archaeological site designation is often understood to include both the high mound (the "acropolis") and the lower (Early Bronze) city enclosure extending south and west from its base. In the following discussion the writer reserves "tell" as the term for Hesi's conical high mound, or "upper city," only. On the varying topographical conventions that have been used for describing the Hesi site, see Matthers 1989 (Chapter II below): note 13. —Editor.
3. The basin is the area referred to by Petrie as "the enclosure," and by the present expedition usually as "the terrace" or "the lower city." See fig. 16 and Matthers 1989 (Chapter II below): note 13. —Editor.
4. The smaller of these large stones has disappeared, having been removed from the site by unknown persons between the 1981 and 1983 excavation seasons. —Editor.

BIBLIOGRAPHY FOR CHAPTER I

Avi-Yonah, M.
  1936 Map of Roman Palestine. *Quarterly of the Department of Antiquities* 5: 139-83.
Begin, Z. B.; Ehrlich, A.; and Nathan, Y.
  1974 *Lake Lisan.* Israeli Geological Survey Bulletin 63.
Beha ed-Din, Ibn Shaddad (Yusef Ibn Rafi)
  1897 *The Life of Saladin* [ca. 1193]. Translated from the French translation of the 1787 Leiden [Schultens] Edition, by C. W. Wilson and C. R. Conder. Library of the Palestine Pilgrim Text Society 32. London: Palestine Exploration Fund.

Bell, B.
  1975 Climate and History in Egypt: The Middle Kingdom. *American Journal of Science* 79: 223-70.
Bliss, F. J.
  1894 *A Mound of Many Cities or Tell el-Hesy Excavated.* London: Palestine Exploration Fund.
Broecker, W. S.
  1968 In Defence of the Astronomical Theory of Glaciation. *Meteorological Monographs* 8,30: 139-41.
Bryson, R. A., and Padoch, C.
  1981 On the Climates of History. In *Climate and History.* Edited by R. I. Rotberg and T. K. Rabb. Princeton, NJ: Princeton University Press: 3-17. Reprinted from *Journal of Interdisciplinary History* 10 (1980), 583-97.
Conder, C. R., and Kitchener, H. H.
  1883 *The Survey of Western Palestine.* Vol. III: *Judaea.* London: Palestine Exploration Fund.
Coogan, M. D.
  1989 Chalcolithic Remains in Field III. In *Tell el-Hesi: The Site and the Expedition,* pp. 169-76. Edited by B. T. Dahlberg and K. G. O'Connell, S.J. Excavation Reports of the American Schools of Oriental Research: Tell el-Hesi 4. Winona Lake, IN: Eisenbrauns.
Dewey, J. F.; Pitman, W. C.; Ryan, W. B. F.; and Bonnin, J.
  1973 Plate Tectonics and Evolution of the Alpine System. *Geological Society of America Bulletin* 84: 3137-80.
Euler, R. C.; Gumerman, G. J.; Karlstrom, T. N. V.; Dean, J. S.; and Hevly, R. H.
  1979 The Colorado Plateau: Cultural Dynamics and Paleoenvironment. *Science* 205 No. 4411: 1089-1101.
Fairbridge, R. W.
  1972 Quaternary Sedimentation in the Mediterranean Region Controlled in Tectonics, Paleoclimate, and Sea Level. In *The Mediterranean Sea.* Edited by D. J. Stanley. Philadelphia: Dowden, Hutchinson, and Ross: 99-114.
Ginzburg, A.; Cohen, S. S.; Hay-Roe, H.; and Rosenzweig, A.
  1975 Geology of the Mediterranean Shelf of Israel. *American Association of Petroleum Geologists Bulletin* 59: 2142-60.

Gvirtzman, G.
1973 The coastal plain and shelf of Israel during the Neogene. *Proceedings of the Annual Science Meeting.* Jerusalem: Israel Academy of Sciences: 73–75 and maps of the Coastal Plain.

Horowitz, A.
1975 The Pleistocene Paleoenvironments of Israel. In *Problems in Prehistory: North Africa and the Levant.* Edited by F. Wendorf and A. E. Marks. Southern Methodist University Contributions to Anthropology 13. Dallas: Southern Methodist University Press: 207–28.

1979 *The Quaternary of Israel.* New York: Academic Press.

Josephus, Flavius
1958 *Jewish Antiquities*, Books XV–XVII [ca. 94 CD]. English Translation by R. Marcus. Completed and edited by A. Wikgren. The Loeb Classical Library No. 140. London: William Heinemann; Cambridge: Harvard University Press.

Kellogg, T. B.
1974 Late Quaternary Climate Changes in the Norwegian and Greenland Seas. In *Climate of the Arctic.* Alaska Scientific Conference, Proceedings No. 24: 3–36.

Klostermann, E., ed.
1904 *Das Onomastikon der Biblischen Ortsnamen.* Eusebius Werke, III. Band, I. Hälfte. Die Griechischen Christlichen Schriftsteller der Ersten Drei Jahrhunderte. Leipzig: J. C. Hinrichs.

Ladurie, E. Le R.
1971 *Times of Feast, Times of Famine.* Second edition. Translated by B. Bray. Garden City, NY: Doubleday.

Lamb, H. H.
1966 *The Changing Climate.* London: Methuen & Co.

Matthers, J. M.
1989 Excavations by the Palestine Exploration Fund at Tell el-Hesi, 1890–1892. In *Tell el-Hesi: The Site and the Expedition*, pp. 37-67. Edited by B. T. Dahlberg and K. G. O'Connell, S.J. Excavation Reports of the American Schools of Oriental Research: Tell el-Hesi 4. Winona Lake, IN: Eisenbrauns.

Molnár, G.
1981 Possible Effects of Long Lasting Absence of Solar Activity on Climate. *Climate Change* 3: 189–201.

Neev, D.
1975 Tectonic Evolution of the Middle East and the Levantine Basin. *Geology* 3: 683–86.

Neev, D., and Emery, K. O.
1967 *The Dead Sea.* Israel Geological Survey Bulletin 41.

Orni, E., and Efrat, E.
1971 *Geography of Israel.* Third Edition. Jerusalem: Israel Universities Press.

Petrie, W. M. F.
1890 Journals of Mr. W. M. Flinders Petrie. *Palestine Exploration Fund Quarterly Statement* 22: 219–46.

1891 *Tell el Hesy (Lachish).* London: Palestine Exploration Fund.

Robinson, E.
1841 *Biblical Researches in Palestine, Mount Sinai, and Arabia Petraea.* 3 Vols. London: John Murray; Boston: Crocker and Brewster. Reprinted at Salem, NH: Ayer Company, 1977.

1856 *Idem.* Second edition, with new maps and plans.

Stearns, C. E., and Thurber, D. L.
1965 Th^{230}–U^{234} Dates of Late Pleistocene Marine Fossils from the Mediterranean and Moroccan Littorals. *Quaternaria* VII: 29–42.

Survey of Israel
1959 1:100,000 Map Series. Jerusalem: Department of Survey, Ministry of Labour, State of Israel.

Survey of Palestine
1924 1:20,000 Topographic Series, Administrative Maps of Palestine. British Mandatory Government.

Toombs, L. E.
1989 The Stratigraphy of the Site at the End of Phase One. In *Tell el-Hesi: The Site and the Expedition*, pp. 125-62. Edited by B. T. Dahlberg and K. G. O'Connell, S.J. Excavation Reports of the American Schools of Oriental Research: Tell el-Hesi 4. Winona Lake, IN: Eisenbrauns.

Van der Hammen, T.; Wijmstra, T. A.; and Zagwin, W. H.
1971 The Floral Record of the Late Cenozoic of Europe. In *The Late Cenozoic Glacial Ages.* Edited by K. K. Turekian. New Haven: Yale University Press.

Volney, M. C.-F.
1787 *Travels through Syria and Egypt in the Years 1783, 1784, and 1785.* 2 vols. Translated from the French. London: G. G. J. and J. Robinson. Reprint. Westmead, Farnborough, Hants., England: Gregg International, 1972.

Wendland, W. M., and Bryson, R. A.
1974 Dating Climatic Episodes of the Holocene. *Quaternary Research* 4: 9–24.

Wollin, G.; Ericson, D. B.; and Wollin, J.
1974 Geomagnetic Variations and Climatic Changes 2,000,000 B.C.–1970 A.D. In *Les méthodes quantitatives d'étude des variations du climat au cours du Pleistocene.* Paris: Colloques internationaux du Centre National de la Recherche scientifique, No. 129: 273–88.

Yallon, D. H., and Dan, J.
1974 Accumulation and Distribution of Loess-Derived Deposits in the Semi-Desert and Desert Fringe of Israel. *Zeitschrift für Geomorphologie* 20: 91–105.

Yallon, D. H., and Ganor, E.
1973 The Influence of Dust on Soils During the Quaternary. *Soil Science* 116: 146–55.

Chapter II

EXCAVATIONS BY THE PALESTINE EXPLORATION FUND AT TELL EL-HESI 1890-1892

by
John M. Matthers (†1981)
Palestine Exploration Fund

THE WORK OF THE PALESTINE EXPLORATION FUND

The survey of Jerusalem carried out by Captain Charles Wilson of the Royal Engineers between June 1864 and May 1865 caused a great deal of public interest and was the stimulus for the founding of the Palestine Exploration Fund.[1] At a meeting in the Jerusalem Chamber, Westminster, on May 12, 1865, it was decided that "an association be formed under the title of the Palestine Exploration Fund for the purpose of investigating the archaeology, geography, geology, and natural history of Palestine" (Minutes, May 12, 1865). The Fund was formally constituted in June of that year.

One of the first actions of the founding committee was to ask Wilson to make a general survey of Palestine in order to determine what projects the Fund could usefully undertake in the future. Consequently, as leader of the Fund's first expedition, Wilson brought a small party in 1866 on a journey from Beirut to Damascus, Galilee, Samaria, and Jerusalem (Watson 1915: 31). Many sites were surveyed, and much information was brought back to the Committee. Wilson was particularly impressed with the site of Tell Hum (Capernaum) on the Sea of Galilee as a place profitable for excavation. In the light of Wilson's reports, the Committee announced (Watson 1915: 39–40) that the objectives of its future work were (1) a detailed survey of both eastern and western Palestine; (2) exploration and excavation of Jerusalem; (3) study of the geology, natural history, and meteorology of Pales-

tine; and (4) excavation of the tells of Palestine.

Between 1866 and 1888 the Fund concentrated on the first three of these objectives. An impressive list of achievements marks those years:

1867–1870	Excavations at Jerusalem by C. Warren.
1870–1871	Explorations in Sinai, Edom, and Moab by E. M. Palmer and C. F. Tyrwhitt Drake.
1871–1877	A survey of western Palestine by R. W. Stewart, C. F. Tyrwhitt Drake, C. R. Conder, and H. H. Kitchener.
1873–1874	An archaeological survey in Jerusalem and southern Palestine by C. Clermont-Ganneau.
1881–1882	A survey of eastern Palestine by C. R. Conder and A. M. Mantell.
1883–1884	A survey of the Wadi Arabah by E. Hull and H. H. Kitchener, and a geological examination of the country from Sinai and Aqaba to the Dead Sea.
1885–1886	A survey of country to the east of the Jordan by G. Schumacher.
1886–1890	Explorations in Jerusalem by C. Schick.[2]

By 1888 the Fund was ready to undertake the remaining objective: excavation of the tells of Palestine. In November of that year A. H. Sayce, the eminent Assyriologist, and Charles Wilson (by then Sir Charles) proposed that definite plans should be made to begin the work. On December 18 it was agreed at a meeting of the Executive Committee that a firman or permit be applied for from the Turkish authorities "for excavation in Jerusalem and on both sides of the Jordan for the purpose of identifying Bible places" (Executive Committee Minutes, December 18, 1888). The application for the firman was made through the British Foreign Office.

Fig. 1. W. M. Flinders Petrie.

W. M. FLINDERS PETRIE (1853–1942)

It must have been about the same time that an informal approach was made on behalf of the Fund to the Egyptologist, W. M. Flinders Petrie (fig. 1). At the age of thirty-five he had already established his reputation with ten years of excavation in Egypt. His first contact with the Fund is recorded in a letter he wrote to the Committee from Medinet el-Fayum on January 28, 1889:

> My dear Sir,
> Your informant has certainly a ready imagination. I have not ever thought of applying for a firman, or of conducting any work on my own account in Palestine, nor have I ever had any relations with a German in my work.[3] The subject of the tells of south Palestine is one which has been mentioned

to me by two office-bearers of your Fund; but beyond that I have not thought of taking up the subject. If however serious work is in prospect, I should be very glad to place a portion of my time at the disposal of the committee as you have suggested.

> The terms of the firman are of course an affair between the committee and the Porte [Ottoman Government]. And if my services should be acceptable to the committee I should be quite satisfied with any agreement between us that they may think suitable. I understand that the winter is not a good season for such work in Palestine; hence probably I could continue my annual work in Egypt from November to March, and then work in Palestine from March to June. But this is not essential.

> I am accustomed to hire and pay every workman myself, and never have any interpreter with me. Nor do I believe in middlemen, and at present I have no one but workmen with me, without any overseer. Hence you will see that in no case do I want a staff of encumbrances about with me.

> Last year and this I have been working in Egypt privately; the expenses and proceeds being shared with some friends. As it is possible that other arrangements might arise which would oblige me to give all my time to Egypt, I do not wish anything in this letter to be understood as binding me in case circumstances should alter.

> Believe me, Dear Sir,
> Yours very sincerely,
> W. M. Flinders Petrie.
> (PEF/Bliss/I/4)[4]

The Committee was soon forced to be more specific in its plans. In February 1889 the Turkish authorities responded that sites would have to be designated before a firman would be granted. In April the Committee was told that the excavators must be named as well, and then in June that a map of the area had to be submitted with the application. The area was not to exceed ten square kilometers. In that same month of June 1889 the Committee formally invited Petrie to direct an excavation for the Fund in the spring of 1890. The choice of the site was delayed until July, when Petrie arrived in London to take part in the discussion of the question at the annual general meeting of the Fund. The Executive Committee made the final decision in August, accepting the recommendation of Petrie, Wilson, and Sayce that the Khirbet Ajlan area was the most promising. They hoped that Khirbet Ajlan and nearby Umm Lakis were the biblical Eglon and Lachish, respectively.[5] A plan of the area including these sites (fig. 2) was sent with the formal application to the Turkish authorities. Petrie returned to Egypt on September 25 still very uncertain about many details of his appointment. He managed to settle some of these problems in correspondence with Sir Walter Besant,

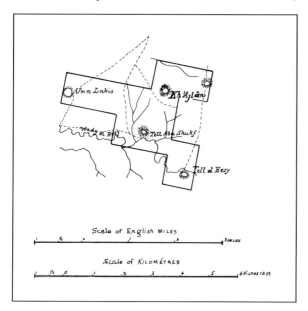

Fig. 2. Area map submitted by the Palestine Exploration Fund with its application for a firman. August 1889.

the Honorary Secretary of the Fund (PEF/Petrie/ 3–6). To fulfill the requirement of regular reports to the Committee during his excavations in Palestine, he decided to make available to the Fund his private journal which he would be sending home regularly to his mother in Bromley, Kent (PEF/ Petrie/3). With a few omissions, that is what was published in the *Quarterly Statement* for 1890 (Petrie 1890c). (The Journal shows that at the same time he also reported most of his activity in letters to George Armstrong, Acting Secretary of the Fund.)

In December 1889 further details concerning the whereabouts of Khirbet Ajlan had to be sent off to the Turkish authorities, since they were unable to locate it. Despite this the Committee heard in January that the firman had been granted. It immediately paid the £50 deposit and £20 fee, sent a telegram to Petrie in Egypt, issued a press release, and sent out a "special appeal" for funds to "all subscribers and friends interested in the work." £1,000 was sought; £1,110 6s. 6d. was actually subscribed[6] (Minutes, July 1, 1890).[7]

Meanwhile, Petrie had been excavating at Kahun and Gurob in the Egyptian Fayum. "I have filled up my time till now very well in finishing off the two towns that I discovered last year," he wrote to

Armstrong on January 11 (PEF/Petrie/7; cf. Petrie 1892b: 112–37). As soon as it became available, Armstrong sent him a copy of the following translation of the firman:

This permission has been given to Mr. Flinders Petrie, Member of the Administration of the British Museum, on his application for leave to search for and excavate antiquities in the place called Khirbet Ajlan in the Kaimakamlik [District] of Gaza in the Metesariflik [Province] of Jerusalem and after all the steps have been taken and all the investigations made which are required by the Regulations for the excavation of antiquities that the antiquities which are excavated in conformity with the said regulation shall belong entirely to the state museum, the Excavator only being able to make drawings or casts from them; that the antiquities found shall be all kept in a safe place, to be pointed out by the local authorities under the charge of an official who shall be appointed, and that the excavators shall not put hands on nor interfere with them; that the sphere of the excavation shall not exceed the boundaries marked on the maps of the locality drawn up by the applicant; that, if after the excavations have been begun any objection is found by the Government and the excavations temporarily stopped the explorers shall have no right to claim any expenses or indemnity; that the guarantee money shall be restored at the expiration of the term of the permission, or before, if it is announced that the excavations are finished and that the conditions of the Regulations have been entirely complied with; that the salary of the official to be appointed shall be paid by the applicant up to the completion of the excavation; that the permission shall be revoked if the excavations are not commenced without excuse within three months from the date of the permission or it having been commenced, they are abandoned without excuse for two months; that the permission shall not be transferred or sold to another, in that all the provisions of the said regulation should be observed and that the permission shall be good for two years to date from February 5/17 of the year 1305/1890. The Minister for Public Instruction.

(PEF/Bliss/1/33/2)[8]

After a weakening bout of influenza and some difficulty with the Inspector of Antiquities in Cairo, Petrie left for Palestine on March 7, 1890. Rough seas made the journey an unpleasant one. The worst part was the disembarkation at Jaffa in the early hours of Sunday, March 9:

There was so much sea on that we bumped heavily against the rocks in the usual anchorage and steam was put on all in a scuffle, and we went and lay further out. Next day we all stood anxiously watching the heavy line of breakers in front of the harbor and fully expected that we should have to go on to Beirut, and take the next steamer back again. However a heavy rain that came up quieted the sea a little and after waiting till 11 we at last saw the boats coming out to meet us. The boats here are large and massive to bear the rough seas; they could not venture through the usual passage which was a mass of breakers, but came over the sand shoals at a risk of sticking and being swamped. The miseries of the waiting in the boats to leave the ship and the long row into the harbour (such as it is) in heavy showers was untellable. For 24 hours after it I was shaking inside and out, and even two or three days have hardly put me right again. (Journal, March 6–19, 1890; unpublished section)

In Jaffa Petrie stayed at the house of a boyhood friend, J. Longley Hall, now a missionary working in the area. On Tuesday, March 11, he went by carriage to Jerusalem. This was his first visit to Palestine, and his immediate impressions were not favorable:

The greyness of everything is oppressive; the hills are mainly bare grey limestone, the villages are equally grey stone houses, and the trees are grey olives. The wild flowers give some bright colour in parts, crimson poppies and exquisite pale purple orchids; in one valley were many almond trees all fully out. In the plain the villages are indistinguishable at a distance, as the houses are covered with earth which is all green with grass so that the village looks like a group of grassy hillocks. (Journal, March 6–19, 1890; unpublished section)

The Committee had insisted on correcting the firman's reference to the British Museum as the sponsoring body of the excavation in place of the Palestine Exploration Fund. The result was a delay that detained Petrie in Jerusalem from March 11 to the 29th. Taking advantage of the presence of Hayter Lewis, Thomas Chaplin, and Conrad Schick, he made a detailed study of the antiquities in Jerusalem (Petrie 1890a). He was most appreciative of these scholars, but became rather skeptical of their general understanding of ancient Jerusalem:

I learnt, I cannot say much, about the antiquities, but rather I found how provokingly little is positively known and in what a vast uncertainty almost every question still remains. . . .If ever the history of the city is to be clearly settled, it must be by learning the archaeology of Syria in other and less complicated sites, and then applying the knowledge of stone-working, of construction and

of pottery to fix the ages of things in Jerusalem. (Petrie 1890b: 160)

Apart from discerning comments on the known sites of the city—analyzing, for example, the methods of cutting stone that he observed in the quarries beneath Jerusalem (Journal, March 19–26, 1890; unpublished section)—his main contribution from these few days was to measure fifty ancient rock-cut tombs in the vicinity of the Kedron valley. Using principles put forward in his book, *Inductive Metrology* (1877), he determined the equivalents in inches for the commonest cubit-measure—and the variations thereof—used by the tomb builders (Petrie 1890b: 160–61).

On March 29 the British Consul in Jerusalem informed Petrie that the amended firman had arrived. They went together to see the Turkish governor, Reshad Pasha. Petrie was pleased with his reception:

Reshad Pasha was as agreeable as could be over the matter, willing to facilitate us in every way, and not in the least grasping as to the question of the pay of the government inspector; I asked to have a native and not a Turk, as I wanted to be able to use Arabic with him, and so he appointed a relative of one of the Jerusalem notables; and, as I hear that he has an affection for the bottle, no doubt a little supply of bakshish will keep him happy. (Journal, March 27–April 2, 1890; unpublished section)

The government inspector appointed was a man named Ibrahim Adham Effendi el-Khaldi (fig. 3), who was to be mentioned frequently in the correspondence of Petrie and his successor, Bliss. Petrie developed a dislike for the man,[9] whereas Bliss had a distinctly positive regard for him.[10]

Two days after this interview, Petrie set off for Jaffa to collect his equipment and a servant. The change of seasons in 1889–90 was late. There had been no rain before Christmas, and when the spring rains started they continued well into April. A violent storm that caused widespread damage along the coast broke during his journey to Jaffa and made it extremely unpleasant for him.

On April 3 a small convoy left Jaffa made up of Petrie, Muhammed (a servant chosen for him by his friend Hall), and the drivers of two equipment-laden camels. It took two days to reach the village of Bureir which was to be the base for Petrie's preliminary survey of the area specified by the firman (Journal, March 31–April 16; unpublished section). The first night in camp was disturbed by a burglar. Petrie awoke to someone leaning in through a gap in his tent. "I challenged, he ran, and four bullets went over his head to improve his pace" (Petrie 1890c: 220).

Fig. 3. Ibrahim Effendi, the Turkish Government Inspector.

For two days Petrie inspected the sites available to him for excavation. On April 7 he wrote Armstrong of his finding:

> *Umm Lakis* is mostly cultivated; but in all parts of it and also in a place a quarter of a mile to the east of it, the pottery all shows the Roman age. I expect to dig here for a short time however in order to organize the work on a near site.
> *Ajlan* is most unsatisfactory. It is all cultivated, the very top being a vegetable garden. There is not much pottery and everything seems to be Roman.
> *Tell Hesy* is a very fine site. The mound is about 60ft high and artificial for at least 20ft, as I saw layers of burnt earth in a section of one side cut away by a stream. I did not see a single trace of Roman times. All the pottery is of earlier styles, mostly like Egyptian pottery of the Ramesside times. The difficulty about work is that it is mostly cultivated so that I shall have to buy out crops from the petty shekh who swaggers about there; and also it is 6 miles from Bureir and there will be difficulty about

camping here. But this is the only place which is clearly promising.
> *Kh. Hazzarah* is very slight and of Roman age.
> *Tell Abu Shukf* is half cultivated; some of the pottery is Roman.
> *Kh. Sommeily* is pre-Roman; but there is only a small amount of pottery.
>
> (PEF/Petrie/12)

A further delay was caused by the failure of Ibrahim Effendi to arrive as arranged on April 7. Finally, on the tenth, Petrie was called to Gaza where he found the Effendi with the local Turkish official. "He (the Effendi) began with every sort of objection to coming or doing anything, evidently wishing to spin out the time of all pay and no work" (Petrie 1890c: 222). After a great deal of bargaining and a threat by Petrie to replace him, Ibrahim Effendi agreed to join the camp on Monday, April 14. The local official took Petrie's part and agreed that work could start on the fourteenth with or without the Effendi.

> . . . So I don't care when he comes. He will be a fearful plague. He grumbles about the bread, about the supplies, about the distance, about a cook, although he has £15 a month in order to pay liberally for horses, servants and all he can want. . . . I am determined that he must either settle civilly or else go.
>
> (Journal, for April 7–16, 1890; unpublished section: Fund copy PEF/Petrie/29D)

Ibrahim Effendi arrived on time, eager to please and to show himself useful.

Petrie excavated at Umm Lakis from April 14 to 16, and found exactly what he had anticipated: "I made trench-pits in many different parts and everywhere the result is 4 to 8 feet of earth and burnt dust, &c., with Roman and Arab pottery. Beneath that is clean untouched red earth, veined with white infiltration, evidently undisturbed soil" (Petrie 1890c: 222). On April 17 he moved camp from Bureir to the vicinity of Tell el-Hesi, six miles away.[11]

The First Season at Tell el-Hesi: April 17–May 31, 1890

Petrie now found himself in Arab country where the Turkish administration was unable to enforce its rule fully. All negotiations about land, workers, and such had to be made with the sheikhs of the neighborhood. He was saved from this ordeal by Ibrahim Effendi, who insisted on taking command of the situation and spent two whole days bartering with the local leaders over terms for the required

Fig. 4. The acropolis of Tell el-Hesi viewed from the west with the terrace of the tell in the foreground (on the site topography, see note 13, page 63). Petrie's camp at right. Spring 1890.

labor. Finally, all was ready for the Fund's first major excavation of a tell in Palestine. Petrie was the director, surveyor, and photographer, with no European on the site to help him. Ibrahim Effendi, Muhammed, and four guards were the only other people in that small camp of three tents (fig. 4). The work force consisted of thirty men, each bringing a woman or girl to carry the baskets of earth. Petrie was unhappy about the standard of work. " . . . I have increased their wages to 1s. a day,[12] but they are poor workers after the Egyptians, not doing more than a half or two thirds of what my old hands in Egypt would have done" (Petrie 1890c: 223). The situation was worsened by the fact that most of the excavation time coincided with the month of Ramadan, and its long fast inevitably slowed down the workers. However, by ruthless dismissal of those he perceived as lazy and troublesome, Petrie gradually brought the standard of

work closer to his liking.

In a letter to Armstrong written on April 21, only three days after starting the work at Hesi, Petrie shows that he had already come to some clear decisions. First, he had set his strategy for the season. He was not going to attempt to excavate the whole tell. "We shall therefore only nibble at it, following walls and clearing the floors of rooms all around the outside where the work is cheapest in proportion." He estimated that four or five weeks of work would be sufficient. Second, he saw his most important task to be that of determining the pottery chronology of the site. "If I do nothing more I shall at least have established a scale of pottery which will enable future explorers to date all the tells and khirbehs." He inspected every sherd and kept any that he thought instructive. His knowledge of Egyptian pottery was his guide. From the so-called cemetery he was to recognize the Cypriot wares he had found in a tomb at Illahun and had dated to 1100 BCE (see below). From the upper levels of the tell he found lamps, store-jars, and Greek wares similar to those he had found at Naukratis and had dated to *ca.* 550 BCE. Petrie's third decision was that he would not continue to work in Palestine after this season. "To me personally, Egypt is such a richer and more interesting field, that having utilized the information which I bring there, I am not interested to work off the Nile again" (PEF/Petrie/13).

"Outside of the town circuit on the south-west, is a sand hill with much pottery buried in it, the purpose of which is not clear" (Petrie 1890: 224). This, one of the first areas he excavated, Petrie conjectured might be a cemetery; moreover, possibly "a cemetery of the sacred animals of the Amorite age."[13] Here he found vessels buried upright in the ground: store-jars "with a basin or cup on the top," with smaller vessels inside, and filled with white sand, "like what they rest on." A few small bones were found in some of them. Petrie had these analyzed by Professor Boyd Dawkins who stated that they were animal bones. "Perhaps where no bones can be found they buried the sacred flies of Baal-zebub!" Petrie wrote whimsically (Petrie 1890c: 224). The present writer's own examination of the pottery of this area shows it to be an interesting collection of LB II wares with a high proportion of imported Cypriot material.

Petrie had decided it was not worth the expense to buy the crops growing on top of the tell. It would have cost £4. He happily settled for the sides and especially for the eastern face which he saw as having great potential (fig. 5). "This is an excellent place to work, as the storm floods have kept up so much scour as to leave the face a clean section from top to bottom, so I can work at any period I wish" (Petrie 1890c: 224). He put groups of six men trenching on the slopes at different levels. One of the first fortification walls that appeared belonged to the earliest level of occupation, which Petrie called "Amorite" (Petrie 1890c: 225), now known to belong to the Early Bronze Age.

On May 3, having completed two weeks of excavation, Petrie reported on the work to Armstrong by letter, enclosing a plan of the site and a section of the northern end of the tell's east face. The latter had taken up a lot of his attention in the second week of excavation. " . . . I have had the surface all cleared down at the north end, and have spent hours there tracing out the sec-

tions of the various brick-wall fortifications of the town" (Petrie 1890c: 227). He identified nine phases of city wall in this section (Petrie 1891: pl.3). It should be noted that the plan (fig. 6) sent with the letter of May 3 to Armstrong contains some information that has not been published.[14] Apart from showing the extent of the cultivated land that was inaccessible to Petrie until the last few days of his excavation, the plan plots the extensive clearance made in the "cemetery" area (see above) and the large number of trenches that were dug to virgin soil within the enclosure area that is pictured in fig. 7. Only a few of the latter were marked on the published plan (Petrie 1891: pl.1), and only passing reference was made to them (Petrie 1891: 13). The plan in fig. 6 demonstrates how thoroughly Petrie probed all the available areas.

Much of the third week was spent in completing the plan of the walls found at the northern end of the tell. At the top of the northwest corner of the tell he started to clear what he took to be a tower or bastion. He also continued to trace the lowest wall by tunneling, "Mainly for the sake of the chance of early pottery in the black ash earth outside of it" (Letter to Armstrong, May 12, 1890; PEF/Petrie/15). However, features were beginning to appear at the southern end of the tell that would engross him for the rest of the season. At the southeast corner he found a doorway of drafted masonry next to a small stairway. Still more exciting was the discovery of a piece of masonry decorated with a relief carving of a pilaster which, in place of a capital, had a volute decoration.[15] This was the first evidence for what Petrie came to refer to as the "pilaster building." He considered it his most important find at Tell el-Hesi. He was particularly delighted by these finds, not only because of his personal interest in masonry techniques, but also because of his belief that they were equal in value to pottery for establishing a chronology.

During this third week Petrie was happy to receive several visitors, one of whom—Camden Cobern from Detroit, Michigan—he had previously met in Cairo. Cobern—"a very pleasant change of society from the continual Effendi" (Petrie 1890c: 230)—wrote a popular account of this visit to Hesi which was published in the *Quarterly Statement* of the Fund (Cobern 1890). In that article he described his first sight of the tell—a description that is surely one of the more purple passages in the literature of Near Eastern archaeology:

Fig. 5. The east face of Hesi's acropolis, used by Petrie as a vertical section, showing the various cuts and trenches he made in it. Spring 1980.

. . . On the morning of the 8th May, I caught sight of the end of my journey—a gashed and broken tell lying by the water-brook like some hurt creature of the geologic ages fallen in its dying agonies. In the distance this fancy was encouraged, because of the many little objects which could be seen crawling in and out of the fresh wounds. On approaching nearer these moving objects took shape as Arabs, who seemed to be mangling the poor carcase in a most reckless way, until the discovery was made that every stroke of the pick was directed "from above," and that every puncture and furrow and tunnel had some definite object.

(Cobern 1890: 166–67)

By the fourth week, Petrie had exhausted all the space available for excavation on the tell. He noted that "all the trenching, sometimes over 20 feet deep, and all the clearing of the section on the east

side, on the valley cliff, had only produced two stone buildings" (Petrie 1890c: 230). He was forced to stop trenching and tunneling along the "Amorite" wall at the northern end of the tell because of the danger of cave-in. He concentrated his work force on the two stone buildings: the northwest tower or bastion, with its roughly built walls of reused masonry, and the "pilaster building." To expose more of the latter, he had his men cut back the east face of the tell in that area by about twenty feet.

The clearance of this "pilaster building" occupied his men for most of the next (the fifth) week of excavation, as well. A further five feet of cliff was cut back, leaving buttresses for support. During all this work in the area of the "pilaster building" other important structures began to appear, and their stratigraphic relationships were carefully noted.

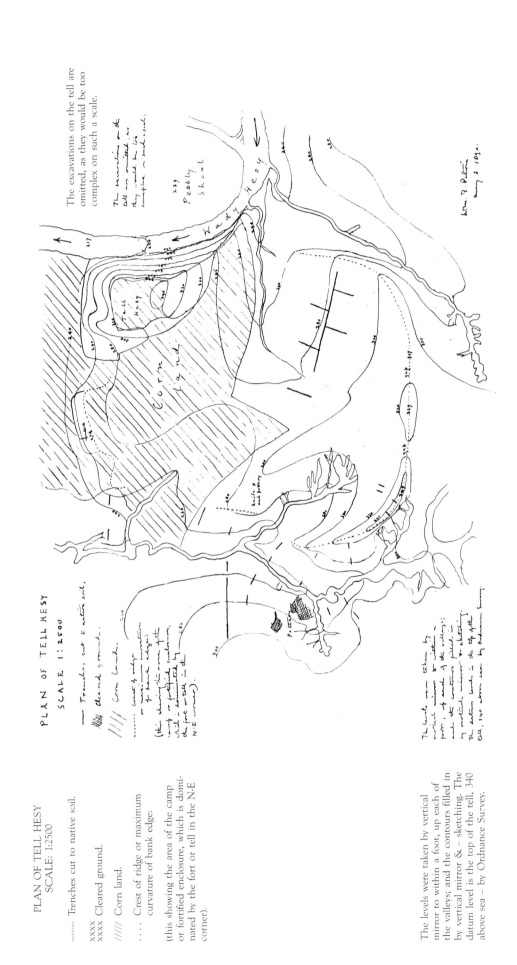

PLAN OF TELL HESY
SCALE: 1:2500

...... Trenches cut to native soil.

XXXX Cleared ground.
XXXX

///// Corn land.

..... Crest of ridge or maximum
curvature of bank edge:

(this showing the area of the camp
or fortified enclosure, which is domi-
nated by the fort or tell in the N-E
corner).

The levels were taken by vertical
mirror to within a foot, up each of
the valleys; and the contours filled in
by vertical mirror & – sketching. The
datum level is the top of the tell, 340
above sea – by Ordnance Survey.

Fig. 6. Plan of Tel el-Hesi drawn by Petrie on May 3, 1890.

Fig. 7. View from the top of the acropolis of Tell el-Hesi to the south over the terrace or "enclosure" area. Spring 1980.

Above, and sealing the "pilaster building," was a brick structure that could be traced for eighty-six feet along the east face of the tell. This long building was in turn sealed under some ten feet of earth by a glacis "at about 40-degree slope" that was formed from blocks of stone and faced with white plaster (fig. 8 and Petrie 1890c: 232). Petrie judged the glacis to be contemporary with the ashlar doorway and steps he had found earlier at the southeast corner of the tell. He based this phasing on the fact that the steps led up to the line of the glacis in which the stairs were probably continued. Later than all these features, and covering them all, was a twenty-five-foot-wide mud-brick wall which he dated to the reign of Manasseh (Petrie 1890c: 232).

The sixth and final week was very busy. The harvest had been gathered, and Petrie had only a few days in which to probe these newly available areas: " . . . So soon as the reapers were over the ground within a few hours I had the men sinking pits all about the crop land, to test the depth of the earth. I find that the ground close to the tell is just like that all over the enclosure; only a few feet of made soil with Amorite pottery and a little later stuff, and then native clay" (Petrie 1890c: 234).

A further cut was made in the cliff above the "pilaster building" but with little result. The plan of the building had to be finished by tunneling along the inside of the northern and southern walls. Finally, in a very hurried operation, the line of the wall system that Petrie attributed to the reign of Manasseh was traced through that area on the top of the tell which had been covered with crops.

Work stopped on Saturday, May 31, and Petrie wrote to Armstrong, "I think that I have done all that is worthwhile here now in our present state of knowledge."[16]

One of the regulations of the firman that had upset Petrie was the stipulation that all the finds

Fig. 8. Detail of the section on the east face of the acropolis, showing the glacis at the southern end. Spring 1890.

should go to the Turkish authorities. He overcame this to some extent by convincing Ibrahim Effendi that the sherd material would be of no use to the authorities and that they only needed the whole vessels. Petrie also made more of an effort to be nice to him. In a letter carried by Cobern to Armstrong, Petrie confided that "by some management he has come to the the point of offering openly to me that I may take whatever I like so long as I do it quietly."[17] This was something of a strain, for he wrote when the official finally left Hesi, " . . . I never realized how much he bored me until I was rid of him. To have to be always humouring a pretentious goose and avoiding offending his whims, while preventing him getting any authority or hold over me, is a wearisome matter and to me most nauseous" (Journal, May 27–June 1, 1890; unpublished section). Before he left, however, Ibrahim Effendi made several attempts to get more money, cornering Petrie and outlining all the extra expenses he

had incurred for the excavations. "I only smole a smile and shrog a shrug," Petrie wrote in the same unpublished section of his journal, "and returned him the inevitable cook and horse reply." This remark referred to the extra expenses that had already been allowed for in the Effendi's salary. The Effendi did not press this too far because, Petrie conjectured, he wanted a good testimonial from him. "We parted the best of friends, he hoping to see me again etc. etc. (I didn't). His absurdity was the only thing that redeemed his loathsomeness" (Journal, June 1–27, 1890; unpublished section [See note 9, p. 63—Ed.]).

Of the pottery found, therefore, all the whole vessels went to the Turkish authorities. These were mostly "Phoenician" vessels, Petrie's term for the Late Bronze Age. From the vast collection of sherds, Petrie assembled representative samples of the different types found and distributed them to the following recipients: the Palestine Exploration Fund, the British Museum, the Louvre, the Berlin Museum, Baron Ustinoff, Conrad Schick, J. Longley Hall, a "Mr. Clarke," and himself.[18] He wrote to Armstrong about that on May 31: "I think that our first consideration should be to diffuse information and stimulate research in every way that may not be directly injurious to the Fund" (PEF/Petrie/18). Against loss of anything in transit he made a complete catalogue of all the forms and variations found, together with a statement of the level at which they had been found.[19] The few small objects that had been discovered were sent back to the Fund, most of them being taken by Cobern.

It was mainly the loss of his workers to the harvest that forced Petrie to close the excavations. At the start of June he found it so difficult to get anyone that he was unable to fill in the probes he had made in the cropland and had to modify his plans for a tour of the sites to the east of Tell el-Hesi. After some delay he managed to get a camel driver for equipment and went with him on a shortened tour through Edh-Dhahariyeh, Beit Jibrin, Tell Sandahanna, and Tell es-Safi.[20] On the road to Edh-Dhahariyeh they were ambushed and robbed by four armed men. Petrie saved his money by dropping it "into two bushes." The worst effect of the incident was a sore throat caused when one of the men grabbed him by the throat and broke the top ring of his windpipe. This caused him trouble for some time. "Altogether," he wrote, "I think the business was conducted quite as pleasantly as such affairs ever are" (Petrie 1890c: 237–38; 1931: 126).

Back in Jaffa, he sent off their equipment to Jerusalem for storage and took a boat for England, where he arrived on June 27. On July 1 he attended the annual general meeting of the Fund, at which his official report was presented. The Chairman took the opportunity of publicly asking him to continue working in Palestine. Petrie declined but promised to help his successor in any way possible (Minutes of the Annual Meeting, July 1, 1890; P. E. F. *Quarterly Statement* for 1890: 153–54).

During the following weeks Petrie was involved in preparing his final report on the excavations at Tell el-Hesi. He also arranged an exhibition of his Egyptian and Palestinian materials for four weeks of public display, beginning on September 15. During this period the Committee of the Fund consulted Petrie about his replacement and about the next site to excavate. He was very definite in advising against another season at Hesi, and argued

that it would be too costly for too few results. His own preference was Tell es-Safi, Beit el-Khallil, or Tell Sandahanna.[21]

On August 5 the Committee agreed that the next excavation would be at the site of Tell Hum (Capernaum) on the Sea of Galilee. However, Professor Sayce opened up the whole discussion again by urging strongly that the excavation should continue at Tell el-Hesi, since inscribed tablets, similar to those from Tell el-Amarna, might well be found there. The Chairman decided to close the debate October 7 and put the choice of Tell el-Hesi or Tell Hum to the Committee. Sayce, Simpson, and Grace voted for Hesi; Morrison and Watson for Hum, with Chaplin abstaining. Many names had been suggested in the quest for a replacement for Petrie, but most of them were unable to accept. At the same meeting of October 7 the Committee agreed to invite Frederick Jones Bliss to direct the next season of excavations at Tell el-Hesi.

F. J. BLISS (1859–1937)

Frederick Jones Bliss (fig. 9), an American by birth and education, had lived a great part of his life in Beirut. His father, Daniel Bliss, had come to Beirut with the American Mission to Syria in 1855 and had founded the college that was to become the American University of Beirut. Frederick, a bachelor, was deeply attached to his family, writing frequent letters to them from wherever he traveled. A collection of these letters was given to the Palestine Exploration Fund in 1964 by a member of the Bliss family, and a summary has been published (Tufnell 1965: 112–27). Bliss was artistic, musical, and fluent in Arabic, but bad health kept him from following any regular career. In 1887, while recovering from a second breakdown, he went to the small town of Ma'lula near Damascus to study the Aramaic dialect spoken there. It was this work that brought him into contact with the Fund, for his friend, George Post, sent the committee a copy of a paper Bliss wrote on Ma'lula (Bliss 1890). In a letter to the Committee dated September 2, Post had praised Bliss's scholarship and thought that it could be of further benefit to the Fund (Armstrong to Post, on behalf of the Committee; PEF/Bliss/I/39A). The Committee subsequently agreed to pay Bliss a fee for an article on the Maronites, which eventually was published in four installments (Bliss 1892d). It was Post who also put forward Bliss's name as a possible replacement for

Petrie, and it was on his recommendation that the Committee decided to invite Bliss to undertake the work. Bliss's reaction was mixed. He was afraid that the work might lead to another breakdown, but he also felt the need of some career or useful work. He wrote the following letter to his father on October 26, 1890:

Fig. 9. Frederick J. Bliss.

My dear Father,

The matter is now reduced to a simple question of health. In Dr. Post's letter I begged him to make strong the points in which I felt myself unqualified; the committee decided to take the risk of my suitability. In 1883 I broke down. In the summer vacation of 1885 I had gained so much, and had stood the year of work so well that I decided to tutor the church boys. I did so—broke down under the daily fret and worry and it has taken me *five years* to get into a somewhat better condition. I can work with some degree of regularity now, certainly better than I could one year ago. Now comes an offer of hard work; to be sure not book work, which I find perhaps the hardest, but one of responsibility with a thousand chances of worry, from which I shall not be able to break away. The last three years I have

had hardly a tie from which I could not ride away on horse-back at any moment: even thus my progress has been slow. Now if I accept this place, it will be with the full knowledge of the risk: the risk of getting another put-back as in the year 1885, but differing from that in that it will probably be my last; I don't mean at all that it will kill me but that it will leave me a comparatively useless member of Society for the rest of my days. I don't say the risk is large, but it exists. I worry more about some things than I used, and less about others I never used to be able to stick and I do not suppose I have changed. Indeed my conscience suggests the question as to whether I ought to let the committee take the risk of my breaking down—however I should probably hold out till the time was over. Notwithstanding, I feel inclined to take the risk, but I confess, very soberly and with no elation. Ambition was long ago knocked out of me. If I decline, I shall simply shrug my shoulders and forget about it. If I accept I shall have plenty of ambition to do the work well for the committee. Now please think over these points and let Dr. Post see this letter.

I may add that one great cause of worry and depression in the last few years has been the sense of my uselessness and that I am not in receipt of a salary as return for honourable service; now I daresay we must allow something for removal of that load for, of course, I shall begin the work with a certain amount of assurance that it will come out all right. Thanks very heartily for your copying the letter. Everything most satisfactory—only one point, work in these southern regions can't go on after June 1st—that is very certain.

As ever, F. J. Bliss.
(PEF/Bliss/152/9a; excerpts also in Tufnell 1965: 113)

Despite his doubts Bliss accepted the position, and an official letter of appointment was sent by the Committee on November 8. One of the conditions of appointment was that he should spend some weeks with Petrie to receive instruction in excavation. Consequently, on January 10, 1891, he joined Petrie at Meidum in Egypt. "My first impression of Petrie was very pleasant," he wrote to his family on January 12, "a clear intelligent eye—black hair and beard and a pleasant but very decided quiet manner" (PEF/Bliss/152/11A). Bliss had an exhausting time accompanying Petrie as he hurried from trench to trench, explaining every detail of the excavations. These tours would go on for as long as eight hours on some days. However, he was greatly impressed by what he saw and expressed his admiration in that same letter home: "His knowledge is marvellous. He manages his men like a good despot—he has an iron will and evidently good judgment" (PEF/Bliss/152/11A). Petrie also instructed him in photography and surveying. The latter Bliss found difficult to grasp until he had practiced on an imaginary tell and worked out the principles for himself. Petrie's final report on his excavations at Hesi arrived from the publishers just as Bliss had planned to leave, so he stayed a fourth week to read the book and discuss it with Petrie.

Petrie seemed pleased with Bliss's progress. On February 7, the day Bliss left for Cairo, Petrie wrote to Armstrong:

> [Bliss] has given great care and attention to all the details of excavation while he was here; and there is not a point in which he has spared any trouble to master it as far as possible. He has made some trials in the form of survey that he will require and has taken my levelling mirror to Cairo to get one made for his use. He has also read and almost learnt by heart the details of my account of Lachish, so as to realise it. So I fully hope that whatever can be found in Tell Hesy will be intelligently examined and recorded.
>
> (PEF/Petrie/26)

During this visit to Egypt, Bliss made friends with several Egyptologists apart from Petrie, including Edouard Naville, Count d'Hulst, Percy Newberry, and George Fraser. He was even offered the post of assistant to Naville.

Bliss's first task was to follow up Petrie's suggestion that he would need some sort of tram (hand-operated railroad cars on tracks) for the large earth-removal operation intended at Hesi. After five days of inquiry in Cairo, he decided to buy ten pairs of secondhand wheels and axles, have them shipped to Jaffa, and have the remaining parts made out of wood there. It took another five days in Jaffa to arrange for a carpenter to make the sixty meters of wooden rail with iron capping and the eight trucks (see fig. 10). The total cost was about £60 (Bliss 1891a: 97; cf. Tufnell 1965: 116). His next task was to settle the question of Ibrahim Effendi's salary; the Committee insisted that the £15 per month paid under Petrie was too much. He visited the Governor of Jerusalem and had a long session of bargaining with the Effendi in his presence. After a struggle the Effendi agreed to a sum of just over £10 per month. While delayed in Jerusalem by storms, Bliss examined all the Hesi pottery left by Petrie.

The Second Season at Tell el-Hesi: March 16-May 15, 1891

On March 5 Bliss and Ibrahim Effendi traveled from Jerusalem to Ramleh where they were joined by Yusif, Bliss's servant from Beirut. The next day they set out for Tell el-Hesi and found that what was normally an easy journey had become hazardous from streams swollen by recent rains. They set up camp that evening to the southwest of the tell. The unsettled weather, arrangements for a work force, and negotiations to buy up the crops delayed the start of excavation for ten more days. The beans growing on the tell were cheap, but the barley in the area to the west was expensive, and the whole operation involved a lot of time and talk. Bliss also spent a great deal of time tracing out Petrie's finds and trenches. He noted that the ashlar stone entrance and the steps at the southern end of the tell had been removed, presumably by the villagers.

Work began on March 16. The workers had started turning up at the camp from Bureir as soon as Bliss had arrived. With the aid of lists given him by Petrie he was able to select a fairly competent group. He appointed Yusif, his servant, foreman. Of the latter, Bliss wrote to Armstrong on April 24: "My man Yusif (who is a perfect treasure—intelligent, keen, honest, politic and enthusiastic) is very clever at detecting brick in situ, fallen brick and brick decay" (PEF/Bliss/3/3; also Bliss 1891b: 209).

Following an earlier suggestion from Petrie, he started the season by excavating the area to the west of the tell,[22] the area which Petrie, in 1890, had also investigated first before attacking the tell itself. With seventeen teams, each consisting of a man with a woman or girl to carry away the earth in baskets and dump it, Bliss spent eight days digging about thirty trenches in the area. The soil depth varied from one to seventeen feet, and he found in it not only the "Amorite" or Early Bronze Age pottery but also a great deal of "Phoenician" or Late Bronze Age material. " . . . Found burials of Phoenician jars similar to those found in Petrie's 'cemetery,' only very much deeper—quite 6 feet—found painted Phoenician pottery at all levels, except the lowest, with Archaic Amorite above it in some cases" (Bliss 1891b: 208; 1894: 87–88 and pl. 4). Bliss managed to isolate only a few features, finding the mud-brick remains in that area too difficult to unravel. This is not surprising, given the complexity of the stratigraphy and the brief period of four weeks that he had studied with Petrie. To finish his excavation in the area Bliss dug a large trench twenty-seven by nineteen feet and twelve feet deep. "A study of the side of this hole revealed a curious irregular stratification, with lines of brick, rough stonework, burning and decay, which indicated the ruins of three or four towns" (Bliss 1891c: 283).

Having completed all that he considered worthwhile in this western area, Bliss started work on the tell. He marked off the northeast quadrant of the tell (an area 100 by 120 feet), intending to extend this area of excavation to the whole of the northern half of the tell. As soon as he began to realize the problems of earth removal he abandoned any idea of excavating more than the quadrant. Even when the tram arrived a few weeks later, he found he could barely manage that. He increased his work force to thirty men, each teamed with two or three women or girls to carry away the earth. It had already become obvious that one basket-carrier for each man was insufficient, because each basket had to be carried to the edge of the tell. The men were placed in areas that were each ten feet square, with no balk or section between the squares, and were told to dig down to the next identifiable layer. With this organization Bliss started the process of peeling off the layers of occupation, applying to this large area the basic principles of stratigraphy that he had learned from Petrie.

During the course of the season Bliss identified the following "periods," starting from the topmost on the tell. The titles are those given in his preliminary report (Bliss 1891b: 209):

1. "The Arab graveyard at the surface": Bliss found many graves within the first three or four feet of earth. In his report he described the position of one of the bodies—"the skull being towards the east" (Bliss 1891c: 284; 1894: 122);[23] the construction of some graves—"a space hollowed out in the shape of a coffin with slabs placed across the top," others also "partially lined with stones" (loc. cit.); and some of the grave furnishings—bracelets of blue glass or twisted brass, anklets, beads and agates, pipe heads, and thin glass. Although this cemetery was similar to Bedouin cemeteries of his own day, Bliss judged it to be one or two centuries old, since none of the local people knew of its existence.

2. "Rough stone dwellings, all fallen, with rough pottery": These structures had been badly disturbed by the graves dug for the cemetery, and only the remains of walls and pavements constructed of stones from the riverbed, and fragments of mud-brick walls, could be found. Pottery included "a large quantity of thin, white-faced sherds of the late Phoenician or Jewish type" (Bliss 1891c: 285).

3. "The town of the ovens": This layer was also in a very fragmentary state and consisted mainly of a series of tanânîr (sing. tannûr) or pit ovens. "A pit is sunk in the floor of the house, or in a hut outside, two or three feet in depth, and is plastered with mud, which is built up for a few inches above the floor. The ground is levelled at the bottom of the pit, and salt is placed upon it before the layer of mud is plastered down" (Bliss 1891c: 285; 1894: 114). Some of the pottery that he attributed to this layer can be identified as Persian grinding bowls, store jars, and lamps, as well as some Greek imported wares (Bliss 1891c: 286; 1894: 117–22). He followed Petrie's example of studying all the pottery, although his main concern was to find inscribed material. "Hundreds of potsherds were turned up and examined by me every day, in the unfulfilled hope of an inscription, the men having strict orders to throw nothing away" (Bliss 1891c: 286).

4. "A lower town, full of granaries": At the northern end of the next stratum Bliss found the first well-preserved mud-brick walls. He carefully planned and described these rooms and the evidence for the different types of storage and industry that took place in them (Bliss 1891c: 286–89; 1894: 108–14). One room contained one of the few uniformly self-contemporaneous assemblages of materials that he was to find in any of his excavations at Tell el-Hesi, a collection of store jars full of seeds. Bliss attributed some large pits or granaries to the same stratum, although he saw also that they might have been dug from a later one. He noted that if they had been dug from the "town of the ovens," they would have been ten feet deep, but if from the (lower) "town of the granaries," only three or four feet deep (Bliss 1891c: 286; 1894: 110). This uncertainty necessarily casts doubt on his attribution to this level of the pottery which was more or less the same as that from the town above, although with a larger proportion of figured pieces among the fine Greek wares (cf. discussion in note 8 to table I).[24] This "town of the granaries" had been destroyed by fire. In the layer of burning and ash he found quantities of barley, wheat, sesame, pulse, grape seeds, and a very large number of snail shells.

In his final report, A Mound of Many Cities (1894), Bliss presented the occupation levels as eight "cities," with several subphases which he numbered from the chronologically earliest to the latest. His plan for City VIII included the "rough stone dwellings" and the "town of the ovens" (Bliss 1894: 115), and his plan for the (lower) City VII (Bliss 1891c: 287; 1894: 111) showed not only the northern group of rooms and ten pits (or granaries),[25] but also other structures cut by the pits.

Far from suffering poor health under the burden of directing the excavations, Bliss thoroughly enjoyed the season and his new sense of responsibility. His first major problem arose six weeks after the start of excavation, when his best workers began to leave for the harvest. The harvest was better and earlier than in 1890, so that by April 25 he had lost most of his trained men from Bureir. He tried to keep them by raising the wages from 9d to 15d a day for men and from 5d to 8d a day for women, but with little effect (Bliss 1891b: 210; 1892c: 193). When he hired raw workers he soon learned why Petrie had complained so bitterly about the work force at the start of the 1890 season. Bliss struggled on, sometimes with as few as seven men, until May 15 when he decided it was all too difficult, paid off the remaining workers, and finished the season. Some of the problems of his City VII may have been exacerbated by this labor problem. Certainly the excavations he made below City VII at the end of the season must have been affected by having inexperienced workers. In his report he stated that the material below City VII was "so consolidated . . . that it is difficult to say whether we are working in the debris of one or of two towns" (Bliss 1891c: 289). He noted that there was a total of about seven feet of fill above his next town and that this accumulation represented a long period of continuous occupation. However, owing to the labor problems, occupation levels that would normally have been found by his workers may well have been missed. This seven feet of confused debris contained many more pits and the same types of pottery discovered at the two levels above (Bliss 1891c: 289–90).

As soon as the season was over, Bliss visited Tell Safi, for the Committee wanted his comments on the possibility of future work at that site. When that task was done, he made his way home to Beirut to rest and to prepare his report on the season's work. In a letter to Armstrong on June 10 he requested the Committee to be careful as to what they published in the *Quarterly Statement*. "Nowadays everybody reads—and someone told him (Ibrahim Effendi) that Petrie made fun of him in the Q.S. You know he *did* rather! I certainly hope he will serve again. I think he is honestly attached to me" (PEF/Bliss/5/1). In this connection, it is indeed astonishing to read some of the things that the Committee published from Petrie's journals—remarks that could not have helped diplomatic relations either with the authorities or with the local people, if they had read them. Bliss, on the other hand, was always sensitive to this in his reports to to the Fund.

On June 16 the Committee invited Bliss to continue the excavations in the autumn and offered him an appointment for twelve months beginning that June 3. Bliss accepted the offer gladly. His main concern at this time was the condition stated in the firman that interruption of the excavations for more than two months would mean cancellation of the permit. So, despite being very tired from the spring season, Bliss had to go to Jerusalem in July prepared to dig at Hesi for a few days to meet the requirement. The governor of Jerusalem, after keeping him waiting ten days, gave permission for the longer break in the work. "My dear Armstrong," Bliss wrote on July 8, forgetting his usual restraint in letters to the Fund, "we must make up our minds that the chief obstacle to our work will always be, as it has always been, the Turkish Government—a bitter pill to swallow daily" (PEF/Bliss/5/4).

Back in Beirut, he sent an article to the *Quarterly Statement* titled, "Excavating from its Picturesque Side" (Bliss 1891d). It is an absorbing and sympathetic account of the local people he met in the neighborhood of Tell el-Hesi. Bliss appears to have had a greater rapport with these people than Petrie had, and his article shows a deep concern with them as individuals. He was certainly on better terms with Ibrahim Effendi, for he wrote to Armstrong on August 10: "Ibrahim Effendi will do anything for me as a friend and was deeply hurt when I offered him a present."[26]

The Third Season at Tell el-Hesi: October 13–December 15, 1891

Bliss left Beirut on September 22 full of enthusiasm and confidence. He was eager to start work at Hesi and had plans for a very long season. He reached Bureir on October 10 after delays in Jaffa, and was given a warm welcome by his workers. When he camped at Hesi on the twelfth he chose a site three-quarters of a mile from the tell to avoid the dangers of malaria from the stagnant water below the tell. In contrast to the freshness and color of the countryside he had seen in the spring, the landscape was now brown and barren.

Work began on October 13 with ninety-six workers. He hoped to increase this to forty trios but was checked from doing so by the Committee of the Fund. Meeting on October 20 the Committee requested him "not to employ more than half that number of people," and instructed him "that his total expenditures including expenses must not exceed £20 a week" (Executive Committee Meeting Minutes, October 20, 1891).

His first upset of the season came with the arrival of a telegram from Beirut on October 15. His young niece Geraldine, daughter of his widowed sister, had died suddenly, and he was asked to come to Lebanon. After giving Yusif detailed instructions on the work to be done, he rode through the night to Jaffa. There he found that if he left Jaffa for Beirut the quarantine restrictions for cholera might prevent his return. Very much divided in loyalty, he decided to stay, and he sent a letter to his family by a friend.

The major problem to bedevil that season was an epidemic of fever that was probably due to the excessive spring rains. Despite all his precautions in situating the camp, all nine of its residents, except Bliss himself, succumbed to the fever. Many of the workers from Bureir were also affected, and the work suffered badly. One of the tents had to be turned into a hospital, in which the main remedies applied were Epsom salts and quinine. The water had to be brought six miles from Bureir, since the local spring water was suspect. On November 2 Bliss wrote to Armstrong, "Thank God I keep well but it is not exhilarating to see one after another drop and it rather takes it out of one to furnish courage for the whole camp" (PEF/Bliss/7/5A). On the thirteenth he wrote to his family, "Frankly I am *not* having a good season but I take genuine pleasure in the hardships of it" (PEF/Bliss/152/19A).

Despite these problems Bliss continued the work in the northeast quadrant of the tell. During this autumn season his workers excavated the occupation levels that he would later call Cities VI and V. Most of the material above City VI had been removed at the end of the previous season, so that the new plan soon emerged. The main feature of this new town was its northern defensive wall. This was the wall that Petrie had attributed to the reign of Manasseh. Bliss was able to describe many details of the wall which Petrie had not been in a position to discern (Bliss 1892b: 97; 1894: 98–100). Within this defensive wall was a group of rooms and some very wide mud-brick walls or pavements. As at the higher levels, he discovered the presence of pits.

The planning of City VI was completed by

November 2. The workers then removed the features of that layer and found four feet of fill above the next occupation level, City V. Bliss attributed the relative thinness of this debris to a rapid rebuilding of City V in which a great deal of material was reused. The main feature of City V was a group of buildings made up of roughly parallel lines of stone blocks and mud-brick walls (fig. 10). Bliss was intrigued by this unusual type of building, gave a very full description of it (Bliss 1892b: 97–100; 1894: 90–98), and suggested that it may have been a group of shops or possibly barracks. Since 1891 similar buildings have been found at other sites in Palestine, and there has been much debate as to their function. The generally accepted view at present is that they were public storehouses (Shiloh 1970: 182–83; Herzog 1973: 23–30). Also included on the plan for City V is a group of rooms that Bliss decided were later than the storehouses (Bliss 1982b: 100; 1894: 97), so at least two phases are represented in that city plan.

By the time City V had been planned, it was nearing the end of the season. The final work of the season involved digging down through another five feet of brick decay. Bliss wrote:

> . . . In the north-east of the excavations there were several jar burials, similar to those in the "Cemetery" described by Petrie, and of the same period. The brickwork was much consolidated and difficult to resolve into walls. In one part, from the nature of the decay between two parallel wallings, 3 feet apart, it looked as if we had found graves with mud brick sides, but of this I cannot be sure, though bones appeared.
>
> (Bliss 1892b: 100)

This mention of jar burials is important; it should be noted that they were found below City V but above City IV, since the latter was not reached until the following season. It is strange that the jar burials are not mentioned in *A Mound of Many Cities* (Bliss 1894), but the author may not have attached any great importance to them. Their significance will be discussed later in connection with the chronology of the site.

At the request of the Committee, Bliss sent a report on November 24 with his recommendations for the future work of excavation to be undertaken by the Fund. The firman was due to expire the following February, and a decision had to be made about the future. He suggested that the excavation of the northeast quadrant should be completed and estimated that it would require renewing of the

Fig. 10. Drawing made from a photograph, taken in the autumn of 1891, of the public storehouses in Bliss's "City V" (foreground shows rail-bed being assembled for earth removal "tram"; see pp. 50-51 and *PEFQS* 1892b: 96).

firman for at least another six months. In this same report he expressed doubts over Petrie's identification of Tell el-Hesi with biblical Lachish. He felt that the smallness of the settlement in post-Amorite times precluded this. On the strength of his recommendations the Committee applied for an extension of the firman for twelve months.

Ibrahim Effendi became ill with fever and stayed in Gaza for nearly two weeks recovering. "The Effendi is still in Gaza and I have borne the fortnight's separation beautifully!" Bliss wrote to his family on December 4 (PEF/Bliss/152/21A). But a few days later he added to the same letter, "Such is the inconsistency of human nature that when the old Effendi rode up at 3 o'clock I was really glad to see him. . .personally I am attached to the old boy" (PEF/Bliss/152/22).

Perhaps the most important work of the season was a probe near the southern end of the tell's east face. This was where Petrie had cut back the cliff to expose the "pilaster building." Bliss cut down the remaining twenty-five feet of debris above virgin soil, in an area fifty by twenty feet, to get a pre-

view of the "Amorite" or Early Bronze Age layers of the tell. He came upon what he called very solidified material and was only able to plan two sets of walls, both of which were of the very earliest occupation levels. His "Level I" was at 286 feet above sea level and was of dark mud brick with little stone. There is no plan of this phase. His "Level II" was at 293 feet and had well-preserved mud-brick walls and the clear outline of rooms. The destruction of the features by fire had preserved their important contents. In one of the rooms there was a hoard of ten metal tools and weapons together with Early Bronze Age pottery and a few objects, including two wooden seals (Bliss 1892a: 38; 1892b: 100–105; 1894: 39–40). The metal hoard is one of the very few Early Bronze Age metal groups found thus far in the Levant. The discovery was made by Yusif while Bliss was on a quick trip to Jaffa. He had gone there to see his mother as she passed through on her way to Beirut.[27]

Heavy rains began to trouble them from the middle of November, and gradually the days became shorter and colder. On one occasion they were confined to their tents for three days by continuous rain. On December 16 Bliss gave instructions to level the ground for ploughing. The season was over. There had been so much rain that the excavation area was filled with pools of water and the supplies from Beirut had been cut off by swollen streams.

Bliss arrived home in Beirut at the beginning of January. He was so exhausted by the season's work and by all the extra problems caused by the fever outbreak and heavy rains that it took him until the middle of February to send off his report to the Committee. In a letter to Armstrong on February 17 explaining his accounts, he spoke of how useful had been the excellent relations that he had established with Ibrahim Effendi: "He is really a friendly, sensible man and you must remember that we really had no legal right to the Amorite weapons he yielded to us" (PEF/Bliss/10/5).

On March 6, 1892, he received the news that the firman for excavations at Tell el-Hesi had been renewed, and he immediately set sail for Jaffa. He was eager to start the spring season promptly and to complete as much work as possible in what he now saw to be the more healthy and pleasant half of the year.

The Fourth Season at Tell el-Hesi: March 28–May 26, 1892

The excavations resumed at Tell el-Hesi on March 28, 1892. In contrast to the previous season everything started well: the standard of the workers was high, the weather fine, the area healthy, and the countryside beautiful. But Bliss then found things turning sour for him. One cause might have been loneliness. Ibrahim Effendi had been sent on another task by the Governor and did not get to Hesi until May 1. In some ways Bliss was pleased to be free of him, but he found that he missed the Effendi's company. "It is lonely this year," he wrote to his mother on April 10, "though the Effendi's absence lessens the worry, it deprives me of my only company" (PEF/Bliss/152/27). The main reasons for his being so ill at ease were probably boredom and the frustration of finding so little. He gave vent to these feelings in his letters home. On March 31 he called the tell a "fraud"; on April 3 he complained that it was "poor digging"; and on the 7th he wrote of his as a "silly life" (PEF/Bliss/152/24,25A,26).

During this season the goal was to get down as far as possible in the northeast quadrant of the

tell. The first task was to remove the rest of the confused debris found below City V at the end of the previous season. At about seven feet below the base of City V the foundations of a very large and symmetrical building began to appear. Bliss described this as a public building and called it his City IV. His workers were able to trace the complete plan of this imposing structure by following the layer of fine sand, half an inch thick, laid under all the walls. This acted as a guide in places where the walls had been obscured by pits or other intrusions. Bliss knew from the section on the east face of the tell that this large building was not very far above the thick ash layer that Petrie had ascribed to alkali burners (Petrie 1891: 16 and pl. III). When he excavated below City IV, however, he found between it and the ash "the remains of at least two other towns, in one of which there was found building in the usually unoccupied central part" (Bliss 1893a: 12). In these ill-defined phases there were a great many lamp and bowl deposits of indeterminate date. Just above the ash layer a well-preserved wine press appeared, with fragments of a second one and several pit ovens (Bliss 1893a: 14–15; 1894: 69–70). "Last week's work was very good in quantity but no results," he complained to his family on April 3, " . . . a barren stupid week" (PEF/Bliss/152/25A).

By April 7 half the excavation area was down into the deep ash layer while the other half was still excavating what Bliss called "difficult walls." The monotony of digging through the ash deepened his gloom. "Of course the novelty has worn off," he wrote to his mother on April 10, "and what was fun in mere superintendency of workmen has become drudgery. But a real find would brisk up matters!" (PEF/Bliss/152/27). More problems were to arise before that wish would be granted. Heavy winds and rain troubled them from about the middle of April. One storm blew down his tent on payday, scattering money in the mud. He had to deal with a strike. As the harvest approached he raised the wages by the usual 30 percent in order to keep the men, but they only demanded more and refused to work. The deadlock lasted through the whole weekend but dissolved on Monday, when he found more applicants for work at his rate than he needed.

He was in very low spirits on May 15 when he wrote to his family, "Now that we have worked a month with hardly any results, there is little to dignify the work, no discovery to sustain me—it is hard, very stupid" (PEF/Bliss/152/30A). He was seriously considering giving up excavation after completion of the work at Hesi. Then, on the very next day, one of his workers discovered an inscribed tablet,[28] the first Amarna tablet to be found in Palestine and the justification of Sayce's earlier suggestions to the Fund. Since the first discovery of the tablets at El-Amarna in 1887, Sayce had hoped that similar archives, containing the other end of the correspondence between Egyptian rulers and their small Canaanite vassal kingdoms, would be found in Palestine. It was for this reason that Sayce and Wilson had proposed the start of excavation on Palestinian tells in 1888 and, in 1890, the continuation of the excavations at Tell el-Hesi. This discovery completely revived Bliss's spirits and interest and sustained him for the rest of his time at the site. He sent home a letter full of jubilation. To the Committee he sent as soon as he could various squeezes and impressions for interpretation by Sayce.[29] Despite pointed and repeated inquiries from the Committee, Bliss insisted that the tablet was made of sandstone. He changed his mind only when he saw the other Amarna tablets in Cairo in March, 1893 (PEF/Bliss/152/17/4; see also Bliss 1894: 57).

The week that followed discovery of the tablet produced little of interest, but the whole mood had changed with the real hope of finding more tablets. Gradually the work force was being reduced by the harvest, but Bliss managed to retain enough experienced workers to continue without any problem. In the week before he closed the season on May 27, the men continued to clear away the deposit below the great ash layer until some of the northern rooms of City III began to appear. Bliss was forced to stop the excavations on account of the harvest, the heat, the mosquitoes, and the degeneration of the local water supply. He summarized the season in a letter to his family on the twenty-seventh: "Hardly any sickness, no quarreling, much loneliness and salaam!" (PEF/Bliss/152/32A).

As a keen horseman he could not resist buying for himself a fine gray Arab stallion in Jaffa while on his way home to Beirut. Three days after his arrival home Bliss became seriously ill with typhoid fever. From then until the middle of July he was too ill to write to the Fund, and his sister acted on his behalf. The report and accounts for the spring season remained untouched until autumn. Though his recovery was fairly rapid, the fever left him very weak and soon exhausted by any physical or mental effort. To regain his strength in time for the autumn season, since he was determined to finish the work at Hesi, he spent the rest of the summer camping in the Lebanon mountains.

The Fifth Season at Tell el-Hesi: September 27–December 16, 1892

Bliss arrived at Jaffa on September 17 in good time for the new season. After being delayed for several days by a very hot spell of weather, work resumed at Tell el-Hesi on the twenty-seventh. Bliss's continuing weakness after typhoid made it a difficult season for him. On the second day of work he wrote to his sister, "I was very much disappointed to find my strength very minus when I tried to skip from hole to hole, and tottered like an old man!" (Letter of September 28, 1892; PEF/Bliss/152/38A). He decided to take life easy, resting and reading in his tent a great deal and only visiting the tell once or at most twice a day. He relied upon Yusif to supervise the work in his absence. "He has learned to trace archaeological levels by pottery, brickwork and the tilt of strata and his induction is admirable and safe. He can carry out any orders a day ahead" (Letter to Armstrong, December 3, 1892; PEF/Bliss/13/4A).

Despite his weakness he was less dependent than in the previous season. The tonic of finding the tablet was still working. "Professor Sayce told the Oriental Congress that the stone proved that I have found my way to the entrance chamber of the Archive Chamber of Lachish!" he wrote to Armstrong on October 2. "The stone was found in no chamber but in debris. I doubt our right to assume the existence of an Archive Chamber, though I devotedly look for it; but I shall be very much disappointed if we turn out no more tablets. I confess before the discovery of the stone the work had grown greatly dreary, but every day now I am full of hope" (PEF/Bliss/13/1A). The Effendi was late in reaching the site, but this time, due to his weakness, Bliss was grateful for his absence. Furthermore, the weather was good, the workers well experienced, and the season a healthy one.

As in the spring season, the work was concentrated in the northeast quadrant of the tell (fig. 11). The workers continued clearing the mud-brick walls of City III, which had been partially uncovered at the end of the previous season. Symmetrical rooms appeared along the inside of a northern defensive wall, and Bliss suggested they were part of some public building, possibly a fort. The debris within them had very few sherds in it. It was in similar

Fig. 11. Tell el-Hesi acropolis viewed from the northeast, showing the quadrant excavated by Bliss. Autumn 1892.

debris at the same level under the ash layer that the Amarna tablet had been found, but no more tablets appeared.

Below the remains of City III, five feet of debris covered the mud-brick walls that Bliss called City II, which he admitted included at least two periods of occupation. It was in this layer or layers that he found sherds of bichrome ware (Bliss 1894: 62–63; also, briefly, 1893b: 105). Included on his plan for City II was an installation first identified as a blast furnace for iron. It was a circular structure about twelve feet in diameter, with mud-brick walls two feet thick which had a series of air channels built into them (Bliss 1893b: 106–10; 1894: 45–51). A later analysis of what he had taken to be slag from iron ore showed that the proportion of iron was too small. John Hall Gladstone, who did the analysis, judged that the "slag" was only a fired brick broken off from the wall of the furnace (Bliss 1893b: 190). Bliss had to leave the func-

tion of the furnace an unsolved problem.

On November 7, when the workers dug below City II, the pottery suddenly changed. They had at last reached the "Amorite" or Early Bronze Age levels of occupation: " . . . Here the ledge-handles, peculiar spouts, comb-facing, thick-brimmed bowls, black-brown smutty surfaces, come in as controlling types, types appearing but not prevailing in the Tell above, and not recognised by that careful observer, Prof. Petrie, in any country" (Bliss 1893b: 106; 1894: 40–41).

Although disappointed at finding no more tablets, Bliss had great hope for some exciting discoveries at these lowest levels. After all, it was at the same level in the southeast probe that he had found the metal hoard in the autumn of 1891. It was about this time that the first rains began, and some of the men left for the ploughing, which had started a month earlier than in the previous year. The rains brought a Bedouin tribe of about thirty tents into the area, and Bliss was somewhat apprehensive when they pitched their tents immediately behind his own. He soon made friends with them, however, and enjoyed spending much time with them.

The main feature to appear at the lowest level (City I) was the large fortification wall that Petrie had traced on the northern side. Bliss was able to correct Petrie's description of the wall in a number of details. Instead of the very wide mud-brick wall described by Petrie, he found a two-room tower or building set into the wall. He agreed with Petrie, however, that the wall had undergone three phases of rebuilding (Bliss 1893b: 110–11; 1894: 27–31). Inside the city, on the west side of his excavation area, Bliss found no signs of buildings. On the east there were two phases of town buildings, but they were so fragmentary that he did not consider them worth planning. Both phases shared similar building techniques and pottery. Once again he felt disappointment at finding hardly any objects at these levels. On December 28 he would report to the Committee that the lowest layers had "yielded nothing but potsherds—not a single weapon turned up, showing that the enemy or else the builders of the second town had searched the ruins, removing all valuables" (Letter of December 28, 1892; PEF/Bliss/13/4C).

December had begun with heavy storms which set back his recovery of health. "I am pretty seedy," he reported to Armstrong on the third, "—had some fever this weekend; since the rough weather began, have ceased to gain strength" (PEF/Bliss/13/4A). This did not keep him from making a last effort to complete the excavation of the lower levels, however. On December 5 he employed as many as ninety-seven workers. The work went more speedily at this time, because the earth could be thrown back onto the areas that had already been excavated to virgin soil. On December 16, satisfied that he had fully explored these Early Bronze Age layers, Bliss ordered the whole area prepared for ploughing. The fifth season and the work of the Palestine Exploration Fund at Tell el-Hesi were finished.

Having returned to Beirut, Bliss wrote to the Committee on December 28 and formally announced the completion of the excavations. "The task which I undertook when I first came to Tell el-Hesy almost two years ago is now accomplished. The artificial mound has now lost about one third of its bulk, as I have cut out a huge wedge at its NE corner, layer by layer, successively uncovering (and necessarily destroying) the bases of eleven or twelve towns, piled above each other" (PEF/Bliss/14A). He strongly recommended that no further work be undertaken at Hesi, since there seemed to be little chance of finding any important groups of objects. Resting and completing his report, Bliss remained in Beirut until March 1893. He then visited Egypt, studying material in the museums, before making his way to London, where he arrived on April 11. He had a most agreeable time in London working on his final report and enjoying a full social life of dinner parties, theaters, and concerts. He attended several committee meetings of the Fund to discuss the future plans of excavation and had long discussions with Petrie on the Hesi material. On June 6 Bliss gave a public lecture on his excavations. Petrie was in the chair and, afterwards, praised him very generously for his work. After a brief interval, Bliss's final report of his excavations at Tell el-Hesi appeared in 1894 with the title, *A Mound of Many Cities*.

CHRONOLOGICAL CONCLUSIONS ON THE EXCAVATIONS AT TELL EL-HESI, 1890–1892

Petrie worked out his elaborate chronology of the site in the following way:

1. From his knowledge of Egyptian pottery, he dated the "Phoenician" pottery of Hesi to 1350–800 BCE, taking the mid-point, 1100 BCE, as representative. He dated the latest (Greek) pottery on the site to *ca.* 450 BCE. These dates formed the starting point for all his calculations. ("Phoenician" was Petrie's term for the Late Bronze Age.)

2. He then formulated the principle that the occupational debris of a tell accumulates at a more or less regular rate. Since 32.5 feet of accumulation represented the 650 years of occupation between the middle of the "Phoenician" levels and the abandonment of the site, he calculated an accumulation rate of five feet per century, which allowed him to place the start of the earliest or "Amorite" level at *ca.*1670 BCE (Petrie 1891: 14–15).

3. His next step was to identify Tell el-Hesi with biblical Lachish (Petrie 1891: 18–20). Once this had been done, he related the observed features of the site with the history of Lachish as given in the Bible: the stone layer was identified with the poverty of the period of the Judges; the deep ash layer was related to the abandonment of the site just before the United Monarchy; and each of the defense

walls found at the northern end of the tell was associated with one of the kings of Judah (Petrie 1891: 21–29).

Bliss was more cautious in his approach. He was dissatisfied with the identification of Hesi with Lachish, and he did not use the biblical references to Lachish. He also ignored Petrie's principle of a calculable growth-rate of debris deposit. Rather, having established the relative sequence of cities or levels, he sought to date them exclusively "by the objects *found clearly in situ* in them." These he ranked in the order of their usefulness for dating, such as (a) the inscribed objects (the cuneiform tablet, the Greek and "Phoenician" inscriptions, the jar-handle, and some of the scarabs), (b) the figured objects (the cylinder seals and the rest of the scarabs), (c) the metal tools and weapons, and (d) the pottery (Bliss 1894: 128–30).

Many archaeologists would disagree with this ranking, but most would adopt the same approach in principle as that of Bliss. With the exception of his City I, Bliss's dating holds up surprisingly well.

This cautious and reasoned approach to chronology was Bliss's greatest contribution to Palestinian archaeology.

The accompanying chart (table 1) offers in three parallel columns a comparison and correlation of the findings of Petrie and Bliss with each other and then gives the present writer's tentative interpretation of them. The interpretation is based solely on a study of observations and artifacts from the 1890–1892 excavations. Though of limited value, this exercise may throw light on that part of the tell that can never be re-excavated and may help define some questions for later excavators at Tell el-Hesi. The correlations with biblical history in column I are, of course, Petrie's; they were part of his method, as explained above.

In table 1 the italicized numbers in parentheses refer to the notes that follow. In the notes, artifacts are referred to by "P" or "B" to designate Petrie or Bliss, followed by the number used to designate the artifact in the respective *final report* of each, i.e., Petrie 1891 or Bliss 1894.

Table 1. The chronological conclusions of Petrie and Bliss compared, with a tentative interpretation of their findings.

PETRIE 1890	BLISS 1891-1892	TENTATIVE INTERPRETATION
AMORITE 1670–	CITIES SUB-I and I 1700– West town: 3 or 4 phases Tell: city wall with tower, 2 house-phases inside Southeast probe: 2 phases, metal hoard *(2)*	EB III *ca.* 2700-2300 BCE *(1)**
		GAP IN OCCUPATION: no signs of MB I–II *(3)*
(Phoenician Pottery 1350–850 BC) JUDGES *ca.* 1300–1100 Stone layer: poor houses of river stones	CITIES SUB-II and II 1550– At least 2 building-phases, one of stone; bichrome pottery	LB I *ca.* 1550– *(4)*
	CITY III 1450– Public building against north wall; Amarna tablet; furnace (City II?)	LB II 14th century
SITE DESERTED, during which time the alkali burners worked on the tell		
ASH LAYER, site abandoned	ASHES from furnaces, spread during a short gap in occupation	

*Figures in parentheses refer to the following legend to the table.

PETRIE 1890	BLISS 1891-1892	TENTATIVE INTERPRETATION
"CEMETERY" with Phoenician pottery from 1000–900 or earlier (5) UNITED MONARCHY 1050– Original use of masonry from pilaster building (6); 5 feet of debris below pilaster building REHOBOAM 970– North wall (291 feet); last phase of pilaster building (7b) DESTRUCTION	CITY SUB-IV 1400– North wall and 2 possible house-phases; wine presses, pit ovens; lamp and bowl deposits CITY IV 1300– Public building in 4-room style; "Phoenician" pottery (7a) 7 feet of "DECAY, ROUGH STONE AND BRICK WALLING": a long period represented Jar burials in northeast similar to cemetery (Bliss 1892b: 100)	Late 14th century (5)
		PROBABLE GAP IN OCCUPATION from early 12th until 10th/9th centuries BCE (7)
JEHOSOPHAT 910– North wall (298 feet) UZZIAH 800– North wall (298–300 feet); long building Destruction 735 BCE AHAZ North wall (300–305 feet) HEZEKIAH North wall (303–305 feet); guard-house, steps and glacis Destruction 701 BCE Period of Poverty MANASSEH 660– Large wall system, with northwest tower/bastion (310–319 feet) Nomadic occupation	CITIES SUB-V and V 1000– Storehouses (7c); at least 2 building-phases; iron CITY VI 800– Large north wall, same as Petrie's Manasseh wall; wide mud-brick pavings or walls; pits (from VII or VIII?) One or two towns in 7 feet of occupational debris CITY VII: "Town of Granaries" 500– Domestic buildings in northeast; pits/granaries (from VIII?); shells, barley, sesame, pulse, etc. Violent destruction by fire	Iron II 10th/9th centuries– (7d) Persian 6th century– (8)
Occupation ends in 5th century BCE	CITY VIII: "Town of Ovens" 400– Pit ovens ROUGH STONE DWELLINGS Traces of mud brick	Hellenistic? (9)
	ARABIC CEMETERY 17th/18th century CE	Arabic cemetery

LEGEND TO TABLE 1

1. The present writer's dating of the Early Bronze Age occupation to EB III is based on conclusions in his unpublished M.A. thesis (Matthers 1974). The earliest material is parallel to the latest levels of Tel ᶜErani (Yeivin 1961),[30] and the latest to Tell Beit Mirsim J (Albright 1932: 1–7; cf. Dever and Richard 1977). Similar groups of material have been found at Tell ed-Duweir, Tell Yarmuth, and other sites in the area. These sites at the designated levels may well represent a distinct regional culture.

Legend to Table 1 (continued)

2. For a discussion of the metal hoard, see Kenyon 1955: 10–18. Of the ten metal objects reported to have been found in this hoard, B69, B70, B75, B76, and B78 are in the collection of the Palestine Exploration Fund. B71, B72, B73, and B77 recently were rediscovered in the basements of the Rockefeller Museum in Jerusalem. B74 has not been traced, nor have the curious wooden seals which were found with the hoard (Bliss 1892a: 38; 1892b: 105; 1894:40).

3. There is a distinct gap in occupation at Hesi between EB III and LB I. Bliss observed that under his City II with its bichrome ware there was a sudden change to the "Amorite" or Early Bronze Age wares (Bliss 1893b: 106). This observation is supported by the fact that there is no record of any pottery or other artifact that is typical of the intervening periods, i.e., MB I (also designated Intermediate Early Bronze–Middle Bronze) or MB II. The two cylindrical juglets, B89 and B90, fit very well into the LB I corpus (Kenyon 1973: 528).

4. The distinctive LB I pottery types recorded are (a) bichrome ware: B106–09 and B189 (a full classification of these sherds is given in Epstein 1966: 7, 15, 16); (b) a truncated dipper juglet: P143; and (c) black lustrous ware: P104 and a fine example published, with an inaccurate drawing, in Bliss 1892b as fig. 46. The latter vessel is mentioned by Oren, though there is no evidence to support his statement that it came from a "homogeneous LB I grave" (Oren 1969: 146).

5. Petrie and Bliss published twenty-six vessels from the "cemetery" area which lay to the west-southwest of the town enclosure (Petrie 1891: 44–45 and pls. VII-VIII; Bliss 1894: 87–88 and pl. 4). Twenty of these vessels are in the collection of the Palestine Exploration Fund and are expected to be republished. As a group they fit well into Kenyon's Late Bronze Age Group D (Kenyon 1973: 529), the best parallels being found in Tomb 216 at Tell ed-Duweir (Tufnell 1958: pls. 52–54) and Tombs 8144–8145 at Hazor (Yadin 1960: pls. 128–38). The date suggested by Kenyon for this group is 1350–1320 BCE. Two Mycenaean pieces in this "cemetery" group (P145, B179) were recently identified by Vronwy Hankey as Mycenaean IIIA2 (private communication). In view of this evidence, the "cemetery" group probably belongs immediately after the post-Amarna ash layer. This would allow for the destruction and abandonment of the Amarna-age town (City III) and its resettlement toward the end of the fourteenth century, represented by the "cemetery" and City Sub-IV. This fits Bliss's comparison of the "cemetery" pottery with that of Cities Sub-IV and IV (Bliss 1894: 87), but does not allow his earlier comparison of the "cemetery" material with the jar burials he found above City IV (Bliss 1892b: 100). The fact that the latter comparison is not repeated in his final report probably implies that it was too hasty and based upon poorly defined ware types.

6. The pieces of masonry found in the "pilaster building" and ascribed by Petrie to an earlier building phase are as follows:

   a. Four cornices or lintels, all of which were found fallen and broken. They were carved with a cavetto that drooped somewhat at the front and with a simple roll. Otherwise, they were undecorated (Petrie 1891: 23, 25).

   b. Four slabs, each with the left side of a pilaster carved in low relief. The tops of the pilaster reliefs had no capitals; each had only a volute, which Petrie compared to a ram's horn. They had been used originally at the sides of doors, for they each had a recessed area for a lock (see n. 15 on p. 64).

   c. Stone jambs for the doors were also found, but how many there were of them is not recorded. Petrie noted that the one found in the "SSE door" had a graffito of an animal on it (Petrie 1890c: 232, 235; 1891: 23). Since the latter was upside down, it must have been inscribed during an earlier use of the masonry. Apart from the rough sketch he made in his journal (fig. 12) and his note that it was one foot long, no other record was made of this graffito, and only allusions to it have been published.

   From the evidence to be studied below under *(7b)* concerning the destruction of the final phase of this building, it is necessary

Fig. 12. A sketch made by Petrie of a graffito found in the "pilaster building" (Journal for May 18-26, 1890; see also Petrie 1890c: 232, 235; 1891:23).

to date the original use of this masonry to no later than the thirteenth century. Petrie considered this masonry his most important find at Hesi, and it is strange that it has been so neglected in the literature. The whereabouts of the masonry is unknown. Petrie did not want to surrender the pieces to the Turkish authorities, and he knew that he could not get them back to England. After taking squeezes of some of them and photographing them, he buried them again somewhere at Tell el-Hesi (see, e.g., Petrie 1890c: 229, 235). Petrie's photographs of these pieces of masonry are in the collection of the Palestine Exploration Fund.[31]

7. One of the major chronological problems at Tell el-Hesi is whether there was a gap in occupation somewhere between the Late Bronze Age and the Iron Age and, if so, for how long. Many scholars have suggested a gap lasting from the thirteenth or early twelfth century until the tenth century BCE. Representatives of this view include W. F. Albright (1932: 55), P. Lapp (1967: 293) and S. Yeivin (1971: 522). The following observations may shed some light on the problem:

7a. Bliss's City IV is generally accepted as being Late Bronze Age, most probably representing a thirteenth-century occupation of the site. This is the impression given by the scanty evidence provided by Bliss from the pottery and other finds. He observed that, with Sub-IV, City IV represented the principal age of "Phoenician" pottery. His account of finding jar burials above City IV similar to those of the "cemetery" (Bliss 1892b: 100) needs qualification, as noted above under (5), but seems to indicate that they were similar enough to be Late Bronze Age even though not contemporaneous with the "cemetery." There is one difficulty with dating City IV to the thirteenth century, however. The plan of the main building has been interpreted as an example of the four-room type (Shiloh 1970: 183–84 and fig. 2), which is normally of a later date. "The time span of this plan is from the end of the eleventh century BCE down to the destruction of Judah" (Shiloh 1970: 180; 1980: 28–29).[32] Several solutions are possible: that the plan of this building has been incorrectly excavated or interpreted, that the four-room type of building had antecedents two centuries earlier than previously realized, or that City IV must be dated to the eleventh century or later. The last solution would certainly alter our understanding of any gap in occupation, probably putting it back into the thirteenth century. Apart from this architectural evidence, however, nothing supports such a radical revision, as will be seen from the subsequent discussion.

7b. In the last phase of the "pilaster building" Petrie found a layer of ash and charcoal from the destruction of the building by fire. The only objects recovered from this layer were "four pottery vases placed in pairs one on the other" (Petrie 1891: 23). Two of these

Legend to Table 1 (continued)

were published (P128, P134). From the general sense of his description and from their find level, these vessels must have been on the floor of the building and must therefore represent the last use of this structure before it was destroyed. P134 is a common bowl form, but P128 is a good chronological indicator. Fig. 13 shows a recent drawing of this vessel, which is now in the collection of the Palestine Exploration Fund. The decoration is in a reddish paint. Very close parallels are found at Ashdod in areas A and H (M. Dothan 1971: figs. 1: 8; 84: 1, 2, 4). It is this pottery that T. Dothan called the "missing link between Mycenaean IIIC1 pottery as known from the eastern Mediterranean and the Aegean, and its local development into Philistine pottery" (T. Dothan 1973: 187). An analysis of some examples of this ware from Ashdod showed it to be of local manufacture (Asaro, Perlman, and Dothan 1971: 175). A destruction at Tell el-Hesi dated by this vessel to the early part of the twelfth century would be a good candidate for the start of a gap in occupation. A gap starting at this time would offer a cogent explanation for the apparent absence at Hesi of any of the developed Philistine wares and other Iron I types.

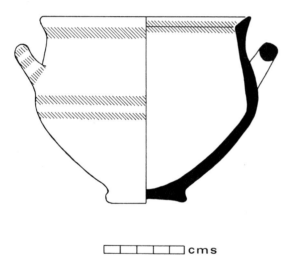

Fig. 13. Bowl found in the destruction level of the "pilaster building" (Petrie 1891: Pl. VIII, No. 128). Drawing by J. Matthers.

7c. City V has usually been dated to the tenth century, since the main structures of that level were compared to the so-called Solomonic stables at Megiddo. It is now generally accepted that the latter are neither Solomonic nor stables. Two recent analyses have been made of this type of building (Shiloh 1970: 182–83; Herzog 1973: 23–30). It is now believed that these buildings were public storehouses and are to be found in use in the tenth, ninth, and eighth centuries BCE. A very close parallel to the structure of City V is the storehouse in use in Stratum II at Beer-Sheba, dated by the excavator to the eighth century (Aharoni 1973: 8). There is, therefore, no necessity to put a tenth-century date on City V from the architectural evidence.

7d. The amount of pottery published by Petrie and Bliss that can be dated to the Iron Age at Hesi is very small. Petrie published about forty pieces and Bliss about twenty. The latter were so badly drawn that it is often difficult to recognize a common type. All that can be said from what has been published and from a study of some of the vessels which are now in the collection of the Palestine Exploration Fund is that there is nothing that needs to be dated to the period between the mid-twelfth and the ninth cen-

turies: P219 is described as "hard red, indian red face, coarsely burnished" (Petrie 1891: pl. 9), but it is in fact wheel burnished and not hand burnished. Indeed, most of the material fits well into the eighth century or later. It is obvious that negative evidence from such a small sample can prove nothing. However, it does allow us to keep open the possibility of a gap in occupation from the mid-twelfth century onwards and to put a question mark against a tenth-century date for City V.

If we accept Bliss's view that the site of Tell el-Hesi was a fort rather than a settlement from the Late Bronze Age onwards, then we must expect it to have been abandoned more frequently and abruptly than any town site. Its fortunes would mirror directly the vicissitudes of political power.

8. Among the pottery attributed to Cities VI–VIII are types that are clearly from the Persian Period: heavy grinding bowls, store jars with high loop handles, very flat lamps, etc. However, it is most likely that the pottery from all these levels was mixed by the deep pits or granaries, so that it is impossible to determine when these types first appeared at Hesi. Bliss's acknowledged uncertainty as to the depths of these pits (Bliss 1891c: 286) strengthens this conclusion.

9. There is no clear evidence for a Hellenistic occupation of the site from the finds of Petrie and Bliss alone.

THE ACHIEVEMENTS OF PETRIE AND BLISS AT TELL EL-HESI

It would be unreasonable to judge the Tell el-Hesi excavations of 1890–1892 by the techniques and standards of later excavations and the accumulated field experience of nearly a century. It is more profitable to look for the lasting contributions they made to the development of Syro-Palestinian archaeology.

Stratigraphy

Petrie can be said to be the founder of stratigraphic excavation in Palestine, since at Hesi he pioneered the study and recording of the relationships between features with the help of vertical sections. His section along the eastern side of the tell was the first section to be cleaned down and drawn in Palestinian archaeology (Petrie 1891: 21 and pl. III)[33], and his immediate grasp of its potential was a stroke of genius. It was from Petrie that Bliss learned the basic principles of stratigraphy, but it was Bliss who applied them for the first time on such a large scale, attempting to peel off the levels of occupation in an area of well over a thousand square yards. He did not have the techniques necessary for maintaining the desired control in such an undertaking, but in his work at Hesi he was pioneering ahead of Petrie.

Pottery

It was in the sphere of pottery that Petrie made what was the most important contribution of these excavations. Within a few weeks he had established a relative chronology for Palestinian pottery that was essentially correct and that was not improved upon until Albright's work at Tell Beit Mirsim. He set standards for the field by insisting on handling every piece of pottery excavated—up to a thousand sherds on some days. He set the standards of publication by presenting pottery drawings with rim profile and stance—an example that was not to be followed until Fitzgerald thus presented the pottery from the 1927 Ophel excavations (Crowfoot and Fitzgerald 1929). Petrie set the standards in pottery classification. His analysis of the Early and Late Bronze Age groups from Hesi presented an amazingly complete corpus for both periods. He introduced many terms which are still used today, such as holemouth jar, ledge handle, and pattern burnishing. Bliss, on the other hand, made little or no contribution to the study of pottery, but relied on Petrie's type series and seldom added to it. The few vessels that Bliss did publish are badly presented for archaeological purposes.

The Employment of Other Techniques and Sciences

Petrie's breadth of knowledge and his abilities were so outstanding that he combined in himself a whole team of experts. He was a surveyor, photographer, draftsman, geologist, an expert in pottery and techniques of masonry, and knowledgeable about weights and measures—to name only his most obvious talents. His contribution to archaeology was in the use of all these abilities to reconstruct the history of the site as completely as possible. Nothing was ignored that could give the slightest help.[34] Bliss was not such a giant, but made a fundamental contribution to the development of archaeology by recognizing that fact and then calling on experts in other fields as often as he could. His final report, *A Mound of Many Cities*, with reports by specialists in metallurgy (J. H. Gladstone), flints (F. C. J. Spurrell), and bones and shells (A. Day), represents the first step toward a multidisciplinary approach to archaeology. Bliss's greatest contribution was his caution in not going beyond the evidence as he attempted to work out the absolute chronology of the site.

The various contributions and abilities of Petrie and Bliss were complementary. Together they laid solid foundations for future archaeological work at Tell el-Hesi and throughout the Near East.

Manuscript completed August 1978.[35]

NOTES

1. The author wishes to thank the Palestine Exploration Fund for allowing him to consult its archives in the preparation of this chapter and for allowing the reproduction of the figures that accompany it.

2. Attesting to the role played by officers of the Royal Engineers in this early exploration is the fact that, in addition to Wilson among the names above, their number included Warren, Stewart, Conder, Kitchener, and Mantell. [On the interplay between international politics and near-eastern archaeology in the nineteenth and early twentieth centuries see now Silberman 1982. —Editor.]

3. "A German." The disclaimer is not explained, unless by Petrie's expressions elsewhere of disdain for Émile Brugsch, assistant director of the Bulaq Museum (Cairo) in the 1880s (Petrie 1931: 29, 63, 77, 84), or of indignation toward "the German—Kruger— who came into the Fayum [in 1888] simply to plunder" (Petrie 1931: 96). See now, also, Drower 1985: 36-7, 157. —Editor.

4. Hereinafter citations beginning "PEF/ . . . " indicate the archival format of the Palestine Exploration Fund (see bibliography in this chapter). Petrie's letter (above) is misfiled there under "Bliss."

5. Tell ed-Duweir, about eight miles east-northeast of Tell el-Hesi, is today generally accepted as the site of ancient Lachish. The range of evidence for this identification is conveniently summarized in Tufnell 1950. Whether the name "Lachish" might have been preserved in the name "Umm Lakis" was held to be a false issue by Charles Clermont-Ganneau, whose investigations among the local Bedouin convinced him that "Umm Lakis" was a phonetic misunderstanding by nineteenth century scholars of what he perceived as the true, local pronunciation, *Mulâkis* (Clermont-Ganneau 1896: 438 n.). On the difficult problems of toponymy in Syria-Palestine, see, for example, Rainey 1978. —Editor.

6. The exchange-rate in 1890 was $4.866 (U.S.) for £1.00 (Whitaker 1890: 631), and $1.00 then was the equivalent of about $10.40 as of November, 1982 (U.S. Bureau of the Census 1975: 199; U.S. Department of Labor 1983: 94). Thus, £1,000 amounted to $4,866 in 1890, or about $50,600 in late 1982. —Editor.

7. *P. E. F. Quarterly Statement* 22 (1890): 141.

8. The archive misfiles this document under "Bliss."

9. Petrie's outrageous comments, here and later, on the subject of the Effendi annoyed and embarrassed Petrie's own colleagues. See, for example, Bliss's reaction (PEF/Bliss/5/1, p. 52). —Editor.

10. "With Ibrahim Adham Effendi el-Khaldi, descendant of the great Khalid who took Syria for Mohammed, my relations were most friendly from beginning to end. He filled his post in a gentlemanly and honourable manner. In an unsettled country of Bedawin his presence was a source of security" (Bliss 1891c: 290). —Editor.

11. "On April 17 I moved a few miles on, to Tell Hesy, so called from the 'gravelly valley,' Wady Hesy" (Petrie 1931: 122). —Editor.

12. In 1890, about $0.24 (U.S.) a day; equivalent to about $2.50 in 1982; see n. 6 above. —Editor.

13. See fig. 6. The area referred to is at the left, marked "pottery" and indicated by the map's legend to be "cleared ground." In Petrie 1891: pl. I, it is the area marked "cemetery" (this latter map is reproduced in Bliss 1894: pl. I), and it is outside and to the west of what is today known to be the Early Bronze Age city, often referred to as "the lower city." This EB city at Hesi formed what Petrie usually referred to as the "enclosure" extending south and west from the base of the tell (see fig. 7). The present Joint Expedition usually refers to this "enclosure" as the "terrace." Petrie's "high mound," or "tell," which stands in the northeast corner of the "enclosure," is today more often referred to as the "acropolis," so that "Tell el-Hesi" is today understood to include both the acropolis and the terrace extending south and west from it. —Editor.

14. Author omitted P.E.F. archive location for the May 3 letter to Armstrong and for the particular plan of the site (now fig. 6) enclosed with it. —Editor.

15. In all, four such pilaster-decorated slabs were found (Petrie 1890c: 229, 231–32, 234, 235–36; Petrie 1891: 23, 35, and pl. IV). A replica of one of them—either one of Petrie's casts or a cast made from one of his casts—has been seen in the collection of the Harvard Semitic Museum in Cambridge, MA, by Daniel Katz (area supervisor at Tell el-Hesi in 1977) and Kevin O'Connell, S.J. —Editor.

16. Author omitted P.E.F. Archive location. —Editor.

17. Author omitted P.E.F. Archive location. —Editor.

18. Baron Ustinoff (Platon von Ustinov), a wealthy private collector of antiquities (Schick 1893), lived in Jaffa as a Russian expatriate. He was the grandfather of English writer and actor-director Peter Ustinov. Hall was Petrie's boyhood friend, by this time a missionary resident in Jaffa and often Petrie's host there (Petrie 1891: 11). Schick, a German-born, Swiss-educated missionary-carpenter living in Jerusalem, was a self-taught expert on the architectural history of the city and became a regular contributor to the *P. E. F. Quarterly Statement*. For his obituary, see Wilson 1902. Conjecturally, "Clarke," otherwise unidentified here, may refer to C. P. Clarke, the Egyptologist who became keeper of the South Kensington (now the Victoria and Albert) Museum in 1892, or, alternatively, to Herbert Clark [sic], agent for Thomas Cook and Son in Jaffa and also a collector of Palestinian antiquities (*P.E.F. Quarterly Statement* 1895: 298; Vester 1950: 63; Drower 1985: 166).

19. Author did not indicate whether this catalogue is located in the Fund archives. —Editor.

20. The tour is described in Petrie 1890c: 237–45. Brief topographical and archaeological survey-type notes on a great many of the sites are given in "Notes on Sites Visited in Southern Palestine, 1890," Petrie 1891: 51–62. —Editor.

21. Author did not indicate source for this information. —Editor.

22. See fig. 6, area marked "pottery"; same as Petrie 1891: pl. I, area marked "cemetery." The latter is reproduced in Bliss 1894: pl. I. —Editor.

23. Recent excavation of the Muslim cemetery at Hesi shows eye-directions of 80 percent of the skeletons to be oriented approximately toward the south-southeast, the direction of Mecca (Toombs 1985: 66–68). —Editor

24. Current investigations of the Joint Expedition have found that the pits are usually 8-1/4 to 11-1/2 ft. deep, which supports the attribution of Bliss's pits to the "town of the ovens" (private communication from L. E. Toombs). —Editor.

25. The plan referred to shows only nine features labeled "pit"; apparently the author interpreted the parabolic dotted line just to the right of the labeled southernmost pit as a tenth one. —Editor.

26. Author omitted P. E. F. Archive location for this letter. —Editor.

27. Author did not indicate the source—apparently a letter by Bliss—for this detail about Yusif's role. —Editor.

28. A worker found the 2.5 inch x 2 inch tablet in debris "to the east of the outer doorway of room (I)," one of a series of rooms against the north wall of "City III." Bliss did not see the tablet *in situ*; it was brought to him in his tent by Yusif, the foreman, who had observed the discovery (Bliss 1894: 51–53, 57). —Editor.

29. The first transcription, transliteration, and translation of the tablet was given by Sayce (1893; reproduced in Bliss 1894: 184–87). Sayce had offered a tentative translation the previous year (Sayce 1892 = Appendix B, pp. 212–214 below). See now W. F. Albright, "Letter from Tell el-Hesi," in J. B. Pritchard, ed., *Ancient Near Eastern Texts* (1969): 490. In "Bibliography of Publications," Part C (pp. 206–9 below), see also Scheill 1893 and 1894; Hilprecht 1896; Knudtzon 1907; and Albright 1942. —Editor.

30. Thus designated on the most recent maps; formerly Tell Sheikh Ahmed el-ᶜAreini—called, for a time, "Tel Gat"—until S. Yeivin's excavations there in the 1950s showed that it could not be the site of ancient Gath. —Editor.

31. John Worrell reports recovering what are possibly a couple of fragments of this masonry in the ruins of Petrie's tunnel, found while trimming the east-face section above the Wadi in 1973. The pieces were entered in the material culture registry of the Joint Expedition; at present they are stored in Jerusalem (private communication). —Editor.

32. This is no longer an objection to a possible thirteenth century date. Recent excavations have shown that the four-room house was already widely attested in twelfth-century Palestine, including some non-Israelite examples (Sauer 1979: 9; Stager 1985: 17; Finkelstein 1988: 254–59). —Editor.

33. Earlier section-drawing by others elsewhere than in Palestine is mentioned by Drower (1985: 160). —Editor.

34. His brief chapter, "The Art of Excavating" (Petrie 1892b: 156–66), provides Petrie's own succinct and engaging summarization of his methods. —Editor.

35. The photographs reproduced in figs. 1–5, 7–9, and 11, as well as the plan in fig. 6, were supplied by the author from unpublished archives with permission from the Palestine Exploration Fund (London). —Editor.

BIBLIOGRAPHY FOR CHAPTER II

Abbreviation: *PEFQS = Palestine Exploration Fund Quarterly Statement*

Aharoni, Y.
1973   *Beer-Sheba I.* Tel Aviv: Tell Aviv University Institute of Archaeology.

Albright, W. F.
1932   *The Excavations of Tell Beit Mirsim.* Vol. I, *The Pottery of the First Three Seasons.* Annual of the American Schools of Oriental Research 12.

Asaro, F.; Perlman, I. and Dothan, M.
1971   An Introductory Study of Mycenaean IIIC1 Ware from Tell Ashdod. *Archaeometry* 13.2: 169–75.

Bliss, F. J.
1890   Ma'lula and its Dialect. *PEFQS* 22: 74–98.
1891a   Reports from Mr. F. J. Bliss. *PEFQS* 23: 97–98.
1891b   Reports from Mr. F. J. Bliss. *PEFQS* 23: 207–11.
1891c   Report of Excavations at Tell-el-Hesy during the Spring of 1891. *PEFQS* 23:282–90.
1891d   Excavating from its Picturesque Side. *PEFQS* 23: 291–98.
1892a   Notes from Tell el Hesy. *PEFQS* 24: 36–38.
1892b   Report of the Excavations at Tell el Hesy for the Autumn Season of the Year 1891. *PEFQS* 24: 95–113.
1892c   Notes from Tell el Hesy. *PEFQS* 24: 192–96.
1892d   The Maronites. *PEFQS* 24: 71–83, 129–53, 207–18, 308–22.
1893a   Report of the Excavations at Tell-el-Hesy, during the Spring Season of the Year 1892. *PEFQS* 25: 9–20.

1893b   Report of the Excavations at Tell El Hesy
         during the Autumn of 1892. *PEFQS* 25:
         103-19.
1894   *A Mound of Many Cities or Tell el Hesy
         Excavated.* London: Palestine Explora-
         tion Fund; New York: Macmillan.
Clermont-Ganneau, C.
1896   *Archaeological Researches in Palestine
         During the Years 1873-74.* Vol. II. Lon-
         don: Committee of the Palestine Explo-
         ration Fund.
Cobern, C.
1890   The Work at Tell el Hesy, as seen by an
         American visitor. *PEFQS* 22: 166-70.
Crowfoot, J. W., and Fitzgerald, G. M.
1929   *Excavations in the Tyropoeon Valley, Jeru-
         salem, 1927.* Palestine Exploration Fund
         Annual, 1927. London: Palestine Explo-
         ration Fund.
Dever, W. G., and Richard, S.
1977   A Reevaluation of Tell Beit Mirsim Stra-
         tum J. *Bulletin of the American Schools
         of Oriental Research* No. 226: 1-14.
Dothan, M., *et al.*
1971   *Ashdod II–III. The Second and Third Sea-
         sons of Excavations, 1963, 1965, Sound-
         ings in 1967.* (ᶜAtiqot, English Series,
         Vols. IX–X). Vol. 1: Text. Vol. 2: Figures
         and Plates. Jerusalem: Department of
         Antiquities and Museums, Ministry of
         Education and Culture.
Dothan, T.
1973   Philistine Material Culture and Its
         Mycenaean Affinities. In *Acts of the In-
         ternational Archaeological Symposium:
         "The Mycenaeans in the Eastern Mediter-
         ranean." Nicosia 27th March–2nd April,
         1972.* Nicosia: Republic of Cyprus, Min-
         istry of Communications and Works,
         Department of Antiquities.
Drower, M. S.
1985   *Flinders Petrie: A Life in Archaeology.*
         London: Victor Gollancz.
Epstein, C.
1966   *Palestinian Bichrome Ware.* Leiden: Brill.
Finkelstein, I.
1988   *The Archaeology of the Israelite Settle-
         ment.* Translated by D. Saltz. Jerusalem:
         Israel Exploration Society.
Herzog, Z.
1973   The Storehouses. In *Beer-Sheba I,* pp. 23–
         30. Edited by Y. Aharoni. Tel Aviv: Tel
         Aviv University Institute of Archaeology.

Kenyon, K. M.
1955   A Crescentic Axehead from Jericho and
         a Group of Weapons from Tell el-Hesy.
         *XIth Annual Report of the Institute of
         Archaeology:* 10–18. London: The
         University of London.
1973   Palestine in the Time of the Eighteenth
         Dynasty. In *Cambridge Ancient History,*
         3rd ed., Vol. 2, Part 1, *History of the Mid-
         dle East and the Aegean Region c. 1800–
         1380 B.C.,* pp. 526–56. Edited by I. E.
         S. Edwards, *et al.* Cambridge: The
         University Press.
Lapp, P.
1967   The Conquest of Palestine in the Light
         of Archaeology. *Concordia Theological
         Monthly* 38: 283–300.
Matthers, J.
1974   *A Reassessment of the Early Bronze Age
         Material Excavated at Tell Hesy 1890–
         1892.* M.A. Thesis in the Library of
         the London University Institute of Ar-
         chaeology.
Oren, E.
1969   Cypriot Imports in the Palestinian Late
         Bronze I Context. *Opuscula Atheniensis*
         [Lund] 9: 127–50.
Palestine Exploration Fund
1895   Notes and News. *PEFQS* 27: 297–304.
Palestine Exploration Fund Archives
1977   *77/46. Report on the Papers of the Pales-
         tine Exploration Fund. Handlist III (1876–
         1914).* Unpublished typescript: NRA
         16370. London: National Register of Ar-
         chives (The Royal Commission on His-
         torical Manuscripts). [In the foregoing
         chapter, citations from the Handlist fol-
         low the format "PEF/. . ." etc.]
Petrie, W. M. F.
1877   *Inductive Metrology.* London: H.
         Saunders.
1890a   Notes on Places Visited in Jerusalem.
         PEFQS 22: 157–59.
1890b   Explorations in Palestine. *PEFQS* 22:
         159–66.
1890c   Journals of Mr. W. M. Flinders Petrie.
         PEFQS 22: 219–46.
1891   *Tell el Hesy (Lachish).* London: Palestine
         Exploration Fund.
1892a   Notes on the Results at Tell el Hesy.
         PEFQS 24: 114–15.
1892b   *Ten Years Digging in Egypt.* London: Re-
         ligious Tract Society.

1931   *Seventy Years in Archaeology.* London: S. Low Marston & Co. Ltd.; New York: Henry Holt (1932).

n. d.   Journals. Unpublished portions archived in the Griffith Institute of the Ashmolean Museum, Oxford.

Rainey, A. F.
1978   The Toponymics of Eretz-Israel. *Bulletin of the American Schools of Oriental Research* 231: 1–17.

Rose, D. G.; Toombs, L. E.; and O'Connell, K. G., S.J.
1978   Four Seasons of Excavation at Tell el-Hesi: A Preliminary Report. In *Preliminary Excavation Reports: Bâb edh-Dhrâᶜ, Sardis, Meiron, Tell el-Hesi, Carthage (Punic)*, pp. 109–49. Edited by D. N. Freedman. Annual of the American Schools of Oriental Research 43, Cambridge, MA: American Schools of Oriental Research.

Sauer, J. A.
1979   Iron I Pillared House in Moab. *Biblical Archeologist* 42: 9.

Sayce, A. H.
1892   The Latest Discovery in Palestine. *The Sunday School Times* (Philadelphia) 34, No. 35 (August 27): 546–47 (Reprinted below, pp. 212–14, as Appendix B to "Bibliography of Publications Concerning Tell el-Hesi.")

1893   The Cuneiform and Other Inscriptions Found at Lachish and Elsewhere in the South of Palestine. *PEFQS* 25: 25–32.

Scheil, V.
1893   Une tablette Palestinienne cunéiforme. *Recueil des Travaux Relatifs à la Philologie et l'Archéologie Égyptiennes et Assyriennes* 15: 137–38; reprinted, *PEFQS* 26 (1894): 47.

1894   La tablette de Lachis. *Revue Biblique* 3: 433–36.

Schick, C.
1893   Baron Ustinoff's Collection of Antiquities at Jaffa. *PEFQS* 25: 294–97.

Shiloh, Y.
1970   The Four-Room House: Its Situation and Function in the Israelite City. *Israel Exploration Journal* 20: 180–90.

1980   The Population of Iron Age Palestine in the Light of a Sample Analysis of Urban Plans, Areas, and Population Density. *Bulletin of the American Schools of Oriental Research* 239: 25-35.

Silberman, N.
1982   *Digging for God and Country: Exploration, Archeology, and the Secret Struggle for the Holy Land 1799–1917.* New York: Alfred A. Knopf.

Stager, L. E.
1985   The Archaeology of the Family in Early Israel. *Bulletin of the American Schools of Oriental Research* No. 260: 1–35.

Toombs, L. E.
1985   *Tell el-Hesi: Modern Military Trenching and Muslim Cemetery in Field I, Strata I–II.* Edited by K. G. O'Connell, S. J. Excavation Reports of the American Schools of Oriental Research: Tell el-Hesi 2. Waterloo, Ontario: Wilfrid Laurier University Press.

Tufnell, O.
1950   Excavations at Tell ed-Duweir, Palestine, Directed by the Late J. L. Starkey, 1932–1938: Some Results and Reflections. *Palestine Exploration Quarterly* 82: 65–80.

1958   *Lachish IV (Tell ed-Duweir), The Bronze Age.* Part I: *Text.* Part II: *Plates.* London: Oxford University Press.

1965   Excavator's Progress: Letters of F. J. Bliss, 1889–1900. *Palestine Exploration Quarterly* 97: 112–27.

U. S. Bureau of the Census
1975   *Historical Statistics of the United States, Colonial Times to 1970.* Bicentennial Edition, Part 1. Washington, D.C.: U. S. Bureau of the Census.

U. S. Department of Labor
1983   Current Labor Statistics: Producer Price Indexes. *Monthly Labor Review* 106: 93–98.

Vester, B. S.
1950   *Our Jerusalem: An American Family in the Holy City, 1881–1949.* Garden City, NY: Doubleday.

Watson, C. M.
1915   *Fifty Years' Work in the Holy Land: a Record and a Summary, 1865–1915.* London: Committee of the Palestine Exploration Fund.

Whitaker, J.
1890   *An Almanack For the Year of Our Lord 1890.* London: J. Whitaker.

Wilson, C. W.
1902   Obituary of Dr. Conrad Schick. *PEFQS* 34: 139-42.

Yadin, Y.
1960   *Hazor II: An Account of the Second Season of Excavations, 1956.* Jerusalem: Hebrew University.

Yeivin, S.
1961   *First Preliminary Report on the Excavations at Tel Gat (Tell Sheykh Ahmed el-* ͨ*Areyny) Seasons 1956.1958.* Jerusalem: The Gat Expedition.

1971   *The Israelite Conquest of Canaan.* Istanbul: Nederlands Historisch-Archaeologisch Institut in het Nabije Oosten.

Chapter III

THE EVOLUTION OF A HOLISTIC INVESTIGATION: PHASE ONE OF THE JOINT EXPEDITION TO TELL EL-HESI

by
John E. Worrell[1]
Sturbridge Village Foundation

This chapter is a position paper that explains the holistic approach followed by the staff of the Joint Expedition to Tell el-Hesi during its first four seasons (1970–75). In the attempt to implement the "new archaeology" at Hesi,[2] there was more method than theory at the beginning of the Hesi project. It took time and experience to understand what it means to reconstruct lifeways from the patterned residues of human behavior, but an interdisciplinary method that had been applied and tested at prehistoric sites was available for adoption at Hesi.

From the outset Hesi has been a cooperative undertaking. Instead of the traditional pattern in which a chief archaeologist conducted a dig as its factotum, an interdisciplinary team of archaeologists and other specialists directed the project in dialogue with one another. The resultant integration of diverse perspectives was viewed as the precondition for a reconstruction of the site's past. However, the difficulty of integrating disparate data generated by an interdisciplinary team of specialists is obvious. No matter how admirable the goal and how well organized the project, "total archaeology" is impossible in practice.

The Hesi expedition is best understood against the backdrop of the archaeological ferment in the period after World War II. On the basis of the increasingly influential "new archaeology," there was a need for rethinking the traditional approach to Palestinian tells. While archaeological method had been improving steadily in the Near East, the main emphasis was on the chronology and political history of a site. Little attention was given to other aspects of the past, such as cultural and ecological history. The Hesi project was one of the front-runners in practicing the "new archaeology" (with its interdisciplinary emphasis) in the context of Palestinian archaeology.

The Hesi project was founded on the conviction that a greatly broadened perspective needed to be brought to bear on the physical site. The traditional archaeological procedures had to be supplemented by a variety of new ones, if the whole cultural history lying beneath Tell el-Hesi was to be recovered. The conventional chronological approach of the past was not adequate of itself to accomplish this end. Consequently, the Hesi expedition was organized according to a multidimensional perspective. To do justice to Hesi with respect to its regional orientation and its societal structure, archaeologists had to collaborate with natural and social scientists in establishing objectives, strategies, and techniques. Not surprisingly, this pioneer attempt to do more than relate strata to historical events often proceeded by trial and error.

The Hesi project was affiliated with the American Schools of Oriental Research (ASOR) from its inception; in fact, the expedition was the creation of ASOR's then president, G. Ernest Wright of Harvard University. Convinced that tells previously dug could profit from the application of new stratigraphic methods, Wright suggested Hesi as an appropriate site for reexcavation. He wanted the project to be patterned after the excavations of Robert J. Braidwood and his interdisciplinary staff, beginning in 1948, at the prehistoric site of Jarmo in Iraq.

ASOR itself was undergoing some adjustments in the aftermath of the Six-Day War of 1967. From 1948 to 1967 ASOR could function only on the Arab side of the international armistice line in Palestine. Immediately after the 1967 war, Israel became accessible to ASOR-sponsored excavators. West Bank sites such as Taanach, Ai, and Shechem, which ASOR had been digging at the outbreak of the war, could no longer be excavated because of UNESCO regulations governing occupied territory.

Hesi is in Israel; its location made it a good candidate for excavation by ASOR archaeologists. Furthermore, as the first tell to be dug systematically in Palestine—by Sir William Flinders Petrie in 1890 and then by Frederick Jones Bliss in 1891–92[3]—it was the foundation and benchmark for all subsequent Palestinian archaeology. Further excavation with modern interdisciplinary techniques was highly desirable.

The Department of Antiquities of Israel welcomed ASOR-affiliated archaeologists and readily granted excavation permits for Hesi and other sites. As president of ASOR, Wright was a distinguished biblical scholar and archaeologist. He had inaugurated and directed the multiseason excavation of Shechem on the West Bank, beginning in 1956; in 1964 he also launched a long-term dig at Gezer in Israel. His Shechem dig was a model of organization and method: the organization he learned from Yigael Yadin's excavation at Hazor; the method represented Wright's refinement of the techniques used at Jericho by Kathleen Kenyon. Wright's greatest contribution to the archaeology of Palestine was the large number of younger colleagues whom he trained; this training was so effective that when he died unexpectedly in 1974 his students were able to fill the gaps left by his death.

As early as his Shechem dig Wright was eager to utilize specialists in the natural and social sciences. His dream was realized to some degree at Gezer under the leadership of William G. Dever, and later came to fruition at Hesi, Hesban, and other digs directed by Wright's students. Most of the archaeologists on the Hesi team had dug at Shechem or Gezer, where they learned Wright's approach to archaeology. Good teacher that he was, Wright was eager to have his students go beyond him by using the more advanced interdisciplinary techniques on Palestinian tells. In the course of

the Gezer excavations in the late 1960s, William G. Dever, the director, and John E. Worrell and Lawrence E. Stager, who later became members of Hesi's first staff, often discussed the advantages to be gained from applying the techniques and strategies of the natural sciences at a historic site in Israel. Despite the difficulty of integrating an extraordinary amount of disparate data, the Hesi staff was convinced that the interdisciplinary approach was the way to recover a complex, interactive, and multileveled human culture.

The original staff of the Hesi expedition included John E. Worrell as director; Lawrence E. Stager; Lawrence E. Toombs; W. J. Bennett, Jr.; and Philip J. King. G. Ernest Wright and Edward F. Campbell served as overseers and advisers. The initial proposal for Hesi was constructed by Worrell in collaboration with the staff. Stager was largely responsible for enlisting the specialists from the physical and social sciences, especially the paleobotanist and the faunal analyst. From the beginning the specialists were integral to the staff and shared in all decisions with respect to strategy and interpretation.[4] Only with a fully integrated staff was it possible to reconstruct the ecosystem for each historically discernible culture and period. Instead of concentrating exclusively on political history, now there was the opportunity to test a wide range of hypotheses with respect to population variances, cultural adaptations, and other phenomena.

Hesi seemed like an excellent testing ground for holistic archaeology. Preliminary investigations revealed a cultural continuum from prehistoric to modern times. Also, ethnographic phenomena were present for testing the validity of various techniques and hypothetical structures. Hesi appeared to have functioned both as an urban center (for example, in the Early Bronze Age) and as a crossroad and frontier community (during most of its subsequent history). Also, its location is conducive to posing questions of a geographic, climatic, ethnographic, and political nature. Situated at the juxtaposition of the fertile Shephelah, the arid Negev, and the Judean hills, it was close to major commercial routes and water sources. In addition, problems of ecosystemic adaptation, cultural process, and spatial utilization present themselves for holistic investigation at Hesi.

Hesi is an excellent subject for a holistic study because of its situation in a natural transition zone, both geologically and meteorologically. In the southern Judean purlieu, it occupies a position where the rolling limestone hill country breaks sharply into the verdant coastal plain. This zone has great variability in rainfall. Directly proximate to major commercial and military routes in antiquity, Hesi was also on a political border, on both north-south and east-west axes, during most periods. Inhabited from the Chalcolithic to the Hellenistic periods (with some notable gaps), the site had been subject to dramatic variation in both its size and the extent of its population. Also, initial paleobotanical study of a substantial ash layer circling the mound indicated that the now arid plain may have been forested in the Early Bronze Age. Herein may be at least a partial explanation for ancient urban centers such as Hesi and Arad in regions which are now desert.

Hesi's location helps to explain its political importance in antiquity. Situated at the extreme southeastern extent of the Philistine Plain, on a natural and political border, close to major commercial and military routes, with a commanding view of its surroundings, Hesi may have been part of a satellite defense network in antiquity.

In terms of modern geography, Hesi is located midway between Beersheba, the capital of the northern Negev, and the Mediterranean port city of Ashdod. It lies four miles south of the mid-plain agricultural city of Kiryat Gat and less than one mile west of the main highway from Jerusalem and Tel Aviv to Beersheba. From the tell the coastal dunes and the sea are visible to the west, while the rising desert can be seen to the southeast. The lush agriculture of the plain today meets the semi-arid grazing land immediately at the foot of Tell el-Hesi. How precisely this phenomenon parallels the environment of antiquity and what changes may have occurred in that frontier during the periods of the site's occupation became subjects of the staff's investigation. Indications are that the challenge of a fluctuating environment was met by cultural adaptations.

Hesi appears to have been a thriving metropolis in its earliest phases; in later periods there was fluctuation between commercial center and border military post. If the initial botanical indicators can be substantiated, it may be possible to demonstrate a curious interplay of environmental factors and cultural distribution bearing on the collapse of the Early Bronze cultures in the south.

Ecological, geographic, and topographic features are therefore ideal for testing both standard assumptions and new hypotheses with respect to cultural and natural environmental factors as they relate to known history and to patterns of settlement, as well as theories concerning urban fluctuation and frontier cultural and economic systems. Comparative ecology provides an effective index to correlations between climatic and population shifts from antiquity to modern times.

Ethnological concerns loomed large on the staff's agenda. Hesi's population fluctuations, its situation in a zone of considerable climatic variation, its location at a cultural crossroad, and its position on a natural frontier between sedentary and transient societies made it ideal for ethnological study. In the course of this study valuable analogies could be drawn from contemporary population groups in the area, including local Bedouin, kibbutzniks, and military personnel. The modern composition of the population can be a valuable index for anthropologists as they try to formulate interpretations with respect to the inhabitants in antiquity.

In the attempt to learn as much as possible about the site and its history, no procedure has been neglected. For example, analyses have been done on floral materials (seeds, fibers, pollens), faunal materials (bones, teeth, shells, even artifacts), human remains, contents of rubbish pits, lithics, and types of pottery fabrication. Studies have also been made of dry farming and grain-storage techniques. Interpretations are based on scientifically controlled procedures applied to massive quantities of data. Every effort has been expended to interpret the data carefully in reconstructing the cultural processes of antiquity. Plans call for publishing the results in detail so as to allow other archaeologists to incorporate them in their own studies. To ensure that the Hesi staff would meet its publication responsibilities, Kevin G. O'Connell assumed the editorial oversight for the whole project in 1975.[5]

The extent of the Early Bronze Age city was evident from the reports of Flinders Petrie and confirmed by preliminary survey of the site by the current excavators. The reports of Petrie and Bliss attest to the intensity of occupation at Hesi during the Early Bronze Age. In later periods there appears to have been a greatly reduced population. The inhabitants and their activities were concentrated on the small acropolis at the northeast corner of the older city.

The extensive activities of the Persian Period date close to the end of the ancient cultural continuum of occupation at Hesi. The Persian Period is not well documented by evidence from other Palestinian sites, at least in comparison with the available data for the Bronze and Iron ages. At Hesi the main concern of the inhabitants in the Persian

Period was agriculture; it is attested by deep and intricate stratigraphy, including many storage pits, and gives the specialists excellent material for study and interpretation.

The most recent phases of occupation at Hesi have also been subjected to analysis in accordance with the approach of the "new archaeology." The Bedouin cemetery at Hesi has been the subject of a special study which sheds light on a modern cultural phenomenon neglected heretofore.[6]

While concentrating on the foregoing concerns, the Hesi staff did not neglect such historical questions as the identification of the site and its occupants in antiquity. Scholars have made several conjectures about the identity of Hesi, but none can yet be put forward with confidence. Petrie was convinced that Tell el-Hesi was the ruin of ancient Lachish, but his successor, Bliss, was less certain.[7] Subsequent research convinced many scholars to identify Hesi with biblical Eglon, reported in the book of Joshua to have been a Canaanite city-state conquered by the Israelites.[8] The present expedition to Tell el-Hesi may eventually be able to clarify the ancient identification of the site.

One of the vital parts of the Hesi program is its educational dimension. Using Gezer as the model, the Hesi staff was eager to involve student volunteers not only in the daily labor of the dig but also in the learning process. Thanks especially to Harry Thomas Frank, an accredited field school has been organized at Hesi. Students have every opportunity to learn field archaeology firsthand; work in the field is supplemented by lectures and seminars.[9] Staff and volunteers from various Hesi seasons are kept informed of further excavation at the site, publication of results (from Phase One and subsequent seasons), and other news by means of a special

newsletter, *Trowel and Patish*.[10]

While Phase One of the Joint Expedition's *excavations* at Hesi came to an end with the completion of the 1975 field season, it also remains unfinished until the results of the first four seasons (1970–75) have been brought to final publication. The present volume is a step toward that goal.[11]

NOTES

1. This essay is an abridged version of the original. Among those whose comments were very helpful in the revision are Philip J. King, W. J. Bennett, Jr., Lawrence E. Stager, D. Glenn Rose, Michael D. Coogan, and Lawrence E. Toombs.
2. See Rose 1989 (Chapter IV, below).
3. See Matthers 1989 (Chapter II, above).
4. Among the scientists who helped form the project's objectives, Jeffrey Schwartz, Robert B. Stewart, Reuben Bullard, Frank L. Koucky, and Michael Hammond deserve special mention. Feedback from the laboratory and the field has continued to be formative. The team concept extends throughout the field, specialist, research, and support personnel. Harry Thomas Frank organized the educational program (see Frank and Horton 1989 ([Chapter V, below]). Field archaeologists who were involved early in the project and took on increasingly responsible roles included D. Glenn Rose, Michael D. Coogan, Ralph W. Doermann, and Linda L. Ammons. Kevin G. O'Connell, S. J., and Charles U. Harris joined the central policy core of the project later in Phase One. See Worrell and Betlyon 1989 (Chapter VI, below), Appendix A, for a complete staff list.
5. See O'Connell 1989b (Introduction, above).
6. See L. E. Toombs, *Tell el-Hesi: Modern Military Trenching and Muslim Cemetery in Field I, Strata I–II*, ed. by K. G. O'Connell, S. J. Excavation Reports of the American Schools of Oriental Research: Tell el-Hesi 2 (Waterloo, Ontario: Wilfrid Laurier University Press, 1985).
7. Lachish is now identified with neighboring Tell ed-Duweir.
8. Josh 10:34–37; an alternative location for Eglon is Tell 'Eitun, SE of Lachish.
9. See Frank and Horton 1989 (Chapter V, below).
10. Edited since its inception in May 1978 by J. Kenneth Eakins, the newsletter has been made possible by the generous financial support of Golden Gate Baptist Theological Seminary, Mill Valley, California. —Editor.
11. See O'Connell 1989a (Conclusion, below).

Chapter IV

The Methodology of the New Archaeology and Its Influence on the Joint Expedition to Tell el-Hesi

by
D. Glenn Rose (†1981)
The Graduate Seminary, Phillips University

INTRODUCTION

The word *methodology* is used a number of different ways in modern archaeology. Sometimes it means a procedure by which excavation takes place, such as the architectural or the debris-layer method of excavation. Both of these methods define procedures for excavation that make use of particular strategies and techniques. At other times methodology means the principles of procedure, and the stress lies on the assumptions and goals of archaeology which are prior to and govern the operating procedures. In this essay, *methodology* will be used in the latter sense of principles that underlie the procedures, strategies, and techniques used in field excavation.

The basis of modern, scientific archaeological method in Palestine was laid at Tell el-Hesi in 1890 by Sir Flinders Petrie. He correlated the layers of soil with the pottery forms they contained (which he knew from Egypt) and thus established a solid basis for determination of the chronology of the site (Petrie 1891). F. J. Bliss, Petrie's successor at Hesi, added a further dimension when he published the site according to its stratigraphic layers (Bliss 1894; Matthers 1989 [Chapter II, above]: 59–60). Since that time, the determination of chronology at a site has been refined through a variety of techniques, and today it is guided by a method whose goal is the historical reconstruction of culture. At Tell el-Hesi, this method was further modified to include such non-chronological goals as the description of the inhabitants' lifeways and culture and the clarification of the relationship between them and the surrounding environment. These changes came about as part of a general concern with methodology in Syro-Palestinian as well as North American archaeology and as a result of the particular interests of the Hesi staff. For a discussion of the increasing concern with methodology in Syro-Palestinian archaeology, see Worrell 1989 (Chapter III, above); for an account of its working out in Phase One at Hesi, see Worrell and Betlyon 1989 (Chapter VI, below).

The Hesi methodology did not come into existence all at once. It developed through a slow, painful process of success and failure, and it continued to be refined in Phase Two of the Joint Expedition. This essay will take as its point of departure the last year of Phase One (1975), when Hesi's methodology was better developed than in the earlier seasons, and will have a retrospective stance. Within this context, the present essay sets out to examine in particular one major aspect of the methodology at Tell el-Hesi: the ways in which the assumptions and goals of the new archaeology movement in North American anthropology affected the principal assumptions and goals of the Joint Expedition.

The impact of the North American debate (Willey and Sabloff 1974: 178–211) is reflected in statements of the initiators of the Joint Expedition. As John Worrell so often put it, Hesi was to practice a holistic approach to archaeology (Worrell

1970; 1989 [Chapter III, above]). Or, as Lawrence Stager has held, the new archaeology is the most creative of the approaches to archaeology. The early statements also stressed the interdisciplinary nature of the staff at Hesi whose contributions were to result in a deeper kind of archaeological understanding. In order to appreciate these statements, we need to look briefly at the history and concerns of the new archaeology movement in North American anthropology.

HISTORY OF THE
NEW ARCHAEOLOGY MOVEMENT

Background

To understand fully the present debate in anthropological archaeology, one must go back to the middle of the nineteenth century to the theories of Darwin and Spencer concerning biological and cultural evolution (Harris 1968: 142–216). Before the end of the century these theories were applied to the archaeological record by E. B. Tylor and L. H. Morgan. According to these early anthropologists, humanity passed more or less uniformly through a series of stages leading from savagery to barbarism and on to civilization (Daniel 1962: 66–68). Assumed in this view is a belief in progress and evolution as the mechanisms of cultural change. According to many archaeologists who accepted the thesis, every artifact dug from the ground could be explained by reference to one of the cultural stages in this unilinear human evolution (Willey and Sabloff 1974: 83–87). This rationalistic approach to the intrepretation of the archaeological record was challenged at the end of the nineteenth century by the anthropological theories of Franz Boas.

Boas argued that the data gathered by ethnology and archaeology would not fit into predetermined categories derived from unilinear evolutionary theory. This judgment was based upon the observation that there were too many differences between the observed data and the categories derived rationalistically from a theory. As a result, Boas argued for a "historical particularism." By this term Boas meant to designate a method that was based upon empirical observation of particulars instead of speculative generalizations. Accordingly, all data must be described objectively before any generalization or interpretation can take place (Harris 1968: 250–392). For many students of Boas this meant that synthesis was not possible until extensive

data had been gathered. As a result, description itself became the goal of archaeological work (Willey and Sabloff 1974: 42–130). It is suggested by many interpreters that Boas was anti-evolutionary; however, others believe that he was only reacting against the form of evolutionary theory that was associated with the name of Spencer. The latter held to a biological reductionism coupled with an emphasis upon parallel evolution and progress (Harris 1968: 290–94). In contrast, Boas and the archaeologists who followed his position argued that each datum must be described in its historical context as a first concern, while development or evolution is a secondary matter. Since Boas trained so many prominent anthropologists who later became heads of major university departments, this approach became the basic methodology in North American archaeology throughout the first half of the twentieth century. Then at mid-century, when stratigraphic methods of digging were introduced, North American archaeologists became more interested in questions of development. The result was an emphasis on the history of cultural particulars with its corresponding concern for typologies of development (Willey and Sabloff 1974: 83– 130). This approach became the dominant one for Near Eastern archaeology as well.

Part of this generally accepted point of view in archaeology was an emphasis upon diffusion as the mechanism of cultural change. When similar ideas or artifacts were found in different places, it was assumed that these ideas or features had been carried from one place to another by migrating peoples or traders.[1] Thus culture in a particular area changed through outside influences. This view was accepted by many Boasians in opposition to the evolutionary view of independent invention as an explanation of culture change. However, most archaeologists did not accept the extreme diffusionist positions of some European colleagues which (for example) accounted for the pyramids of Central America by positing Atlantic sea voyages there from ancient Egypt. But a theory of generalized diffusion coupled with historical particularism became the interpretative matrix for both North American and Near Eastern archaeological explanation. The development of North American cultural areas, based upon typological similarities, followed. This general view of cultural history as proceeding by diffusion was one against which the new archaeology movement was to protest (Wilson 1974: 274–90; Willey and Sabloff 1974: 178–211).

The New Archaeology

The basis for the new archaeology's reaction was laid in the forties and fifties of this century. Dissatisfaction with the prevailing emphasis on cultural history surfaced in anthropological writing. Some of this uneasiness appeared also in new approaches to archaeological data and their interpretation. First, since artifacts were to be understood as the material remains of human behavior, archaeologists were led to emphasize the context of the artifact and the function it played in human culture. Second, the introduction of settlement-pattern studies suggested that the larger area context of an artifact supplied economic, technological, and cultural data for understanding the recovered evidence for human behavior in a particular occupation level. Finally, a new emphasis was placed on the relationship between culture and the natural environment. Environment was to be understood as more than a passive context for human development and behavior. These approaches obviously affected the implicit historical goal of archaeology, that is, the concern with the political-cultural history of a particular tell or site. Along with these changed approaches came an increasing emphasis upon archaeology as an interdisciplinary enterprise. Laboratory scientists began to make significant contributions to archaeological analyses and techniques by entering the field with sophisticated equipment to collect the data themselves (Willey and Sabloff 1974: 131–60).

These changes in archaeology were fueled by the writings of two social anthropologists in particular, Julian Steward and Leslie White. Practitioners of the new archaeology often appeal to the theories of these scholars as support for their own concerns. Both were neo-evolutionary thinkers who rejected historical particularism in favor of a reemphasis on evolution.

Julian Steward developed an approach that came to be called "cultural ecology" (Harris 1968: 654–87; Kottak 1974: 31–33). It included an emphasis upon multilinear evolution and the role of environment in cultural change. For Steward, similar environmental conditions will cause similar cultural responses. If this is so, then one can account for cultural similarities between different regions and different times as the result of multiple invention (convergent or parallel evolution) rather than of diffusion. Thus culture works by a different mechanism than that posited either by the older evolutionary view of universal stages (unilinear evolution) or by the diffusion position (transfer of cultural traits by movement of population or ideas). An investigation of the relationships between environment and human culture can lead to an understanding of cultural process as opposed to cultural history. Steward's ideas are more complex than these few remarks indicate; however, their basic thrust as described here was most important to the new archaeological movement.

Leslie White, whose influence on North American archaeology operated in part through the work of his student, Betty Meggers (Willey and Sabloff 1974: 179), took an approach to evolution that focused on the efficient use of energy in a society. In his view, society moves from dependence upon human energy alone to levels where technological discovery and economic innovation allow ever-increasing efficiency in the use of such energy. White argued that cultural advance is directly proportional to the amount of energy harnessed per person (Kottak 1974: 31). He surveyed the development of humanity in these terms and suggested that such movement was evolutionary in nature. White also believed that his approach could be used to evaluate contemporary social movements. He stressed the interdependence within a culture of such elements as technology, economics, social organization, and ideology. A change in any one of these will cause corresponding changes in the others. This emphasis upon the subsystems of a culture and their interrelationships became extremely important in the new archaeology movement. Previously it had been supposed by many that culture is the product of a closed system whose components are identifiable and quantifiable in the archaeological and ethnographic records. By the late fifties and early sixties, these ideas of White and Steward were beginning to influence both anthropologists and archaeologists of various persuasions.

The new developments in archaeology and anthropology all came together in 1965 at the meeting of the American Anthropological Society in Denver. A group of younger archaeologists conducted a seminar on "The Social Organization of Prehistoric Communities" (Binford and Binford 1968: vii). Although the term "new archaeology" had been used earlier, the concepts associated with the movement seem to have crystalized at Denver and to have received a favorable audience among more than just a few "rebels" (Binford 1972: 12–13). Lewis R. Binford was involved in organizing the symposium, and since that time his name has become almost synonymous with the new archaeology. He and his group have been vocal about the movement, and from them have come a number of theoretical essays that deal with the assumptions and goals of archaeology (Redman 1973; Leone 1972b; Watson, LeBlanc, and Redman 1971). Many of the group acknowledge that their method rests upon the philosophical epistemology of Carl G. Hemple (1966). This approach to the philosophy of science criticizes an older "narrow empirical approach" which assumed that each object contained within itself a meaning that was independent of presuppositions. Hemple, by contrast, argued that the only proper scientific approach is deductive. The meaning of an object must be discovered in relationship to the presuppositions of the observer and the questions with which one approaches the object. Instead of a single objective meaning that can be inductively grasped, there are a multitude of possible meanings whose elucidation depends upon the particular questions asked by the investigator. Therefore one formulates questions, problems, or hypotheses to which the data supply answers (Hill 1972: 64–70). This approach has led the new archaeologists to refer to their discipline as a deductive science in opposition to the older inductive archaeology. Sometimes, as well, they speak of themselves as the only genuinely scientific archaeologists. They also prefer to call themselves process archaeologists, since the goal of their work is the explanation of cultural change in general rather than the description of actual changes within specific cultures. It is the general law or rule that is important rather than the particular example. Most of the ideas of the new archaeology have been presented in strongly apologetic terms. At times this has evoked ill will in the profession, but it has also forced archaeologists to become more self-conscious about their methodology (Willey and Sabloff 1974: 210–11).

This brief historical survey must suffice for our purposes. A more comprehensive history with a systematic listing of themes can be found elsewhere (Willey and Sabloff 1974: 178–211; Wilson 1974).

Reactions and Anticipations

It is possible to argue about the "newness" of the new archaeology movement. In 1948 Walter W. Taylor published *A Study of Archeology*, in which he called for a conjunctive approach to the discipline. In more recent works, Taylor has suggested that much of the new archaeology was anticipated in that book (Taylor 1972). In their *History of American Archaeology*, Willey and Sabloff support Taylor's priority only in some areas. Not to be found in his work, they point out, are "a cultural evolutionary point of view; a systematic view of culture which incorporates this evolutionary point of view; and a battery of new methods, techniques, and aids that were not available in 1948" (Willey and Sabloff 1974: 184–85).

It is also possible to speak of developments in Europe, especially in England, that anticipated the new archaeology movement. There archaeology developed within the fields of history and classics. These disciplines emphasized a chronological or diachronic approach; however, this was modified in England by the work of V. Gordon Childe. For him, much of the archaeology then current was not scientifically sound since it involved unwarranted assumptions about the nature of history. For Childe, history was the development of technology, not the ideas of great people or the story of political movements (Childe 1951: 9–19). Drawing his own ideas from the realm of social evolutionary thought, he argued that cultural change is the product of modifications in technology and economic systems. He combined this understanding with a modified diffusionism and used it to demonstrate the movement of culture from the Ancient Near East to Europe (Wilson 1974: 18–21, 297–301). Only now is that model of European prehistory being challenged by one whose outlook is similar to that of the new archaeologists, namely, Colin Renfrew (1973; 1974). But Childe's emphasis on technology and economics anticipated similar elements in the new archaeology. The work of Grahame Clark at Star Carr, which stressed ecological studies in addition to economic/technological patterns, also has connections with the new archaeology's emphasis (Clark 1954). The concern of this essay is not to trace these connections; however, one must remember that some of these views found their way to Syria-Palestine through the work of the British School in Jerusalem before they were introduced there from the North American debate.

The polemics of the North American discussion not only divided archaeology into two camps—the older archaeology's diachronic/chronological view versus the new archaeology's synchronic/nomothetic approach—but it also created divisions within the new archaeology movement itself. Kent Flannery has recently suggested whimsically that the movement is now made up of "law and order" and "Serutan" ("nature's" spelled backwards, as in the commercial tonic advertisement) groups. The first is interested in formulating and testing general or covering laws, analogous to the laws of the natural sciences, by which cultural change operates. The demonstration of these laws is usually supported by statistical data. The "Serutan" group is less convinced that general laws can be discovered and demonstrated. Instead, it concentrates on the "natural regulation" of subsystems which creates cultural change. The universal principles of subsystem relationships and cultural feedback are accepted, and systems theory is regularly used to explain cultural change. From the point of view of the "older archaeology," this division is one of emphasis only. Flannery also castigated the whole movement for its failure to produce excavation reports to back up its theoretical pronouncements (Flannery 1973: 50–53). Obviously, this debate will continue in North American archaeology and anthropology, and new methodological insights will evolve from it. However, our concern is with the initial debate since it is the one that affected the early leaders of Hesi.

Other persons, such as Robert J. Braidwood, also had some influence on Hesi method. Braidwood emphasized environmental studies at Jarmo in Iraq (Braidwood 1960). Even though he was the target of some polemic from the new archaeology (Binford 1972: 11–12), he early brought a number of its concerns to his own work in the Near East.

The New Archaeology at Hesi

The work at Tell el-Hesi is indebted to this whole complex background, but it is certainly the polemics of the sixties which had the greatest impact (Worrell 1989 [Chapter III above]). For the purposes of this essay, the new archaeology can be characterized in terms of four aspects. These have already been mentioned in the foregoing summary of the history of the movement, and together they make up a holistic approach to archaeological methodology. The first aspect is a concern for process, for cultural change itself rather than for the cultural history of a site or area. The second is an understanding of archaeology as a science in the sense of the natural sciences. The third aspect is ecological, a focus on the intrinsic relationships between human beings and their natural environment and a conviction that these relationships can be understood through ecosystems analysis, (i.e., by examining the mutual interactions of a culture's subsystems). Fourth, the new archaeology has a

particular understanding of the role of explanation in archaeology. Explanation is not mere description of what is found or inductive inference as to its meaning. It involves an interpretation of the process of cultural change in terms of general or covering laws of culture; i.e., it is an explanation of cultural change that holds true whenever there are similar relationships present in similar cultural systems. The explanation seeks to produce universal laws of culture. Culture is "nomothetic."

To suggest that these aspects of the new archaeology influenced the Tell el-Hesi field staff is not to say that they were adopted uncritically. To see the particular impact they had, it is necessary to examine briefly the archaeological context in Syria-Palestine. The early leadership of Hesi came largely from Tell Balatah (Shechem) and Tell Gezer where discussions were already underway concerning the proper goals and techniques of Syro-Palestinian archaeology. G. Ernest Wright had indicated that the main purpose of the excavation of Shechem was "to learn how to dig in accordance with the methodology employed by Kenyon at Jericho" (Wright 1969: 132). Shechem made some modifications in that methodology, and further refinements were made at Gezer. William Dever has noted that these changes at Shechem and Gezer have resulted in something no longer to be called by the names of Wheeler and Kenyon (the initiators of the "Wheeler-Kenyon method" used at Jericho; cf. Kenyon 1957 and Wheeler 1954). Instead, the procedure should be called the "balk/debris-layer method" (Dever 1973: 3). This had already been suggested by Wright when he identified G. A. Reisner as the initiator in Palestine of the procedure that was later reintroduced independently by Kenyon at Samaria (Wright 1969: 121). This approach excavates within square areas bounded by control balks. The layers of earth are traced to the vertical balk which retains a cross-section record of the excavation. The chief modifications made in Kenyon's procedure by ASOR digs are a more specialized ceramic analysis, based upon the work of Albright and Wright, and the introduction of the team concept of supervision of the work (Dever 1973: 3). These modifications were being introduced and discussed at Shechem and Gezer when future Hesi personnel were staff members at those excavations. These discussions took place within the accepted methodology whose goal was the recovery of the cultural history of Syria-Palestine. However, at times the discussions turned to the larger concerns generated by the new archaeology, and this helped prepare the way for the Tell el-Hesi project. John Worrell and Lawrence Stager, in particular, felt more could be done to incorporate new-archaeology insights into excavation technique and strategy.

The context for this methodological discussion is bound up with the history of the American Schools of Oriental Research (ASOR), whose involvement in Syro-Palestinian archaeology has been sketched in a number of places (Wright 1970; King 1983). The perspective for this involvement during the last half century has been the methodological outlook of William F. Albright and G. Ernest Wright together with the insights of the historian of Syria-Palestine, John Bright. Their archaeological work created a movement of scholarship often referred to as the Albright/Wright/Bright school of archaeological and biblical studies, noted for its emphasis upon archaeology as a means of assessing the essential historicity of the biblical texts (Albright 1957: 1–3; Wright 1962; Bright 1956; 1972: 69–76). The Bible was also the context out of which Syro-Palestinian or Biblical Archaeology developed in the United States (Wright 1970), and it is the context out of which many of its practitioners still operate. Currently there is something of an in-house debate over the appropriateness of this context for the developing field of Syro-Palestinian archaeology (Dever 1974). However, ASOR has largely retained this general orientation, and archaeological digs associated with ASOR continue to attract to their staffs persons whose basic background is, at least to some degree, that of biblical studies (Campbell 1977).

The present debate was sparked in part by objections to a type of archaeology that seems to be more interested in "proving the Bible" than in establishing the cultural history of Syria-Palestine. While Albright and Wright cannot fairly be accused of this orientation, those who do set out to "prove the Bible" from archaeology have sometimes supposed they could look to their writings for support. There is also a counter-tendency which attempts to show that Palestinian archaeology is essentially an independent discipline practicing a "scientific" approach to the data. This latter tendency can be seen developing from Shechem, under the leadership of Wright, through Gezer, under the leadership of Dever, to Hesi under the leadership of Worrell. While these digs did not abandon all interest in the relationship of their findings to the Bible, they did move away from a primary interest in the Bible as a context for archaeology to an interest that deals with the data on their own terms and applies them to the Bible only secondarily.

Furthermore, the Hesi leaders with biblical training were not always at home in the dominant Albright/Wright tradition of Syro-Palestinian archaeology or the Albright/Wright/Bright tradition of biblical studies. One was more representative of the British tradition of Palestinian archaeology which did not necessarily sustain a close link with biblical studies. At least one had been influenced by the Alt/Noth tradition of biblical studies in which archaeology plays a quite different role with regard to the Bible than it does in the Albright/Wright tradition. The archaeological data are taken equally seriously in both traditions, but different philosophies of history often lead to different evaluations and conclusions (Bright 1956; Noth 1960: 46–48; 1964: 139–44). Still another, while trained under the Albright/Wright tradition, came to be more at home in the new archaeology. These different perspectives all contributed to the concern over methodology at Hesi where the archaeological goal was beginning to be understood differently. The development of procedures for ASOR digs had taken place within the context of ASOR concerns, or those of the British, where either a critique of history, as recorded in the Bible, or the cultural history of Syria-Palestine was the basic goal for archaeological work. At Hesi this context itself was challenged in part. The goal was not merely the history of the biblical period or the cultural history of Syria-Palestine, but the total history and life of the people and their activities considered from a regional-environmental perspective. The lifeways of the people were to be taken as seriously as their history.

One of the changes implied was an emphasis upon a multidisciplinary approach to archaeology, something anticipated on the ASOR scene by the use of a geologist at Gezer and at Tell Balatah in the sixties. Hesi, in 1970, entered the field with a specialist staff that included a geologist, a paleoethnobotanist, and cultural and physical anthropologists. The purpose of this staff expansion was the practice of a holistic approach to archaeology that was directed to the goal of understanding Tell el-Hesi in terms of its people and the surrounding environment. The theory to support this change came more slowly, and it came from persons on the Hesi staff who themselves represented more than one position among past ASOR methodological traditions in Palestinian archaeology.

ASPECTS OF THE NEW ARCHAEOLOGY AT HESI

With this context in mind, we can return to the previously mentioned four aspects of the new archaeology to examine their influence at Hesi. Most of the discussions of the new archaeology have been theoretical and abstract or applied to prehistoric times and sites. At Hesi, the conversation has developed in terms of specific field strategies and techniques. In what follows we will present those four categories of the new archaeology and show how each was treated at Hesi. This will involve a glance backward to 1970 as well as a view forward to the concerns of Phase Two of the Joint Expedition.

Archaeology as the Study of Lifeways and Process

It has been said that archaeology has three aims: "(1) the reconstruction of culture history, (2) the detailing of the daily lifeways of earlier cultures; and (3) the elucidation of cultural processes in a broader sense with emphasis on the dynamic aspects of culture" (Deetz 1970: 115). The new archaeology movement has emphasized the latter two aims; sometimes, only the last. The purpose of archaeology is often defined as the understanding of cultural change rather than of the history of he culture at a site. The goal of archaeology is then the trajectory and cause of change. Sometimes this assertion has been accompanied by a polemic against the goal of history and chronology that the older archaeology sought (Binford 1962; Leone 1972a; Renfrew 1973; 1977). Others have protested that this sharp dichotomy presupposes a nineteenth-century view of history and is not valid (Trigger 1970). At Hesi, especially in the early days, this concern for process and lifeways was sometimes set over against history and chronology, although in retrospect it is now clear that lifeways rather than process were the real concern. Process, as the new archaeology defines it, was never really brought into focus.

Translated into field terms, this theoretical concern was expressed by emphasizing the horizontal dimension of digging equally with the vertical dimension. The Wheeler-Kenyon method, even as modified at ASOR sites, is basically concerned with the vertical dimension of digging and pays great attention to the balk-sections for vertical control. The use of elaborate pottery typologies also reinforces this emphasis upon the separation of layers according to their relative and absolute chronological sequence. In other words, the techniques traditionally employed at ASOR digs in Palestine were primarily meant to trace the history of the site through its successive occupational layers. Within the context of ASOR this history was usually explained in political terms drawn from biblical and Near Eastern records. Therefore, the larger monumental buildings were dug, and attention was focussed on site destructions and building phases which could be connected with events known from other sources. Important as this information is, it does not adequately reveal or explain the experiences of the people, especially the common persons, who lived and died on the site. To investigate this aspect of a site, it is necessary to give more attention to the horizontal aspects of digging, i.e., to isolate activity areas and to relate them to social and environmental factors. Thus, it is just as important to dig the domestic area of the city as its royal or governmental area. Only by studying the interrelationships of the various parts of a site is it possible to lay the groundwork for later studies of the causes of cultural change itself. Thus, to help recover the lifeways of a people, the decision was made in the first season to dig the Bedouin cemetery as carefully as a temple or palace would be dug. The burial patterns of a group of later occupants of the site were felt to be fully as significant as the data from any underlying levels. The fruits of this decision for Phase One are described in Toombs 1985.[2] In a sense, the goal at Hesi has been to learn to dig the site as prehistorians, i.e., as if without access to historical records and with an emphasis on the horizontal dimension.

In the early days of digging it proved difficult to translate this concern for the horizontal into field technique. Most of the techniques for horizontal control were developed on single-layer North American or European prehistoric sites. Previously, some horizontal concern in Palestinian excavation had been expressed in terms of greater exposure of buldings, but little effort was expended on the isolation of activity areas. The Wheeler-Kenyon procedure, as modified, allows for the subdivision of layers into horizontal loci, but seldom were the units small or restricted enough to permit the kind of statistical analysis needed to compare and understand cultural behavior. The recording system, while sophisticated in the vertical dimension, was less adequate for the horizontal.

The anthropologists at Hesi carried on a running dialogue with other staff concerning horizontal control that would allow them to plot activity areas and deal functionally with cultural remains.

That dialogue led to an experiment during the 1975 season in which one of the probes into the Early Bronze Age remains was used to pinpoint the problems of horizontal control. Field V was divided into small units and dug in arbitrarily set levels according to the procedures of prehistorians. It soon became apparent that this technique was too slow for the depth of human debris at Hesi (at least twenty meters on the acropolis, three meters or more in Field V) and for the present state of our recording procedures. A second experiment was carried out by W. J. Bennett, Jr., field archaeologist, and James Whitred, photographer, to see if photography would enhance horizontal control when working with tightly stratified material. Sequential layers of pottery were photographed in situ and then reassembled on the basis of the photos after removal from the soil. Through this experiment a fire pit was identified. It had been overlooked in the digging because the ash had washed out and was visible only on the underside of the pottery. These experiments suggested that some compromise in technique was needed. The traditional vertical methods of digging were still best for sterile material and fill where little human activity had taken place, but a system with greater horizontal control was demanded for living surfaces (Rose and Toombs 1976: 53).

At the end of Phase One there was general agreement that the recovery of the lifeways of the people was a primary goal of the expedition and that we wished to know more about cultural change. But after five seasons it was even more apparent that this must be done within the context of competent stratigraphic research. The horizontal and vertical dimensions are really two different sides of one coin in archaeological work. This corresponds to Trigger's theoretical conclusion that history with its particularizing concerns is not so very different from social science with its nomothetic or generalizing concerns (Trigger 1970). Equally appropriate is Irving Rouse's suggestion that there are three kinds of archaeology: the analytical (dealing with history), the synthetic (dealing with lifeways), and the comparative (dealing with process). All three are necessary, but the comparative and synthetic tasks cannot be done until the analytical or historical is completed (Rouse 1973). This needs to be considered along with the insight of

the new archaeologists that unless the comparative and synthetic concerns are present at the beginning, the data collected will not be adequate to answer such questions at a later date (Hill 1972). Thus Hesi has sought to combine the best vertical digging possible with new ways of gaining better horizontal control, in order to deal with all dimensions of the archaeological task and the human record.

These remarks might suggest that technique in vertical digging has reached perfection and that we are in a position to deal scientifically with the chronology of southern Palestine. Of course this is not so. While directed to the field of prehistory, remarks by Colin Renfrew oversimplify this very problem. Renfrew suggests that the introduction of the Carbon-14 dating technique has solved the problems of chronology and that therefore archaeologists should turn to questions of lifeways and cultural process, something they should have been doing from the beginning (Renfrew 1974: 1–40). Among Palestinian archaeologists there is likewise a fairly common assumption that the basic outlines of chronology are set and are scientifically sound. As a result, some would call upon Palestinian archaeology to deal with issues other than chronology. But the matter is not that simple. Hesi is certainly committed to the principles of stratigraphic digging which have been so clearly laid down under the direction of Lawrence Toombs, the archeological director at Hesi. We also accept the general chronological outline of Palestinian culture. However, we are also well aware of the difficulty of defining so basic a stratigraphic feature as a horizontal surface. The rule of thumb that defined a surface by "three flat-lying potsherds" only points up the problem. Those who locate surfaces differ in their abilities to make distinctions as to compaction and color, two keys to recognition of a surface. This simple fact sets a question mark over our ability to produce final descriptive statements about soil layers. When one adds to this the complexity of the stratigraphy at Hesi, one is hesitant to make final chronological pronouncements. The changing chronological interpretation of features at Hesi in our published reports illustrates this. If it were possible to be more assured of the definition and relative sequence of surfaces in all cases, it would then be possible to be more responsive to Renfrew's summons to turn more fully to other concerns.

But the issue of chronology goes beyond this. In Palestinian archaeology, we have relied almost exclusively on pottery typology to establish absolute chronology. Undoubtedly we are "within the ball park" on most of our judgments. But what are not always examined closely are the assumptions by which a pottery typology operates. For example, we assume that pottery form and style are conservative by nature and that cultures tend to retain the initial forms over at least brief periods of time. Thus the discovery of the same form in two different places is taken to indicate contemporaneity. One wonders if this is as true as is commonly thought. Again, we assume that pottery types can be explained on the basis of biological analogy in which forms reproduce and deliver offspring. By tracing these offspring we can trace the chronological movements of people. The assumption seems to be that there can only be one origin for any one form of pottery and its derivatives. This leaves no room for the possible multiple origin of pottery forms (Adams 1968: 1188, 1190). Thus it is a question whether our assumptions about origins and diffusion are correct.

Even if we accept these assumptions as true, we find that pottery can give us dates only within a spread of 50 to 100 years. This does not provide the accuracy needed to write reliable history. From these chronological data we can produce a general history of culture, but the chronological precision we demand from good history writing is wanting. Precision depends upon written records, especially chronicles, which are not available for most sites. In most cases in southern Palestine, we are for all practical purposes engaged in prehistoric archaeology, since records are either non-existent (e.g., the Early Bronze period in Palestine) or do not pertain to the site being dug (e.g., the Late Bronze period) or have only limited or disputed historical value (e.g., the Iron Age). These factors, among others, make it difficult to plot precisely the chronological history of a site.

Renfrew points to the emergence of Carbon-14 as a cure-all for such chronological problems. Carbon-14 has not yet been used at Hesi due to the cost of processing and to the fact that greater precision can be obtained from pottery typology. This is so despite the fact that Carbon-14 dating has become more precise through dendrochronological corrections. The basic problem for the historical period in Palestine is the fact that Carbon-14 contains a substantial "plus or minus" factor attached to each reading. In addition, the chance of the real date falling within the limits of those upper and lower readings is only 65 percent. The probability can be raised to 85 percent only if the plus or minus factor is increased considerably. Carbon-14 is a major breakthrough in prehistory where plus or minus factors are less troublesome because of the larger time spans involved. However, in historical periods it is less precise than present pottery typologies.

This lack of chronological precision does not mean that it is impossible to write the history of a site. History always involves assumptions about data. Hesi will continue to interpret the data historically using the resources that are available. Associated with this will be a continued effort to refine the procedures and techniques that yield historical data and historical explanation. At the same time, Hesi has learned from the new archaeology that historical explanation is only one of the obligations laid upon archaeologists. Historical explanation must be expanded to indicate those environmental, economic, and social factors that affect human populations. The activities of people create culture and make history. The interrelationship of social, ideological, economic, and technological factors produces cultural change. Whether this change is nomothetic remains to be seen, but the possibility that culture changes according to laws means that archaeology must collect the data needed to discern and test such laws. To this end, Hesi will continue to experiment with the horizontal dimension of digging until it produces a system applicable to the great depths of human debris present on most Near Eastern sites. This concern for lifeways and process which was part of the initial thrust at Hesi will not be allowed to slip away.

Archaeology as Science

A related aspect of the new archaeology, especially in contrast to the humanistic focus of much older archaeology, is its similarity to the natural sciences. According to the new archaeologists, the discipline is to be so "explicitly scientific" that it will be able to produce general covering laws of human behavior and culture change (Watson, LeBlanc, and Redman 1971). J. Hill argues that a paradigm shift has occurred in archaeology like one of those in natural science that Thomas Kuhn termed "scientific revolutions" (Kuhn 1970). The new archaeology has changed its scientific methodology from an inductive to a deductive approach. According to Hill only the latter approach is really scientific and able to produce laws of universal applicability (Hill 1972: 61–70). Because these laws of behavior and culture operate in the same way as, for example, the laws of thermodynamics, they allow the complete predictability of human culture. This emphasis on deductive science in the new archaeology yields two elements for our consideration: a theoretical model concerning the proper way to do archaeology and a field procedure that is designed to put the model into practice.

One of the best examples of this new emphasis is found at Koster, an American Indian site in the lower Illinois River valley near Kampsville, Illinois. It is one of the showplace sites of the new archaeology (Streuver and Carlson 1977). The Koster operation prides itself on the fact that more people are analyzing the data in the thirteen laboratories than are digging new data out of the ground. All of the information from the laboratories and from the field is put into two computer banks daily so that it can then be instantaneously available to field and laboratory personnel. This computer usage requires a large budget, but it means that laboratory data are brought into relationship with field data daily, something which the ordinary dig needs months or years to accomplish. My own experience at Koster indicated that an excessive reliance was placed upon the computer capabilities. It seemed that little was done in the field to relate strata to one another or to distinguish and trace surfaces visually, as is traditionally done in the Middle East. Instead, it was assumed that the computer would take the data fed into it and do whatever was necessary to indicate stratification. This turned archaeology into a laboratory science in the highest degree. More to the point, around 1974 a new laboratory was established, the sole purpose of which was to play with computer profiles and projections. Cultural and behavioral laws that could have been in operation at Koster were generated. These theoretical laws were fed into the computer to produce a profile of how the culture would have looked if such laws had been in operation. Then the actual data from the laboratories and the field were set alongside this profile to see if there was a "fit." A statistical correlation would "prove" that the law applied. This approach brought process to center stage in the field operations and made the dig something of an experimental laboratory. One must hasten to add, however, that a good deal of attention was given to producing a history of the culture of the lower Illinois River valley as well.

As indicated earlier, the theory for this field operation derives from Carl Hemple's positivistic philosophy of science, which is quoted regularly as the basis for the new archaeology (Hill 1972: 66–70). In this approach, archaeology is a deductive science that formulates hypotheses to be tested in the field. In fact, Lewis Binford has declared that the only valid archaeological knowledge is that which is testable in the field (Binford 1968: 89–90). This view is held so strongly by some in the new archaeology movement that it has led Flannery to characterize it as one side of a split in the movement: "The law and order archaeologists receive their nickname from the fact that they not only believe that Carl Hempel rose from the dead on the third day and ascended to heaven—where he sits at the right hand of Binford—but, to use their own words, they 'have made the formulation and testing of laws [their] goal' " (Flannery 1973: 50). The hyperbole emphasizes the role of a particular philosophy of science in the new archaeology movement. Archaeology's humanistic and prior scientific concerns have been relegated to a past era.

A concern for scientific archaeology was already present in the ASOR tradition when the Hesi project began, but it existed within a humanistic context. The scientific approach was construed largely in inductive and objective terms, so that attempts were made to assure controlled conditions in the field and to produce the most objective recording system possible. Scientists were asked to identify materials in the field and to assess their function within the limits provided by a chronological methodology. Basically, the thrust of this scientific archaeology was to remove subjectivity from the digging process as much as possible by concentrating on those objective factors that science could handle, and by stressing an inductive approach to function and meaning of data. When Hesi entered the field, it continued this emphasis by insisting on objective criteria such as, for example, Munsell color designations by which soil colors could be scientifically described in terms of hue, value, and chroma (Munsell 1975).[3] In this, Hesi was simply continuing a program that was already well underway there, one which implemented an inductive understanding of science.

The work at Tell el-Hesi benefited from the new archaeology's field procedures more than from its theory. Thus, one difference of approach from the ASOR tradition was the extensive use of a problem-solving (deductive) approach to the strategy of excavation. Staff strategy sessions in the United States and conversations in the field tended to stress a problem—usually one that had arisen out of earlier findings at the site—to be solved by the work of a single or several seasons. Though no inductive-deductive terminology was used in these discussions, they did reflect the new archaeology's concern to generate hypotheses that could then be tested in the field. Over the seasons, the focus of these problems has expanded to include more and more input from the scientists associated with the dig. The hypotheses to be tested have been generated by both scientific and humanistic concerns. For example, as a result of such input Hesi has begun to test the hypothesis that the demise of the large EB III city was the result of an environmental change in the region (Rose 1974; Rose, Toombs, and O'Connell 1978).

Another development in the ASOR tradition at Hesi was the increased use of scientific specialists at the site. Each scientist would have a small laboratory in the field, and much material was shipped home after the dig for further laboratory analysis. Over the years these specialists have become more and more involved with the digging process itself, even to the point of suggesting samples needed for analysis, strategy for the season, and digging techniques helpful for carrying the research through to a conclusion (Stewart 1978 [Chapter XI, below]). Successful attempts were also made to increase conversation in the field between the scientists and the humanists of the Hesi staff.

In all of this debate over "scientific" versus "humanistic" concerns there is something of a false dichotomy. Scientists work by both inductive and deductive principles, and their methods are not so very far removed from those of humanistic scholars. However, there *is* a difference of focus. Hesi has approached the problem largely through the dialogical process that takes place in strategy conferences, field work, and the field laboratory. Each of the student volunteers, moreover, is encouraged to learn as much from the laboratory experience as from the field work. The discussions between scientific specialists and archaeologists are open discussions to which the volunteers listen and sometimes contribute. Often the suggested explanations bear witness to the imaginative powers of the scientists and the factual rigor of the humanists. Hesi began its operation by bringing more scientists into the field to help make archaeology scientific. It ended Phase One by placing more trust in the scientific-humanistic field dialogue while spending less energy in debate over questions about the meaning of scientific archaeology.

Archaeology as Environmental Studies

A third aspect of the new archaeology is the ecological perspective which understands cultural change in terms of "systematic responses to empirical, measurable environmental variables" (Hill 1972: 76). In the literature of the new archaeology, this emphasis is most often set over against theories of diffusion and the observation and collection of cultural traits by which cultural change is explained in the older archaeology. For the new archaeology the human being is an adaptive animal, and human culture reflects responses to the environment in which one lives. Changes in this environment cause changes in the cultural subsystems as they respond to the necessity of being in balance with the environment. This emphasis has been a primary ingredient of the new archaeology even though the ecological approach appeared earlier in England in the work of Grahame Clark and in some North American studies. The new archaeologists using the ecological approach have divided into two groups. One views the relationship between the environment and culture in terms of a strict determinism in which cultural change is the product of adaptive responses to environmental change and little else. A second group is less committed to this principle and works with an open-system model in which cultural change can result from the interaction between different human cultures as well as from environmental shifts (Trigger 1971). However, both of these groups see culture as a whole composed of various subsystems that interact with each other. Some of these subsystems are technology, economics, social and political structures, and ideology. The subsystems form variables in the study of human culture that can be approached by systems-theory analysis. The emphasis upon environment has also led new archaeologists to engage in settlement or locational studies as well as to work with ecologists to recreate the ancient environments of a site or region.

Again, this aspect of the new archaeology at Tell el-Hesi is expressed by the field techniques used. One of the reasons for the selection of Hesi as an excavation site was its location in a marginal environmental zone. The variations in yearly rainfall mean that the site lies in a transition zone where the climatic conditions fluctuate between semi-arid and wet (Koucky 1989 [Chapter I, above]: 10-11, 14-19). The expedition wished to study this variation in order to see what effect it had upon the culture and history of Hesi. To this end, a paleoethnobotanist and a geologist were members of the team from the beginning. Flotation techniques were developed in the first season (Stewart and Robertson 1973), and the subsistence base for each stratum of occupation was recorded. In 1971, an attempt was made to establish a botanical profile for the tell by wet-screening all the soil from one area on the acropolis. This concern with the environment expressed itself also in initial efforts at a regional survey to examine the settlement patterns, subsistence potentials, and economies of the region. Some of the results appear in the geologist's essay on the geographic/geomorphic context of the site and the historic geology of the region (Koucky 1989 [Chapter I, above]: 6–10, 11–14, 20–34).

In 1975, similarly, two probes were dug into the Early Bronze Age materials at the southern end of the site to test ecological and historical hypotheses concerning the abandonment of EB III sites in the south of Palestine. In most of the literature it is assumed that the hiatus at these sites was due to some historical-political cause, such as an invading army, a migration of people, or some other human movement. Despite the failure to identify any group in the region from the EB III period that could have been the destructive agent required by such a hypothesis, that sort of explanation was thought adequate.

Such an understanding seemed called for at Tell el-Hesi. A deep ash layer lies around the south edge of the site, and this was believed by some to be destruction ash, thus providing evidence to support an invasion theory. Yet others believed the demise of Hesi during EB III had a different explanation, related to the ecology and climate of the region. In this view, the abandonment of the site related to a declining rainfall and gradual deforestation of the region that resulted in its desiccation and the loss of a subsistence base for the site. These hypotheses were tested in the probes with conflicting results (Rose and Toombs 1976: 52–53). However, the excavated data did lead to the establishment of Fields V and VI to explore the Early Bronze site during Phase Two of the Hesi expedition (Rose, Toombs, and O'Connell 1978: 141–42).

These examples indicate that Hesi has adopted a "both-and" attitude towards the question of the relative importance of historical and ecological factors in human culture. There is no rigid determinism presupposed in the testing of hypotheses, and this is due in part to the fact that both scientists and humanists are involved in the process from the formulation of the problem to its resolution.

Nevertheless, the "new archaeology" has indeed influenced Hesi's methodology in the direction of a wider investigation of ecological factors that affect human history and culture.

The Explanatory Function of Archaeology

The final aspect of the new archaeology—its particular concept of "explanation"—has already been introduced at several points in the preceding discussion. In the literature of the new archaeology, explanation is usually set over against description. For the new archaeology, description is not really an explanation of the data, nor is it relevant to our present interest. Rather, it is necessary to be explicitly scientific (deductive) in our logic in order to explain culture rather than simply describe it (Watson, LeBlanc, and Redman 1971). The descriptive approach is one that collects data and assumes that both problems and solutions will appear in the process. As Hill (1972: 67) says, "This approach restricts us to describing artifacts and features, dating them, and comparing their forms in time and space; analysis becomes description, taxonomy, and the pigeonholing of assemblages into time charts . . . ." One can read many excavation reports for which this is a fair description of the contents. That is, what has been found is described in great detail, but nothing further is ventured. The question arises whether the data have really been explained.

The explanatory or deductive approach, on the other hand, assumes that the meaning of data lies in their relationship to problems posed by the archaeologist. The underlying assumption is that the problems are relevant to the present. These problems focus on the lifeways of human beings who produce culture and on the processes that cause culture to change. Therefore, explanation deals with issues that the descriptive approach avoids or cannot handle. By inference these issues have more relevance to and therefore priority for our understanding of humanity than do those inferred from inductive logic. Genuine explanation deals with generalizing principles as do ethnology and the social sciences instead of particularizing principles as do history and the humanities.

Clearly one can be critical on theoretical grounds toward this polarization of approaches to archaeological reasoning (Willey and Sabloff 1974: 193–97). The theoretical debate has not yet produced any clear alternatives to descriptive excavation reports at the practical publication level, and as a result it has not influenced Hesi in an obvious way. Some other concerns such as problem solving and hypothesis testing have already been mentioned. A further example of the latter aspect of the new archaeology at Hesi is described in an article by Lawrence Stager dealing with the large number of grain storage pits on the tell during the last Persian subphase. Instead of giving them an inductive explanation based upon historical assumptions (e.g., they served military needs), Stager argued that examination of the storage pits in light of the environmental evidence ("vagaries of rainfall" with the consequent threat of drought) suggested that their function was to stave off famine conditions (Stager 1971). This examination involved the testing of alternative hypotheses. While not fully in the deductive framework, it was a first attempt to go beyond mere description to the "why," i.e., to the activities of people that would account for the evidence. It did so in terms of an ecological understanding rather than a particularizing historical approach. However, at the end of Phase One of the expedition, the implications of this explanatory aspect of the new archaeology had yet to be brought into clear focus.

SUMMARY

The thesis of this essay is that Hesi stands solidly within the tradition of ASOR digs that have emphasized a historical model using inductive science. However, Hesi has added a new element to the tradition that is a combination of the various aspects of the new-archaeology discussed here. The concern is not only for time and space but also for the activities of people and, to some extent, for cultural process. Yet Hesi has not adopted uncritically the new-archaeology "package," the anthropological concerns of which must be adapted to a complex multilayered tell in the Ancient Near East where western civilization finds its historical roots. At the same time we who are involved with the excavations at Hesi continue to monitor and evaluate the debate over the new archaeology in order to develop a clear and consistent archaeological method.

NOTES

1. In a private communication, Lawrence Stager has cautioned against the confusion of "diffusion" (transmission of ideas) with "migration" (physical movement of people) or with "trade" (physical movement of goods). — Editor.

2. A continuation of the work on the Bedouin cemetery in Phase Two at Hesi is being prepared for publication by J. Kenneth Eakins. —Editor

3. As elsewhere, it is acknowledged at Hesi that use of the Munsell system does not obviate observer subjectivity in color-comparisons or variant results due to differences in light conditions. Nevertheless, a Munsell designation limits the range of possible misunderstanding by users of the data, while it records precisely what the *observer* understood the color to be at the time of observation. —Editor

BIBLIOGRAPHY FOR CHAPTER IV

Adams, R. McC.
1968   Archeological Research Strategies: Past and Present. *Science* 160: 1187–92. Reprinted in *Corridors in Time*, pp. 52–63. Edited by B. M. Fagan. Boston: Little, Brown, 1974.

Albright, W. F.
1957   *From the Stone Age to Christianity.* Garden City, NY: Doubleday.

Binford, L. S.
1962   Archaeology as Anthropology. *American Antiquity* 28: 217–25. Reprinted in *Contemporary Archaeology*, pp. 93–107. Edited by M. P. Leone (which see, below).

1968   Archaeological Perspectives. In *New Perspectives in Archaeology.* Edited by S. R. and L. S. Binford (which see, below). Reprinted in *An Archaeological Perspective* (see next title, below).

Binford, L. S., ed.
1972   *An Archaeological Perspective.* New York: Seminar.

Binford, S. R. and Binford, L. S., eds.
1968   *New Perspectives in Archaeology.* Chicago: Aldine.

Bliss, F. J.
1894   *A Mound of Many Cities or Tell el Hesy Excavated.* London: Palestine Exploration Fund.

Braidwood, R. J.
1960   The Agricultural Revolution. *Scientific American* 203: 130–48.

Bright, J.
1956   *Early History in Recent History Writing: A Study in Method.* London: SCM.

1972   *A History of Israel.* Second Edition. Philadelphia: Westminster.

Campbell, E. F., Jr.
1977   Biblical Archaeology—an Appraisal. Mimeographed. Unpublished paper

delivered before Society of Biblical Literature Southwest Region at Phillips University, Enid, OK.

Childe, V. G.
1951 *Man Makes Himself*. Revised Edition. New York: New American Library.

Clark, J. G.
1954 *Excavations at Star Carr: an Early Mesolithic Site at Seamer near Scarborough, Yorkshire*. Cambridge: Cambridge University.

Daniel, G. E.
1962 *The Idea of Prehistory*. London: Watts.

Deetz, J.
1970 Archaeology as a Social Science. In *Current Directions in Anthropology*, pp. 115–25. Edited by A. Fischer. Washington: American Anthropological Association. Reprinted in *Corridors in Time*, pp. 11–23. Edited by B. M. Fagan (which see, below); reprinted also in *Contemporary Archaeology*, pp. 108–17. Edited by M. P. Leone (which see, below).

Dever, W. G.
1973 Two Approaches to Archaeological Method—the Architectural and the Stratigraphic. *Eretz-Israel* 11: 1–8. Jerusalem: Israel Exploration Society.
1974 *Archaeology and Biblical Studies: Retrospects and Prospects*. Evanston, Illinois: Seabury-Western Theological Seminary.

Dever, W. G; Lance, H. D.; and Wright, G. E.
1970 *Gezer I*. Jerusalem: Hebrew Union College Biblical and Archaeological School.

Fagan, B. M., ed.
1974 *Corridors in Time*. Boston: Little, Brown.

Flannery, K. V.
1973 Archaeology with a Capital 'S.' In *Research and Theory in Current Archaeology*, pp. 47–53. Edited by C. L. Redman (which see, below).

Harris, M.
1968 *The Rise of Anthropological Theory*. New York: Thomas Y. Crowell.

Hemple, C. G.
1966 *Philosophy of Natural Science*. Englewood Cliffs, NJ: Prentice-Hall.

Hill, J. N.
1972 The Methodological Debate in Contemporary Archaeology: A Model. In *Models in Archaeology*, pp. 61–107. Edited by D. L. Clarke. London: Methuen.

Kenyon, K. M.
1957 *Beginning in Archaeology*. Revised Edition. New York: Frederick A. Prager.

King, P. J.
1983 *American Archaeology in the Mideast: A History of the American Schools of Oriental Research*. Philadelphia: The American Schools of Oriental Research.

Kottak, C.
1974 *Cultural Anthropology*. New York: Random House.

Koucky, F. L.
1989 The Present and Past Physical Environment of Tell el-Hesi, Israel. In *Tell el-Hesi: The Site and the Expedition*, pp. 5-36. Edited by B. T. Dahlberg and K. G. O'Connell, S.J. Excavation Reports of the American Schools of Oriental Research: Tell el-Hesi 4. Winona Lake, IN: Eisenbrauns.

Kuhn, T. S.
1970 *The Structure of Scientific Revolutions*. Revised Edition. Chicago: University of Chicago.

Leone, M. P.
1972a Issues in Anthropological Archaeology. In *Contemporary Archaeology*, pp. 14–27. Edited by M. P. Leone (which see, below).

Leone, M. P., ed.
1972b *Contemporary Archaeology*. Carbondale: Southern Illinois University.

Matthers, J. M.
1989 Excavations by the Palestine Exploration Fund at Tell el-Hesi, 1890–1892. In *Tell el-Hesi: the Site and the Expedition*, pp. 37-67. Edited by B. T. Dahlberg and K. G. O'Connell, S.J. Excavation Reports of the American Schools of Oriental Research: Tell el-Hesi 4. Winona Lake, IN: Eisenbrauns.

Munsell, A. H.
1975 *Munsell Soil Color Charts*. 1975 Edition. Baltimore: Macbeth Division of Kollmorgen Corporation.

Noth, M.
1960 *The History of Israel*. Second Revised Edition. Translation by P. R. Ackroyd. New York: Harper & Row.
1964 *The Old Testament World*. Fourth Edition. Translated by V. I. Gruhn. Philadelphia: Fortress.

Petrie, W. M. F.
1891   *Tell el Hesy (Lachish)*. London: Palestine Exploration Fund.

Redman, C. L., ed.
1973   *Research and Theory in Current Archaeology*. New York: John Wiley and Sons.

Renfrew, C.
1973   *Before Civilization*. Hammondsworth: Penguin.
1974   *British Prehistory*. London: Duckworth.
1977   Ancient Europe is Older than We Thought. *National Geographic* 152: 615–23.

Rose, D. G.
1974   A Funding Proposal to the National Endowment for the Humanities. Mimeographed. Unpublished.

Rose, D. G., and Toombs, L. E.
1976   Tell el-Hesi, 1973 and 1975. *Palestine Exploration Quarterly* 108: 41–54 and pls. I–V.

Rose, D. G.; Toombs, L. E.; and O'Connell, K. G., S.J.
1978   Four Seasons of Excavation at Tell el-Hesi: A Preliminary Report. In *Preliminary Excavation Reports: Bâb edh-Drâᶜ, Sardis, Meiron, Tell el-Hesi, Carthage (Punic)*, pp. 109-49. Edited by D. N. Freedman. Annual of the American Schools of Oriental Research 43. Cambridge MA: American Schools of Oriental Research.

Rouse, I.
1973   Analytic, Synthetic, and Comparative Archaeology. In *Research and Theory in Current Archaeology*, pp. 21–31. Edited by C. L. Redman (which see, above).

Stager, L. E.
1971   Climatic Conditions and Grain Storage in the Persian Period. *Biblical Archaeologist* 34: 86–88.

Stewart, R. B.
1978   Archaeobotanic Studies at Tell el-Hesi. *Economic Botany* 32: 379–86 [reprinted as Chapter 11, below].

Stewart, R. B., and Robertson, W., IV
1973   Applications of the Flotation Technique in Arid Areas. *Economic Botany* 27: 114–16.

Streuver, S., and Carlson, J.
1977   Koster Site: The New Archaeology in Action. *Archaeology* 30: 93–101.

Streuver, S., and Holton, F. A.
1979   *Koster: Americans in Search of Their Prehistoric Past*. Garden City, NY: Doubleday.

Taylor, W. W.
1948   *A Study of Archeology*. Memoir Series of the American Anthropological Association (*American Anthropologist* 50, no. 3, pt. 2). Menasha, WI: American Anthropological Association.
1972   Old Wine and New Skins: A Contemporary Parable. In *Contemporary Archaeology*, pp. 28–33. Edited by M. P. Leone. Carbondale, Illinois: Southern Illinois University.

Toombs, L. E.
1985   *Tell el-Hesi: Modern Military Trenching and Muslim Cemetery in Field I, Strata I-II*. Edited by K. G. O'Connell, S. J. Excavation Reports of the American Schools of Oriental Research: Tell el-Hesi 2. Waterloo, Ontario: Wilfrid Laurier University Press.

Trigger, B. G.
1970   Aims in Prehistoric Archaeology. *Antiquity* 44: 26–37. Reprinted in *Corridors in Time*, pp. 24–38. Edited by B. M. Fagan (which see, above).
1971   Archaeology and Ecology. *World Archaeology* 2,3: 321–36. Reprinted in *Corridors in Time*, pp. 98–112. Edited by B. M. Fagan (which see, above).

Watson, P. J.; LeBlanc, S. A.; and Redman, C. L.
1971   *Explanation in Archaeology: An Explicitly Scientific Approach*. New York: Columbia University.

Wheeler, M.
1954   *Archaeology from the Earth*. Baltimore: Penguin.

Willey, G. R., and Sabloff, J. A.
1974   *A History of American Archaeology*. San Francisco: W. H. Freeman.

Wilson, D.
1974   *The New Archaeology*. New York: The New American Library.

Worrell, J. E.
1970   The Expedition to Tell el-Hesi: A New Joint Project. *Newsletter No. 8* (April 1970) of the American Schools of Oriental Research: 1–4.
1989   The Evolution of a Holistic Investigation: Phase One of the Joint Expedition to Tell el-Hesi. In *Tell el-Hesi: The Site and*

the Expedition, pp. 68-71. Edited by B. T. Dahlberg and K. G. O'Connell, S. J. Excavation Reports of the American Schools of Oriental Research: Tell el-Hesi 4. Winona Lake, IN: Eisenbrauns.

Worrell, J. E., and Betlyon, J. W.
1989   Phase One at Tell el-Hesi: A Season-by-Season Account. In *Tell el-Hesi: The Site and the Expedition*, pp. 97-124. Edited by B. T. Dahlberg and K. O'Connell, S.J. Excavation Reports of the American Schools of Oriental Research: Tell el-Hesi 4. Winona Lake, IN: Eisenbrauns.

Wright, G. E.
1962   *Biblical Archaeology*. Revised and Expanded Edition. Philadelphia: Westminster.
1969   Archaeological Method in Palestine—an American Interpretation. In *Eretz-Israel* 11: 120–33. Jerusalem: Israel Exploration Society.
1970   The Phenomenon of American Archaeology in the Near East. In *Near Eastern Archaeology in the Twentieth Century*, pp. 3–40. Edited by J. A. Sanders. Garden City, NY: Doubleday.

Chapter V

THE VOLUNTEER AND EDUCATIONAL PROGRAM:
1970-1975

by
H. Thomas Frank (†1980)
Oberlin College
and
Fred L. Horton, Jr.[1]
Wake Forest University

The purpose of an archaeological excavation is to recover the material remains of a given site and by interpretation of them to relate the site to its cultural and geographical context. In fulfillment of this purpose, however, other and ancillary intentions may be pursued. An important secondary purpose of the Joint Expedition to Tell el-Hesi has been to give students, scholars, and other interested persons an opportunity to gain field experience in archaeology under the direction of talented teachers and skilled archaeologists. This article reviews the history of the volunteer program at Hesi from 1970 to 1975.

BACKGROUND

In principle the volunteer program at Hesi followed the precedent of the Drew-McCormick Joint Expedition at Shechem (modern Tell Balatah), affiliated with the American Schools of Oriental Research (ASOR). An expressed purpose of the Shechem dig (1956-1969) was to train younger scholars in the cultural history and archaeology of the Near East, and in so doing to provide competent leadership for one major aspect of the work of ASOR (Wright 1965: 35-36). However, fluctuating historical and political circumstances caused the undertaking at Hesi to develop along somewhat different lines from the example at Shechem.

After the 1948 Arab-Israeli war, the changed political and military situation made it impossible for the American School in Jerusalem, then divided, to undertake archaeological work in Israel. After the 1967 war and a major reorganization of ASOR's structure necessitated by the new political conditions, field work in Israel became possible for that institution. An expanded account of the 1967 reorganization of ASOR is given by King (1975: 63; 1983: 184-215). Continuing its tradition of political neutrality but recognizing the new opportunities for scholarship afforded by access to the wider region, ASOR decided to excavate in Israel. The site chosen for excavation was Tell el-Hesi, an important location which had not been scientifically explored since 1893.

Playing on the title of Frederick Bliss's 1894 volume on Hesi, *A Mound of Many Cities*, John Worrell, the first director of the present excavation, renamed the site "a mound of many surprises" (Worrell 1970). Among the surprises was the cost of labor in Israel. It was not possible, as it had been at Shechem and places elsewhere on the West Bank and in Jordan, to recruit farmers and villagers glad to find short-term work in the summer at what by American standards was the very low wage such expeditions could afford to pay. Previous excavators in Israel had tried various solutions to the problem, and one of the most successful was the recruitment of the first large-scale international volunteer staff by the Masada Expedition in 1955 (Yadin 1966: 13-14). The idea of using unpaid volunteers who would find their own way to Israel was also adopted by the Hebrew Union College-Harvard Semitic Museum excavation at Tell Gezer in 1964, but the Gezer staff, many of whom were later to dig at Hesi, added an educational component to their volunteer program. Volunteers, who in many if not most cases were without previous excavation experience, could earn academic credit by completing their share of the field work, visiting other archaeological sites, and writing a paper.

The volunteer program at Tell el-Hesi profited from the experience of the Masada and Gezer expeditions. Indeed, Gezer was still in the field when Hesi began, and H. Darrell Lance of the Gezer staff was helpful in offering suggestions for Hesi. At the same time, the Hesi volunteer program developed along its own lines as it evolved season by season.

As preparations went forward for the first field season it became clear to the staff that the ambitious educational program envisioned for Hesi could not be accomplished all at once. Nevertheless, from the outset there was a firm commitment to a strong educational program, and refinements over the years went a long way toward realizing it.

The staff leadership rejected any idea that the volunteers were on the site merely to do the physical work of the dig, so it expended a great deal of time and effort on volunteer training. At least three ends were kept clearly in view:

(1) **Personal Enrichment:** For some—perhaps most—of the volunteers, the experience at Hesi and the travel associated with it constituted the opportunity of a lifetime. The staff sought to insure that volunteers, many of whom were at Hesi at personal sacrifice, had the most valuable total experience possible.

(2) **Academic Quality:** The staff aimed to design a program that met the demanding standards of the institutions offering academic credit for the experience at Hesi.

(3) **Field Training in Archaeology:** The staff sought to provide excellent field training in archaeological methods and techniques for students, younger scholars, and other interested persons.

Anyone unacquainted with Hesi may wonder whether its volunteer training program could be worth the investment of time, energy, and financial resources put into it, but at no time has the staff doubted its commitment to the program or regretted its costs.

THE FIRST SEASON

The 1970 dig season was particularly difficult. Not only was it the first season in the field with all of the attendant "shake-down" problems, but the necessity of living in Kiryat Gat, a development (i.e., government-created) town some six miles from the site, magnified even routine difficulties. Transportation was a problem, since limited funds made it impossible for staff and volunteers to return to the site in the late afternoon. As a consequence, time that would otherwise have been available for work and training was lost. To make matters worse, the bare minimum in requirements for living facilities promised earlier in the year by town authorities was only partially provided. Living space was only about half of what the dig organizers considered adequate and had expected, and of special concern to those responsible for the educational program was a lack of a suitable place for lectures and other educational activities. Under those circumstances, survival rather than education became the order of the day.

In spite of the obstacles a strong beginning was made toward realization of the educational goals of the volunteer program. John E. Worrell, who as Project Director skillfully guided the excavation in those difficult early days, and Philip J. King, who had to cope with many unexpected crises as Administrative Director, refused to retreat from the commitment to education. They saw to it that lectures and seminars were held for the volunteers in spite of the inadequate physical arrangements, and they sought occasions for volunteers to work with the specialists, technicians, and stratigraphers.

Thus, even with the problems encountered in the first year, a good start was made toward a program that combined readings and lectures with on-site work experience. This allowed the volunteers to understand the work of the excavation within the context of Near Eastern history and archaeology, and enabled them to gain some firsthand knowledge of the modern social, political, and religious situation in Israel and the Near East. The chartered flights for volunteers, which began with the first season, were required by airline rules at the time to stop in Paris or London before passengers proceeded to Israel. Thus some volunteers, as time and money allowed, were able to make more extensive European trips at that point. The European stopover remained a feature of the volunteer program through the 1977 season, after which low-cost group flights directly to Israel became available.

SUBSEQUENT SEASONS

The 1971 season was very different from its predecessor, because a tent village was established at the excavation site, and because an orientation period was arranged in Jerusalem for the volunteers before the season began. The tent camp at Hesi provided sleeping and dining quarters for volunteers and staff, as well as bathing and toilet facilities. It also included extensive work areas for registration of pottery and artifacts and for preservation, reconstruction, drawing, and various other tasks. The specialists, including a botanist, a geologist, an osteologist, and an expert in pottery restoration, all had specific work space for themselves and those assisting them.

The new facilities brought substantial benefit to the educational program. Volunteers could observe and participate in the activities of the specialist teams. They could attend pottery reading, in which the newly found sherds were identified as to type and probable date, thus helping to date the debris-layer in which they were found. Perhaps no other camp activity drew as much volunteer interest as did the daily call for each digging team to come to pottery reading for a discussion of the materials found in their area. With everyone living next to the site, field supervisors were now able to lead tours of the excavation to explain to the volunteers the problems that had arisen in each field and the techniques being used to solve them. The tempo and pace of the entire operation quickened in the 1971 season as increased time became available for the work of the excavation and the task of education.

With the establishment of the camp there came housekeeping duties. Susan Simms, who as camp director had supervised the setting up of camp, developed an afternoon rotation which allowed volunteers to alternate housekeeping chores with archaeological tasks. Pottery washing, balk drawing, restoration, skeletal analysis, and the like went on side by side with more mundane chores, such as policing the camp, cleaning the showers and latrines, and washing dishes.

The new facilities made it feasible to hold an evening lecture series, and the practice that developed was to schedule these lectures for Tuesday and Thursday evenings. Although most of the presentations were given by the field staff and the specialists, such events were also graced by distinguished visitors who had been invited to speak about some aspect of the history or methodology of excavation in the Middle East. A massive, creaking, yet faithful old generator provided current for lights and refrigeration. Electricity in the field also made it possible for the evening lecturers to illustrate their talks with projected slides.

Besides the tent camp, another innovation of the 1971 season was an orientation period for volunteers before they went to the Hesi site. Its purpose was to familiarize them with the principles of archaeological method, with the scope of archaeological work in the Middle East, and with the city of Jerusalem where they would spend much of their weekend when the dig was not in operation.

The expedition was particularly fortunate to be able to find space for the volunteers in a small hotel within easy walking distance of the Albright Institute, the École Biblique, and the Rockefeller Museum. The Jordan House Hotel and its gracious hosts, Farid and Doris Salman, were to become firm fixtures in the Hesi operation.[2]

Orientation was an intense experience. Small group walking tours under the guidance of scholars familiar with the history and archaeology of Jerusalem alternated with exploration of the Israel Museum and especially the Rockefeller Museum. The latter also provided the orientation program with well-equipped lecture rooms. An important aspect of the orientation was the program of lectures by experts in various areas of archaeology. Perhaps nowhere else in the world could such a series of lectures have been put together. Through the generosity and thoughtful good efforts of the staff of the Department of Antiquities of the State of Israel, not only were lecture facilities made vailable and museums opened to the Hesi volunteers, but a glittering array of archaeologists and others took part in the orientation lectures, both at the Rockefeller Museum and in the garden of the Albright Institute. Because of this the volunteers not only learned about ceramics, archaeological method and interpretation, and various archaeological sites, but they also heard from various resident archaeologists of the Department of Antiquities about work going on in every part of Israel. Moreover, they learned details not widely known outside of Israel, such as that archaeological interest on some kibbutzim has resulted in the establishment of valuable collections and museums which have made new resources available to scholars.

Special appreciation is owed Avraham Biran and Moshe Dothan, the former Director and Associate Director, respectively, of the Department of Antiquities, for their great help in the establishment of so solid an orientation program. Grateful mention must also be made of the thoughtfulness, the suggestions, and the efficiency of Hannah Katzenstein, who contributed significantly to the success of the Jerusalem orientation.

In addition, the orientation program was materially aided by the Fathers of the École Biblique and by the scholars of the Albright Institute. The volunteers were welcomed by both institutions and treated to lectures by members of their staffs. For these and many other favors, appreciation is due Robert J. Bull and William G. Dever, the successive directors of the Albright Institute, and Fr. Roland de Vaux, the late doyen of the École. One remembers with pride and sadness that Pere de Vaux's last public lecture was given to Hesi volunteers in his classroom at the École. With sparkling wit and characteristic insight, Fr. de Vaux spoke on the topic, "In Honor of the Lowly Potsherd."

The Jerusalem orientation ended with the bus ride to Hesi, where, after further orientation, the volunteers were divided into field teams. At the tell the volunteers were introduced to actual field methods and to the history of the site. Stratigraphy was demonstrated in "Bliss's Cut" (see Matthers 1989 [Ch. II above]: 51, 58. See also Ch. I, p. 25 and figs. 10-12 and 16.), where the stratigraphic sequence is quite clear and striking, and where balk trimming technique can be demonstrated and practiced. Staff members led the volunteers on tours of the tell to explain what had been found by the earlier excavations of Petrie and Bliss and by the present excavators in their work to date. Volunteers were introduced to the record-keeping system at Hesi, and the "sanctity" of the pottery-drying area was emphasized. Field staff and medical personnel stressed health and safety precautions.

The purpose of orientation was to enable volunteers to participate intelligently in the work of excavation. The real job of working and learning took place in the daily routine of archaeological work. The schedule in 1971 and 1973 had everyone awakened at 4:00 a.m. in order to be at work by 5:00. A light breakfast at 4:30 was followed by a more substantial "second breakfast" at 8:30. Early morning is quite pleasant at Hesi in the summer,

and a productive time for work, but by 9:00 temperatures normally become quite warm. The increasing heat of late morning is relieved only by breezes from the Mediterranean some twelve miles to the west, which rise around 11:00 but are of little comfort to those who may be working in a deep trench on the tell. Thus, the period from 11:00 a.m. to 1:00 p.m., when field work ended, was very hot and took its toll in energy and efficiency.

At the close of a day's field work some would race for the showers and others for the few cold soft drinks and beers on ice at the excavation's non-profit canteen, dubbed the "Peace Bar," situated under Hesi's single tree—a great, spreading tamarisk. Some would line up for lunch; others would be content to find a shady place to rest. At 3:00 the afternoon's work would commence—the archaeological and the housekeeping chores previously detailed. This work ended at 5:30 each day, with dinner following at 6:00. Twice a week, lectures followed dinner; on other nights the volunteers enjoyed free time while staff members reviewed the day's work, made drawings, and discussed plans for the following day. At 9:00 the chugging of the generator would stop, and the camp became immersed in the stillness of the night—occasionally broken by the clank of a tractor doing night plowing, or by the far-off sounds of army reservists holding nighttime drill.

The Israeli army provided an unexpected addition to the dig experience. It was not unusual to wake up in the middle of the night to hear sounds in the dining area of soldiers discussing how to find their assigned destination by dawn. Few of the 1971 Hesi group will forget the night when a detachment of armored half-tracks somehow drove onto the top of the tell in total darkness and stopped just short of plunging into Bliss's cut or into the deep Persian Period pits then under excavation. There is a path of sorts down Bliss's cut which descends some sixty feet at an incredible angle. Once each week in the daylight, as a training exercise, the army would bring neophyte drivers to the cut to test themselves and their vehicles on the steep, sixty-foot slope. On each such occasion archaeological work would stop on the tell, and all would gather at the edge of the cut to watch the exercise. As each half-track reached the bottom of the steep incline and then took the remaining, less-steep sixty feet down to the Wadi Hesi, cheers would go up from the Hesi folk, to be returned by the soldiers below.

There was a carefully scheduled alternation between free weekends for the volunteers and organized field trips. Trips were made to important sites in the Jordan valley and the Dead Sea area—Jericho, Qumran, Masada, and ʿEn Gedi—and to sites north of Jerusalem such as Tell en-Naṣbeh, Beth-el (Beitin), ʿAi (et-Tell), and Gibeon (el-Jib). The return trips to Hesi saw stops at places such as Ramat Rahel, Bethlehem, the Herodium, Hebron, and Lachish (Tell ed-Duweir). There was also a longer trip to the Galilee over three days and two nights, traveling as far north as Tell Dan and including stops at Shechem (Tell Balatah), Taʿanach, Megiddo, Beth Alpha, Tiberias, Hazor, the Wadi el-Mughara (Mount Carmel caves), and Caesarea Maritima, among others. At every site under excavation the excavation director, by previous arrangement, would give the Hesi crew a personal tour of the dig. At sites not then under excavation, an accompanying Hesi staff member was prepared to introduce the volunteers to the site and guide them through it.

With some refinements, the basic pattern of the 1971 program was followed in 1973 and 1975. In 1973, under the direction of Larry and Dorothy Ingalls—a retired engineer and a registered nurse, respectively—who had been volunteers in 1971, the camp underwent a major upgrade of its facilities—including, most importantly, the installation of a flexible water line from an existing permanent line in a nearby orchard. The year 1973 also saw the beginning of the "Hesi Survey," a systematic exploration over a wide region around the tell to find further clues concerning its natural and archaeological context. Participation in the survey allowed volunteers to experience yet another phase of archaeological activity. In 1975 D. Glenn Rose, one of the most enthusiastic supporters of the educational program on the Hesi staff, became Project Director. Under his guidance new emphasis was placed on field instruction and on the in-camp lecture series.

Two other major improvements were instituted in 1975 that have been of help to the volunteer program. A split work schedule, which stopped the digging at 11:00 a.m. and resumed it at 4:00 p.m., avoided the discomfort and the diminished productivity occasioned by the midday sun. In this season also the Galilee trip was placed at the end of the dig, so that the volunteers and accompanying staff would not have to return to a week of excavation following an exhausting trip. Finally, full bus service to and from Jerusalem was instituted for the weekend convenience of volunteers and staff.

The period following the 1971 season saw a diversification of functions and the addition of staff to handle those functions, as the workload involved in setting up the volunteer program increased. In 1973 Louis Gough served as Associate Volunteer Director with the particular responsibility of counseling and advising volunteers in the personal problems that inevitably arose for some of them. In 1975 Jack van Hooser joined Volunteer and Educational Director H. Thomas Frank as a second Volunteer Director to assist with administration and serve as counselor to the volunteers. Since 1973 many of the administrative tasks associated with the volunteer program have been efficiently handled by the dig's administrative director, Kevin G. O'Connell, S.J. The many tasks which had to be shared by these people included advertising the excavation (for volunteer recruitment); handling the volumes of mail generated by the process of selecting volunteers; arranging the group flights; sending volunteers bulletins concerning clothing, insurance, medical matters, and the like; and planning the volunteer program in consultation with the Project Director. Once in Israel, these staff members had to attend to the hiring of buses, the arrangement of excursions, lectures, the rotation of volunteer assignments, and a myriad of other tasks that included handling crises like loss of a passport or even an emergency trip home.

During the years 1970–1975 the volunteer program achieved its definitive shape and, with the inevitable small adjustments one might expect, has served the Expedition well during the second phase of excavation, which began in 1977 and is still in progress at this writing (January, 1983).

THE VOLUNTEERS

Over the first four seasons (1970, 1971, 1973, and 1975) some 256 volunteers (counting "repeaters" only once) participated in the Hesi program. They represented eight countries and more than eighty-five institutions of higher learning. The youngest volunteer was eighteen and the oldest sixty-nine. Beginning in 1971, a change in policy brought to the volunteer staff a number of persons forty-five years old or older, although the majority of volunteers continued to be undergraduate and graduate students.

The academic and vocational interests of the Hesi volunteers varied widely, but, as one might expect, archaeology, anthropology, geology, art history, Biblical studies, and Middle Eastern history headed the list. For some reason there has been a large number of pre-medical students on the volunteer staff. Some volunteers have become vocationally interested in archaeology or in an associated field while at Hesi and have changed their career directions accordingly. At least two older volunteers shifted professional careers as a result of their experience at the dig. Eight persons who began their field experience at Hesi subsequently joined the Expedition as area supervisors or in other capacities. Other volunteers who received their first training at Hesi found staff positions on other digs.

It is satisfying to cite the volunteers who have so significantly contributed to the success of the first four seasons of the Joint Expedition's work at Tell el-Hesi. Their names form an impressive list:

1970
(Photo in Ch. 6, below, fig. 1)

Bamberg, Juliann
Bouchard, Marcel
Brenner, Alice
Burger, John
Burr, Liza
Busch, Vincent
Carlson, Frank
Clark, Kevin
Connelly, Tom
Conton, Leslie
Dickinson, David
Drons, Michael
Dunn, Ed
Epley, Carol
Gautier, Linda
Goldstein, Steve

Grimm, Joan
Helms, Christine
Holman, David
Johnson, Gordon
Johnson, Steve
Kaufmann, Aaron
Kaye, Michèle
Lampert, Emily
*Lass, Egon
Lerner, Lucia
Lewis, James
Luchs, Richard
McCabe, Edward
Marfoe, Leon
Maxmin, Jody
Michaelis, Susan

Raines, Holly
Redmont, Jane
Reid, Patrick
Reif, Robin
Root, Meganne
Saltz, Diane (Daniella)
Schottenfeld, Judy
Schumacher, Fred
Shapiro, Anita
Smith, Simon, S.J.
Ward, Marjorie
Weinberg, Suzanne
White, Vera
Wickland, Robert
Wilson, Carol

*Appointed area supervisor during the 1970 season.

1971
(Photo in Ch. 6, below, fig. 5)

Allen, Ronald
Augustinowitz, Mic
Ballou, Nancy
Blakely, Jeffrey
Bolton, Marilyn
Boxwell, David
Bray, Michael
Brown, Martha
Burr, Liza
Campo, Juan
Clark, Kevin
Dall, Ellen
Edwards, Jim

Eisentrout, Virginia
Eshkenasy, Polly
Falkenburg, Claudia
Feigenbaum, Susan
Gold, Richard
Haass, Richard
Hancock, Debbie
Hart, Patricia
Hayes, Deborah
Hershberger, Christine
Hirsch, Mark
Ingalls, Dorothy
Ingalls, Lawrence

Johnson, Christine
Johnson, James
Kolts, Kathryn
Kriens, Ronald
Larsen, Jean
LeDuc, Louise
Lichtwardt, Ron
Lipman, David
Long, Mark
Luker, Ann
Luker, Maurice
Lynch, Paul
Lyon, David T.

1971
continued

Michaelis, Susan
Naidoff, Bruce
Newcombe, Lydia
Nunemaker, Kathy
O'Connell, Kevin, S.J.
Parker, Thomas
Peterson, John
Popp, Tom
Redmont, Jane
Redmount, Carol

Reznikoff, Allen
Richard, Sue
Rogers, Christopher
Ross, Sarah
Sanders, Wayne
Schottenfeld, Judy
Schweitzer, Peter
Silberstein, Paula
Smith, Ellen
Specht, Olga

Startup, Charles
Wall, Kate
Walters, Henry
Ward, Marjorie
Weeks, Linda
Willcox, Shelley
Woodruff, Preston
Zeckser, Clifford
Zipris, Arthur

1973***
(Photo in Ch. 6, below, fig. 9)

Alt, Arthur
Barnet, Walter
Batchelor, David
Beamer, Janice
Bean, Theodore
Beardsley, Mark
Bertoni, Louis
Betlyon, John
Biggs, Edward
*Blakely, Jeffrey
Bobker, Michael
Brown, Bruce
Cassels, Donna
Celum, Connie
Cheloff, Alice
Clayton, Janine
Cole, Stephen
Collins, Michael
Cook, Sally
Dart, Barbara
Davies, Mary Ellen
Davis, Hunt
Doermann, Roger
Eakins, J. Kenneth
Engle, James
**Epley, Carol
Fessler, Sally
Fisher, Stephen

Fraser, Stuart
Freund, Deborah
Frick, Frank
Fry, Ralph
Gandelman, Alan
Gard, Linda
Hirsch, Deborah
Hobson, Gregory
Hodges, James
Holland, Albert
Hubbard, Frank
Hursch, Marian
Kaiser, Tema
Kimpel, Stephen
Kirby, James
Kirschenfeld, Jon
Klick, David
Kohls, Paul
Krulick, Monique
Kwon, Ohyun
Lambert, Debra
Langaa, Lynn
Linde, Lorraine
McClellan, Murray
Magel, Judith
Maharam, Stanley
Maitland, R. Edward (Ted)
Mangus, Warren

Muncie, Margaret
Myers, Robert
Nealon, Donald
Olsen, James
Ready, Charles
Reed, Rosanna
Richman, Paula
Robinson, Bruce
Roudabush, David
Rubsys, Anthony
Runge, Janey
Saunders, Nancy
Schwartzman, Amy
Schwinn, Beverly
Sipe, Richard
Specht, Olga
Smith, Martha
Smukler, David
Storr, Anne
Swendseid, Margaret
Tarpley, Kent
Walstadt, Kirk
Ware, Donna
Weiss, Margaret
Williams, O. Ernest
Young, Robert

*Area supervisor for two weeks in 1973.

**Area supervisor for four weeks in 1973.

***Jeffrey Yarus, a student from the College of Wooster, worked under the supervision of geologist Frank Koucky but was not a participant in the Volunteer Program.

1975***
(Photo in Ch. 6, below, fig. 10)

Anderson, Gary	Katz, Daniel	Rutledge, Lawrie
Augustine, Louise	Kidd, Paul	Schimpf, Alice
Bloom, Joanne	Kirby, James	Schultz, Louis
Bloomer, Howard	Klein, Marjorie	Scott, Jere Lee
Bloomer, Kristi	Klingshirn, William	Shapiro, Letitia
*Blow, Dorothea	Koenig, Isolde	Shirley, Homer
Bradley, Karen	Lambert, Debra	Showers, Jack
Brank, Claude	Landis, Sandra	Shuell, Michèle
Bubolz, Jerry	Leffingwell, Charlie	Smyers, Karen
Burbank, Robert	Levin, Katya	Sorrel, Blair
**Claviez, Christian	Levinson, Ronnie	Stock, Irene
Coffey, Jonathan	Luker, Maurice	Stork, Paul
Coffey, Julie	Markens, Robert	Stork, Sharon
Cummings, Annabelle	Matijascic, Ernest	Terhune, Paul
Decker, Paul, S.J.	Menees, Katie	Tiffany, Frederick
Diven, Benjamin	Michelson, Ruth	Tjardes, Doris
Dunn, Ruth	Neff, Jonathan	Toller, Brenda
Grimm, Robert, S.J.	Nock, Richard	Ward, Lavanna
Hall, Robert	O'Dea, Arthur	Weeks, Linda
Hershberger, Christine	Raaflaub, Vernon	Westerfield, Karen
Hodgman, Robert	Roberts, Cheralyn	Windisch, Meredith
Hoffman, Suanne	Ronsheim, Marian	Ziman, Alice
Hutton, Rod	Ross, Mark	
Imhof, Paul, S.J.	Rowland, Kathie	

*Area supervisor for four weeks in 1975.
**Participant in the Volunteer Program for one week.
***David Budd and Karen Havholm, students from the College of Wooster, worked under the direction of Dr. Frank Koucky but were not participants in the Volunteer Program.

EPILOGUE AND A SPECIAL WORD

Excavation reports tend to be impersonal and factual, but anyone who has participated in an excavation knows that it is a very human venture. Extraordinary relationships develop. Some frictions occur when so many different people live and work together under unusual and sometimes difficult conditions. But, more often, firm friendships are made, and many such have developed at Hesi. Additionally, there has been a high level of morale, owing, at least in part, to the democratic nature of the dig—both in its administration by the continuing staff and in the mutual sharing of the site's physical privations. What has brought unity out of the extreme diversity in personalities and backgrounds among the volunteer staff, and focus to the entire operation, has been the determination to dig at Tell el-Hesi in a style consistent with the finest traditions of Middle Eastern archaeology. The decision made in 1969 to combine this central purpose with a manifold educational opportunity for volunteers was a wise one which has stood the test of experience.

Finally, a special word of appreciation is gratefully offered by the Hesi professional staff and by the volunteers to Barbara Turek of Oberlin College, who has processed hundreds of volunteer applications, answered queries, handled many thousands of dollars in flight and volunteer accounts, and offered sound advice in the selection of volunteers. And she has done all this with great and good spirit. "Thanks" seems so little for so much.

NOTES

1. H. Thomas Frank died before he could complete the final draft of this essay, and so the final draft was entrusted to me. I have attempted to retain as much of the style and wording of the original as possible in light of the various editorial comments the author had received on his first draft, but I would be remiss were I not to point out his inestimable contribution to the Joint Expedition as director of its Volunteer and Educational Program during the years covered in this essay. Professor Frank's own characteristic modesty prevented him from doing justice, in his writing, to his own contribution. Though I have felt constrained to follow his wishes in the text, I could not in honesty leave the writing of this piece without expressing the heartfelt gratitude of the Expedition staff for his unstinting effort that achieved the excellent volunteer program described here.—F. L. H., Jr.

2. Farid Salman died on July 1, 1982.

BIBLIOGRAPHY FOR CHAPTER V

Bliss, F. J.
    1894   *A Mound of Many Cities or Tell el Hesy Excavated.* London: Palestine Exploration Fund; New York: Macmillan.

King, P. J.
    1975   The American Archaeological Heritage in the Near East. *Bulletin of the American Schools of Oriental Research* 217: 55–65.

    1983   *American Archaeology in the Mideast: A History of the American Schools of Oriental Research.* Philadelphia: The American Schools of Oriental Research.

Matthers, J. M.
    1989   Excavations by the Palestine Exploration Fund at Tell el-Hesi, 1890–1892. In *Tell el-Hesi: The Site and the Expedition*, pp. 37–67. Edited by B. T. Dahlberg and K. G. O'Connell, S.J. Excavation Reports of the American Schools of Oriental Research: Tell el-Hesi 4. Winona Lake, IN: Eisenbrauns.

Worrell, J. E.
    1970   Tell el-Hesi: Mound of Many Surprises. *Newsletter Number 5* (December 1970) of the American Schools of Oriental Research: 1–4.

Wright, G. E.
    1965   *Shechem: The Biography of a Biblical City.* New York and Toronto: McGraw Hill.

Yadin, Y.
    1966   *Masada: Herod's Fortress and the Zealots' Last Stand.* New York: Random House.

Chapter VI

PHASE ONE AT TELL EL-HESI: A SEASON-BY-SEASON ACCOUNT

by
John E. Worrell
Sturbridge Village Foundation
and
John W. Betlyon
Smith College

The time following the Arab-Israeli War of 1967 was difficult and confusing for American archaeologists. Archaeological activity in Israel and Jordan was measurably affected. All projects then based in the Jerusalem School of the American Schools of Oriental Research (ASOR) were being conducted at sites on the West Bank and were thus paralyzed by the new political situation. ASOR's president, G. Ernest Wright, worked energetically to evaluate the changed conditions and to modify ASOR's activities accordingly. His aim was to stabilize ASOR's relations with all parties in order to foster more comprehensive archaeological research throughout the Near East. This led in 1970 to the reorganization of the Jerusalem School as the W. F. Albright Institute of Archaeological Research (AIAR), sponsoring expeditions and research in Israel, and to the organization of separate ASOR-affiliated centers for research in Jordan, Cyprus, and Tunisia. In Israel, Hesi was the first expedition to take the field under ASOR's new structure.[1]

Preliminary Surveys in 1968 and 1969

Israeli officials had strongly encouraged Wright's proposals to field an ASOR dig in Israel. Wright wished to refine the work of an earlier expedition using the new methods tested at Shechem (Tell Balatah) and Gezer. He was particularly interested in reexamining the southern sites of Tell el-Hesi

and Tell Jemmeh, both originally dug by Petrie.[2] In August, 1968, following the Gezer and Shechem field seasons, Lawrence E. Stager, Robert G. Boling, and John E. Worrell set off for a preliminary look at each site. The limited objective was to evaluate each tell for possible excavation. Hesi was Wright's first choice; it was closer to Lachish and might shed some light on the Biblical conquest narratives, and it had been the first site excavated by an American (Frederick J. Bliss) in Palestine in the nineteenth century. With Wright's encouragement, Worrell proceeded immediately to spread enthusiasm for the proposed project and the site. W. J. Bennett, Jr., was enlisted to augment the period specializations of Stager and Worrell, and Lawrence E. Toombs was invited to add the extensive experience he gained in stratigraphic excavation at Jericho under Kathleen Kenyon and at Tell Balatah. Toombs, moreover, possessed a well-known pedagogical ability to train young archaeologists. The need for someone with administrative capabilities was met by Philip J. King. Thus the nucleus of a staff was formed.

A two-week preliminary season with exploratory objectives was first planned to follow the Gezer season in 1969. Financial and staffing problems combined to cancel that plan, however, and its goals were reformulated to allow a core staff of three people to survey the area in a six-day period in August. Geologist Reuben Bullard, stratigraphic technician Nasser Diab Mansur (Abu ʿIssa), and Worrell probed, observed, and recorded surface data during that trip. They also cut a section on the wadi face (the east slope of the tell, eroded by the Wadi Hesi) and another in Bliss's old excavation area (the northeast quadrant of the acropolis). Samples were collected, photographs taken, and plans sketched, prior to the formulation of the strategy for a regular field season in the summer of 1970. The survey results provided a basis on which an application for funding from the Smithsonian Institution could be made (Worrell 1970a).

Three principal objectives were met in the preliminary surveys. First, the site's potential for an extensive project was assessed, and information useful for designing a research strategy was studied. Hesi's location, the evidence there for its early floral and faunal life, its traces of human occupation from many different periods, and the apparent diversity in the extent of human activity at the site in different periods promised varied and interesting excavation. Second, signs of change in the extent of the site over different historical periods were surveyed, and surface pottery provided some corroboration of Petrie's earlier observations. Finally, Hesi's relationship to its wider environment, including several smaller, neighboring sites, was examined. This research would lead to much more extensive work in subsequent years.

The 1970 Field Season

The Joint Archaeological Expedition to Tell el-Hesi began its first six-week excavation season on June 15, 1970. Working from the surface in Fields I (atop the acropolis) and II (on the southern terrace), the season's first work moved ahead quickly. In Field II, however, four millennia of erosion and modern deep plowing had almost completely destroyed the occupational remains (see Coogan 1989 [Chapter VIII, below]). The design for achieving lateral exposure of Early Bronze Age strata therefore had to be revised. Field III was opened nearer the base of the tell's acropolis, but here later remains obscured any Early Bronze Age material. Surface surveys in 1971 and 1973, augmented by preliminary soundings in 1973 and 1975, identified substantial undisturbed EB material elsewhere on the tell, and investigation of these remains would become a cardinal objective of the project's Phase Two.

Another early discovery was a series of surfaces and associated pits in Field I from the Persian Period. Four distinct substrata were eventually observed within this era, usually undifferentiated at other sites (Toombs 1989 [Chapter VII, below]: figs. 12–13).

Other major discoveries included the Muslim cemetery in Field I on the acropolis and the massive fortification complex in Field III on its southern slope. Intrusions from the many graves of the cemetery nearly decimated multiple Hellenistic phases of occupation and everything more recent (see Toombs 1985; 1989 [Chapter VII, below]: 125, 128), but the cemetery also provided the expedition with the most complete compendium of stratigraphic, ethnographic, and physical data yet derived from the excavation of a Bedouin burial grouping in the Levant (Toombs 1985). Investigation of the fortification complex in Field III made unexpectedly large demands on staff time and energies. By 1975 the fortification wall had been traced for over eighty meters, and two sections through its width had clarified its three-stage construction. It proved to be one of the largest mud-brick structures from the Iron Age thus far discovered in Palestine (see Rose and Toombs 1976; Amiran and Worrell 1976).

During the first season the expedition staff was quartered in a schoolhouse in Kiryat Gat, a "development town" some six miles from Hesi. At the excavation site itself there was an open pavilion to house the registry and field laboratory. Some of the specialist, drawing, and recording activities were carried on both at the site and in the schoolhouse; this work continued in the remote but more controlled Jerusalem environs of the Albright Institute or the Hebrew Union College on weekends and after the close of the dig season.

An egalitarian team model evolved throughout that initiatory season. Staff and student volunteers alike accomplished the work of the dig. For the latter, a field school program was begun through the efforts of many of the staff. Harry Thomas Frank screened and accepted close to fifty volunteer applicants (see fig. 1; also Frank and Horton 1989 [Chapter V, above]: 89–90, 93). Philip J. King, assisted by Susan Simmons, saw to the numerous details of scheduling and logistical coordination for the entire staff. Specialists in the field included Abdulhossein Baharlou, geologist; Jeffrey Schwartz and Janet Sawyer, physical anthropologists (with Schwartz also doing faunal analysis); William Robertson, botanist; Theodore A. Rosen, photographer; David Voelter and Bishara (Fouad) Zoughbi, surveyor-draftsmen; Muff Thomsen,[3] artist and registrar; and Nasser Diab Mansur (Abu ʿIssa), chief technical man.

Fig. 1. Staff and volunteers for the 1970 season. Photo by T. Rosen.

W. J. Bennett and John Worrell directed the work in Field I (see fig. 2). Six 5 m. x 5 m. areas separated by balks one meter wide were opened in 1970 and were supervised, respectively, by Linda Ammons, Richard Kuns, Ellen Messer, Mark Papworth (two weeks), Cymbrie Pratt, Robert Rhoades (four weeks), and D. Glenn Rose. The six units formed an L, generally parallel to Bliss's cut on the north and to the wadi face on the east. Areas inside the lines formed by that right angle of contiguous squares were plotted for later expansion. Areas 1, 2, 3, 11, 21, and 31 were the ones opened this first season (see fig. 4 and Toombs 1989 [Chapter VII, below]: fig. 2). Occupation layers well down into levels that would be labeled Stratum V (Persian Period) were reached in all squares. The grain silos of Va provided the most spectacular finds, since their contemporary use-surfaces and fill contained abundant material culture remains. All superimposed strata and materials were excavated and recorded, and their interrelationships carefully analyzed, under the overall guidance of L. E. Toombs. The expedition was committed to the recovery and

study of every piece of archaeological evidence, no matter how slight or ordinary, from every archaeological period, in order to obtain the most complete record possible of the site's history and cultural development.

The remains of some periods are better preserved than others, or are more interesting to staff members, so that equality of treatment is not easily achieved. The modern military installations (Stratum I), for example, lacked the ancient allure, and they intruded into and hindered the stratigraphic differentiation of earlier levels. The Stratum II cemetery involved both historical archaeology and ethnology. However, lack of care in placing the latest interments, complicated by military trenching from Israel's War of Independence, made the recovery of individual burials in Stratum II very difficult (Toombs 1985). Those burials, in turn, disturbed crucial stratigraphic connections in the Late Arabic agricultural phase (Stratum III) and in the underlying Hellenistic phases of Stratum IV (Toombs 1989 [Chapter VII, below]: 136-140). Each burial was nevertheless carefully excavated, and

Fig. 2. Field I being opened in 1970 (Areas 1-2, 11-12, 21-22). Photo by T. Rosen.

important information was thus gained through the use of meticulous field techniques and systematic recording.

Under L. E. Stager's direction Field II was opened to explore the stratification inside the southern perimeter of the fortification line observed in the preliminary survey. A depression in the line of hills suggested the possibility of an entryway through an ancient wall protecting the site. The evidence was lost, however, for with the exception of two truncated EB III pits all cultural remains had been eroded or destroyed by modern deep plowing. The marks of the agricultural work were clearly etched into the caliche-compacted virgin soil (Coogan 1989a [Chapter VIII, below]: 163).

Stager, Toombs, and Worrell conferred and decided to open another area in which features were visible *in situ*. Therefore, excavation began in Field III on the southern flank of the acropolis, where erosion from the Wadi Hesi had exposed extensive mud-brick construction and detritus. (Fig. 3) Stager's team of Dorothea Brooks, Michael Coogan, Ralph Doermann, David Freedman, and Egon Lass undertook the exposure of what has proven to be Hesi's most imposing feature thus far (see fig. 4 and Toombs 1989 [Chapter VII, below]: fig. 2; Areas 1, 2, 3, 4, 5, 5A, 13, 14, 18, and 23 of Field III were opened in 1970). The wall—of unfired mud brick—was found to have been built in three distinct construction phases, with a total breadth of nearly thirteen meters. Foundation trenches produced slight ceramic evidence which, though limited, initially suggested to the excavators that the construction was all or partially dated to the Iron II Period. Subsequent excavations and analyses raised the question of a possible later date in the Persian Period, contemporary with Stratum V (and more specifically, Vd) in Field I (cf. Worrell 1970b; Toombs

Fig. 3. Tell el-Hesi under excavation in 1971 (Field III wall, E corner, on the face above wadi). Photo by T. Rosen.

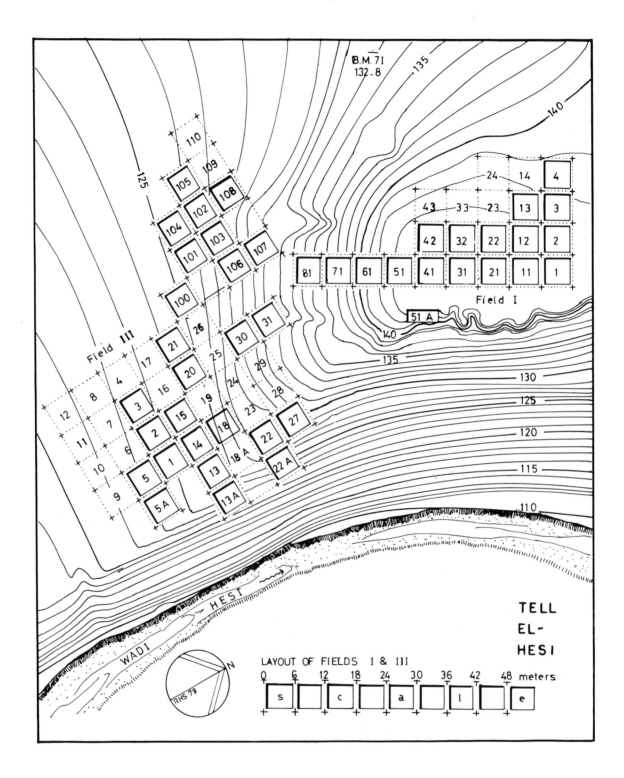

Fig. 4 Contour plan of the acropolis at Tell el-Hesi, showing the layout and numbering of all squares opened in Fields I and III during Phase One. Drawing by R. Spytek.

1974). However, as exposure of the wall system continued, the Iron II date was confirmed. The construction phasing and detail were dramatically revealed in a section along the wadi face (Area 5A) where the wall's foundations and an earlier drain beneath it were also unearthed (Toombs 1974: 28–31; 1987 [Chapter VII, below]: figs. 17–18; Worrell 1970b: 3–4). Clearly, the Iron II inhabitants of the tell went to great lengths to shore up the slopes against the erosion caused by winter rains. This may have been part of a military "watch tower" operation linked to the defense of Lachish (modern Tell ed-Duweir), about eight miles east-northeast of Hesi.

Chronological limits for the Field III wall were established in this season with the discovery of the foundation of a Chalcolithic domestic structure outside the wall and late Persian Period burials dug into its topmost level (for the Chalcolithic structures see Coogan 1989 [Chapter IX, below]; Toombs 1989 [Chapter VII, below]: 144–5; Worrell 1970b; for the Persian Period burials see Coogan 1975 [Chapter X, below]).

An important innovation in this season was a new adaptation of Stuart Struever's flotation techniques (Struever 1968), as modified for an arid environment by Stewart and Robertson (1973). This had been tried, using only test pits, at Gezer and other locations. At Hesi, botanist William Robertson took soil samples from any layer that potentially might contain plant remains (usually seeds). This provided a more complete sampling from the beginning.[4]

In sum, this initiatory field season saw the dig staff clarifying its objectives and refining its methods. On the whole it was an auspicious beginning.

The 1971 Field Season

An eight-week season was fielded from June 13 to August 5, 1971. After these first two seasons, which fell in consecutive years, excavation would move to an alternate-year program. This would allow more time for the processing and analysis of data in the intervening years. The staff decided in favor of the two successive field seasons at the beginning of the project in order to test field methods more intensively from the start. This helped to solidify the interdisciplinary collaboration begun in 1970 and to insure the accumulation of sufficient data for off-season analysis.

The 1971 field season continued and expanded the 1970 work in Fields I and III (see figs. 3–4). On the acropolis (Field I), exposure of the Persian and later strata was expanded by opening Areas 4, 12, 13, 22, 32, and 41. This doubled the number of squares under excavation. In Field III, to determine better the details of the wall-system's construction, Areas 20, 21, and 23 were opened, and work continued in the areas first opened in 1970 (see fig. 4 and Toombs 1989 [Chapter VII, below]: fig. 2 for all areas in both fields). Several teams traced the course of the wall, investigated its method of construction, and sought stratigraphic connections between the wall and the heavily eroded slope of the acropolis. Some sixty-eight students participated in the dig's comprehensive training program in field archaeology (see fig. 5). The Hesi format for student field education, initiated under Harry Thomas Frank's supervision with input and involvement by the entire staff, became a model for archaeological projects elsewhere. It has been followed and amplified through succeeding seasons at Hesi (Frank and Horton 1989 [Chapter V, above]).

The educational program was a field school in the best sense. Beginning with a full week of orientation and instruction, first in Jerusalem and then at the site, it was conducted by staff members and included lecturers from the Israeli Department of Antiquities and discussions by noted archaeologists and historians from various academic and scientific institutions. Topics included the history of Syro-Palestinian archaeology, ceramic typology, techniques of excavation appropriate to sites featuring mud-brick construction, and an introduction to the contemporary life of the modern host country. After this formal introduction, students began their work at Hesi. They received work assignments that rotated between the field, the technical shed, and the pottery table. Without compromising archaeological standards, all staff were encouraged to conduct field work in such a way as to make it a part of the volunteers' educational experience. During the season a series of lectures, seminars, demonstrations, and simulations were combined with weekly progress reports and with tours of all the areas under excavation. The student volunteers also participated in visits to other important archaeological sites and took part in surface surveys conducted by the staff at Hesi's nearest neighbors in the area, Tell Sheqef and Tell Qeshet. While many of the volunteers came from sponsoring schools in the Hesi consortium, additional volunteers included teachers, ministers, and men and women of other backgrounds. The

Fig. 5 Staff and volunteers for the 1971 season. Photo by T. Rosen.

age span of the group in that year ranged from about nineteen up into the fifties. Some 1971 volunteers were to return in subsequent years as area supervisors, camp managers, and staff members in a variety of other field and administrative posts.

In 1971 the expedition staff and the volunteers lived in tents at the site for the first time, and expanded registry and technical facilities were now constructed there, as well. This logistical improvement made possible more efficient use of time and personnel. It thereby enhanced the work of the entire field team.

The major financial underwriting for the first two field seasons and the 1972 interseason activities came from counterpart funds granted by the Smithsonian Institution. Principal American institutional sponsorship came from Oberlin College and the Hartford Seminary Foundation, which formed the original nucleus of a nascent supporting consortium. Additional monies were received from Christian Theological Seminary (Indianapolis) and from Phillips University (Enid, Oklahoma).

A Canada Council grant for the 1971 season supported an innovation in computerized recording and retrieval of ceramic data. Under Toombs's direction, a team from Waterloo Lutheran (now Wilfrid Laurier) University in Ontario registered and coded all ceramics in the field and produced 650 finished drawings at a scale of 1:1. After the field season, Toombs and Norman Wagner continued to refine the coding procedures—intended to computerize the ceramic data (Toombs 1971b; Wagner 1971)—and the result was a total registration of 7,178 ceramic items, of which 5,927 were coded and 1,140 drawn. In the end, however, Toombs concluded that a more traditional approach to the study of the ceramic data would be necessary to accomplish final processing and publication. Drawings made under difficult field conditions often did not meet publication standards. Similar procedures developed by Toombs and Schwartz for coding burials and osteological information from the Stratum II cemetery and the burials in other strata were much more successful, and they have been used in later seasons (Toombs 1974: 22; also, 1985).

The core field staff continued in their respective 1970 capacities for the 1971 season. Robert B. Stewart joined the team to direct the recovery of botanical samples by the flotation technique and to perform the necessary analysis. Jeffrey Schwartz was assisted by physical anthropologist Lynn Fischer; Reuben Bullard consulted in the areas of geology and stratigraphy; Joel Plum, a ceramist, did

pottery reconstruction and demonstrated the ways in which various ancient ceramic vessels were produced. Bishara Zoughbi (Fouad) became the project's chief architect and surveyor and was assisted by Mark Hirsch; together they completed most of the basic grid and contour plan of the site (Toombs 1989 [Chapter VII, below]: fig. 2). Theodore Rosen was again the photographer and, in cooperation with the Gezer Project, continued to use darkroom and other facilities at the Hebrew Union College in Jerusalem. As in 1971, the Albright Institute generously provided work space on weekends and logistical support.

Melvin K. Lyons became the permanent medical advisor during the 1971 season; he and Alfred M. Donovan served as camp physicians. Mary Bennett became the objects registrar for the duration of Phase One and, along with W. J. Bennett, organized a highly efficient system of material culture registration (see Bennett 1974; Bennett and Bennett 1976; Blakely and Toombs 1980). Anne Carter was ceramics registrar. Nasser Diab Mansur (Abu 'Issa) headed a contingent of technical men from Balatah. Philip J. King managed the complex fiscal and logistical details of camp life and organization, while Lawrence Toombs provided archaeological advice in the field, at the pottery-reading table, and in the technical shed (a pavilion where objects were registered and the specialists worked).

A scientific innovation in 1971 was the trace-element analysis of ceramics by neutron activation. A controlled sampling of common wares, representative imports, and fine sherds was selected, along with some other wares having unusual characteristics. Dorothea Brooks performed the laboratory work of neutron activation under the direction of Edward Sayre and Garmon Harbottle of the Brookhaven (New York) National Laboratories. A great deal of information concerning the origins of the ceramic materials, the patterns of ancient commerce, and the use and function of different vessels has resulted from this research (Brooks 1975; cf. Brooks *et al.* 1974; Bieber *et al.* 1976).

Excavation in Field I was again directed by Bennett and Worrell. Supervisors Linda Ammons, Richard Kuns, and D. Glenn Rose were joined by Carol Epley, Yechiel Lehavy, and Burton MacDonald. By the end of the season, the six areas that had first been opened in 1970 were consistently brought into phase with each other in the third or fourth substratum of the Persian Period (Stratum V), while the teams in the six new areas were still excavating the Arabic levels (Strata II and III) and beginning to expose fragments of the Hellenistic remains (Stratum IV). In this process, the staff was becoming more experienced in isolating multiple phasings of unfired mud brick amid mud-brick detritus and the derangement of materials occasioned by the pits, graves and—most recently—trenches dug from higher levels. The sorting and recording of burials and their contents was complicated by the frequent disruption of earlier burials by later ones. However, the staff remained committed to the careful retrieval of all possible data from this excavated material (Worrell and Toombs 1971; Toombs 1974: 23–25; 1985).

Field III investigations by Lawrence Stager involved the analysis of monumental architecture as well as continued excavation. Michael Coogan and Ralph Doermann were joined on the supervisory staff by Lucia Lerner and Daniella Saltz. The complexities of the wall-system construction in that field were recognized as falling into three phases. The sequence of these phases was established, and the differences in their composition carefully noted (Toombs 1989 [Chapter VII, below]: 145–49).

The 1972 Interseason

The time between the 1971 and 1973 field seasons saw several staff engaged in analysis and evaluation. Senior staff came to understand the practical implications, advantages, and disadvantages of the holistic method. It required maximum cooperation between all levels and specializations in the team organization. Techniques had to be reassessed and priorities reassigned. Costs in time, energy, and money were more realistically seen, while the experience of the first two seasons had illuminated the site's archaeological potential and possible historical significance. The fact that the Smithsonian grant was about to expire and could not be renewed gave new urgency to planning for the future. One result was a successful proposal to the National Endowment for the Humanities, prepared by John Worrell, which stressed the possibilities of the expedition's interdisciplinary approach for the investigation of such a site.

A few specific endeavors of 1972 deserve special note. Ceramic analysis, including comparative study and drawing, was undertaken by students at the University of Southern California and at Wilfrid Laurier University, working, respectively, under W. J. Bennett and L. E. Toombs. John

Worrell sorted and catalogued artifactual materials in Jerusalem and, in the United States, began a project of conservation on some of them at the Hartford Seminary Foundation Museum. Philip King began research into the early work of Petrie and Bliss and into the subsequent history of ASOR's work in the Near East. The study of Hesi's first excavations in the nineteenth century brought him into collaboration with John Matthers, whose own conclusions are found in Matthers 1989 (Chapter II above; see King 1975 and 1983 on the history of ASOR). Toombs continued to study the materials from the cemetery and refined the burial codification system. Robert Stewart and Jeffrey Schwartz worked with the floral and faunal data, respectively, developing conventions and criteria for assessment of the ecosystem to which Hesi belongs.

The most ambitious undertaking of 1972 was research by Dorothea Brooks to achieve correlation of the neutron activation analysis of Hesi's stratified ceramic materials with those already studied and catalogued on the computer. She worked with Sayre and Harbottle at Brookhaven, with Worrell at Hartford, and with archaeologists, geologists and local potters in Israel and on the West Bank. She collected ceramic materials and clays from twenty-two sites in the vicinity of Hesi, as well as from likely clay sources immediately adjacent to the tell. The object of her work was to obtain a variety of analytical profiles of base materials from different sites in order to identify sources and patterns of exchange (fig. 6). At each site sherds were collected from as many time periods as possible. Where available, samples of mud brick were also collected. Clay samples for each site were gathered from wadi beds, while clay mines, clay deposits in fields, and limestone pockets were located and sampled. From present-day potters' shops she obtained materials for controlled testing of the neutron activation technique with modern Palestinian wares, and in so doing she learned about methods and materials used in ceramics today. The collected materials, including representative Hesi sherds and clays, were then analyzed and computer-sorted at Brookhaven according to methods originally developed by Sayre and Harbottle (fig. 7; see Sayre 1972).

The procedure can be summarized as follows: A small portion of a sample sherd is drilled, or sliced, and ground into a powder; it is then weighed and sealed in an individual container. The material is irradiated in an atomic reactor for a period of

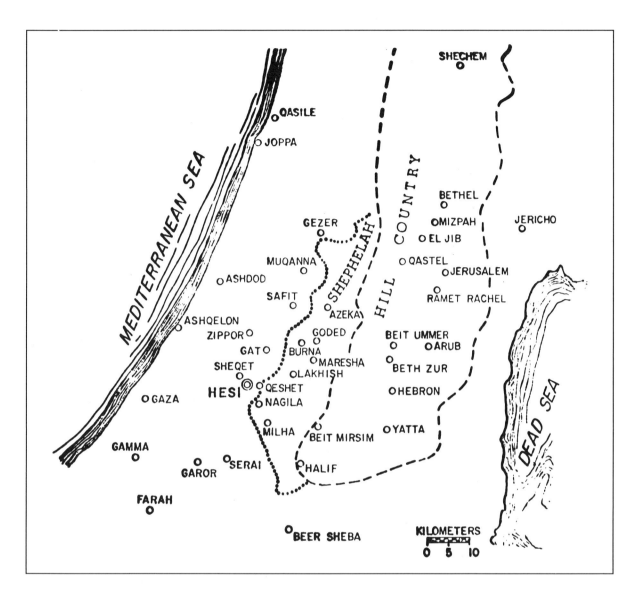

Fig. 6. Map showing sites sampled in D. Brooks's project (from Brooks 1975: xxii).

time determined by the elements being analyzed. Resulting gamma radiation is counted by a lithium-drifted, germanium-crystal detector connected to a multi-channel analyzer, and the data are recorded on magnetic tape for processing and plotting. By comparison with charts that record values for the Hesi area and for many other clay sources, the wares are then separated into groups according to whether they were produced at Hesi or imported from elsewhere. Further separation of imports into those manufactured nearby and those from more remote sources provides information about commercial relationships, the extent of external involvements, and economic networks.

Brooks also employed other methods of chemical analysis, including X-ray fluorescence. Studies were extended to include finishing materials such as slips and paint. Finally, all this information was compared to relevant data derived from archaeological findings at the respective sites and at Hesi. To this was added an in-depth study of the documentary record in order to develop a complete picture of the economic and political relationships of Hesi's inhabitants with their neighbors and with foreign countries during each time period (see Brooks 1975 for an extensive application of these processes to the Persian Period materials from Hesi).

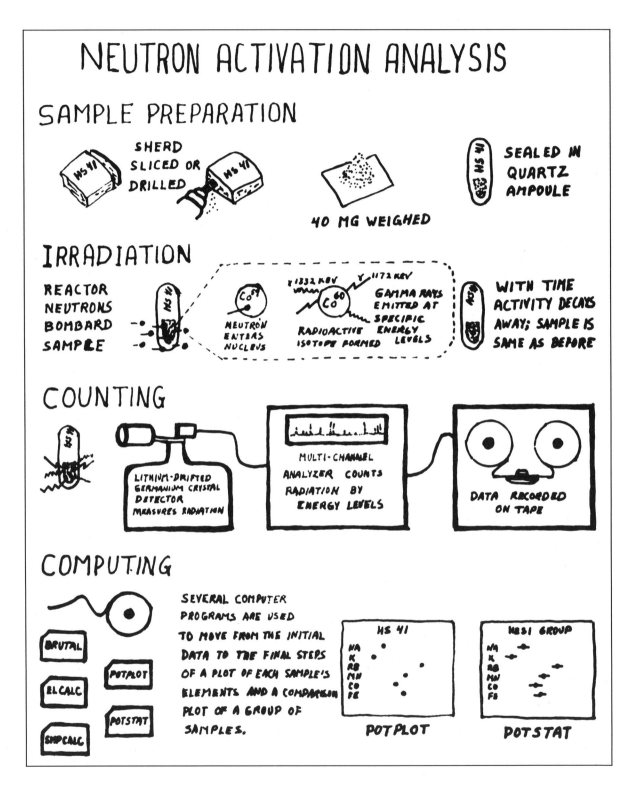

Fig. 7. Diagram of the neutron-activation process (from Brooks 1975: 138).

The 1973 Field Season

The third full-scale season was fielded from July 1 to August 20, 1973. Strategies had been refined for Fields I and III, and further excavation was planned for both (fig. 8). A survey was also proposed, including a systematic surface sampling of the site and its environs together with a limited probe through the stratigraphy of the lower city in the depression west of the acropolis on the western edge of the terrace.

General Theological Seminary and Seabury-Western Theological Seminary joined Waterloo Lutheran University (now Wilfrid Laurier University) as full Hesi consortium sponsors in 1973. Important additional funding was contributed by grants from Ashland Theological Seminary, Oberlin College (one of the original consortium members), the Lutheran Theological Seminary, and the Smithsonian Institution. A major grant was received from the National Endowment for the Humanities. Charles U. Harris became the director of this expanded consortium. As camp administrators, Larry and Dorothy Ingalls attended to the innumerable details of set-up and maintenance. This was a complex and difficult task, because more participants came to the field than in any other season. Several new specialists joined the staff in the field to improve cooperation and information flow between the field and the technical shed. In addition to the enlarged staff with expanded technical facilities, thirteen local personnel were hired for technical assistance, and eighty-two student volunteers came to the site (fig. 9). Harry Thomas Frank organized an ambitious educational program with Louis Gough as his assistant. Continuing a practice begun in the preceding years of the Hesi program, the staff frequently conferred before and during the season on the subject of education, to devise good opportunities for student involvement in the various archaeological processes. Nine advanced archaeological students

Fig. 8. Tell el-Hesi under excavation in 1973 (uppermost Iron II occupation levels in I.51). Photo by W. Nassau.

Fig. 9. Staff and volunteers for the 1973 season. Photo by W. Nassau.

took on modified supervisory roles, and others shared specialists' responsibilities. For the first time the teams worked split days in the field (5:00 a.m. to noon, and again from 4:00 to 6:00 p.m.). Thus, they took advantage of the day's best light (for photography, balk reading, etc.) but avoided having to work during the hottest hours. In previous seasons the 5:00 a.m. to 1:00 p.m. schedule had been followed.

Kevin G. O'Connell, S.J., became the administrative director at the start of the 1973 season, when Philip J. King's new responsibilities as president of the Albright Institute of Archaeological Research removed him from the field and made him limit himself to an advisory role. Jeffrey Schwartz and Lynn Emmanuel continued as the physical anthropologists; Robert Stewart was again the paleo-ethnobotanist; and Bishara Zoughbi (Fouad) once more served as the architect-surveyor. Michael Hammond joined the staff as lithics analyst and cultural anthropologist. In addition to processing stratified and survey-derived lithics for the season, he worked through the previous season's samples and provided methodological suggestions concerning the regional survey. Frank L. Koucky became the staff geologist, assisted in the survey, and began a topographic study of the region (Koucky 1989 [Chapter I, above]). John L. Peterson directed the survey, assisted by Lydia Newcombe. Richard Finman was the ceramist and demonstrated various techniques of pottery-making and of the analysis and reconstruction of excavated ceramic remains. Other staff members included Wilhelm E. Nassau as the photographer, Judy Hammond as the artist and draftsperson, Richard Kuns as the conservator, and Melvin Lyons as the camp physician. Nasser Diab Mansur (Abu ʿIssa) continued to direct the team of stratigraphic "technical men" and local workers. Mary Bennett handled the material culture registry, Carol Toombs was the objects registrar, and Anne Pritchard, assisted by Martha Smith, took care of the pottery registry.

Lawrence E. Toombs, W. J. Bennett, and John Worrell again assumed field responsibilities, with some adjustments of assignment. Toombs was more directly involved in the survey than the others. Lawrence Stager withdrew from field involvement at Hesi during this season in order to direct the Idalion project on Cyprus. Worrell, therefore, moved from Field I down the slope to direct Field III, where Stager had supervised, and this field was now subdivided into western (III-A) and eastern (III-B) sectors. These were placed under Michael

Coogan and Ralph Doermann, respectively, who became field supervisors, assisted by Daniella Saltz and Peter Jenkins. S. Thomas Parker, Carol Redmount, and Peter Schweitzer supervised areas in Field III.

W. J. Bennett directed Field I while he also attempted to sort out the intricate and frequently disjointed stratigraphy of Strata IV and V uncovered over the first three seasons. Field I was subdivided into northern (I-A = Areas 1, 2, 11, 12, 22) and southern (I-B = Areas 21, 31, 32, 41) fields on the top, and a new sector (I-C = Areas 51, 61, 61A, 71) stepping down the slope to the south toward Field III (see fig. 4). Linda Ammons, D. Glenn Rose and John Matthers became field supervisors for I-A, I-B, and I-C, respectively. They were assisted by Richard Kuns, W. Boyce Bennett, and Larry Herr. Jeffrey Blakely, Kevin Clark, Carol Epley, Hank Lay, and Maurice Luker were the area supervisors in Field I.

Excavation atop the acropolis was completely taken up with the Persian and later periods. Nearly 100 burials were excavated, recorded, and analyzed, for a three-season total of more than 400 (Rose and Toombs 1976: 47; Toombs 1985; Worrell 1974: 140). No new areas were opened in I-A or I-B, and those continued from previous seasons were cleared to the earliest Hellenistic levels or below (Strata IV and V). One early Hellenistic structure was discovered, partially preserved in spite of intrusive burials and trenching. It was a crude stone building similar to those described by F. J. Bliss in his City VIII (Bliss 1894: 115, 123). Some substantial areas of relatively undisturbed stratigraphy were associated with this building complex and an earlier drainage system. Gradually three distinct Hellenistic subphases became clear (cf. Rose and Toombs 1976: 46–47; Toombs 1989 [Chapter VII, below]: 136–40). Artifactual material, including impressive imported ceramics, suggested the relative affluence of the Hellenistic residents and indicated the extent of trade and cross-cultural contacts. From the numerous excavated pits came debris which included an ostracon, domestic items, and a wealth of floral and faunal remains, all of which contributed to the understanding of life styles, nourishment patterns, and ecological conditions (Rose, Toombs, and O'Connell 1978: 128; Stewart 1978; Toombs 1989 [Chapter VII, below]: 137, 139; Worrell 1974: 140).

The areas most extensively worked during the three seasons were all excavated well down into Stratum V, and a fourth substratum (Vd) was discovered. It contained the first evidence for spatial reorganization and major architectural features initially thought to be associated with the Persian Period (Worrell 1974: 140; Rose and Toombs 1976: 43–44). Moreover, a deep probe in Area 31 provided further information about the enigmatic "long range of chambers," which Petrie had noticed but could not explain functionally (Petrie 1891: 34 and pl. III, top). They were found to lie well under Stratum V, and apparently they were built to a height of three meters or more to retain dirt fill and debris—for no other purpose than to elevate and consolidate the tell's summit (see Worrell 1974: 140; Amiran and Worrell 1976: 519; Rose and Toombs 1976: 45). Subsequent excavation would prove that the date of this series of "chambers" was Iron II rather than Persian (see, e.g., Rose, Toombs, and O'Connell 1978:116).

Field I-C was the major area of expansion in the 1973 season. Excavations were moved southward, down the slope, to examine the fortifications described by Petrie and evidenced in the wadi face on the east side of the tell. Both Petrie and Bliss had traced the course of a wall on the north slope of the acropolis which Bliss assigned to his City VI, but which Petrie thought was from the time of Manasseh (Petrie 1891: 29, 32–33 and pl. 3; Bliss 1894: 98–100; cf. Matthers 1989 [Chapter II above]: table 1). Petrie had traced the wall around the western and southern sides of the acropolis to the point of its evident loss to erosion at the wadi face. By evidence from one of his trenches on the south slope, he related it to two other fortifications lower down, which he suggested had belonged to Uzziah and Rehoboam, respectively. In 1973, Areas 61 and 71 were opened between Petrie's trenches, and a section through the large wall complex at the wadi (61A) was prepared in order to gain some definition of the architectural remains (see fig. 8 and Toombs 1989 [Chapter VII, below]: figs. 20–21). Preliminary indications led the staff to believe that Petrie's dating for the major structure was probably more nearly correct than that of Bliss, although the other phases of fortification on the slope were seen to be far more complex structurally than Petrie had guessed (Worrell 1974: 140).

One feature that Petrie overlooked was a double layer of cobble-sized stones and brick-and-fill construction on the top of his "Manasseh" wall, which can still be traced all the way around the southern and possibly the western slopes of the tell to a point where it is lost to Petrie's and Bliss's excavations. Area 61 exposed this feature from the top, probed it stratigraphically, and cut one section through it

all the way down to the top of the large "Manasseh" wall. It proved to be part of an Iron II glacis. The Area 71 strategy was to work on the larger wall in similar fashion, utilizing step-trenches to expose contiguous phases and to reach the southern face—then to define relationships to features farther down the slope. The section at the wadi face (61A) clearly revealed the 7.5-m. breadth of the large wall from its northern (internal) to its southern (external) limits (Rose and Toombs 1976: 50-52; Toombs 1989 [Chapter VII, below]: fig. 20). This season's excavation established the relative phases in the architecture of this massive structure. More precise dating, however, would have to await future work.

In Area 51 at the crest of the mound a structural complex was found preserved immediately beneath the burials. The building had an exterior wall nearly a meter in breadth on the east side that continued for more than four meters into Area 41. The 0.50-m.-wide southern wall which extended across Area 51 was constructed of small stones set on brick with a well-preserved, fine threshold. Beneath this structure and its floors, and at points disturbed by them, was another structure with a heavy layer of ash and destruction debris both inside and out (cf. Rose, Toombs, and O'Connell 1978: 119–20; Toombs 1989 [Chapter VII, below]: 149–51 and fig. 19:D, C). From the ash came several nearly intact late Iron II juglets. Interestingly, excavation appeared to be moving horizontally rather than vertically through time—Persian to ron II—as excavation progressed southward. A strange picture was emerging of a tell intentionally built up by sections (Amiran and Worrell 1976: 518–19).

Field III strategy for the 1973 season called for further definition of the three construction phases of the vast southern wall complex. Specifically, teams were assigned to trace the course of the wall to the west and to explore its enigmatic "piers," discovered previously to be cutting into the fill against the rise of the acropolis.

The most surprising discovery of the season was the ancient engineering activity inside the main line of the wall excavated in III-B. While not entirely unlike the chamber-and-fill activity found atop the acropolis, the construction in III-B was initially thought to be later—from the Persian Period (Rose and Toombs 1976: 47–50, fig. 3, and fig. 3:A, items F and G; cf. Toombs 1989 [Chapter VII, below]: fig. 15). Erosion caused by surface water running off the acropolis through the centuries had apparently done heavy damage. Two probes in the wadi face (Area 22A) showed heavy build-up of water-laid sediment against a retainer which was now almost entirely lost to erosion. The layers built up by the run-off were laden with Late Bronze Age materials, including a Hathor figure molded on an LB bowl rim (see Rose and Toombs 1976: pl. 4:B:1). But most significant for dating purposes were Iron II sherds found dispersed to the lowest levels of the water-laid striations, dating the period of exposure—and probably of construction—for the wall now vanished into the wadi. Farther up the slope a stone foundation ran northward. At its southern end it merged with the stone foundation of the innermost part (Zone A) of the three construction zones of the major wall system in Field III. Enough of the N-S foundation survived in the two probes in 22A and in another in 13A (near the juncture of the N-S and E-W walls) to show that it had been cut in stepped fashion into earlier fill material. Ceramic evidence dated the E-W foundation securely to the late Iron II or early Persian Periods. Area 23, farther to the west of these probes, showed that a series of piers had been built up against Zone A of the wall. They were never free standing, but were also cut in stepped fashion up the slope into and upon earlier fill materials (or occasionally into virgin soil). The material between the piers was neither water-laid nor occupational debris, but solid fill brought in from below the occupational areas on the site's apron. The sparse ceramic evidence from this voluminous mass of fill included Iron II pottery throughout. Within the fill material was found a series of crudely-laid, mud-brick working platforms, which were set at intervals of about 1.25 m. to 1.5 m. up the slope. Apparently, the wall or pier building and the filling operation were contemporaneous. Evidence from Areas 23 and 28 further indicated that the entire structure may have been capped by a (presumably sloping) brick platform, a sort of mud-brick glacis, that extended well up the south face of the mound. This massive operation, inside the earlier wall and evidently following on heavy erosion, was probably directed more against natural than against military enemies.

In III-A to the west, the outer face of the apparently Iron Age wall construction was exposed, and walking or working surfaces of brick were encountered in Areas 21 and 100 adjacent to it (see fig. 4 and Toombs 1989 [Chapter VII, below]: fig. 2). A line across the three zones of the wall in Areas 101, 103, and 106 yielded dimensions corresponding to those found in III-B. Excavation in Areas 106 and 107 continued the exposure up the slope, inside the line of the massive three-zone wall. The same evidence of pier-and-fill activity was evident as in III-B to the east (Rose and Toombs 1976: pl. 2:A, item G; Toombs 1989 [Chapter VII, below]: fig. 15).

The entire southern base of the acropolis, therefore, appears to have undergone revamping and extensive inward expansion in the Iron II Period for the purpose of consolidating the lower slope and, perhaps, of expanding the ancient settlement's usable space (see Worrell 1974: 140). An initial dating of this consolidation assigned it to the Persian Period. However, continued ceramic analysis and comparison with data from other sites, as well as continued excavation, determined that the earlier dating to the Iron II Period was the more accurate.

Field IV was a 2 m. x 2 m. probe in the depression to the west of the acropolis. It was a point suggested by geological and survey information as possibly preserving undisturbed occupational debris (see plan in Toombs 1989 [Chapter VII, below]: fig. 2). Modern deep plowing had disturbed the context, however, and destroyed all stratigraphy to a depth of at least 0.75 meters. Sherds from all major periods known at Hesi were mixed in the disturbed plow zone. Beneath this, two substantial phases of stratified material remained. Both were Early Bronze in date and produced structural fragments one meter or more in height. Beneath this level, to a depth of five more meters, although not yet to bedrock, no occupational materials were encountered. The probe showed that remains later than EB were unlikely to have survived subsequent plowing in this part of the site. Significant lateral exposure of EB levels could easily be achieved in the future by removal of the soil already disturbed by the plowing.

The survey project was initiated in 1973 to determine settlement patterns within the confines of the wadi system bracketing the acropolis and lower city (the tell terrace). The entire expanse, with the exception of the areas under excavation and the camp site, was plotted on a grid of 30 m. x 50 m. areas that was keyed to the overall contour map of the site. A standard method of collection was devised, and a record of probable date and possible usage was maintained for the samples collected in each area. In addition to determining the use patterns of the site for different periods, the survey provided some evidence for the ancient functional divisions of the site as well. Substantial EB remains were confirmed on the southern ridge at the opposite end of the lower city from the acropolis. In addition, many earlier, Upper Paleolithic objects and faunal remains were recovered in the vicinity of the site (Koucky 1989 [Chapter I, above]: 21, 32).

The third season had been the largest in terms of participants and integrated activities at Hesi. The size of the 1973 staff caused new logistical problems which forced the team to adapt its archaeological methods to the new situation. The experience over three seasons had led to a general movement from theoretical aims to organized practice. The interpretation of the upper five strata on the acropolis was becoming clearer and internally more consistent, and directions for future excavation were more easily set. The massive constructions on and around the acropolis in Fields I and III would need further investigation to determine their precise dates and purposes. The survey and the probe in Field IV would shape the approach to the EB lower city through further probes in 1975 and a major effort at lateral exposure in Phase Two.

The 1974 Interseason

The 1974 interseason was a time of evaluation, coordination, and reorganization. The principal goal was to process and assimilate the three-season accumulation of material so that Phase One could be concluded after one more season with as many complete units of information as possible. The staff hoped to demonstrate the values of the holistic approach by unifying the data as much as possible, thus lessening the fragmentation often caused by reporting each season as a distinct unit or by presenting data separated according to scientific disciplines. It was becoming apparent that Phase One official publications would run to several volumes. Preparation of the materials was needed so that one more field season would complete the necessary data for that phase of the excavations. At the same time, Phase One's completion was the logical preparation for Phase Two. The initial program called for Phase One to extend from 1969 to 1976, while Phase Two tentatively would cover 1976 to 1983. A grant from the National Endowment for the Humanities supported the year's efforts to process and prepare material culture and ceramics for eventual publication.

Various members of the field and specialist staffs continued their own research, which culminated in several preliminary reports, as well as some more specialized publications. Kevin O'Connell was appointed the managing editor of all publications at this time. Dorothea Brooks and Michael Hammond were involved in innovative analyses of ceramic and lithic materials, respectively. Their projects were processing important material for Hesi and became significant, interdisciplinary Ph.D. dissertations. Brooks's doctoral project derived from the neutron activation analysis program described above. Harbottle and Sayre at Brookhaven and Worrell at Hartford directed the dissertation. Its multidimensional nature is indicated in the title: *Persian Period Relationships of Tell el-Hesi as Indicated by Neutron Activation Analysis of Its Imported Ceramics: Implications for Archaeological and Biblical Research* (Brooks 1975). Hammond's project at Columbia University utilized a special analysis of lithics excavated from Field I. Sets of hypotheses were tested scientifically and weighted by the stratigraphic, historical, and other evidence of the material culture to elucidate behavior patterns that changed through time. Selection of materials, functional use, techniques of fabrication, and socioeconomic ramifications (both internal and external) were quantified and analyzed. Field and specialist personnel from Hesi, as well as scientists, anthropologists, and prehistorians from Columbia University, were called upon for guidance. The title of Hammond's thesis was *The Raw and the Chipped: An Analysis of Correlations Between Raw Material and Tools of a Lithic Industry from Tell el-Hesi, Israel* (Hammond 1977).

The 1974 Winslow Lectures at Seabury-Western Theological Seminary highlighted work at Tell el-Hesi. In keeping with the team model of organization, precedent was broken to make this a joint lectureship with Wright, Toombs, Stager, Peterson, and Worrell giving major presentations, while technical demonstrations were given by Richard Kuns ("Restoration of Archaeological Artifacts") and Richard Finman ("Ancient Methods of Pottery Making, Using the Potter's Wheel"). In these discussions emphasis was placed on dialogue with the various relevant scientific disciplines.

In other areas, Kuns and Worrell continued the conservation and restoration of artifactual materials during the year. Katharine Korrell and Richard Finman produced an audio-visual program on Hesi, which John Peterson made available to colleges and other institutions. The consortium Director, Charles Harris, more than doubled the consortium base of participating institutions, necessitating readjustment of the structure of administrative and directorial responsibilities. Following Worrell's decision for personal reasons not to go back into the field in 1975, D. Glenn Rose was named acting director and immediately devoted himself to the task of organizing and staffing the final season of Phase One. This transition was a time of crisis for the dig, since planning for the 1975 field season had already begun. Several additional staff meetings were held to assist Rose in assuming his new responsibilities for the approaching season. Toward this end the administrative director, Kevin G. O'Connell, undertook substantial, extra organizational responsibilities throughout 1974–75.

The 1975 Field Season

The fourth season of excavation was conducted from June 26 to August 15, 1975. The consortium of institutional supporters now had eight full members: Oberlin College, Seabury-Western Theological Seminary, College of the Holy Cross, Smith College, Wilfrid Laurier University, Lutheran Theological Seminary, The Protestant Episcopal Theological Seminary in Virginia, and the Consortium for Higher Education in Religious Studies (Ohio). The grant from the National Endowment for the Humanities was substantially depleted, so consortium fees and student volunteer payments provided most of the project's financial support. Staff efforts to draw on services and resources available from their own institutions added to the income of the expedition. Thirty-seven staff members, seventy student volunteers (plus two student geological assistants), and ten local workmen from within Israel and the West Bank comprised the total work force for the 1975 season under Rose's direction (see fig. 10).

Lawrence Toombs was retitled Archaeological Director in the new structure, and Kevin O'Connell continued as Administrative Director. Larry and Dorothy Ingalls again organized and managed the camp. H. Thomas Frank was joined by Jack B. Van Hooser in the direction of the Volunteer and Educational Program. Frank Koucky, Fouad Zoughbi, John Peterson, Melvin Lyons, Mary Bennett, Abu 'Issa, Carol Toombs, and Martha Smith continued to fill the positions assigned them in the preceding season. Scientists joining geologist Koucky included Susan Ford, physical anthropologist; Stuart Peters, lithicist and anthropologist; and Elizabeth Porter, ethnobotanist. James Whitred and Eugenia Nitowski were the photographers, and Carolyn Rose joined Martha Smith

in the ceramics registry.

Field work in 1975 was conducted in three sectors: Field I, Field III, and the Survey (see fig. 11). Field I was again overseen by W. J. Bennett, but it was divided into two subfields. The western sector, supervised by Karen Seger, included those areas (12, 22, 32; see fig. 4) having the most materials remaining from Strata IV and V. The eastern sector (Areas 1, 11, 21, 31, 41, 51, 51A; see fig. 4), supervised by John Matthers, had varied Stratum V materials to clear. Jeffrey Blakely, Lydia Newcombe, and Burton MacDonald returned as area supervisors, joined by J. Kenneth Eakins, R. Edward (Ted) Maitland, Valerie Fargo, and Cherie Howard Lenzen. The objective in Field I was to complete all remaining Persian Period excavation atop the acropolis.

The direction of Field III, as subdivided the preceding season, was continued under the supervision of Ralph Doermann (III-A) and Michael Coogan (III-B). S. Thomas Parker and Carol Redmount continued as area supervisors with Barbara Dart, Marjorie Ward Mahler, Dorothea Ditchfield Blow, Carol Schulte, and Eugene Roop (supervisor in training). The strategy in Field III-B was to cut two sections through the entire fortification complex from top to bottom, in order to ascertain the full range of structural sequencing and to determine dating, where possible. Areas worked this season included 1, 5A, 14, 18, and 23 (see fig. 4). The plan for III-A was to determine the degree to which sequencing to the west paralleled the apparent sequencing near the eastern corner. Additionally, Ralph Doermann was to locate, if possible, the corner where the wall system turned northward around the western base of the acropolis and examine the pier-and-fill feature in that western sector. Areas worked were 26, 31, 102, 103, 105, 107, 108, 109, and 110 (see fig. 4).

Utilizing the information gained in 1973 by the surface survey and the Field IV probe, the 1975 survey sought to determine the extent of stratified Early Bronze Age remains on the southern perimeter of the lower city. High concentrations of EB materials and geological evidence of minimal erosion loss indicated that significant Early Bronze Age stratification had probably survived undisturbed. Fields V and VI (See plans in Toombs 1989 [Chapter VII, below]: fig. 2) were opened as probes on the south-central and southeastern hills under John Peterson's direction, assisted by Lydia Newcombe. Frank Koucky and his assistants, David Budd and Karen Havholm, carried on surface

Fig. 10. Staff and volunteers for the 1975 season. Photo by E. Nitowski and J. Whitred.

Fig. 11. Tell el-Hesi under excavation in 1975 (view from SW over Field III toward the acropolis). Photo by E. Nitowski and J. Whitred.

collection of materials to identify sites farther away. They also probed for data bearing on the geological history and morphology of the site, as well as for evidence of prehistoric cultures and any information concerning the ancient environment (see Koucky 1989 [Chapter I, above: 21, 32] for the results of these investigations). A geological probe on the westernmost of the three southern hills disclosed stratified cultural evidence from the Early Bronze Age and was designated Field VII (Rose, Toombs, and O'Connell 1978: 142 and fig. 17:C; Toombs 1989 [Chapter VII, below]: 158). The anthropologists also visited more recent sites, especially Bedouin encampments, in search of comparative ethnographic data.

Field I had been brought uniformly into phase in early Hellenistic and Persian levels the preceding season. In 1975 the only new information for later strata to be derived atop the acropolis came from twenty additional burials encountered in the removal of the few remaining crossbalks. Notable

clarification of Stratum IV emerged, however, from the western line of squares. Use-surfaces and associated architectural features were discovered substantially intact. Later trenching and burials had destroyed all major connections in the Stratum IV remnants elsewhere. Surfaces were uncovered that were associated with the building discovered the previous season in Areas 22 and 32. It was confirmed to be a Stratum IVa structure; its removal exposed a IVb structure and associated features, including the drainage system partially excavated the previous season and several pits filled with kitchen debris and sealed by IVa materials. These discoveries provided the Expedition's most extensive exposure of domestic material from Hesi's Hellenistic levels thus far. Interpretation of the relationships among all three substrata (a–c) presented a picture of common orientation. The several building phases and the associated drain were consistently one above the other within each of the Areas 12, 22, and 32.

Further excavation in the same areas led to the conclusion that the three later Persian substrata (Va–Vc) should be taken together, because, architecturally, the building orientation established in Vc is simply continued in Vb and Va. The phases are differentiated by their associated surfaces. Some rather simple constructions of sun-dried mud bricks with associated cobble- or flag-stone surfaces were unearthed. An interpretation of these Persian Period walls is not yet possible, but they sit atop a more complex structure from Substratum Vd (Toombs 1989 [Chapter VII, below]: 140–44.

Stratum Vd had the fewest use-surfaces of the four Persian phases but provided the most substantial architectural remnants. The latter appear to correspond to Bliss's City VII (see Bliss 1894: 111; also Matthers 1989 [Chapter II, above]: 51–52, 60; cf. Rose, Toombs, and O'Connell 1978: 121; Toombs 1989 [Chapter VII, below]: 141). Architectural features in the southeastern section of the acropolis were linked when elements uncovered in Areas 22 and 32 could be connected to those previously excavated in 21 and 31. This established the construction and orientation of Subphase Vc structures and their subsequent modification and repair in Vb and Va. However, the Vd orientation was completely different. The primary alignment was east-west, rather than north-south as in the later phases. A major Vd structure discovered previously in Areas 31 and 41 was now understood to continue in 32, and all of it was cleared. Well-compacted surfaces and patches of plaster were associated with it (Toombs 1989 [Chapter VII, below]: 141 and fig. 12:A).

Features and strata earlier than Stratum V began to be exposed, including a thick ash layer at the southern extremity of the acropolis and evidence of successive earlier alterations of the mound, such as the preparations for Vd and probably Petrie's "long range of chambers" (see Rose, Toombs, and O'Connell 1978: 115–21). However, since the priorities of Phase One focused attention on Strata I–V, earlier materials were not explored in 1975. The section exposed in the wadi face (51A) confirmed clearly that the filled chambers were prior to Vd. It further demonstrated that the enigmatic pier-and-fill operation was earlier than the glacis with its overlying "Manasseh Wall" on the south slope (sectioned in 61A in 1973: see Toombs 1989 [Chapter VII, below]: 152–5 and figs. 20–21). This was, indeed, an appropriate juncture at which to conclude the first phase of the excavations. Certainly questions were raised from

which work could continue in Phase Two.

Down the slope from the acropolis, Area 5A excavators in Field III had exposed the construction zones and associated features of the massive lower fortifications during the first season, when the wadi face was closely studied and a clean section prepared (Worrell 1970b: 4). At that time the rounded, sloped, and plastered corner tower of Zone B was left exposed (Toombs 1989 [Chapter VII, below]: fig. 18). In this final season of Phase One, the section through the corner was completed and provided a consistent exposure through all three zones down to the founding stonework (see Toombs 1989 [Chapter VII, below]: fig. 17). During this season a second cut through Areas 1, 14, 18, and 23 (see fig. 4) sectioned the entire wall through the foundations and down to virgin soil—Petrie's "golden sands of Hesi" (see Toombs 1989 [Chapter VII, below]: fig. 16). Further information about the construction of the wall was obtained from these two cuts. The materials and techniques employed in constructing the wall were studied, and the sequencing of the wall's three phases was confirmed. The sections displayed concrete evidence that the entire enterprise—the three phases of Field III wall and the construction platforms up the slope—might date to the same period (Rose and Toombs 1976: 49–50, and see below). Excavations in Field III-A provided more information about the filling operation behind the wall system. The preceding season's excavations had strongly suggested a brick surface running up the slope, on top of the piers and fill (see Worrell 1975: 269; Amiran and Worrell 1976: 519). This capping was found preserved in Areas 31 and 107 (see fig. 4). The whole massive combination of piers, fill, and capping, together with the wall, appears to have been built for the purpose of erosion control. Remains of still earlier occupation were noted, as well as another wall line (see Toombs 1989 [Chapter VII, below]: 158, 160 note 16 and fig. 24), but their excavation was held for a later season when it was planned to explore the earlier strata. Excavation of Areas 108, 109, and 110 and information in hand from 102 and 105 (see fig. 4) raised in the minds of the excavators the possibility of a tower or corner in the wall, similar to the one exposed at the wadi. The 1975 season ended before the western extent of the wall could be located or the possible tower confirmed or delineated.

There are three hills or dunes that define the southern perimeter of the lower city (see plan in Toombs 1989 [Chapter VII, below]: fig. 2; cf. Koucky 1989 [Chapter I, above]: 28–9 and figs. 10–12). Field V was opened on the center hill of the three, where two large, worked stones were observed on the surface in the topsoil. A probe trench 7 m. x 2 m. was opened here, but the tones were found to lie in secondary locations. he primary objective was to determine the extent of remaining stratification with some possible lateral exposure of the EB strata to follow in Phase Two. A probe to a depth of 3.5 m. revealed six distinct stratigraphic phases. At least the lower four had architecture and associated surfaces (Toombs 1989 [Chapter VII, below]: 155–7 and fig. 22; cf. Rose, Toombs, and O'Connell 1978: fig. 16:2 for photo). The uppermost phase was again part of the Muslim cemetery. The second phase, though not well preserved, surprised excavators with a previously undemonstrated presence of Late Bronze Age activity in this part of the site; its nature was not determined. The lower four strata were all Early Bronze; preliminary pottery calls indicated that they were probably EB III in date. Virgin soil was not reached in the Field V probe in 1975. The field's promise for future excavation seemed very good.

Field VI added to the surprise and promise of Field V. It was opened on the southern slope of the easternmost hill of the south ridge, just behind the dig camp and near the *weli* of Sheikh el-ᶜUreibat. A thick band of ash was exposed there on the surface, and in each season newly eroded quantities of EB III pottery were exposed downslope. Only a few centimeters of overburden were removed before a massive mud-brick wall was encountered, deeply penetrated from above by several of the cemetery graves. The heavy ash was observed to be related to this major wall structure. Initial sedimentological and biotic analyses indicated an ecosystem dependent upon wetter and cooler conditions than at present (cf. Koucky 1989 [Chapter I, above]: 31). Beneath the nine courses extant in the wall, two and possibly three EB strata were found above virgin soil. Stratigraphic correlation with similar heavy ash in Field V suggested that the uppermost stratum remaining in Field VI and the lowest one probed in Field V constituted a single stratum in common between the two fields (see Toombs 1989 [Chapter VII, below]: 156–7 and fig. 23; an initial stratigraphic section plan for Field VI appears in Rose, Toombs, and O'Connell 1978: pl. 17A). Should that interpretation prove to be correct,

as many as seven EB strata may survive in the southern extent of the lower city. Thus a primary objective of the project—broad exposure of substantial Early Bronze stratification for purposes of a comprehensive analysis—had begun. This work would continue in the second phase of the archaeological investigations at Tell el-Hesi.

The 1976 Interseason

Staff members continued their preparation of publications after the end of the field season. Toombs and Coogan worked in Jerusalem through 1975–76, processing finds. They were succeeded by Doermann in 1976–77. A four-season preliminary report was prepared and published in the *Annual of the American Schools of Oriental Research* (Rose, Toombs, and O'Connell 1978). Additional preliminary reports on the 1975 season were prepared and submitted to *Israel Exploration Journal* (Rose and Toombs 1975), *Palestine Exploration Quarterly* (Rose and Toombs 1976), and *Revue Biblique* (Toombs and Rose 1976).

Strategies for future digging in Phase Two were developed in conjunction with specialists trained in paleoethnobotany, anthropology, and geology. Surface evidence and the data from the initial probes in Fields V and VI indicated that extensive EB remains probably lie beneath the surface. These excavations began in 1977.

APPENDIX TO CHAPTER VI

Staff Members of the Hesi Expedition (1970–1975)

Project Director
    John E. Worrell (1970–74; on leave 1974–75), Hartford Seminary Foundation; Holy Cross College
    D. Glenn Rose (*Acting Director*, 1974–75), Phillips University
Senior Archaeologist (title changed to *Archaeological Director* for 1974–75 season)
    Lawrence E. Toombs (1970–75), Wilfrid Laurier University
Administrative Directors
    Philip J. King (1970–73), St. John's Seminary; Boston College
    Kevin G. O'Connell, S.J. (1973–75), Weston School of Theology
Volunteer and Educational Program Directors
    Harry Thomas Frank (1970–75), Oberlin College

Louis Gough (*Assistant*, 1973), Ashland Theological Seminary

Jack B. van Hooser (*Associate Director*, 1975), Seabury-Western Theological Seminary

Camp Managers
Susan Simmons (1970–71)
Lawrence and Dorothy Ingalls (1973–75)

Consortium Director
Charles U. Harris (1971–75), Seabury-Western Theological Seminary

Overseers and Consultants
G. Ernest Wright (1970–74), Harvard University

Reuben Bullard (1970–73), University of Cincinnati

Edward F. Campbell, Jr. (1970–75), McCormick Theological Seminary

Michael Hammond (1973–75), Columbia University; Duke University

Garmon Harbottle (1971–75), Brookhaven National Laboratory

Philip J. King (1973–75), St. John's Seminary; Boston College

Frank Koucky (1973–75), College of Wooster

Edward Sayre (1971–75), Brookhaven National Laboratory

Jeffrey Schwartz (1970–75), Columbia University; University of Pittsburgh

Lawrence E. Stager (1973–75), The Oriental Institute, University of Chicago

Robert Stewart (1970–75), Sam Houston State University

John E. Worrell (1975), Holy Cross College

Medical Director
Melvin K. Lyons, M.D. (1970–75)

Camp Doctors
Melvin K. Lyons, M.D. (1971–73)
Alfred M. Donovan, M.D. (1971)

Camp Nurse
Dorothy Ingalls (1973–75)

Field Supervisors
Linda Ammons (1973), Harvard University

W. J. Bennett, Jr. (1970–75), University of Southern California

Michael D. Coogan (1973–75), St. Jerome's College; The Albright Institute of Archaeological Research

Ralph Doermann (1973–75), Lutheran Theological Seminary

John Matthers (1973–75), The Institute of Archaeology (London)

D. Glenn Rose (1973), Phillips University

Karen Seger (1975), Hebrew Union College

Lawrence E. Stager (1970–71), Harvard University; The Oriental Institute, University of Chicago

Survey Director
John L. Peterson (1973–75), Seabury-Western Theological Seminary

Surveyor
Bishara Zoughbi (1970–75), The Albright Institute of Archaeological Research

Architects
David Voelter (1970)
Bishara Zoughbi (1970–75), The Albright Institute of Archaeological Research

Photographers
Theodore Rosen (1970–71), Hebrew University

Wilhelm Nassau (1973–74), Wilfrid Laurier University

James Whitred (1975), Wilfrid Laurier University

Eugenia Nitowski (1975), Andrews University

Geologists
Abdulhossein (Alan) Baharlou (1970), Phillips University

Reuben Bullard (1971), University of Cincinnati

Frank Koucky (1973–75), College of Wooster

Botanists
William Robertson (1970), Sam Houston State University

Robert Stewart (1971–74), Sam Houston State University

Elizabeth Porter (1975), Texas A & M University

Cultural Anthropologists
Robert Rhoades (1970), Phillips University

Michael Hammond (1973–74), Columbia University

Stuart Peters (1975), State University of New York

Physical Anthropologists
Jeffrey Schwartz (1970–74), Columbia University; University of Pittsburgh

Janet Sawyer (1970), Harvard University

Lynn Fisher/Emmanuel (1971–73), New York City University

Susan Ford (1975), University of Pittsburgh

Ceramists
Joel Plum (1971)
Richard Finman (1973–74), Northwest Connecticut Community College

Neutron Activationist
Dorothea Brooks (1971–74), Brookhaven National Laboratory; Hartford Seminary Foundation

Artists
Anne Carter/Pritchard (1970), Wilfrid Laurier University

Judy Hammond (1971–73), Columbia University

Dorothy Ingalls (1975)

Peter Jenkins (1971), Wilfrid Laurier University

Patricia Koeber (1970), Wilfrid Laurier University

Katharine Korrell (1974), Northwest Connecticut Community College

Tom Stone (1970), Wilfrid Laurier University

Shelly Wilcox (1971), University of Southern California

Coders (1971)

Erika von Conta, Patricia Koeber, Patricia MacLaughlin, and Joel Nordenstrom, all of Wilfrid Laurier University

Registrars

Mary Bennett (1971–75)

Anne Carter/Pritchard (1971–73), Wilfrid Laurier University

Carolyn Rose (1975)

Mary Schmieder (1970), Wilfrid Laurier University

Martha Smith (1973–75), Seabury-Western Theological Seminary

Muff Thomsen (1970)

F. Carolyn Toombs (1973–75), Wilfrid Laurier University

Area Supervisors

Linda Ammons (1970–71), Harvard University

W. Boyce Bennett (1973), General Theological Seminary

Jeffrey Blakely (two weeks in 1973, 1975), Oberlin College; University of Wisconsin

Dorothea Ditchfield Blow (4 weeks in 1975), Wilfrid Laurier University

Dorothea Brooks (1970), Hartford Seminary Foundation

Kevin Clark (1973), Claremont Graduate School

Michael D. Coogan (1970–71), St. Jerome's College; The Albright Institute of Archaeological Research

Barbara Dart (1975), Wilfrid Laurier University

Ralph Doermann (1970–71), Lutheran Theological Seminary

J. Kenneth Eakins (1975), Golden Gate Baptist Theological Seminary

Carol Epley (1971, four weeks in 1973), Phillips University

Valery Fargo (1975), The Oriental Institute, University of Chicago

David Freedman (1970), Occidental College

Larry Herr (1973), Harvard University

Peter Jenkins (1973), Wilfrid Laurier University

Richard Kuns (1970–73), Hartford Seminary Foundation

Egon Lass (four weeks in 1970)

Hank Lay (1973), Claremont Graduate School

Yechiel Lehavy (1971), University of Pennsylvania

Cherie Howard Lenzen (1975), Johns Hopkins University

Lucia Lerner (1971)

Maurice Luker (1973), Emory and Henry College

Burton MacDonald (1971, 1975), St. Francis Xavier University

Marjorie Ward Mahler (1975), Oberlin College; Duke University

R. Edward Maitland (1975), Oberlin College

Ellen Messer (1970), University of Michigan

Lydia Newcombe (1973–75), Wilfrid Laurier University

Mark Papworth (two weeks in 1970), Oberlin College

S. Thomas Parker (1973–75), University of California in Los Angeles

Cymbrie Pratt (1970), Wayne State University

Carol A. Redmount (1973-75), Oberlin College; Harvard Divinity School

Robert Rhoades (four weeks in 1970), Phillips University

D. Glenn Rose (1970–71), Phillips University

Diane Saltz (1971–73), Harvard University

Carol Schulte (two weeks in 1975), Brandeis University

Peter Schweitzer (1973), Oberlin College

Supervisor-in-Training

Eugene Roop (1975), Earlham School of Religion

Volunteers

Volunteers over the 1970-75 seasons ranged in number from forty-eight to eighty-two, many of them students from consortium schools as well as many from other institutions. A complete list of volunteers is given in Chapter V, above, pp. 93–95.

Other Personnel

"Technical men" each season were Nasser Diab Mansur (Abu ᶜIssa) and Jabber Muhammad Hasan (Abu ᶜAbid) from the village of Balatah, assisted as necessary by other technical men and workmen from Balatah and Taᶜanach.

Important support services were provided each year by Doris and Farid Salman of the Jordan House Hotel in Jerusalem, and by Samir Khayo of Jerusalem in 1973 and 1975.

In 1970 the expedition lived in the city of Kiryat Gat (10 km. distant); thereafter, in a tent camp on the site. The cooks for 1973 and 1975, Muhammad Ali Sourki (Abu 'l ᶜEz) and Harbi Marzouk Tanbour (Abu Najjar), were particularly important to the success of the expedition in those two seasons.

NOTES

1. For more detailed and technical information regarding the archaeological results of Phase One, see Rose and Toombs 1976; Rose, Toombs, and O'Connell 1978; Toombs 1974; 1985; 1989 (Chapter VII, below). For capsule notes on each season, see Worrell 1970b; Toombs 1971a; Worrell and Toombs 1971; Worrell 1974; Rose and Toombs 1975. Principal staff responsibilities and staff changes are described below for each season. For the complete cumulative staff roster for Phase One see the appendix to this chapter; for the volunteer roster, see Frank and Horton 1989 (Chapter V, above: 93–95).
2. Lawrence E. Stager in a personal communication indicated that only these two sites were proposed to him and Worrell by Wright.
3. The familiar form of a first name is cited herein only where the individual so designated habitually used it, and the expedition's occasionally informal administrative lists did not record—and the authors could not recover—the formal name. —Editor
4. Private communication from Lawrence E. Stager; see further Stewart 1978 (Chapter XI, below).

BIBLIOGRAPHY FOR CHAPTER VI

Amiran, R., and Worrell, J. E.
1976   Hesi, Tel. *Encyclopedia of Archaeological Excavations in the Holy Land.* Vol. 2: 514–20. Jerusalem: Israel Exploration Society; London: Oxford University Press; Englewood Cliffs, NJ: Prentice Hall.

Bennett, M., and Bennett, W. J., Jr.
1976   The Material Culture Registry at Tell el-Hesi. *Journal of Field Archaeology* 3: 97–101.

Bennett, W. J., Jr.
1974   The Field Recording of Ceramic Data. *Journal of Field Archaeology* 1: 209–14.

Bieber, A. M., Jr.; Brooks, D. W.; Harbottle, G.; and Sayre, E. V.
1976   Compositional Groupings of Some Ancient Aegean and Eastern Mediterranean Pottery. In *Applicazione dei metodi nucleari nel campo delle opere d'arte—Congresso internazionale, Roma—Venezia 24–29 Maggio 1973*, pp. 111–43. Roma: Accademia Nazionale dei Lincei.

Blakely, J. A., and Toombs, L. E.
1980   *The Tell el-Hesi Field Manual.* Edited by K. G. O'Connell, S.J. Excavation Reports of the American Schools of Oriental Research: Tell el-Hesi 1. Cambridge, MA; 2nd printing (1983), Philadelphia, PA: American Schools of Oriental Research.

Bliss, F. J.
1894   *A Mound of Many Cities or Tell el Hesy Excavated.* London: Palestine Explora-tion Fund; New York: Macmillan.

Brooks, D. W.
1975   *Persian Period Relationships of Tell el-Hesi as Indicated by Neutron Activation Analysis of Its Imported Ceramics: Implications for Archaeological and Biblical Research.* Hartford, CT: The Hartford Seminary Foundation. Unpublished Ph.D. dissertation.

Brooks, D. W.; Bieber, A. M., Jr.; Harbottle, G.; and Sayre, E. V.
1974   Biblical Studies through Neutron Activation Analysis of Ancient Pottery. In *Archaeological Chemistry*, pp. 48–80. Edited by C. W. Beck. Advances in Chemistry 138. Washington: American Chemical Society.

Coogan, M. D.
1975   A Cemetery from the Persian Period at Tell el-Hesi. *Bulletin of the American Schools of Oriental Research* 220: 37–46. Reprinted in the present volume as Chapter X, below.

1989a   Field II. In *Tell el-Hesi: The Site and the Expedition*, pp. 163–8. Edited by B. T. Dahlberg and K. G. O'Connell, S.J. Excavation Reports of the American Schools of Oriental Research: Tell el-Hesi 4. Winona Lake, IN: Eisenbrauns.

1989b   Chalcolithic Remains in Field III. In *Tell el-Hesi: The Site and the Expedition*, pp. 169–76. Edited by B. T. Dahlberg and K. G. O'Connell, S.J. Excavation Reports of the American Schools of Oriental Research: Tell el-Hesi 4. Winona Lake, IN: Eisenbrauns.

Frank, H. T., and Horton, F. L., Jr.
1989   The Volunteer and Educational Program: 1970–1975. In *Tell el-Hesi: The Site and the Expedition*, pp. 88–96. Edited by B. T. Dahlberg and K. G. O'Connell, S.J. Excavation Reports of the American Schools of Oriental Research: Tell el-Hesi 4. Winona Lake, IN: Eisenbrauns.

Hammond, W. M.
1977   *The Raw and the Chipped: An Analysis of Correlations Between Raw Material and Tools of a Lithic Industry from Tell el-Hesi, Israel.* New York: Columbia University. Unpublished Ph.D. dissertation.

King, P. J.
1975   The American Archaeological Heritage in the Near East. *Bulletin of the American Schools of Oriental Research* 217: 55–65.

1983   *American Archaeology in the Mideast: A History of the American Schools of Oriental Research*. Philadelphia: The American Schools of Oriental Research.

Koucky, F. L.
1989   The Present and Past Physical Environment of Tell el-Hesi, Israel. In *Tell el-Hesi: The Site and the Expedition*, pp. 5–36. Edited by B. T. Dahlberg and K. G. O'Connell, S.J. Excavation Reports of the American Schools of Oriental Research: Tell el-Hesi 4. Winona Lake, IN: Eisenbrauns.

Matthers, J. M.
1989   Excavations by the Palestine Exploration Fund at Tell el-Hesi 1890–1892. In *Tell el-Hesi: The Site and the Excavations*, pp. 37–67. Edited by B. T. Dahlberg and K. G. O'Connell, S.J. Excavation Reports of the American Schools of Oriental Research: Tell el-Hesi 4. Winona Lake, IN: Eisenbrauns.

Petrie, W. M. F.
1891   *Tell el-Hesy (Lachish)*. London: Palestine Exploration Fund.

Rose, D. G., and Toombs, L. E.
1975   Tell el-Hesi, 1975. *Israel Exploration Journal* 25: 172–74.

1976   Tell el-Hesi, 1973 and 1975. *Palestine Exploration Quarterly*. 108: 41–54.

Rose, D. G.; Toombs, L. E.; and O'Connell, K. G., S. J.
1978   Four Seasons of Excavation at Tell el-Hesi: A Preliminary Report. In *Preliminary Excavation Reports: Bâb edh-Dhrâᶜ, Sardis, Meiron, Tell el-Hesi, Carthage (Punic)*, pp. 109–49. Edited by D. N. Freedman. Annual of the American Schools of Oriental Research 43. Cambridge, MA: American Schools of Oriental Research.

Sayre, E. V.
1972   Activation Analysis Applications in Art and Archaeology. In *Advances in Activation Analysis*, Vol. 2, pp. 155–84. Edited by J. M. A. Lenihan, S. J. Thomson, and V. R. Guinn. New York: Academic Press.

Stewart, R. B.
1978   Archeobotanic Studies at Tell el-Hesi. *Economic Botany* 32: 379–86. Reprinted in the present volume as Chapter 11.

Stewart, R. B., and Robertson, W., IV
1973   Applications of the Flotation Technique in Arid Areas. *Economic Botany* 27:114–16.

Struever, S.
1968   Flotation Techniques for the Recovery of Small Scale Archeological Remains. *American Antiquity* 33: 353–62.

Toombs, L. E.
1971a   Tell el-Hesi. *Israel Exploration Journal* 21:177–78.

1971b   Coding Pottery in the Field. Appendix to *Coding & Clustering Pottery by Computer* by N. E. Wagner, pp. 25–28. Waterloo, Ontario: Waterloo Lutheran (now Wilfrid Laurier) University.

1974   Tell el-Hesi, 1970–71. *Palestine Exploration Quarterly* 106: 19–31.

1985   *Tell el-Hesi: Modern Military Trenching and Muslim Cemetery in Field I, Strata I–II*. Edited by K. G. O'Connell, S. J. Excavation Reports of the American Schools of Oriental Research: Tell el-Hesi 2. Waterloo, Ontario: Wilfrid Laurier University Press.

1987   The Stratigraphy of the Site at the End of Phase One. In *Tell el-Hesi: The Site and the Expedition*, pp. 125–62. Edited by B. T. Dahlberg and K. G. O'Connell, S.J. Excavation Reports of the American Schools of Oriental Research: Tell el-Hesi 4. Winona Lake, IN: Eisenbrauns.

Toombs, L. E., and Rose, D. G.
1976   Tell el-Hesi. *Revue Biblique* 83: 257–60.

Wagner, N. E.
1971   *Coding & Clustering Pottery by Computer*. With an Appendix, "Coding Pottery in the Field," by L. E. Toombs, on pp. 25–28. Waterloo, Ontario Lutheran (now Wilfrid Laurier) University.

Worrell, J. E.
1970a   The Expedition to Tell el-Hesi: A New Joint Project. *Newsletter No. 8* (April 1970) of the American Schools of Oriental Research: 1–4.

1970b   Tell el-Hesi: Mound of Many Surprises. *Newsletter No. 5* (December 1970) of the American Schools of Oriental Research: 1–4.

1974   Tell el-Hesi. *Israel Exploration Journal* 24: 139–41.

1975   Tell el-Hesi. *Revue Biblique* 82: 268–70.

Worrell, J. E., and Toombs, L. E.

1971   Tell el-Hesi. *Israel Exploration Journal* 21: 232–33.

Chapter VII

THE STRATIGRAPHY OF THE SITE

by
Lawrence E. Toombs
Wilfrid Laurier University

INTRODUCTION

The purpose of this chapter is to provide an overview of the stratigraphy and architecture associated with the archaeological periods represented at Tell el-Hesi (fig. 1), insofar as they have been investigated by the Joint Expedition during Phase 1 of its operations, that is, during the seasons of 1970, 1971, 1973, and 1975. It is designed as a general introduction and background essay to the more detailed and technical volumes in the series.

The text of the chapter reflects the state of knowledge at the end of Phase 1. Considerable new information bearing on the stratigraphy of the site has been obtained in excavation subsequent to 1975 (1977, 1979, 1981, and 1983), and research undertaken for the publication of the Arabic, Hellenistic, and Persian strata has led to refinements in the stratigraphy. These alterations are, in the main, matters of detail rather than substance. Revisions in the stratigraphy made since 1975 are indicated in the notes.

The perennial fascination of excavation is the manner in which, as solutions emerge and some problems are laid to rest, other unsolved problems crowd in to take their place. This summary of the stratigraphy of Tell el-Hesi after four seasons of excavation, therefore, has a Janus-like quality. It is a backward look at the results obtained during Phase 1 of the Joint Expedition. This view shows five strata on the acropolis fully excavated and ready for publication, and the investigation of the construction and lateral extent of the wall system at the base of the southern slope completed.

It is also a forward look toward the second phase (1977, 1979, 1981, and 1983), during which the Early Bronze Age remains in the lower city were examined and Fields I and III were connected by means of a stratigraphic trench on the south slope of the mound (fig. 2).[1]

For the purposes of a summary of this kind, simple block plans of the various strata and phases (figs. 9, 12, 13, and 19) suffice as illustrations. Detailed architectural drawings and the major sections, which provide the supporting evidence for assigning structures and artifacts to the appropriate stratum and phase, will be published in the volumes devoted to the separate strata.

SPECIAL PROBLEMS OF EXCAVATION

Before a summary of the stratigraphy of the site is presented, some comment should be made on the special problems of excavation encountered at Tell el-Hesi and the methods adopted for dealing with them.

Intrusive Features

A persistent set of problems arose from the unusual number of intrusive features encountered in all areas excavated on the acropolis. "Intrusion" in this context refers to any feature whose construction involved excavation into and, consequently, partial destruction of earlier remains. The sequence of strata encountered in Field I included intrusive features of three main types. The first was the military trenching of Stratum I, which

125

Period	Date	Characteristics	Stratum or Phase
Chalcolithic	Ca. 3200 BCE	Circular structure in Field III, Area 5. Two pits in Field III, Area 3	
EB I and II		No clear evidence	
EB III	27th–24th cent. BCE	Fields II, IV, V, VI and VII. Several occupational phases. Fortification wall in Fields V and VI. Abandonment during EB III	
EB IV and MB		A few sherds in fills	
LB I		No clear evidence	
LB II		Ceramics abundant in fills	
Iron I		No Philistine pottery in fills. Other Iron I forms present, especially 12th cent. BCE	
Iron IIA		Ceramics abundant in fills	
Iron IIB		Ceramics in fills	
Iron IIC	9th–7th cent. BCE	Large structure with narrow chambers, founded 9th cent. BCE? "Manasseh Wall," glacis and Field III wall	Pre-Stratum V, Phase 4 (now Stratum VIId)
	8th–7th cent. BCE	Brick-built house with pit in Field I, Areas 41 and 51. Wall system continues?	Pre-Stratum V, Phase 3 (now Stratum VIIb)
	7th–6th cent. BCE	House with long rooms in Field I, Areas 41 and 51. Wall system continues?	Pre-Stratum V, Phase 2 (now Stratum VIIa)
		ASH LAYER	
	6th cent. BCE	Building on bricky platform in Field I, Areas 41 and 51	Pre-Stratum V, Phase 1 (now Stratum VI)
Persian	540–332 BCE	Casematelike building in SE quadrant of Field I. Open-air surfaces and fragmentary walls to the north	Stratum Vd
		Building in S of Field I. Fragmentary walls elsewhere. Agricultural residues and outside surfaces	Stratum Vc
		Extension and elaboration of Stratum Vc with widespread use of cobbled surfaces	Stratum Vb
		Building plan of Stratum Vb retained. Many brick-lined grain storage pits	Stratum Va
Hellenistic	332–37 BCE	Brick building on partial stone foundation. Stone-built drain. Field I only	Stratum IVc
		Stone building. Drain filled and out of use. Probably some pit digging. Field I only	Stratum IVb
		Cultural decline with much pit digging and few recoverable structures. Field I only	Stratum IVa
Late Arabic	?	Pits, hearths, packed-earth surfaces, and fragmentary walls, probably associated with agriculture	Stratum III
Late Arabic	Ca. 1500–1800 CE	Muslim cemetery in Fields I, V, and VI. Burials of both children and adults in a prepared cemetery area	Stratum II
Modern	1948 and after	Israeli military trenching, originating in 1948	Stratum I

Fig. 1. Stratigraphic summary.

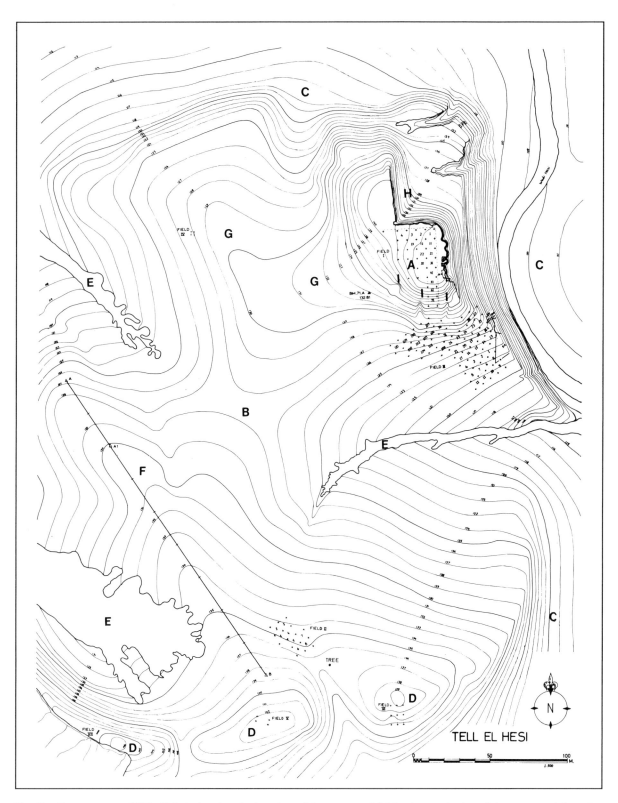

Fig. 2. Contour map of Tell el-Hesi, showing the location of the excavated fields, the numbering of the areas, and the principal physical features of the site: A—the acropolis, B—the central depression, C—the Wadi Hesi, D—the southern dunes, E—internal ravines, F—the southwestern ridge, G—the northern ridge, H—Bliss's cut, I—the southern and eastern slopes of the acropolis. Map by B. Zoughby.

zig-zagged across all but two of the excavated areas and penetrated from the surface into Stratum IV and, occasionally, Stratum V. The second type of intrusion was the graves of the Muslim cemetery (Stratum II), which almost obliterated Stratum III and did severe damage to Stratum IV and sometimes to the upper levels of Stratum V. The third involved the presence of over forty pits dug during Strata III, IV, and V. These pits cut through and penetrated below Stratum V levels.

Fig. 3 (pocket insert) illustrates the extent of the three types of intrusion, and the havoc which they produced in the earlier stratigraphy. The drawing is a simplification of part of the main west balk of Field I, Areas 1–51, shown in fig. 5. For the present purpose it is unnecessary to give the detailed stratigraphy and locus identifications. These may be recovered by consulting fig. 5. In Areas 11 and 21, shown in fig. 3, two segments of military trenching (Stratum I) pass through the balk. They cut through Hellenistic pits (Stratum IV) and Muslim graves (Stratum II). The section shows thirteen Stratum II graves. Some of these intersect Hellenistic pits, others cut into earlier graves, and still others disturb the top of the Persian stratigraphy (Stratum V). In the center of the section is a large conglomerate of intersecting Hellenistic pits. On the left is a single large pit of the same period. On the extreme right is a brick-lined pit constructed in the Persian Period (Stratum V) and reused in the Hellenistic (Stratum IV). The pits cut all levels as yet excavated. The parts of the section marked with question marks are deposits of loess accumulated after the Hellenistic period. These pockets may contain some Stratum III material.

The simplified section (fig. 3) shows at a glance the disruption of *in situ* stratigraphy caused by the intrusive features. One has only to remove in imagination the colored portions of the section to realize how distressingly little survives of the upper levels of the acropolis. Stratum III has, to all intents and purposes, been destroyed in the area represented by the section; the only possible survivals are incorporated in the scattered loess pockets. One orphaned fragment of *in situ* Stratum IV material appears to survive near the left of the section, but this may be illusory, since the layers in question show no evidence of construction and may be part of a pit. Three extensive patches of Stratum V (Persian Period) appear on the section, isolated from one another by Stratum IV pits.

In its first season the Joint Expedition decided to

treat the intrusive features with full archaeological seriousness. This decision obviously complicated and slowed down the excavation process and made heavy demands on the ingenuity and powers of observation of the supervisory staff. However, the wealth of anthropological and biological data recovered fully justified the investment of time and effort.

Balks

The extensive intrusions made it virtually impossible to clear any phase or stratum as a coherent unit. The phasing of walls, surfaces, and debris layers had to be carried out by tracing the soil layers around the intrusions, often on narrow catwalks of earth, and by establishing their connections in the balks. By this procedure a composite picture of each stratum was assembled on plan, and the structures, artifacts, and pottery were assigned to their proper contexts. This exacting process is clearly possible only when careful digging techniques are combined with an elaborate and controlled recording system (see Blakely and Toombs 1980: 87–109).

The balks, the crucial elements in the interpretive process, were cut with the greatest care. Prompt tagging of the levels as they were exposed proved to be essential, since even brief exposure rendered soil layers, originally clearly visible, virtually impossible to detect. An approximation to the original condition of the balks could sometimes by obtained by spraying them gently with water, but, when a balk was to be reexamined or drawn, it usually had to be scraped back about 0.5 cm. Since the balk profiles are the only means by which stratigraphic conclusions can be demonstrated in publication, they were recorded both by drawing and by photography.

The difficulties created by the intrusions necessitated repeated reexamination and reinterpretation of the balk sections as new pieces of evidence were recovered in the excavation. Daily study sessions and many evening post-mortems, involving the supervisory staff from project director to area supervisor, were devoted to the study of the balks in each area. The interpretations offered in this chapter are, therefore, consensus decisions, often arrived at after extended debate, and not the conclusions of a single observer.

Military Trenching

The military trenches of Stratum I were usually

visible as depressions on the surface of the mound, although in a few cases the trench was completely filled. The first task of the excavators was to establish the width, depth, and construction features of the trench, area by area. This was done by cutting two narrow probes across each segment of the trench which occurred in a given area. Where possible the probes were placed at the points where the trench intersected the balks of the area.

In the excavation of the probes special attention was given to determining the location, composition, and slope of the sides of the trench, and to ascertaining whether external features, such as parapets or earth throw-out, were associated with the trench. Excavation of the trench fill concentrated on unraveling the history of the trench during and after its period of use. The fill layers were isolated, and their origin and method of deposition (whether naturally by the action of wind and water or as part of a deliberate filling process) were investigated. Excavation of the lowest levels of the trench fill was done with special care in an effort to isolate the layers deposited during the use-period of the trench. These layers contained surviving traces of roofing and siding and the remains of the floor, or sequence of floors, of the trench.

On both sides and at the bottom the probes were overcut; that is, they were excavated about 0.05– 0.10 m. beyond the boundaries of the trench into the earlier remains through which the trench had been cut. Overcutting proved to be a useful technique in the excavation of graves and pits as well as military trenches. It insured that the limits of the feature had in fact been reached, it allowed a full examination of the sequence of sidings and floorings in the trench, and it provided a probe into the earlier remains, which frequently turned out to be a valuable guide to subsequent excavation into those levels.

When the probes had been excavated in the manner just described, the lateral extent of the trench was cleared stratigraphically, according to the layers revealed by the probes. The intersection of the military trench with the balk was tagged as soon as its position had been accurately determined, since experience showed that brief exposure made the outline of the trench on the balk almost indistinguishable from the surrounding earth.

As each segment of the trench was excavated, it was accurately drawn on plan. Assembly of these drawings gave a complete picture of the system within the excavated areas and became the basis for interpretation of the history of the system and the tactical concepts which it represented.

Graves

During the first season of excavation the decision was taken to excavate and examine every grave as an archaeological unit. This decision created three kinds of problems. The first involved the excavation of the graves themselves; the second, the recording of the grave and skeletal data; and the third, the treatment of the skeletal remains after removal.

Grave Excavation. Since numerous burials had to be cleared before excavation could proceed to a lower level, the interments had to be excavated with the maximum speed consistent with full recovery of the grave and skeletal data. It soon became clear that excavation of the burials by the team regularly assigned to an area slowed down the process unduly and did not always retrieve all the data available. These problems were met by the training of a special burial-excavation team during the first days of each field season. The osteologist and his assistant selected certain volunteers who had expressed special interest in osteological work and coached them in the proper method of clearing a skeleton and preparing it for in-field examination and photography.

Because the grave shafts were of the same soil color and texture as the surrounding loess, they were rarely detected, and the first indication of a burial was usually the stone cappers of the grave or the bones themselves. At this point the specially trained team was called in and assumed responsibility for the clearing, recording, and removal of the skeletal remains.

When the skeleton had been lifted, the earth remaining in the grave was removed. The grave was then overcut by 0.05–0.10 m. and was used as a probe trench into the earlier remains through which the grave had been cut.

Field Recording. The experience of the first season indicated that, with the best of intentions, different excavators made and recorded differing sets of observations. It was obvious that, in order to preserve the maximum amount of data in a consistent form, a standard set of observations was required for each burial. The system which was eventually developed involved ten observations on the grave and ten on the skeletal remains. The required grave observations were (1) location on the site, (2) number of burials in the grave, (3) vertical relationship to other graves, (4) shape of cist, (5) length of cist, (6) width of cist, (7) depth of cist, (8) type of covering, (9) type of lining, and (10) degree to which the grave was contained in the excavated area. The ten required observations on the skeletal remains were (1) location on the site, (2) sex, (3) age, (4) degree of articulation of the skeleton, (5) position of the arms, (6) position of the legs, (7) direction of the eyes, (8) posture of the body, (9) location in the area, and (10) orientation of the skeleton. These observations were given numerical designations and encoded on a simple form that had a series of boxes into which the appropriate numbers could be entered. This system of recording is more fully described in Blakely and Toombs 1980: 55–59. Its use in the field permitted observations to be recorded rapidly.

In addition to the standard coded observations, the area supervisor kept a separate locus sheet for each burial, on which were listed any distinctive features of the grave or skeleton not included among the standard observations. The locus sheet also recorded the material culture items, including ceramics and artifacts, found in association with the burial.

Treatment of the Skeleton after Removal. The standard coded observations were made during the excavation of the burial. From the field the bones were taken to the field laboratory, where they were cleaned, assembled, and studied by the osteologist. This aspect of the study of the skeletal remains is described in Eakins 1980: 89–93. The additional observations made in the field laboratory were entered in the osteologist's notebook, which was available to the area supervisors, in case they wished to enter any of the osteologist's observations on the locus sheet.

Pits

By far the most destructive form of intrusion was the ubiquitous pits, dug mainly from Hellenistic and Persian levels (Strata IV and V). However, these pits were a highly valuable source for the study of the crops grown, the wild plants used, and the animals raised or hunted for food, as well as for details of the agricultural and storage practices of the Persian and Hellenistic farmers of the inner Philistine Plain (see Stewart 1978 [Chapter XI, below, pp. 188–94]).

The method eventually adopted for the excavation of these pits was evolved during the 1970 and 1971 seasons and was refined in detail during subsequent years.

The existence of a pit could usually be detected soon after its top was reached by the fact that its fill was coarser, darker, and less compact than the surrounding earth. The top of the pit and the area surrounding it were leveled, troweled, and swept, and the limits of the pit on the surface were carefully delineated. When the size of the pit permitted, the pit fill was divided into halves along a convenient diameter. One half of the fill was removed fairly rapidly to the pit bottom, with observations being made on the stratification of the fill and on the nature of the lining and bottom of the pit. The contents of the pit were wet-sieved by layers as accurately as the initial excavation permitted. The presumed bottom of the pit was cut through in order to determine whether the actual bottom of the pit had, in fact, been reached.

The vertical face of the unexcavated fill was then trimmed and treated as a balk. The study of this face yielded information as to the nature of the pit bottom, whether the pit contained a residue left from the period of its use, and whether it had been filled in one operation or had filled up in stages by natural or artificial processes.

The second half of the pit was then excavated according to the stratigraphy revealed by the section. Each significant layer was wet-sieved as a separate unit, and the ceramic, artifactual, and material culture items from each layer were recorded separately.

Attention was then directed to the lining of the pit. This was removed in one half of the pit only, and the composition and construction of the lining was studied before the second half was removed. The pit was then squared off, and the sides of the rectangular hole were trimmed to serve as a probe trench into the earlier remains.

In the case of smaller pits it was necessary to remove most of the fill in the first operation, but a sector of the fill was always left to provide a stratigraphic profile of the contents of the pit.

Ideally, the pit section should have been drawn in every case. In practice this was done only in the case of the more elaborate pits.

Mud-Brick Construction

An ever-present problem was the use of unfired mud brick even in major construction. The brickwork differs only slightly in color and consistency from the debris in which it is embedded, and stone foundations are rarely present to aid in the establishment of wall lines.

Experience showed that, where the existence of brickwork was suspected, the best procedure was to level, trowel, and sweep the top and immediate surroundings of the presumed brickwork. This process usually allowed the excavators to distinguish between the coarser debris, which normally contained randomly distributed ingredients such as sherds, brick fragments, and pieces of plaster, from the more compact and relatively artifact-free brickwork. A probe trench was then sunk into the debris at right angles to the presumed face of the bricks and carried down until a surface was reached. The surface could then be traced to the wall or walls which constituted its limits.

Exposure for a day or two would frequently confirm or deny the existence of brick construction. The action of sun and wind, combined with frequent sweeping, removes some of the mortar and leaves the outlines of individual bricks more clearly visible.

LEVELS COMPLETELY EXCAVATED

In the interest of clarity of presentation, the stratigraphic data will be presented under three headings: levels completely excavated during Phase 1, levels partially excavated, and levels indicated but not excavated. Remains belonging to the first category are found on the acropolis (Field I). These have been analyzed into five strata that range in date from the Persian to the modern period (see fig. 1). Each stratum will be described briefly.

In addition to the stratified remains on the acropolis, a small Chalcolithic structure, uncovered in Field III, was completely excavated prior to the 1975 season.

Stratum I—Modern Military Trenching

Some part of the trench system (fig. 4) appeared in every excavated area except Areas 1 and 32. A series of ovoid or roughly circular depressions indicated the location of the main firing points. Two of these were found near the eastern edge of the mound overlooking the Wadi Hesi. A third was dug near the center of the south side of Bliss's excavation. Three more were located along the western side of the mound. A larger depression, part-way down the western slope in the unexcavated Area 23, probably marked the position of the command post. The firing points were con-

nected with one another and with the command post by zig-zag trenches, 0.90–1.50 m. wide at the top. This trench system was widened at intervals to provide auxiliary firing positions. A single roughly circular pit, belonging to Stratum I, was found on the southeastern dune in Field VI. This was either an isolated observation post designed to give a field of view over the dead ground south of the dunes or part of a chain of firing points, the remainder of which have not been isolated. The whole forms a coherent system, sited so as to deal with an attack from any direction.

The flooring of the trenches consisted of a buildup of two to four hard-packed earth surfaces, separated by layers of water-laid soil. In several places there was evidence of the use of slatted duckboards over the floors and of wooden supports for the walls. The trenches contained the debris of their use: iron nails, tin cans, cellophane bags, and spent cartridge cases.

According to local report, trenches were dug on the mound by the Turkish army just before and during World War I. The unified defense system described above belongs to the War of Independence (1948), during which heavy fighting took place between Israeli and Egyptian forces in the Hesi area. The trench system may have remained in use for some time after 1948, but primarily as a troop training area. Located as they are at a considerable distance from the frontier, the trenches ceased to have strategic value after the close of hostilities.[2]

Stratum II—The Muslim Cemetery

The Muslim cemetery has considerable anthropological significance. It is the largest single collection of Muslim graves yet excavated, a sample sufficiently large to allow statistical analysis of the demographic characteristics and burial practices of the population, probably semi-nomadic, which used the cemetery.

Muslim burials are found in profusion in all areas excavated in Field I. F. J. Bliss reported "many graves made in the rubbish of the last constructions" in the large area which he removed from the northeast quadrant of the mound (Bliss 1891: 284). The cemetery, therefore, covered almost the whole acropolis, at least on its eastern side. The burials are not confined to the summit of the mound, but occur with great frequency on the tops of the southern dunes in Fields V and VI. A group of graves at the foot of the southern slope of the

Fig. 4. Military trenching (Stratum I) in Field I at the beginning of excavation. Photo by T. Rosen.

mound constitutes a small Persian Period cemetery, belonging to Stratum V (Coogan 1975: 37–46 [Chapter X, below, pp. 177–87]). In Field VI, just east of a large tamarisk, the only tree on the site, stands the ruin of a small *weli*, the tomb of a minor Muslim saint. *The Survey of Palestine* (1947) map (1:20,000, Sheet 12/10—Jammama) identifies it as Qabr el-'Ureibat. The date of the holy man has not been established at the time of writing, nor is it clear whether his *weli* attracted the Muslim cemetery to the vicinity or whether the shrine was erected after the cemetery was already in use.

The combined catalogue of graves from Fields I, V, and VI contains 410 entries, consisting of 296 well-defined burials, 22 clearly secondary burials, 6 burial pits, and 86 graves where the state of preservation was too poor to allow significant observations to be made.[3] Many graves in the last category may, in fact, be secondary burials. The density of the burials is greater than one per square meter. The cemetery was obviously used over a long period of time, since earlier graves are often cut by later burials, two to five graves frequently intersecting one another in this way.

The Muslim burials are at the bottom of shafts, each designed in length and shape to accommodate the body of a single individual. The shafts are dug from near the present surface through a deep layer of loess and into Stratum IV and V remains. The deposition of the loess layer began with the end of Stratum IV, when settled occupation on the summit of the mound ceased. Between then and the present a thick deposit of wind-blown soil accumulated over the ruins. It forms a continuous deposit, extending from the surviving tops of the Hellenistic remains to the present surface of the mound. On the sections it is often broken down into two layers: disturbed surface soil overlying wind-deposited earth. From the point of view of origin, however, the two layers are essentially one. The west balk drawing of Areas 1–51 (fig. 5, pocket insert) illustrates the typical stratigraphy. Layer 68 is the loess deposit overlying the compact levels of Stratum IV (layers 70a, 70b, and 70c). Graves 11.058 and 11.029 cut this layer, in both cases penetrating into Stratum Va (layer 70d). The same situation is seen farther south in the section, where the loess layer (32 and 42) is cut by Graves 41.211, 41.217, 32.127, 32.122, and 32.125.

The graves are oriented with the long axis lying in a general east-west direction, but in many cases tending to a northeast-southwest orientation. Later grave diggers almost invariably encountered

earlier burials, the precise location of which had perhaps been forgotten. They treated the bones with respect, either placing them in a shallow grave near the newly dug burial or interring them in the shaft of the new grave after the primary burial had been made. When large numbers of bones from several graves had been exhumed, the grave diggers placed them together in a shallow pit. Not being osteologists, they treated all bones with the same respect, and two carefully formed graves were found which contained only disarticulated animal bones.

A place was prepared for the body at the base of the shaft. In the simplest burials the bottom and lower sides of the shaft were packed hard, and the body was placed in the bare earth. Sometimes the burial chamber was covered with five or six stone slabs. In other graves the stone covering was missing, but the base of the shaft was lined with slabs. The most elaborate burials had both stone lining and stone covering (fig. 6). The floor of the grave was never lined with stones.

The body was placed in the grave with the head, occasionally resting on a stone pillow, to the west. Three body positions seem to have been acceptable to the community or communities using the cemetery. The body might be extended on the back with the head turned to the south, extended on the right side, or flexed on the right side. All these positions aligned the eyes in a south to southeast direction. Eighty-two percent of the burials had the eyes oriented in this way. Since Mecca lies to the south-southeast of Hesi, the attempt was clearly and consistently being made to direct the eyes of the dead toward the Holy City.

The position of the hands and feet does not show the same consistency as eye direction. The arms might be extended, or one or both might be crossed over the abdomen with the hand sometimes resting on the pelvis. When the body was placed on the back, the legs were usually extended. When interment was on the side, the legs were normally crossed at the ankles and, in about 50 percent of the burials, slightly flexed.

Grave furnishings are modest or nonexistent. They consist of the adornments worn in life: bracelets, anklets, finger and toe rings of glass or copper or iron, a few coinlike metal disks, metal balls, and numerous beads (fig. 7). The jewelry was almost entirely confined to the burials of adolescent and adult females, although there were a number of cases where jewelry was found in the graves of infants and even of adult males.

Fig. 6. Muslim burial (I.32.038) in a stone-lined grave (Stratum II). A later child burial (I.32.040), also stone-lined, has been cut into the adult burial and has removed the legs of the skeleton. Photo by T. Rosen.

Forty-six percent of all burials were children under three years, testifying to the high infant mortality in the society to which the cemetery belonged. Among the adult burials 54 percent were female, probably the result of the practice of polygamy.

The characteristics described above predominated in the cemetery, but exceptions occurred in every category of data. For example, in Grave 11.211 a female over twenty-four years of age was buried in a position exactly the reverse of the normal. She lay in a simple earth grave flexed

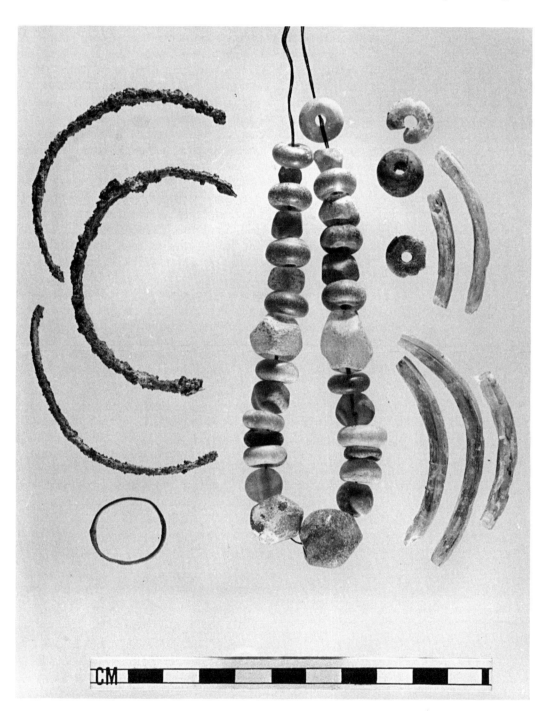

Fig. 7. Typical objects from Stratum II burials. The beads, ring, and bracelets shown here come from the burial of an adult female (I.22.207). Photo by E. Nitowski.

on her *left* side with her eyes directed *northward.* Eighteen percent of the burials were anomalous with respect to eye direction, and 8 percent with respect to body position. The most anomalous was the burial of a young female whose decapitated head rested, cranium upward, on her abdomen.

Multiple burials were rare, but at least five clear cases are known. In one of these an infant rested in the arms of an older child. In a second, three infants lay in a common grave. There were two instances of adult females buried with infants, perhaps the burials of women who died in childbirth. The apparent interment of an adult male and an adult female in the same grave was probably a case of intersecting graves rather than of a multiple burial (Toombs 1974: 27).

The skeletal type was quite uniform throughout the cemetery, the principal exception being several cases of unusually elongated skulls. In these burials the bones were stained a reddish hue.

The cemetery contained only one example of an infant burial in a jar.[4] Bliss reported several similar burials (1891: 285–86), and other instances have been reported from Muslim cemeteries in Israel (see, e.g., Stern 1978: 4–5 and pls. 6: 4–5; 21). The only other occurrence of meaningful pottery in a grave context was the presence of six side-spouted water jars, the familiar *ᶜibrîq* (plural *ᶜabâriq*), in Grave 4.020. Gaza potters recognized the kinship of these vessels to their own workmanship but maintained that they came from an earlier time, although they could not give even an approximate date.

The burial practices witnessed to by the Hesi cemetery correspond closely to those of seminomadic Muslim communities (Ashkenazi 1938: 110–13). The cemetery was already old at the time of Bliss's excavation. His Bedouin workers did not know of its existence and showed no special reverence for the site. Indeed, when Bliss began his work, the summit of the mound was under cultivation (Bliss 1891: 282–84). Until the movements of the Bedouin under Turkish administration can be studied, and until the date of the sheik whose *weli* stands on the site can be established, the cemetery can be dated only by conjecture to 200–400 years ago.[5]

Stratum III—Late Arabic

Some time after the abandonment of Stratum IV (Hellenistic), crude attempts were made to adapt the summit of the mound for agriculture. They consisted of filling in the depressions caused by the subsidence of the fill in the Hellenistic pits and gathering the larger stones into random piles.

The structures to be assigned to Stratum III can be recognized stratigraphically by their location *within* the loess layer which accumulated on the acropolis after the destruction of Stratum IV. An installation in Area 1, the only coherent unit belonging to the stratum, is typical of the situation. A large two-handled water jar was partially enclosed by a low wall of mud plaster. A drain, scarcely more than a water runnel, ran alongside the jar, and a fragment of packed-earth surfacing was associated with it (fig. 8). Sandy loess lay above and below the installation. It predated the cemetery since the nearest graves were cut through the associated surface. The installation probably provided drinking water for agricultural workers.

Apart from this installation, no Stratum III structures worthy of the name were found. Rough lines of stone may have served as plot dividers. Clumps of bricky soil, red, in sharp contrast to the yellowish-brown of the loess, occurred frequently, but they were mere fragments, and their function is unknown. Pits for the disposal of garbage, rude hearths (the sites of campfires), and two small ovens were evidently the casual and scattered remains of the sporadic use of the mound for agricultural and camping purposes. Such surfaces as survived were of tramped earth and were apparently open to the air.

Since structures in the strict sense of the word do not exist in Stratum III, and since the pottery is mainly body sherds from large jars, the date of the stratum is difficult to determine. It could theoretically extend from the end of the Hellenistic to the modern period. The most important clue is the water jar found in Area 1. Although of a very long-lived type, it resembles modern forms. It is probable, therefore, that the remains assigned to Stratum III belong to the Turkish period, immediately prior to the establishment of the cemetery.

Stratum IV—The Hellenistic Period

The Stratification of Stratum IV. The remains of the latest Persian Period structures were covered by a layer of compact, bricky earth, the leveled debris of their collapse. On this layer a buildup of hard-packed earth surfaces occurred, particularly in Areas 1, 3, and 12. These surfaces blended into one another and were difficult to trace, but, where they were well preserved, two clear stages in their deposition could be distinguished, separated by a thin layer of loess.

Pits such as I.2.069, I.2.037, and I.12.081 cut both phases of surfacing. On the basis of these observations three substrata may be recognized, the two earliest being defined by the packed-earth surfaces and the latest by pit-digging activity. The structures of Stratum IV, which are found principally in Areas 22 and 32, are assigned to their appropriate substrata by their relationship to the basic sequence of layers.

Stratum IVa. The latest Stratum IV remains consisted of approximately twelve pits, clustering at the center of the field and thinning out to the north and south (fig. 9B).[6] They were inferior in construction to the Persian pits of Stratum Va and smaller in size. They were normally lined with compacted mud, rather than with brick, as was generally the case with the Persian pits.

The stratigraphic history of the Stratum IV pits is complex. Pit I.22.111, for example, originated in the Persian Period (Stratum V) and continued in use through Stratum IVc, when it served as a sump for a stone-built drain (fig. 9A). In the course of Stratum IVb it was filled up, and Pit I.11.179 was dug through the fill of both Pit I.22.111 and an earlier Stratum IV pit (I.21.159). Towards the end of Stratum IVa, Pit I.11.179 was itself filled, and a much smaller pit (I.11.112), associated with a small oven, was later dug in the fill. The digging, filling, and redigging of pits make it impossible in many cases to determine to which substratum their original use belongs. We have cut the Gordian knot by placing them all in Stratum IVa, but this is clearly an oversimplification which will be modified when the detailed study of Stratum IV is completed. Some pits may have originated in Stratum IVb, or even Stratum IVc, and been reused in Stratum IVa.

The original use of the pits was almost certainly for grain storage. The area around them was honeycombed with rodent runs, and the bottoms were covered with layers of ash produced by the burn-

Fig. 8.   Stratum III installation. An Arabic storage jar lies beside an adobe wall. Photo by T. Rosen.

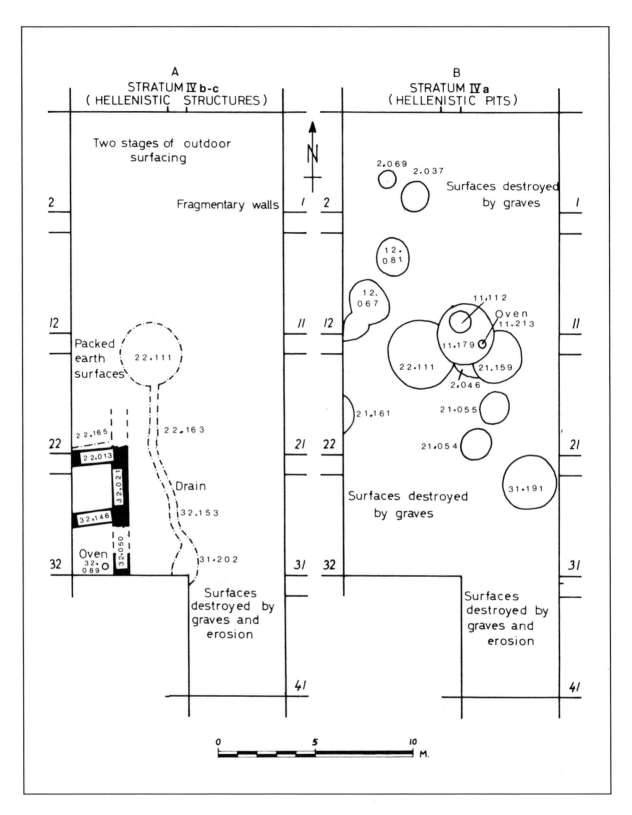

Fig. 9. Schematic block plans of the Hellenistic remains (Stratum IV). Broken lines indicate conjectured walls. Broken lines with dots indicate Stratum IVc structures. Drawing by L. E. Toombs.

ing of straw and chaff in the process of fumigating the pits to rid them of vermin (Stager 1971). Pit I.12.067 had an ovoid platform on its southern side, about 1.50 m. from the floor, to assist in shoveling out the grain when the contents of the pit were low. At the end of Stratum IVa, however, the pits were used for garbage disposal, and the final fill was refuse from the end of the Hellenistic era.

No permanent structures belong clearly to Stratum IVa. If such structures existed within the excavated areas, they were of adobe or low-quality mud brick and have either eroded away during the long period of abandonment at the end of Stratum IV or have been destroyed by the Muslim graves of Stratum II and the military trenching of Stratum I. Isolated mounds of reddish earth, bricklike but without clearly defined individual bricks or discernible wall lines, may represent the remains of flimsy buildings. Bliss reported the discovery of similar "mouldy and decayed" brickwork in the upper four feet of his excavation (Bliss 1891:285).

Stratum IVb. The base of this substratum is a compact, bricky layer covering the Stratum IVc remains and sealing the Stratum IVc drain. This layer appears in the west balk section of Areas 2–32 (fig. 10, pocket insert) as layer 10, underlying the Stratum IVb building (layer 11) and extending over a Stratum IVc wall (layer 13).

In the western half of Areas 22 and 32 a stone-built structure, of which portions of two rooms were preserved, clearly belongs to Stratum IVb (fig. 9A; fig. 10, layers 3 and 11). The foundations of this building were dug into the bricky layer, and the fragments of surfaces associated with it overlay Stratum IVc layers (fig. 10, layer 13). The 1.00-m.-wide outer wall of the building (I.32.021/.050) ran north-south and was constructed of two faces of fieldstones with rubble fill between. Two narrower interior walls (I.22.013 and I.32.021/146) extended westward from the main wall out of the excavated area. The northern limits of the building, considerable portions of its walls, and almost all the associated surfaces have been destroyed by Muslim graves (Stratum II), which clustered thickly in this area.

To the east of the stone building a small fragment of a finely metalled surface overlay the Stratum IVc drain and should, therefore, be assigned to Stratum IVb. North of the building, the upper phase of the buildup of surfaces, referred to above, should also be placed in this substratum. With less certainty two short segments of stone-built walls in Area 1 may be assigned to Stratum IVb.

The extensive use of stone (a scarce commodity in the immediate vicinity of Tell el-Hesi), the large size of the building in Areas 22 and 32, and the good quality of the metalled surface, all indicate that the Stratum IVb settlement was more prosperous and culturally more advanced than the deplorable state of preservation of its remains would at first suggest. It may with justice be called the main phase of Hellenistic occupation on the site.

Stratum IVc. The earliest Hellenistic occupation is only meagerly represented. Its most prominent feature was a stone-built drain (22.163=32.153) running from an oval catch basin (31.202) in the south along a meandering northward course to discharge through a plastered spout into Pit I.21.111 (fig. 9A). The catch basin was floored with stone slabs, and the drain was lined with field stones and capped with slabs, four of which were cut from old basalt grinders.

Stratigraphically, the drain predated the stone building of Stratum IVb, because it was sealed by the bricky layer into which foundations of that building were cut. It was later than Stratum Va, because its foundation trench cut Va surfaces.

A short length of mud-brick wall (I.22.165) belongs to the same period as the drain. This wall appears in fig. 10 as layer 13 and can be seen, resting on its stone foundation, in fig. 11. It lay directly beneath the northern interior wall of the Stratum IVb building (fig. 9A, I.22.013; fig. 10, layer 11), and its foundation trench disturbed Stratum Va levels. In fig. 10, for example, it clearly postdates layer 12a, which is a Stratum Va–b mud-brick wall. The northern face of Wall I.22.165 was founded on a single course of field stones. That it was part of a large building is indicated by an oven (I.32.089) sealed below the surface in use in Stratum IVb. In Stratum IVc, therefore, a residential building, of which the brick wall and oven were features, occupied much the same area as the later stone structure. The drain flanked this building to the east.

The lower phase of the buildup of earth surfaces may also be assigned to Stratum IVc. The stratigraphic placement of two short walls of unfired mud brick, which corner in Area 11, and a section of mud-brick wall on a stone foundation in Area 2 remains uncertain, but they probably belong to Statum IVc. Because of their fragmentary nature and the uncertainty of their stratigraphic assignment, they do not appear in fig. 9A.

Fig. 11. Stratum IVc wall (A) and drain (D) in the north balk of I.22. The stone foundation (B) of the wall underlies a hard, bricky layer (C) which seals the upper stones of the drain lining. Photo by J. Whitred.

The chronological limits of Stratum IV are defined by the pottery from beneath the Stratum IVc surfaces, on the one hand, and the pottery from the filling of the Hellenistic pits, on the other. On the basis of the field analysis of this pottery the stratum may be dated to the third to first centuries BCE.

Stratum V—The Persian Period

The Stratigraphy of Stratum V. Four definable substrata (Va, Vb, Vc, and Vd) represent the Persian Period at Tell el-Hesi. Since the evidence for this division into substrata depends on the reading of the sections, it will be presented in the order in which the layers involved were excavated, that is, from the latest to the earliest.

The separation between Stratum IV (Hellenis-

tic) and Stratum V (Persian) is, in general, a layer of compact soil 0.10–0.30 m. in thickness, often containing stones and decayed bricks. This layer appears at numerous points on the sections, for example, fig. 5, layer 70d, and fig. 10, layer 5. Occasionally, however, the separating layer thins out virtually to the vanishing point, and the two strata are almost directly superimposed on one another.

The upper three substrata are closely related both stratigraphically and structurally. Walls I.31.058 and I.22.149 were common to all three (figs. 12B, 13). The distinguishing feature was the sequence of surfacing, particularly to the east of Wall I.31.058. The uppermost Stratum V surface (I.31.070) was of good quality flagstones (fig. 13B). This overlay a similar pavement (I.31.095), only partially preserved (fig. 13A), which in turn covered a series of packed-earth surfaces separated by layers of ash (fig. 12B). These three phases of surfacing represented Strata Va–c in Area 31. Unfortunately, they did not reach the section, but layers 59 and 70 on fig. 5 show a corresponding sequence of surfaces along the west balk of Areas 1–51. Figs. 12B and 13 illustrate the changes in wall alignment and construction which accompanied the changes in surfacing.

Whereas Strata Va, Vb, and Vc displayed a continuity in building plan and closely contiguous surfaces, Stratum Vd stood apart from its successors. No walls of Stratum Vd were reused in Stratum Vc. Stratum-Vc surfaces directly overlay Stratum-Vd remains or were separated from them by a layer of debris (fig. 5, layer 36; fig. 10, layer 7). The break at the beginning of Stratum Vd was as dramatic as that at its end. The major building of this substratum was located in the south of the excavated area (fig. 12A). Fig. 5 shows the foundation trench (layer 29) for the southern wall (layer 28) of this building cutting deeply into the remains of earlier strata (layers 21, 22, 24, 25, 26). The surface contemporary with this wall (layer 37) rested directly on top of an earlier mud-brick structure (layer 38). Farther to the north the corresponding layer 70r overlay a thick deposit of loose soil and debris (layer 71). It is clear from fig. 5 that the walls and floors of the Vd structure cut into and removed substantial portions of the pre-Persian remains north of Wall I.41.162 (layer 28), while leaving them intact south of that wall line.

In view of the continuity among the substrata of Stratum V, particularly Va–c, the evolution of the structures and the nature of the occupation will be clearer if they are described in the order of their construction.

Stratum Vd. The principal structure of Stratum Vd was located in the southern part of Field I in Areas 31, 32, and 41. It consisted of two parallel mud-brick walls without stone foundations (I.41.162 and I.31.225=I.32.158 on fig. 12A), and about 4.50 m. apart. They were connected by two cross walls of similar but somewhat slighter construction (I.41.229 and I.32.176 on fig. 12A). The vertical faces of the walls showed traces of plastering. Portions of three rooms were preserved, and a doorway gave access to the central chamber from the north. The flooring of all three rooms was compact earth with traces of plaster surfacing. Although only 11.00 m. of the east-west extent of the structure lay within the excavated area, it gave the appearance of a casemate forming the southern

limit of occupation on the summit of the mound. The 9.00-m. space between Wall I.41.162 and the southern edge of the acropolis was evidently regarded as outside the enclosure and served as a walkway and a place for shallow garbage pits.

North of the casematelike structure, only scraps of walls were found: the corner of a chamber formed by Walls I.1.144 and I.1.200 and a wall fragment (I.11.264) which may possibly have formed part of the southern wall of the same chamber (fig. 12A).

The Stratum Vd plan bears a general resemblance to Bliss's City VII (Bliss 1894: 111). His plan shows a complex of rooms running along the northern edge of the mound and another near its eastern edge. The remainder of the excavated area was empty of construction. It may be suggested with a fair degree of probability that in Stratum Vd the acropolis was not a town in the ordinary sense of the word, but was designed and built as an occupational unit. An outer casemate limited the area, chambers were constructed adjacent to the casemate, and a large, open courtyard lay in the center. The layout suggests a barracks or storage area for military or other supplies. If this was indeed the function of the acropolis in Stratum Vd, its use may have been connected with the Persian interest in an invasion of Egypt during the early decades of the Persian Empire.

Stratum Vc. The Stratum Vc walls (fig. 12B) were new constructions on lines altogether independent of those in use during Stratum Vd. The northeast corner of a substantial building, bounded by Walls I.22.149 and I.31.058, was located to the south in Areas 31 and 32. To the north, Wall I.1.137 and the poorly preserved fragment I.2.054 may have formed the southeast corner of a similar room. All these walls were of gray, unfired mud brick without stone foundations and were slighter than the earlier walls of Stratum Vd, averaging about 0.75 m. in width.

Along the eastern edge of the field curious striated bands, formed of alternating layers of packed earth and ash, extended from Area 31 north through Area 11. These layers were cut off by Pit I.11.048 (fig. 13B) and did not reappear north of the pit. The ash contained burnt animal dung, wheat, and barley. The layering seems to have resulted from the burning of the residues of agriculture or stock-raising on a succession of earthen surfaces. Along the west side of the field the striations did not occur in Areas 12, 22, and 32. Here the Stratum Vc surfaces were of compact

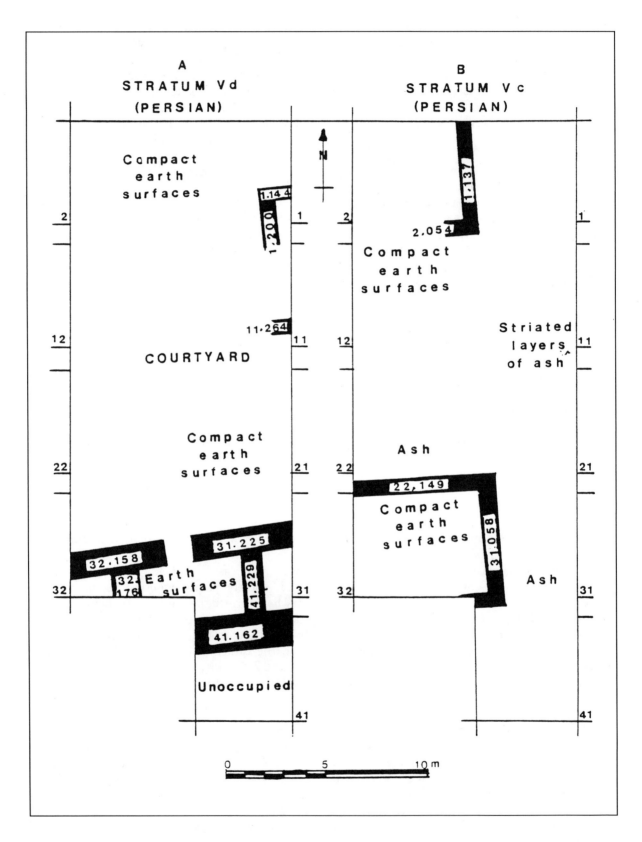

Fig. 12. Schematic block plans of the earliest Persian levels (Strata Vd and Vc). Drawing by L. E. Toombs.

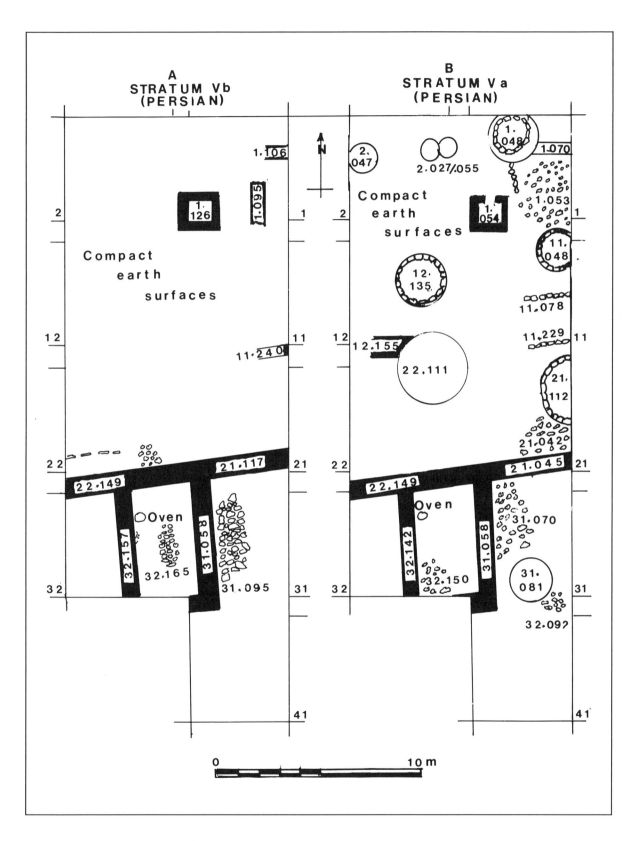

Fig. 13. Schematic block plans of the later Persian levels (Strata Vb and Va). Drawing by L. E. Toombs.

earth with little or no ash. These surfaces were open-air activity areas, probably associated with agriculture or animal husbandry.

It seems clear that between Strata Vd and Vc the function of the acropolis changed from a public or military use to an area primarily devoted to agricultural or pastoral pursuits.

Stratum Vb.[7] Building activity in the southern part of the acropolis increased markedly in Stratum Vb, although structural continuity with the previous substratum was maintained by the retention of Walls I.22.149 and I.31.058 (fig. 13A). Part of the area formerly occupied by the striated layers of ash was incorporated into the new structure by the extension eastward of Wall I.21.149 as Wall I.21.117. The new room thus formed had a flagstone pavement (I.31.095). The western room was divided into two chambers by the addition of Wall I.32.157. In the easternmost of these chambers, an oven and a deposit of ash on the floor nearby indicated that the room was used for domestic purposes.

Additional chambers appear to have existed farther to the north, where fragmentary Walls I.11.240, I.1.095, and I.1.106 survived. West of Wall I.1.095 a square structure with thick walls of red mud brick (fig. 13A, I.1.126) functioned as an underground storage chamber, possibly with an above-ground superstructure. This building appears in section in fig. 5, layer 77, and the thick accumulation of Stratum Vb surfaces can be seen along its north wall (layers 80b–e). Except for patches of flagstones in Areas 1, 22, 31, and 32, all surviving surfaces were of hard-packed earth.

Stratum Va. Stratum Va (fig. 13B) retained the basic ground plan of Stratum Vb. The southern building remained practically unchanged, even to the position of the oven in the central room. This room and the chamber to the east were surfaced, at least in part, with cobblestones (I.32.150 and I.31.070). The eastern room housed Pit I.31.081.

North of the southern building the only well-preserved feature was the square brick structure (I.1.054) which had originated as an underground storage chamber in Stratum Vb. The underground portion was filled, and the fill was covered by a beaten-earth surface (I.1.054). The foundation trench for the repair of the building is shown in fig. 5, cutting Stratum Vb–c layers 80b–g and sealed by the buildup of Stratum Va surfaces (layer 80a). The structure, now a small room, was entered through a doorway to the north.

A distinctive feature of the stratum was the presence of numerous pits north of the southern building. Seven pits occurred in the excavated areas. Four had carefully constructed mud-brick linings (I.1.048, I.11.048, I.12.135, I.21.112). Three were unlined (I.2.047, I.2.027/.055, I.22.111).

The diameters of the brick-lined pits varied between 1.20 and 2.80 m., and their depths were between 2.50 and 3.50 m. In the construction of these pits, irregularly shaped fieldstones were partially embedded in the raw clay which formed the side of the excavation for the pit. Against the jagged exposed edges of the stones, the bricks were pressed while still plastic, and the lining was allowed to dry in place. The lining of Pit I.1.048 was rebuilt at least twice. This pit had a domed roof, part of which was found collapsed in the pit fill. In order to prevent water from surface runoff entering the pits, they were generally provided with low, mud-plastered rims.

The brick-lined pits undoubtedly served for grain storage. Like the Hellenistic pits (see above, p. 136–40), their lower levels contained heavy ash layers, the residue of a fumigating process. The clay-lined pits were used for supplementary storage or for garbage disposal.[8]

Date and Duration. Evidence for the relative duration of the four substrata is provided by the thickness of the surfacing associated with each. This is best studied in fig. 5, layers 37, 59, 70, and 80. The average depth of the surfacing was: Stratum Vd, 0.05 m.; Stratum Vc, 0.10–0.20 m.; Stratum Vb, 0.15–0.35 m.; Stratum Va, 0.10–0.20 m. Strata Va–c were a succession of layers, but Stratum Vd was a single surface that showed no discernible layering, except in Area 11. On this evidence, admittedly by no means conclusive, Stratum Vd was the shortest and Vb the longest of the Persian phases, while Strata Vc and Va were of approximately equal and intermediate duration. The ceramic evidence places the whole sequence in the sixth to fourth centuries BCE.

The Late Chalcolithic Structure (Field III)

In Field III, Area 5 (fig. 2), a circular structure, 2.50 m. in diameter, was uncovered (fig. 14). Its walls were of packed mud and were preserved to a height of 0.40 m. No surfaces survived, but the pottery associated with the building was the earliest found on the site. It was dated in the field to the end of the Chalcolithic or the beginning of the Early Bronze Age (see Coogan 1989b [Chapter IX, below]).

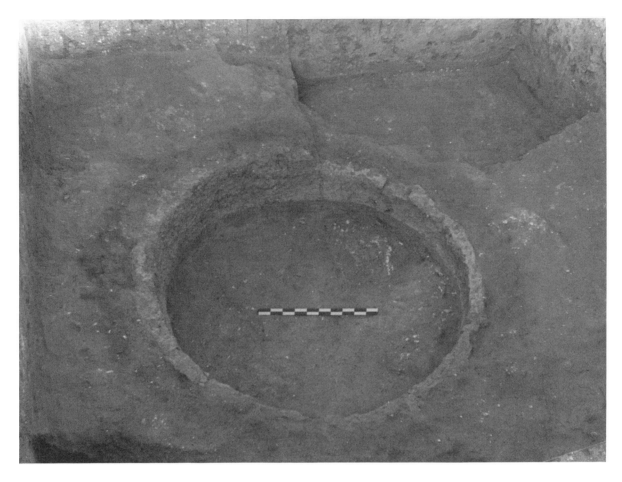

Fig. 14. The Chalcolithic structure in Field III, Area 5. Photo by T. Rosen.

LEVELS PARTIALLY EXCAVATED

Location

In three locations on the acropolis, extensive excavation was carried out prior to and during the 1975 season:

1. the wall system at the foot of the southern slope in Field III

2. the pre-Stratum V levels in Field I, Areas 41 and 51

3. the walls on the southern slope of the mound in Field I, Areas 51A, 61, 61A, and 71

In all of these locations a great deal of work has been done since 1975. While the report given here includes only the results obtained in the seasons 1971–1975, the presentation of the data is inevitably colored by the conclusions reached in later seasons.

The Southern Wall (Field III)

An 11.00-m.-wide mud-brick wall was traced or 60.00 m. along the base of the southern slope. At its eastern end it turns north along the wadi face, but after a short distance the northward extension has been carried away by erosion and is lost. The stone foundation can be traced some distance farther before it, too, disappears. At the western end of the field, the southwest corner of the wall has not yet been reached. In order to study the construction of the wall, two sections were cut through it: the one (A-A') near its eastern extremity at the wadi face; the other (B-B') a little farther to the west. The lateral extent of the wall and the location of both sections are shown in fig. 15, and the B-B' section is given in fig. 16 (pocket insert). The discussion which follows is limited to data bearing on the stratigraphy and relative

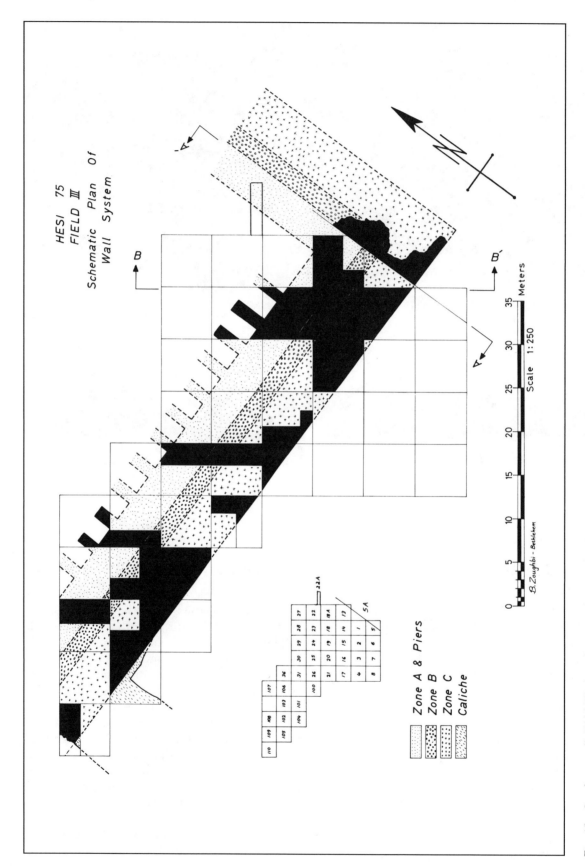

Fig. 15. Southern wall (Field III), lateral extent, showing the three zones of construction. Solid portions were excavated; the remainder is a reconstruction. Drawing by B. Zoughby.

chronology. Additional details are given in the preliminary report of the first four seasons (Rose, Toombs, and O'Connell 1978: 132–35).

The B-B′ section (fig. 16) shows the composite nature of the wall. It consists of three distinct zones of construction, labeled, from north to south, Zones A, B, and C.

For the construction of Zone A the builders cut away the lower portion of the existing slope almost to virgin sand, creating a steep artificial scarp and exposing the earlier soil layers. These appear as fill and wash layers (9a and 9b) at the left of the section. The water-deposited layers must have accumulated against the face of an earlier wall, removed when the Zone A wall was built. That such a wall followed the line of Zone A along at least a portion of its length is strongly suggested by the evidence uncovered in Field III, Area 22A, a stratigraphic cut on the wadi face adjacent to Area 22 and north of the main wall line (figs. 2 and 15). Here the wall itself has been lost to erosion, but the same sequence of layers (fill, a thick layering of wash, and still earlier fill) was observed.

Further evidence for the presence of earlier structures along the line of Zone A was provided by the remains of a drain (fig. 17:E), lined and roofed with stones, near the eastern end of the wall. It passed under the foundations of Zone C, and its bed could be traced under Zone B, but it was cut off altogether by the Zone A foundation (fig. 17:D, A′). The drain must, therefore, have functioned in connection with an earlier structure that was destroyed when Zone A was constructed.

Zone A was founded on a massive stone platform, 2.00 m. high and 4.50 m. wide. Its south or outer face was vertical, but its north face followed the contour of the artificial scarp. On this platform the brickwork of Zone A was laid, with both its inner and outer faces rising vertically. Fig. 16 shows the Zone A brickwork apparently climbing the slope of the scarp in the same manner as the north face of the stone foundation. This is an illusion, created by the fact that the B-B′ section cuts through one of the piers which are a feature of the inner face of Zone A. These piers were evidently devices for stabilizing the wall by keying it into the slope. They were set at intervals of about 2.50 m. along the northern face of Zone A. Since they were bonded into the Zone A brickwork, they were contemporary with the Zone A wall. Their bases climbed step-wise up the scarp as shown in fig. 16. The empty spaces between the piers were filled as the building progressed, and the top of the

filling was sealed with a heavy layer of mud bricks to provide either a walkway inside the wall or a consolidating surface for the slope of the mound. In contrast with the earlier layers exposed when the scarp was cut, the filling between the piers was contemporary with the construction of Zone A.

Zone B paralleled Zone A for its entire length and, like Zone A, turned the corner at the east end and began to run northward along the wadi. The north face of Zone B rested flush against the vertical brickwork of Zone A. Its south face, however, was battered at an angle of 30 degrees and was covered with plaster facing from its preserved top to 1.20 m. above its foundation. The lower portion of the wall, presumably the portion below ground level, was unplastered. The foundation of Zone B was a single course of tightly packed stones laid over a sand fill (fig. 16).

Three lines of evidence converge to show that Zone A is prior to Zone B. The first is the intrinsic improbability that the builders would have cut the back of Zone B vertically and put in a foundation so much more elaborate than that of Zone B, merely to effect a repair or strengthening. In any case the wear and tear would have been on the exposed south face of Zone B, rather than on the earth-backed northern face. The second line of evidence is that the bricks of Zone B were not cut, as they would have been if Zone A had been inserted behind Zone B. They were whole bricks, butted against the Zone A face. The most convincing evidence for the priority of Zone A is shown in fig. 17. The lowest layer of stones (D), at which the excavation stopped, is associated with the Zone A foundation (A′) in a way not altogether clear. Perhaps it functioned as the base of a corner tower during the Zone A period. Its stratigraphic significance is that it *underlay* the Zone B foundation (B′), from which it was separated by an earth fill (F).

Zone B evidently had a tendency to settle forward and pull away from Zone A. In several places the gap thus created was plugged with plaster. Perhaps it was to correct this tendency that Zone C was constructed. Zone B clearly did not have a period of disuse before the building of Zone C. Its plaster face (fig. 16, layer 15a) was found in an excellent state of preservation, but, where the expedition exposed it, it was cut to pieces by the rains of two winters only. Zone C was, therefore, added to a wall system still in use.

Zone C stood on a foundation of plaster (fig. 16, layer 21) laid over a sand fill (fig. 16, layer 22) which

Fig. 17. Southern wall (Field III), section A-A'. A, B, and C represent the three zones of the wall; A' and B' represent the stone foundations of the two earlier zones. D is the stone layer abutting the Zone A foundation, E is the truncated and destroyed drain, and F is the earth layer beneath the Zone A foundation and above the stone layer (D). Photo by J. Whitred.

raised it almost a meter above the Zone B foundation stones (fig. 16, layer 16). Its outer face was vertical, but the brickwork (fig. 16, layer 20) on its northern side was laid directly against the sloping face (fig. 16, layer 15a) of Zone B. Thus, there can be no doubt that Zone C was later than Zone B. If further proof were needed, it is forthcoming from the A-A' section near the wadi face (fig. 18). The Zone B plaster (B) merged with the surface of a walkway or working platform (D) at the edge of the wadi. The Zone C brick (C) rested directly on this platform.

The evidence just presented demonstrates that the order of construction of the three zones of brickwork was A/B/C and strongly suggests that little, if any, time passed between the disuse of one phase and the construction of the next. After the wall system had been abandoned and had weathered down to a fairly regular slope, a large pit was cut into the tops of all three zones, probably for the mining of bricks (fig. 16, layer 8ab). After the robber pit had been filled in by soil washing down the slope, graves were dug into it and into the brickwork of the walls (fig. 16, layers 3–7).

The dating of the lower wall system, its function, and its relationship to the "Manasseh wall" farther up the slope have proved to be difficult problems, and a variety of hypotheses have been advocated at different stages of the excavation.

The graves dug into the top of the wall provide a *terminus ante quem* for the construction. M. Coogan (1975: 46 [Chapter X, below, p. 185]) has dated the cemetery to the Persian Period. The lower wall must have deteriorated and its decayed top been used as a brick mine before the cemetery was established. This would push the date for the disuse of the wall back toward the end of the Iron Age.[9]

The foundation date of the wall system is harder to establish. The best evidence comes from the fill between the piers. The small number and size of the sherds from this fill makes dating difficult, but the evidence points to the 9th-8th century BCE. The latest sherds from the horizontal wash layers, exposed by the Zone A foundation trench, and those from the foundation trench for the drain demolished by the Zone A builders, appear to belong to an earlier date. The large quantity of 10th-9th century BCE pottery found below the wall system at its eastern end may indicate that the first wall construction at the foot of the slope belongs to that period.

As a tentative hypothesis to account for the phenomena just described, it may be suggested that the earliest wall system at the foot of the southern slope was constructed in the 10th-9th century BCE. It was obliterated, possibly in the 9th or 8th century BCE, by the three-phase wall system, the remains of which still survive. This system, extended successively through Zones B and C, was in use until the destruction of the city at the end of the Iron Age.[10]

Pre-Stratum V Phases (Field I)

Pre-Stratum V structures survive principally in Field I, Areas 41 and 51, in a 9.00-m.-wide strip along the southern edge of the mound. The Stratum Vd building cut into and destroyed the continuation of the structure north of this strip. The stratigraphy of the three latest phases of pre-Stratum V remains, as they were known after the 1975 season, is illustrated at the left of the west balk section of Areas 1–51 (fig. 5) and on the block plans in fig. 19.

Layer 28 in fig. 5 is the Stratum Vd Wall I.41.162. Its foundation trench (layer 29) cuts pre-Stratum V layers 21, 22, 24, 25, and 26. The pre-Stratum V remains under consideration, therefore, lie to the left of the foundation trench. Unfortunately, they are badly disturbed by the ubiquitous Muslim graves. The crucial stratigraphic feature of these levels is an ash layer which extends from the southern edge of the section to the base of layer 16 (Wall I.51.144) and reappears farther north as layer 22. This ash layer allows a gross separation of the pre-Stratum V remains into a pre-ash and a post-ash phase.

To the post-ash phase belong Wall I.41.158 (layer 21), Wall I.51.144 (layer 16) and Wall I.51.079, a brick wall on a stone foundation (layer 9). The surviving fragmentary surfaces are involved in layer 13. These features belong to a building erected after the destruction represented by the ash layer. Its ground plan is given in fig. 19D.

The pre-ash phasing is less secure, because excavation had not reached the bottom of these levels. There are clearly at least two pre-ash phases, defined by superimposed walls and surfaces. Along the east balk of Areas 41 and 51, Wall I.51.099 overlay Wall I.51.159, and the stone-covered Surface I.51.098 overlay a beaten-earth surface (I.51.151; fig. 19B-C). On the west-balk section (fig. 5) the situation is not so clear, but cobbled Surface I.41.183 (layer 24) probably belongs to the earlier of the

Fig. 18. Southern wall (Field III), section A-A', at an earlier stage of excavation than in fig. 17. The plaster face (B) of the Zone B wall is seen at its rounded eastern corner. The plaster is continuous with the surface of the walkway (D) at the right of the photograph. This walkway directly underlay Zone C brickwork (C). The Zone A wall (A) appears at the top of the photo. E is a probe trench into the erosion gulley below the Zone C wall. Photo by T. Rosen.

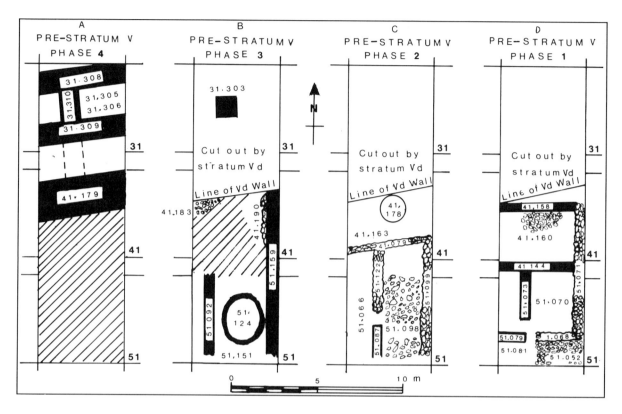

Fig. 19. Schematic block plans of pre-Stratum V levels. Diagonal lines indicate unexcavated area. Drawing by L. E. Toombs.

two phases. The ground plans of the two pre-ash phases are given in fig. 19B-C.

The principal area of uncertainty is in the extreme south of Area 51. Fig. 5, layer 4 is a mudbrick wall (I.51.088) perched on the edge of the slope and, hence, badly eroded, so that its relationship to the ash layer is unsure. Layer 5 (Wall I.51.116) is definitely pre-ash, but whether it belongs to the earlier or later phase has not been established. In the block plans published in the four-season report (Rose, Toombs, and O'Connell 1978:118), Wall I.51.088 was assigned to the pre-ash phase. However, in view of the uncertainty, both walls have been omitted in fig. 19.

The stratigraphic analysis leads to the recognition of four pre-Stratum V phases, defined by a continuous sequence of layers in Field I, Areas 41 and 51.[11]

Pre-Stratum V, Phase 1 (fig. 19D; now Stratum VI) consisted of a narrow chamber on an east-west axis, with a cobbled surface. South of this room were two interconnecting chambers with beaten-earth floors. Against the southern wall a surface of cobblestones formed a walkway along the edge of the southern slope. This building was erected on a platform of bricky material which directly overlay the heavy ash layer. If, as seems likely, the ash resulted from the destruction of the site by the Babylonians, this phase should be dated to the 6th century BCE.

Pre-Stratum V, Phase 2 (fig. 19C; now Stratum VIIa). The building plan of this phase is markedly different from that of its successor. Beneath the ash and debris of its destruction lay a building of which one room and part of a second were preserved. The room with cobbled Surface I.51.098 was long and narrow, and its main axis ran north-south. North of the building was beaten-earth Surface I.41.163, into which an oval pit (I.41.178) was sunk. As indicated above, the southern limit of the structures is uncertain. Assuming that the ash layer resulted from the Babylonian destruction of the city, the terminal date of this phase would be 587/586 BCE. Its foundation date is not yet established, but probably fell within the 7th century BCE.

Pre-Stratum V, Phase 3 (fig. 19B; now Stratum VIIb) was represented by two north-south walls

(I.51.159 and I.51.092) with a large oval pit (I.51.124) between them. The walls were of hard gray mud brick and were superior in construction to either of the later phases. Since excavation of the northern portion of the complex was incomplete in 1975, the entire outline of the building to which these walls belonged was not then known, nor was its foundation date established.[12]

The wall fragment I.31.303 (fig. 19B) has been tentatively assigned to this phase. It existed without associated surfaces between the Stratum Vd floor and the tops of the pre-Stratum V, Phase 4 walls described below. All that can be said is that it predated the Persian Period and immediately postdated the "long range of chambers" in pre-Stratum V, Phase 4.[13]

Pre-Stratum V, Phase 4 (fig. 19A; now Stratum VIId) gave the excavation on the acropolis its first firm connection with the work of Sir Flinders Petrie. In his exploration of the eastern face of the mound, Petrie encountered what he called a "long range of chambers" (see Petrie 1891: 28-9, 31). Pre-Stratum V, Phase 4 consisted of the tops of the three southernmost east-west walls of these chambers (I.31.308, I.31.309, I.41.179). The first two of these walls appear in section in fig. 5 as layers 51 and 38, and Wall I.41.179 belongs immediately beneath layer 29. One north-south cross wall (I.31.310), connecting Walls I.31.308 and I.31.309, was also uncovered.

A deep probe was made into the fill of one chamber. The field reading of the pottery was late Iron II. The walls of the chamber were constructed of large, flat mud bricks, carefully laid, but without doors or windows in the relatively small area exposed. At a depth of 2.50 m. a surface of compact reddish earth was encountered, but at this point excavation ceased in 1975. The surface showed no evidence of use as either a living or a working surface, and it may have been merely a stage in the filling process.[14]

In 1975 work on this important structure had just begun, and excavation up to that date provided more questions than answers. Whether the structure was a freestanding building or a series of subterranean chambers and how it functioned were matters of conjecture. Excavation since 1975 has shown that the pre-Stratum V, Phase 4 walls were part of the interior structure of a huge earthen platform constructed in order to raise the level of the mound and to extend the occupied area to the south (O'Connell, Rose, and Toombs 1978: 82–84; O'Connell and Rose 1980: 80–82; Toombs 1983:31).

Ceramic evidence for the foundation date of the phase was scanty, but Matthers's tentative interpretation of the conclusions of Petrie and Bliss places it in the late ninth or early eighth centuries BCE (see Matthers 1989 [Chapter II, above]: 62).[15]

Walls on the Southern Slope (Field I)

During the 1975 season the decision was made to excavate a trench from the summit of the acropolis down the southern slope of the mound to connect Area 51 of Field I with Area 107 of Field III. This procedure would physically connect the occupational phases on the summit of the mound (pre-Stratum V, Phases 1–4) with the wall at the foot of the southern slope and would produce a continuous profile from the summit to the base of the mound.

In order to obtain a preview of the results likely to be obtained by this procedure, a vertical section was cut along the eastern face of the mound in Field I, Areas 51A and 61A. Fig. 20 shows the structure exposed in the 61A section. There are three principal features in the section:

1. the remains of a glacis, described by Petrie as composed of "blocks of stone, bedded in earth, and faced with white plaster" (Petrie 1891: 27)
2. "Manasseh's Wall," founded on, and at points apparently cut into, the glacis
3. an "upper structure," unrecognized by Petrie, of badly decayed mud brick on a stone foundation, separated from "Manasseh's Wall" by a thin layer of water-deposited earth and a thicker layer of brick debris

An initial indication of the relationship of these structures to one another and to the phases recognized on the summit was provided by Area 51A. The 51A section exposed both the top of the southern wall (fig. 21:B) of the "long range of chambers" and the upper end of the glacis (fig. 21:A). A layer of compact reddish earth (fig. 21:C) originated near the top of the southern wall of the "long range of chambers" and sloped sharply downward below the level of the glacis. This dictated the conclusion that the order of construction was the "long range of chambers," the glacis, the "Manasseh Wall," and the upper structure. Whether these features were all part of the same construction process or belonged to separate phases of occupation remained unknown. The only bit of evidence available in 1975 was the occurrence of a reddish soil layer similar to that exposed in the 51A

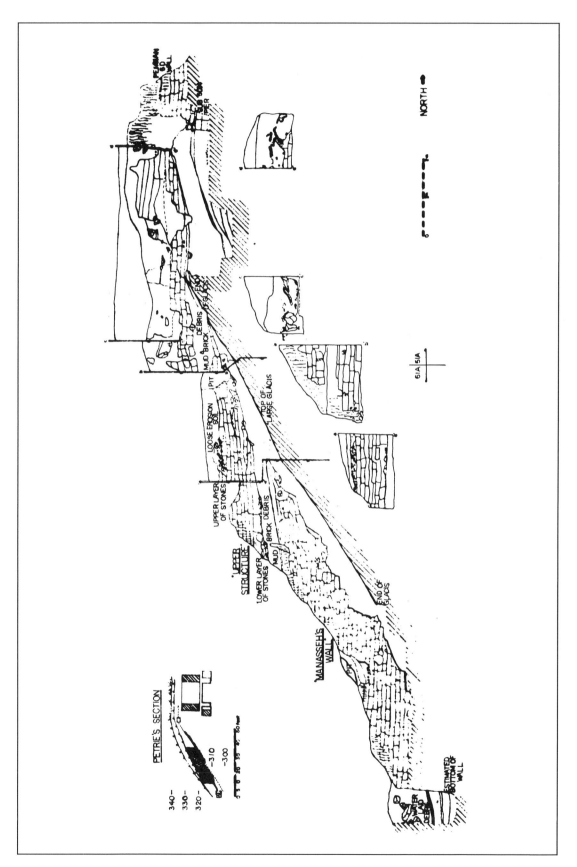

Fig. 20. West-balk section, Field I, Areas 51A and 61A, showing walls on the upper levels of the southern slope. An adaptation of Petrie's section of 1890 appears as an insert at the upper left. In the course of the excavation, the section was stepped back four times. The subsidiary sections a-a', b-b', c-c', and d-d' are the east-west sections along the faces of the cutbacks and show the connection of the four north-south segments of the section with one another. Adapted by K. Kruschen from an original by J. Matthers.

Fig. 21. Segment cut back along the east face of the mound in Field I, Area 51A. The meter stick rests on the top of the pre-Stratum V, Phase 4 wall (B), from which a layer of compact earth (C) is seen sloping below the glacis surface (A). The northward extension (D) of the "Manasseh Wall" (E) overlies the glacis surface. Photo by J. Whitred.

section. This layer was immediately below the pre-Stratum V, Phase 3 cobbles in Area 41 and immediately over the walls of the "long range of chambers" (pre-Stratum V, Phase 4). It appears in fig. 5 as layer 25. Taken at face value, this observation would seem to place the glacis and "Manasseh's Wall" at the end of Iron II and to bring them into association with pre-Stratum V, Phase 3.[16]

LEVELS EXPLORED BUT NOT EXTENSIVELY EXCAVATED

Aims and Methods

The trenches dug by Petrie and Bliss in the Lower City uncovered deposits of Early Bronze Age remains that varied in depth, according to Bliss's report, from one and one-half to seventeen feet. From the evidence found in his largest trench Bliss suspected the presence of "three or four towns" distributed through twelve feet of debris above the "native clay" (Bliss 1891: 282–83).

Since the investigation of the Lower City was to be a major emphasis of the second phase of the Joint Expedition, it seemed desirable, while the first phase was still in operation, to conduct preliminary explorations with a view to establishing locations where more extensive excavation would be most informative. The first stage in this process was a surface survey of the Lower City. The largest concentrations of Early Bronze Age sherds were found to occur in five locations: on a ridge of high ground west of the acropolis (fig. 2:G), on a similar but narrower ridge southwest of the acropolis (fig. 2:F), and on the summits of each of the three dunes on the southern edge of the Lower City (fig. 2:D). Along the sides of the internal ravines (fig. 2:E) and on the low ground (fig. 2:B), erosion and deep plowing had probably destroyed most of the Early Bronze Age remains. Confirmation of this suspicion was obtained in Field II (fig. 2). The field was laid out with a view to investigating simultaneously the structures at the foot of the central dune and the ravine between the central and eastern dunes, where a gateway into the Lower City might have been located. In Field II the occupational remains had been completely eroded, leaving only the bottom of two pits whose fill yielded EB III pottery (see Coogan 1989a [Chapter VIII, below]). Pits dug for the disposal of camp garbage on the slope north of the eastern ravine disclosed abundant EB III pottery, but no surviving walls.

Of the five locations pinpointed by the survey, the three southern dunes were intrinsically the most interesting. On their southern faces, where erosion had cut into the remains, a continuous layer of fine black ash, containing numerous large EB III sherds, could be traced along all three dunes. Here, prior to excavation, was evidence of a possible general destruction, at least of the southern portion of the Lower City, during the Early Bronze Age.[17]

Four of the five "promising" locations were explored by means of small probes. Field IV was a 2.00 m. x 2.00 m. square on the southwest flank of the northern ridge (fig. 2) at a point where the geologist advised that a considerable depth of earth was likely to have been preserved. Field V, on the summit of the central dune, began as an area 7.00 m. x 2.00 m., but under the pressure of time it was contracted in the lower levels to 2.00 m. x 1.00 m. Field VI, on the southern slope of the eastern dune, was a trench 2.00 m. wide, limited at its southern end by the drop-off of the slope. Field VII, on the western dune, took advantage of one of the geologist's narrow, exploratory cuts and squared its sides to produce a section.

Field IV

In Field IV, Early Bronze Age remains were encountered immediately below the plow zone. Two distinct phases of construction, represented by house walls, were found. They were distinguished from one another by completely different wall orientation. The earlier phase had two clear subphases, defined by the resurfacing of floors. The pottery, including two whole vessels, consisted of common EB III domestic ware. Field IV shows that the northern ridge (fig. 2:G) was occupied by domestic structures, of which at least two phases survive in a good state of preservation. Since virgin soil was not reached, an earlier sequence of phases is possible.

Field V

The Field V probe was laid out in relation to two large, round, well-cut stones that were visible on the surface. The shape of these stones suggested column bases, and the initial expectation was that, after a fairly shallow excavation, the major building to which they belonged would come to light. In Field V all guesses in advance proved wrong. Far from encountering a large building, the probe penetrated 3.50 m. of complex stratigraphy without reaching virgin soil. The cut stones proved to have been put in their present position in very recent times.

Fig. 22 shows the east-balk section of Field V. Because of the contraction in the size of the field, the portion of the section above the 140.35-m. level steps back 2.00 m., and the section is, therefore, not continuous. The small area of the probe made phasing difficult, but on the basis of the section six phases may be provisionally recognized.

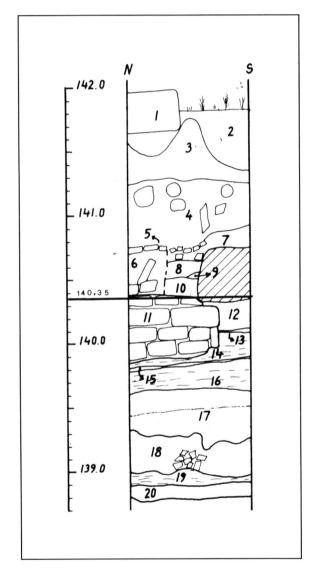

Fig. 22. East-balk section, Field V. For details concerning the layers, see accompanying legend. Above the 140.35-m. level the section steps back 2.00 m. to the east. Diagonal lines indicate a block of unexcavated material at the face of the section. Drawing by B. Zoughby, after an original by L. E. Toombs.

Phase 1 is the Muslim cemetery, associated primarily with layer 2, but penetrating into the lower levels as well. The large cut stone (layer 1) was put in its present position during the cemetery phase or later.

Phase 2 is a layer of decayed brick (layer 3) whose source is unknown. A few sherds of the Late Bronze Age were found in association with this layer, and wider horizontal exposure may reveal Late Bronze Age structures.[18]

Phase 3 is represented by a badly decayed wall (layer 6) and a small patch of surfacing contemporary with it (layer 9). The phase almost certainly belongs to EB III.

Phase 4 is represented by a mud-brick wall (layer 11) and its associated surface (layer 13). The date of the phase is EB III.

Phase 5 is without walls. It consists of an ash-covered surface (layer 15) beneath which is an ash layer (16), probably produced by the decay of surfaces similiar to layer 15. Most probably layers 15 and 16 represent a buildup of living surfaces, since sherds of EB III domestic pottery were recovered from them.

The earliest Bronze Age phase (still EB III) reached in Field V (Phase 6) is a heavy layer of black ash (layer 19) overlying a hard, bricky deposit (layer 20). Whether the latter is the top of a wall or a brick surface cannot be settled without further excavation. Above the ash is a mixed debris layer (18) which appears to be the result of wall collapse.[19]

A crucial question for the interpretation of Field V is, "Which layer or layers correspond to the ash

LEGEND FOR FIGURE 22
(East-Balk Section, Field V)

1. Large cut stone
2. Hard-packed brick detritus
3. Decayed brick
4. Fallen and eroded brick with many rodent burrows
5. Close-packed, fallen brick
6. Probable wall
7. Loose, ashy, with fallen brick
8. Loose, ashy
9. Grey, ashy surface
10. Grey, ashy
11. Mud-brick wall
12. Loose, ashy
13. Sandy surface
14. Dark, ashy
15. Ash-covered surface
16. Dark, ashy
17. Ash and sand mix
18. Mixed debris layer
19. Black ash
20. Solid, bricky

level traced along the southern slope of the dunes?" The most likely candidate is layer 19, since it is at approximately the right level. The argument is, of course, invalidated if (a) the general ash layer did not extend as far north as Field V or (b) it has not yet been reached.[20]

Field VI

In Field VI, coherent Early Bronze Age remains were much closer to the surface than in Field V. The Muslim graves penetrated deeply into a massive mud-brick wall whose top was only a few centimeters below ground level (fig. 23). The wall ran from southeast to northwest along the edge of the slope. It was composed of bricks of various colors and textures, and 2.09 m. of its width were exposed. Against its southern (outer) face and running southward away from the wall was a layer of black ash that contained large, flat-lying EB III sherds and artifacts such as basalt grinders, limestone mace heads, and ceramic animal figurines. The compact ash rested on a layer of well-laid mud bricks. Below the bricks, hard earth filled with limestone flecks, apparently virgin soil, was reached.[21]

The obvious explanation of this structure was that it was a major defensive wall surrounding the Lower City. The ash layer was interpreted in 1975 as the destruction debris of the EB III city.[22]

Fig. 23. Field VI. The Early Bronze Age mud-brick wall (A) is seen in section, but by a Stratum II grave (B). The wall continues (unexcavated) below the meter stick. In the foreground are the ash and sherds of the destruction layer (C). The lower Early Bronze Age phases have not yet been excavated. Photo by J. Whitred.

Field VII

The western dune, on which Field VII is located (fig. 2), is a peculiar formation. It is flanked by deep ravines on both its northern and southern sides, and its summit is a narrow ridge composed of brickwork and bricky debris. F. L. Koucky, the expedition's geologist, suggested that this dune originally had a level summit on which Early Bronze Age structures stood. Centuries of erosion had carried away most of the summit, particularly into the southern wadi, and had left only a ridge of brickwork which probably represents the northern limits of the eroded buildings.

The small probe into the ridge of brickwork on the summit of the dune confirmed these suggestions. The uppermost level of occupation was a plaster surface. It overlay six courses of a mud-brick wall. The wall rested on a layer of water-laid earth, below which was a second wall that was preserved only three courses high. Underlying the wall were two thin ash layers separated by a pebble surface. These ash layers appeared to be part of the general ash deposit traced across the southern slopes of the three dunes. The walls in the probe ran east-west along the ridge, as would be expected if they were the northern walls of structures otherwise destroyed by erosion. It is assumed that the sequence of levels belongs to EB III, although the probe was too small to yield pottery evidence.

LEVELS INDICATED BUT NOT EXPLORED

Two types of data are included under this category: (1) levels indicated by the presence of structures and (2) levels indicated only by the ceramic content of later fills.

Unexplored Structures

Excavation of the three-phase wall on the southern slope of the mound (Field III) brought to light a number of structures belonging to earlier periods.

Walls Exposed in the Foundation Trench of the Field III Wall. The most potentially significant of these earlier structures occurred in Field III, Area 107 (fig. 15). The clearing of the fill between two piers of the Zone A wall exposed the sides and bottom of the foundation trench. In the side of the trench two superimposed walls appeared.

The uppermost (fig. 24:A), which consisted of six courses of dark-colored bricks bearing traces of fire, ran east-west in a line roughly parallel to Zone A. Similar brickwork appeared in the same stratigraphic situation in Field III, Area 31 (fig. 15). The lower wall (fig. 24:B) was at right angles to Zone A and, hence, appeared in section in the side of the trench. Eight courses of yellow, sandy bricks stood on a foundation of rough stones. Evidence of heavy destruction was found on both sides of the wall. Apart from their existence and the fact that they predated Zone A, nothing was known in 1975 of the date and function of these walls.[23]

Brickwork below the Field III Wall. The bottom of the foundation trench in Field III, Area 107, was covered by a platform of brickwork on which the bases of the piers were founded. A similar platform was uncovered in the Zone A foundation trench in Field III, Area 23 (fig. 15). Since in neither case was the brickwork investigated to its foundation, it is impossible to say whether it was the top of an earlier wall, sheared off in the construction of Zone A, or a stage in the building of Zone A itself. The fact that the platform was, in places, at least ten courses deep seems to favor the first alternative.

Brickwork within the Field III Wall. A patch of light-colored brick, embedded in the darker brickwork of Zone C in Field III, Area 105 (fig. 15), is not so readily dealt with. To determine whether it was a fragment of an earlier wall encased in Zone C or a casual variation in the color of the bricks used by the Zone C builders would require a section through the wall in Area 105.

Unexplained Features. At the eastern extremity of the Field III wall some unexplained features remain. The stone platform which abutted the Zone A foundation (see above, p. 147 and fig. 17) was probably contemporary with Zone A and may have functioned as the base of a corner tower that was removed during the construction of Zone B. Since only the surface of the stone work has been exposed (fig. 17), this conclusion cannot be demonstrated.

The stone-built drain, truncated and rendered useless by the stone platform (see above, p. 147 and fig. 17) is without a stratigraphic home and, apart from an unpredictable piece of good fortune, will remain so.

An ancient watercourse was sealed under the foundation of Zone C at its eastern end. The date of its construction, its original function, and its stratigraphic significance may never be known.

Fig. 24. Two earlier walls (A, B) and the stone foundation (C) for the lower wall (B) that were exposed in the foundation trench of Zone A (Field III, Area 107). Photo by J. Whitred.

The Pottery of the Fills

The pottery of the numerous fill layers on the acropolis raises important stratigraphic and historical questions. Only three or four sherds of possible Middle Bronze Age origin and an equally small number which may be dated to EB IV have appeared. LB II was abundantly attested, but no sherds of classical bichrome ware have been found. Although tenth- and ninth-century pottery was plentiful, typical Philistine pottery was absent from the fills. Only a few sherds of degenerate Philistine-type bowls have been recovered.

When, and under what conditions, did the Late Bronze Age occupation of the site begin? When, and for what historical and cultural reasons, did it come to an end? What was the situation at Hesi at the beginning of the Iron Age? When, and with what motivation, did Israelite occupation of the site take place? This catalogue of questions, which could be extended almost indefinitely, indicates that Tell el-Hesi still has much to contribute to an understanding of the cultural and archaeological history of the southern Coastal Plain.

NOTES

1. Preliminary reports for the 1977, 1979, 1981, and 1983 seasons were published in O'Connell, Rose, and Toombs 1978; O'Connell and Rose 1980; Toombs 1983; and Doermann and Fargo 1985. These reports serve to supplement and bring up to date the material included in the present text.
2. A detailed study of the trench system and its use during the Israeli War of Independence is contained in Toombs 1985: 5–14, 159–61.
3. Excavation in Fields V and VI since 1975 has almost doubled the number of graves available for study (O'Connell, Rose, and Toombs 1978: 85–87; O'Connell and Rose 1980: 83–85; Toombs 1983: 44; Doermann and Fargo 1985: 22–23). The skeletal materials from these burials are under study by J. K. Eakins.
4. Several additional examples of jar burials of infants have been found in the Field V and VI cemeteries (O'Connell and Rose 1980: 83; Toombs 1983: 44).
5. The starting date for the cemetery is still a matter of conjecture, but research subsequent to 1975 indicates that it went out of use about 1800 CE. The final report is contained in Toombs 1985: 15–158, 162–250.
6. Seven additional Hellenistic pits were excavated in the 1981 season in Field I, Areas 2 and 3 (Toombs 1983: 35).
7. W. J. Bennett, Jr., has completed a detailed study of the Persian Period stratigraphy (to appear as part of Bennett and Blakely, 1989). He now divides Stratum Vb into two substrata (Vb1 and Vb2). The plan presented in this paper (fig. 13A) is essentially his Stratum Vb1. The plan of the earlier stratum (Vb2) does not include Building I.1.126 and shows fragmentary walls and cobbled surfaces in Areas 1 and 11. These do not appear on the plan included in the text.
8. A very productive pit belonging to Stratum Vd was excavated in Area 2 in 1981 (Toombs 1983: 33–35).
9. Coogan dated the cemetery "toward the end of the Persian Period" (1975: 46 [Chapter X, below, p. 185]). He was influenced in this conclusion by the view, prevalent then, that the Field III wall was early Persian Period (Stratum Vd) in date (idem.). Of the fourteen sherds published on fig. 8 of Coogan's paper, one (#9) is classified as Iron I, six (#1, 4, 7, 10, 11, 13) as Iron II B–C, one (# 14) as late Iron II or early Persian, four (#3, 5, 8, 12) as Persian Period, and one (#2) as late Persian (although the form can appear earlier). It is, therefore, an active possibility that the cemetery belongs to a date about the middle of the Persian Period at Tell el-Hesi (i.e. during the fifth century BCE). This would make it all the more likely that the Field III wall was abandoned sometime in Iron II.
10. There is no direct proof of the final date of the wall system. It may have gone out of use earlier in Iron II.
11. In the 1977 season it became clear that there was in Areas 41 and 51 a third pre-Stratum V phase between pre-Stratum V, Phase 3 and Phase 4, cut through by and, hence, predating Pit I.51.124. This subphase was contemporary with a large building preserved beneath the Persian Period (Stratum Vd) remains in Areas 22 and 32 (O'Connell, Rose, and Toombs 1978: 79–82; O'Connell and Rose 1980: 77). In 1977 the rather awkward designation pre-Stratum V was dropped and the phases were designated by stratum numbers: pre-Stratum V, Phase 1 = Stratum VI; pre-Stratum V, Phase 2 = Stratum VIIa; pre-Stratum V, Phase 3 = Stratum VIIb; the intermediate pre-Stratum V phase recognized in 1977 = Stratum VIIc; and pre-Stratum V, Phase 4 = Stratum VIId.
12. The structure was established as a separate phase and given the designation Stratum VIIc, and its northern limits were clarified, in 1977.
13. As indicated in Notes 11 and 12, a new phase (Stratum VIIc), to which the large building in Areas 22 and 32 belongs, was isolated in 1977. Wall fragment I.31.303 is the sole surviving representative of the eastern half of this building.
14. The surface proved to be part of the fill. The walls were over 6.00 m. high (Toombs 1983: 31).
15. Field analysis of the pottery removed in 1981 from below the foundation levels of Wall I.41.179 tends to confirm Matthers's suggestions.
16. During the 1977, 1979, 1981, and 1983 seasons a major effort was made to deal with the problems raised by this complex of structures. Evidence has been accumulating to show that the Field III wall, the "Manasseh Wall," the glacis, and the chamber-and-fill system on the summit of the mound, with the massive fills required to consolidate these structures, were all part of a single engineering enterprise designed to elevate the mound and to provide it with a double circumvallation (O'Connell, Rose, and Toombs 1978: 82–84; O'Connell and Rose 1980: 80–82; Toombs 1983: 25–33; Doermann and Fargo 1985: 1–6). The relationship of the upper structure to the rest of the system is not absolutely clear. It is most likely part of the consolidating and leveling terraces above the "Manasseh Wall" (Toombs 1983: 32–33).
17. Subsequent excavation in Field VI showed that the ash layer on the southern slopes of the dunes was not destruction debris, but probably ash of industrial or agricultural origin that had been washed and blown against the southern (outer) face of the EB III city wall (O'Connell, Rose, and Toombs 1978: 87–88; O'Connell and Rose 1980: 86–87).
18. Excavation in Field V in 1981 indicated that no LB structures were present. The occurrence of the LB pottery was probably the result of transients moving across the area (Toombs 1983: 35).
19. In the stratigraphic analysis of the probes the tendency is to over-refine the stratigraphy. In the light of more extensive excavation it can usually be greatly simplified. In the case of Field V, it is probable that excavation will show two principal occupation levels, one corresponding to layers 6–15 and the other to layers 18–20.
20. Excavation in Field V after 1975 concentrated on the removal of the Muslim burials (Stratum II) which occurred everywhere in the field. One hundred forty-six graves were excavated, but no extensive penetration into earlier levels was undertaken. However, it is clear that an EB III city wall, analogous to that found in Field VI, extended along the southern edge of Field V also.

21. The work of the 1977 season demonstrated that this deposit lay on the floor of a chamber *within* the EB III wall (O'Connell, Rose, and Toombs 1978: 87).
22. The relative ease of access to the EB III remains in Field VI led to extensive excavation in the field in 1977, 1979, 1981, and 1983. The result of this work has been the uncovering of the massive defensive wall of the EB city, a portion of which the 1975 probe had already encountered. The nature of the wall, its associated glacis, and the mainly industrial occupation which abutted it on the north side are described in O'Connell, Rose, and Toombs 1978: 86–88; O'Connell and Rose 1980: 85–88; Toombs 1983: 35–44; and Doermann and Fargo 1985: 13-22.
23. In the 1981 season the walls in question were shown to belong to EB III, but no additional information was obtained (Toombs 1983: 33).

BIBLIOGRAPHY FOR CHAPTER VII

Ashkenazi, T.
1938   *Tribus semi-nomades de la Palestine du nord*. Études d'Ethnographie, de Sociologie, et d'Ethnologie, Tome II. Paris: Libraire Orientaliste Paul Geuthner.

Bennett, W. J., Jr., and Blakely, J. A.
1989   *Tell el-Hesi: The Persian Period (Stratum V)*. Edited by K. G. O'Connell, S.J., with F. L. Horton, Jr. Excavation Reports of the American Schools of Oriental Research: Tell el-Hesi 3. Winona Lake, IN: Eisenbrauns.

Blakely, J. A., and Toombs, L. E.
1980   *The Tell el-Hesi Field Manual*. Edited by K. G. O'Connell, S.J. Evacation Reports of the American Schools of Oriental Research: Tell el-Hesi 1. Cambridge, MA; 2nd printing (1983), Philadelphia, PA: American Schools of Oriental Research.

Bliss, F. J.
1891   Report of Excavations at Tell el-Hesy During the Spring of 1891. *Palestine Exploration Fund Quarterly Statement* 23:282–90.
1894   *A Mound of Many Cities*. London: Palestine Exploration Fund.

Coogan, M. D.
1975   A Cemetery from the Persian Period at Tell el-Hesi. *Bulletin of the American Schools of Oriental Research* 220: 37–46. This article has been reprinted as Chapter X in the present volume (pp. 177–87, below).
1989a   Field II. In *Tell el-Hesi: The Site and the Expedition*, pp. 163–68. Edited by B. T. Dahlberg and K. G. O'Connell, S.J. Excavation Reports of the American Schools of Oriental Research: Tell el-Hesi 4. Winona Lake, IN: Eisenbrauns.
1989b   Chalcolithic Remains in Field III. In *Tell el-Hesi: The Site and the Expedition*, pp. 169–76. Edited by B. T. Dahlberg and K. G. O'Connell, S.J. Excavation Reports of the American Schools of Oriental Research: Tell el-Hesi 4. Winona Lake, IN: Eisenbrauns.

Doermann, R. W., and Fargo, V. M.
1985   Tell el-Hesi, 1983. *Palestine Exploration Quarterly* 117: 1–24.

Eakins, J. K.
1980   Human Osteology and Archaeology. *Biblical Archeologist* 43: 89–96.

Matthers, J. M.
1989   Explorations by the Palestine Exploration Fund at Tell el-Hesi 1890–1892. In *Tell el-Hesi: The Site and the Expedition*, pp. 37–67. Edited by B. T. Dahlberg and K. G. O'Connell, S.J. Excavation Reports of the American Schools of Oriental Research: Tell el-Hesi 4. Winona Lake, IN: Eisenbrauns.

O'Connell, K. G., S.J.; Rose, D. G.; and Toombs, L. E.
1978   Tell el-Hesi, 1977. *Palestine Exploration Quarterly* 110: 75–90 and pls. V–IX.

O'Connell, K. G., S.J. and Rose, D. G.
1980   Tell el-Hesi, 1979. *Palestine Exploration Quarterly* 112: 73–91 and pls. IV–VII.

Petrie, W. M. F.
1891   *Tell el Hesy (Lachish)*. London: Palestine Exploration Fund.

Rose, D. G.; Toombs, L. E.; and O'Connell, K. G., S.J.
1978   Four Seasons of Excavation at Tell el-Hesi: A Preliminary Report. In *Preliminary Excavation Reports: Bâb edh-Dhrâᶜ, Sardis, Meiron, Tell el-Hesi, Carthage (Punic)*, pp. 109–49. Edited by D. N. Freedman. Annual of the American Schools of Oriental Research 43. Cambridge, MA: American Schools of Oriental Research.

Stager, L. E.
1971   Climatic Conditions and Grain Storage in the Persian Period. *Biblical Archaeologist* 34: 86–88.

Stern, E.
1978   *Excavations at Tel Mevorakh (1973–1976); Part One: From the Iron Age to the Roman Period*. Qedem: Monographs of the Institute

of Archaeology 9. Jerusalem: The Institute of Archaeology, The Hebrew University of Jerusalem.

Stewart, R. B.
1978   Archeobotanic Studies at Tell el-Hesi. *Economic Botany* 32: 279–86. This article has been reprinted as Chapter XI in the present volume (pp. 188–94, below).

The Survey of Palestine
1947   1:20,000 Map Series.

Toombs, L. E.
1974   Tell el-Hesi, 1970–71. *Palestine Exploration Quarterly* 106: 19–31 and pls. I–VI.
1983   Tell el-Hesi, 1981. *Palestine Exploration Quarterly* 115: 25–46.
1985   *Tell el-Hesi: Modern Military Trenching and Muslim Cemetery in Field I, Strata I–II.* Edited by K. G. O'Connell, S. J. Excavation Reports of the American Schools of Oriental Research: Tell el-Hesi 2. Waterloo, Ontario: Wilfrid Laurier University Press.

Chapter VIII

FIELD II

by
Michael David Coogan
Stonehill College

The lower city of Tell el-Hesi is defined in the south by a high dune ridge in three segments, divided by two depressions or ravines. The eastern and western ridges have elevations higher than the acropolis which rises from the northeast corner of the site. These ridges show evidence of mud-brick construction on their eroded southern slopes, and a surface survey in 1969 of both the ridges and the area they enclose revealed a dense concentration of Early Bronze pottery. In the 1970 season Field II was opened to the north of the central ridge near the depression separating it from the eastern ridge (see fig. 1), where there might have been a gateway to the lower city. It was hoped that the field would expose both the fortifications of the Early Bronze lower city and the domestic quarters immediately within the walls.

The removal of the freshly plowed topsoil, ranging in depth from 0.10 m. to 0.25 m., revealed the parallel grooves made by a harrow in the more compact subtopsoil. Seven probes were made within Areas 1–7 (see fig. 2 for their locations and final levels). Five of these probes provided no occupational remains and exposed a layer of subsoil which contained a high concentration of caliche. This layer was probed in Area 3 and was found to be 2.75 m. deep, after which the caliche gradually diminished until one reached the sterile sand, which at Hesi is the equivalent of bedrock.

The only evidence of occupation was in Areas 1 and 4, where the bottoms of two pits were uncovered. The smaller, II.1.004, was 0.40 m. deep as preserved and contained sandy soil and a few randomly distributed body sherds whose ware suggested an Early Bronze date. The larger pit,

II.4.006–.007 and .009, was about 1.00 m. in diameter. It contained the body sherds of two large store jars which showed evidence of burning—probably within the pit itself—and several rims and bases from other vessels (see below).

The excavations of Petrie and Bliss, as well as work by the Joint Expedition in 1973 and subsequently, have shown that there was occupation within the walls of the Early Bronze Age lower city (as at Arad); if this occupation also extended to Field II, as seems likely, then erosion and modern deep plowing have removed all traces of it apart from these pits. Since only the bottoms of the pits were found, the occupational levels from which they were dug must have been higher, in the zone subsequently disturbed by plows or above. Excavation in Field II was halted after one week.[1]

POTTERY

Forty-three sherds (belonging to 38 separate vessels), all from Area 4, were registered. For loci II.4.001–.005 and .008, consisting of soil layers without primary occupational deposits, the sherds constitute a sample of the material found in the entire field. They include the following characteristic Early Bronze Age forms: 4 white-slipped, combed body sherds, 3 holemouth jar rims, 1 platter rim, 4 flat-bottomed jar bases, and several bowl and juglet rims. Most of these sherds are too worn or too small to draw; numbers 1, 2, and 7 in fig. 3 are a selection of the better-preserved forms.[2]

The pit in Area 4 was dug in three layers, loci 4.006, .007, and .009. Again, most of the

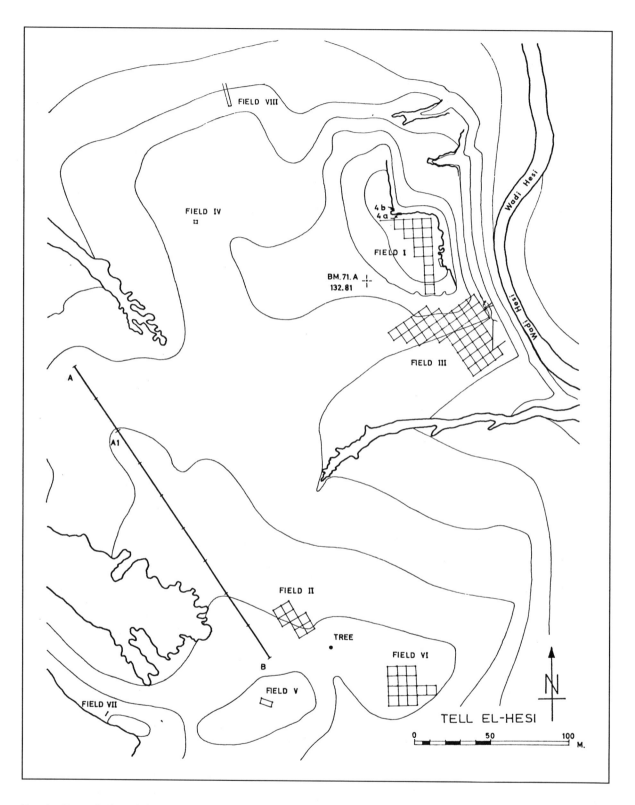

Fig. 1. General plan of the Tell el-Hesi site, showing the location of the various fields. Drawing by B. Zoughbi.

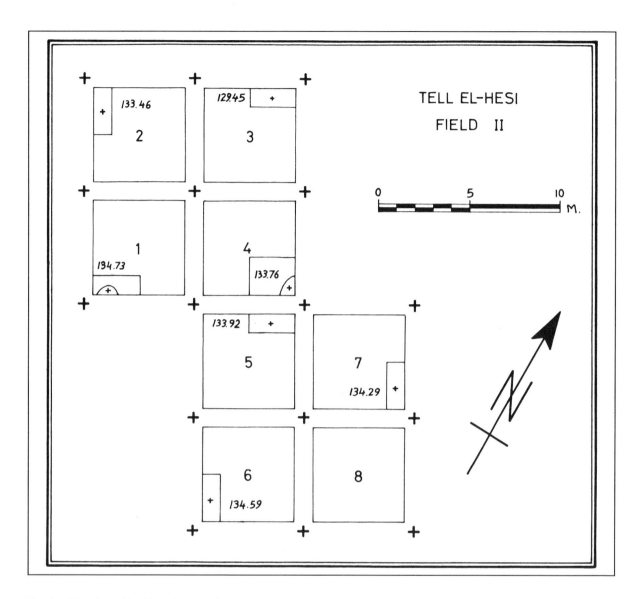

Fig. 2. Top plan of Field II, showing final elevations and the location of the pits in Areas 1 and 4.

registered sherds are too worn or broken to draw; numbers 3, 4, 5, 6, and 8 in fig. 3 are the best-preserved examples.

The vessels shown here fit into Early Bronze II–III; the small size of the sample makes more precise dating difficult.

(completed May 1976; revised May 1979)

CATALOGUE OF LOCI[3]

Area 1

.001 Loose, freshly cultivated topsoil 0.10 m. deep, covering entire area.
Pottery pail: 1 (Arab, EB*).

.002 Probe trench 1.00 m. x 2.50 m. in SW corner of area.
Layer 1: compacted loess (subtopsoil) ca. 0.10 m. deep.
Pottery pail: 2 (Rom, EB*).
Layer 2: loess with high concentration of caliche.
Pottery pails: 4, 6, 7 (EB, ud).

.003 = .002.1 in entire area.
Pottery pail: 3 (Hell, EB*).

.004 Pit 1.00 m. in diameter, 0.40 m. deep as preserved, filled with sandy soil and randomly distributed body sherds.
Pottery pail: 5 (EB).

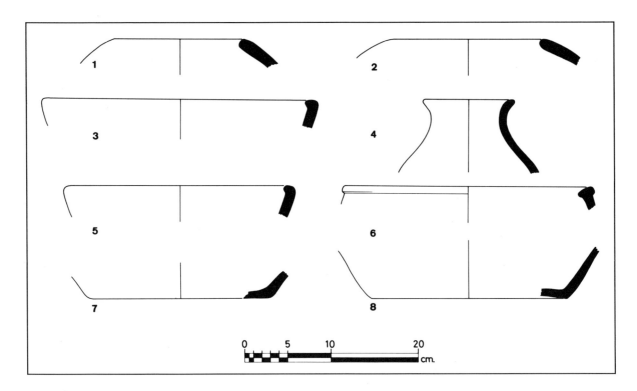

Fig. 3. Pottery from Field II (see accompanying legend).

LEGEND FOR FIGURE 3

No.	Vessel Type	Reg. No.	Locus	Description
1	Jar	139	4.002	Ext gray (10 YR 5/1), int very pale brown (10 YR 7/3), ware brown (7.5 YR 5/2), core dark gray (5 YR 4/1), grit freq 6.
2	Jar	38	4.005	Ext reddish yellow (5 YR 7/6), int pink (7.5 YR 7/4), ware yellowish red (5 YR 5/6) near ext and light yellowish brown (10 YR 6/4) near int, grit freq 6.
3	Bowl	253	4.007	Ext and int pink (7.5 YR 7/4), ware reddish yellow (5 YR 6/6), core grayish brown (10 YR 5/2), grit freq 4.
4	Jar	1741	4.006	Ext white (2.5 Y 8/2) slipped, with traces of horizontal combing on shoulder, int pink (7.5 YR 7/4), ware reddish yellow (5 YR 7/6), grit freq 4.
5	Bowl	214	4.007	Ext and int reddish yellow (5 YR 7/6) with traces of red (2.5 YR 4/6) slip, ware reddish yellow (5 YR 6/6), core pale brown (10 YR 6/3), grit freq 5.
6	Bowl	251	4.007	Ext and int pink (7.5 YR 7/4), ware reddish yellow (5 YR 6/6), grit freq 5.
7	Jar	33	4.002	Ext and int reddish yellow (5 YR 7/6), ware light yellowish brown (10 YR 6/4) near ext and gray (10 YR 5/1) near int, core very dark gray (5 YR 3/1), grit freq 6.
8	Jar	219	4.006	Ext and int pink (7.5 YR 7/4), ware brown (7.5 YR 5/2), core grayish brown (10 YR 5/2), grit freq 5.

Area 2

.001 Probe trench 1.00 m. x 2.50 m. in NW corner of area.

Layer 1: loose, freshly cultivated topsoil ca. 0.10 m. deep.

Pottery pail: 1 (Arab, EB*).

Layer 2: compacted loess (subtopsoil).

Pottery pails: 3, 4, 5 (Byz, EB*, ud).

.002 = .001.1 in entire area.

Pottery pail: 2 (Byz, EB*).

Area 3

.001 Loose, freshly cultivated topsoil ca. 0.10–0.25 m. deep, covering entire area.

Pottery pail: 1 (Arab, EB).

GRIT FREQUENCY

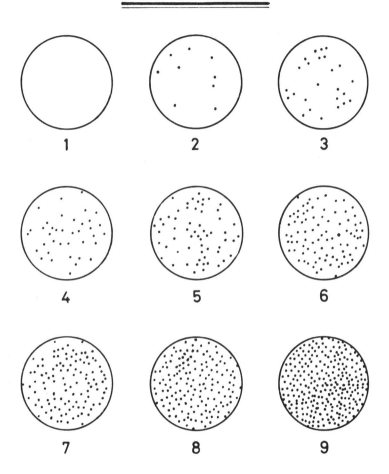

Fig. 4. Grit frequency chart (adopted from Wagner and Toombs 1971).

.002 Probe trench 1.00 m. x 2.50 m. in NE corner of area.
    Layer 1: = .001.
    Layer 2: compacted loess (subtopsoil) ca. 0.25 m. deep.
    Layer 3: loess with high concentration of caliche, denser toward bottom, ca. 2.75 m. deep.
    Layer 4: sand mixed with caliche ca. 0.10–0.50 m. deep.
    Layer 5: pure sand.
    Pottery pails: 2, 5, 6, 7 (Byz, Rom, Iron 2, LB, EB).
.003 = .002.2.
    Pottery pails: 3, 4 (EB*, ud).

Area 4
.001 Loose, freshly cultivated topsoil ca. 0.10 m. deep, covering entire area.
    Pottery pail: 1 (ud).
.002 Probe trench 2.00 m. x 2.50 m. in SE corner of area.
    Layer 1: = .001.
    Pottery pail: 2 (Arab, EB).
    (Remaining layers assigned separate locus numbers)
.003 Compacted loess (topsoil) ca. 0.10 m. deep, covering entire area.
    Pottery pails: 3, 4, 7 (Arab, EB).
.004 Compacted loess (subtopsoil) ca. 0.06– 0.10 m. deep, covering entire area.
    Pottery pails: 5, 6, 9, 23 (Arab, EB*, ud).

.005 Loess with high concentration of caliche ca. 0.30 m. deep, within .002.
Pottery pails: 6, 8, 10, 11, 12 (LB, EB*, ud).

.006 Pit 1.00 m. in diameter, 1.00 m. deep as preserved, containing sandy loess with some ash and flat-lying sherds near the top; within .002.
Pottery pails: 13, 14, 18, 19, 22 (EB).

.007 Lens of soil with high clay content in .006 which had been in contact with fire, ca. 0.03 m. deep.
Pottery pails: 15, 20 (EB).

.008 = .005.
Pottery pail: 16 (EB, ud).

.009 Sandy loess with concentration of caliche and some charcoal flecks in .006 under .007, ca. 0.25 m. deep.
Pottery pails: 12, 20, 21, 24 (EB).

Area 5

.001 Probe trench 1.00 m. x 2.50 m. in NE corner of area.
Layer 1: compacted topsoil ca. 0.20 m. deep.
Layer 2: loess with high concentration of caliche, excavated to a depth of 0.45 m.
Pottery pails: 1, 2, 3 (Arab, EB*).

Area 6

.001 Probe trench 1.00 m. x 2.50 m. in SE corner of area.
Layer 1: compacted topsoil ca. 0.10 m. deep.
Layer 2: loess with high concentration of caliche, excavated to a depth of 0.35 m.
Pottery pails: 1, 2 (Arab, Byz*, Hell, EB).

NOTES

1. L. E. Stager was Field Supervisor, and the Area Supervisors were D. W. Brooks, M. D. Coogan, R. W. Doermann, and D. M. Freedman; the author is grateful to V. M. Fargo for assistance in the description of pottery.
2. The parenthetic notation following a color description gives the more precise Munsell color-code designation (Munsell 1975). For the descriptions of pottery in this and the next chapter, the following abbreviations have been used:
   ext = exterior
   int = interior
   grit freq = grit frequency, i.e., the proportion of inclusions to fabric according to the chart in fig. 4.
3. The following abbreviations have been used in the field identifications of the pottery as reported in this catalogue:
   * pottery from this period predominates
   Arab Arabic (from Umayyad to modern)
   Byz Byzantine
   EB Early Bronze
   Hell Hellenistic
   LB Late Bronze
   Rom Roman
   ud undetermined

BIBLIOGRAPHY FOR CHAPTER VIII

Munsell, A. H.
1975 *Munsell Soil Color Charts.* 1975 Edition. Baltimore: Macbeth Division of Kollmorgen Corporation.

Wagner, N., and Toombs, L. E.
1971 *A Handbook for Coding Palestinian Pottery.* Waterloo: Waterloo Lutheran (now Wilfrid Laurier) University.

Chapter IX

CHALCOLITHIC REMAINS IN FIELD III

by
Michael David Coogan
Stonehill College

During the 1970 season, in the course of probes to determine the direction of the southern face of the fortification system in Field III, remains of earlier occupation were uncovered in Areas 3 and 5 (see fig. 1 for the location of these areas); limited excavation was continued in Area 3 in 1971.[1]

AREA 3

In a probe trench in the northeast corner of Area 3, a small refuse pit was partially excavated in 1970. The locus (3.003; see fig. 2) contained several soil layers, the lowest of which (3.003.4; fig. 3: 9, pocket insert) was a layer of very pale brown (10 YR 7/4)[2] dune sand with occasional water-rolled limestone pebbles, but otherwise sterile. Directly over this was a layer of brownish yellow (10 YR 6/6) sand (3.003.3; fig. 3: 8), about 0.50 m. thick, containing chert pebbles and cobbles. These layers antedate occupation of the site and represent the equivalent of bedrock. Similar geological strata have been probed in Areas 1, 5, and 5A.

The fill of the pit itself consisted of a matrix of pale brown (10 YR 6/3) soil (3.003.2; fig. 3: 7), averaging 0.75 m. in depth, with a high concentration of light gray (5 YR 7/1) and dark gray (5 YR 4/1) ash. Within this soil were found randomly distributed sherds, fragments of charred and uncharred bones, including a sheep or goat vertebra and a long bone, perhaps of a domestic bovine, and, at the top, several large sandstone and limestone boulders (see fig. 2, upper right) which showed traces of burning on their lower side. These stones were covered by a layer of ashy soil (fig. 3: 6), and

then by windblown, brownish yellow (10 YR 6/6) sand (fig. 3: 5).

The outline of the pit was clearly distinguishable. It was cut into pale brown (10 YR 6/3) sand containing caliche nodules which decreased in frequency at lower depths. Over the entire area was a layer of topsoil and wash from the slopes of the tell above (fig. 3: 1–2). The irregular shape of the locus and its contents indicate that it was a refuse pit, dug from ground level (about 121.7 m.), with layers 5 and 6 subsequently having accumulated over the charred stones.

The pottery from this pit (fig. 4: 1–6) all belongs in the Chalcolithic period. No. 1 is a small fragment of the rim of a delicate bowl or perhaps of a footed goblet (see Mallon, Koeppel, and Neuville 1934: pls. 42: 13 and 49: 98); nos. 2 and 3 are the rims of large bowls, with parallels at Meser (Dothan 1959a: fig. 6: 1, 5) and elsewhere. The rudimentary knob handles on no. 4 are similar to examples found at Horvat Beter (Dothan 1959b: fig. 10: 15–18) and Arad (Amiran 1978: pl. 5: 17). No. 5 is the rim of a holemouth jar of a common Chalcolithic type; the thumbnail impressions are most probably part of a continuous decoration circling the shoulder of the jar (cf., for example, Dothan 1959a: fig. 5: 3; Pritchard 1958: pls. 26: 10; 33:7; de Vaux 1961: fig. 2:3).

To the west of Pit 3.003 was another refuse deposit, but, unlike the other features in the area, it seems to have been a midden or refuse heap, largely above ground level (about 121.40 m.). This deposit (3.002; fig. 3:4) was similar in composition to Pit 3.019, .021 (see below), with small amounts of charred and uncharred animal bones, charcoal,

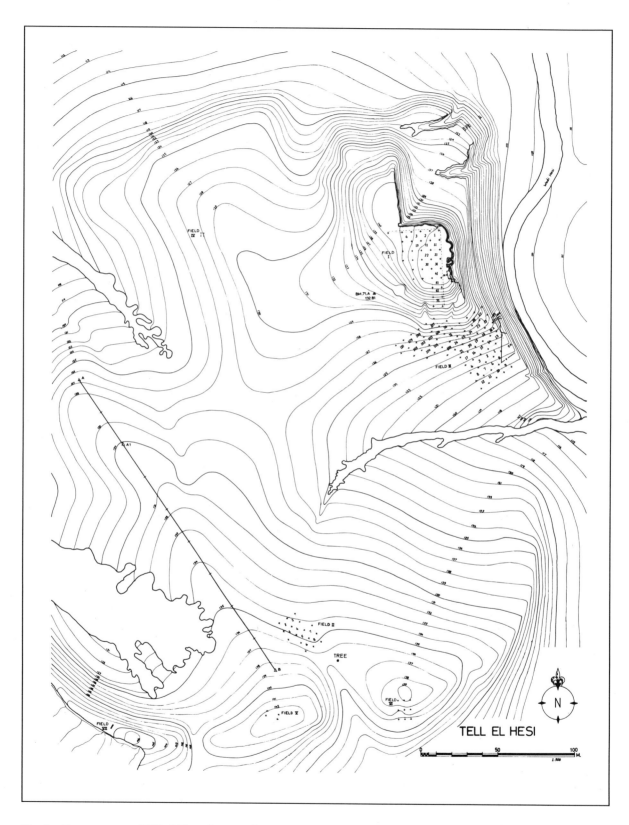

Fig. 1. Contour map of Tell el-Hesi, showing the location of Areas 3 and 5 in Field III. Plan by B. Zoughbi.

TELL EL-HESI

FIELD III AREA 3

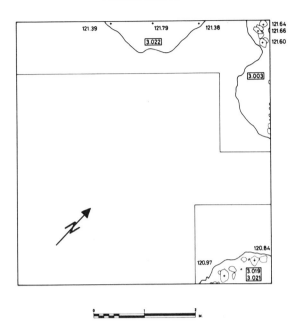

Fig. 2. Top plan of Area 3.

and a few coarse body sherds.

To the south of Pit 3.003 was a second pit (3.019, .021; fig. 3:10), which was also only partially excavated. It was dug into brownish yellow (10 YR 6/6), sterile sand from a level of about 121.25 m. and contained fragments of fired brick, charcoal, charred bone, and sherds concentrated in a band of gray (5 YR 6/1), ashy soil between two layers of mottled, very pale brown (10 YR 7/4); pale brown (10 YR 6/3); and light gray (5 YR 7/1) clayey and sandy soil. The pottery from this pit (fig. 4: 7–11, 13) is best dated to the Chalcolithic period. Noteworthy forms include no. 7, a rounded bowl with close parallels at Gezer (Dever *et al.* 1974: pl. 2: 15), Horvat Beter (Dothan 1959b: fig. 12: 1), and Tell el-Farᶜah (N) (de Vaux 1955: fig. 3: 3); no. 8, the rim of a holemouth jar with the scalloped decoration known from many sites of the Ghassul-Beersheba culture (see the discussion in Dever *et al.* 1974: 12), including Arad (Amiran 1978: pl. 6: 5); and nos. 11 and 13, two large store jar bases. No. 10, if not an intrusion, may be an early example of a type of juglet more characteristic of the Early Bronze Age.

AREA 5

Embedded in the sterile dune sand (5.024) in Area 5 was a circular installation (5.033; see figs. 5 and 6), with diameters from exterior to exterior of 2.55 m. N-S and 2.50 m. E-W. This structure consisted of a wall made of pale brown (10 YR 6/3) mud plaster with straw temper, with a thickness of about 0.16 m. at the bottom and about 0.10 m. at the top of its preserved height of about 0.40 m. (elevation 120.75 m.).

No clearly defined occupational surface was found in association with this installation.[3] It was filled with layers of water-deposited soil alternating with debris layers containing randomly distributed pebbles, cobbles, sherds (some of which had been secondarily burnt), bone fragments, and charcoal flecks, as well as carbonized wheat, lentil, emmer, and grape seeds in small quantities; small finds included a worked chert ballista and a chalk mortar. The bottom layer within the structure was water-deposited, and the fill within it as well as the walls were covered by about 0.25 m. of wash (5.029) which also contained some sherds as well as a limestone mortar fragment. This suggests that the entire fill was secondary to the structure's use.

The associated pottery (fig. 4: 12, 14–16) is all handmade and coarse. No. 12, from the water-deposited soil over the installation, is the slightly everted rim of a large V-shaped bowl; the form occurs in Chalcolithic deposits at Azor (Perrot 1961: fig. 37: 28), Horvat Beter (Dothan 1959b: fig. 7: 21, 30), Tell el-Farᶜah (N) (de Vaux 1955: fig. 3: 2), and Arad (Amiran 1978: pl. 1: 3), and continues into EB I (see Callaway 1972: 74, no. 11). Also noteworthy is no. 15, the rim of a store jar with the thumb-indented, scalloped decoration characteristic of several forms in the Chalcolithic repertoire; see de Contenson 1956: fig. 1: 3, 5, 10; Dever *et al.* 1974: pl. 3: 1; Dothan 1959b: fig. 7: 31, 32. The large bowl (no. 14) and the holemouth jar (no. 16) are also typical Chalcolithic forms. All of this pottery comes from the material which had secondarily accumulated within or just above the structure, but this cannot have been long after its abandonment in view of the preservation of its walls. The installation is, therefore, to be dated to the Chalcolithic period.

Since no occupational surfaces were found in association with this Chalcolithic installation, its function is difficult to determine. Parallels from the same period suggest that it was the foundation of a small dwelling whose superstructure was probably

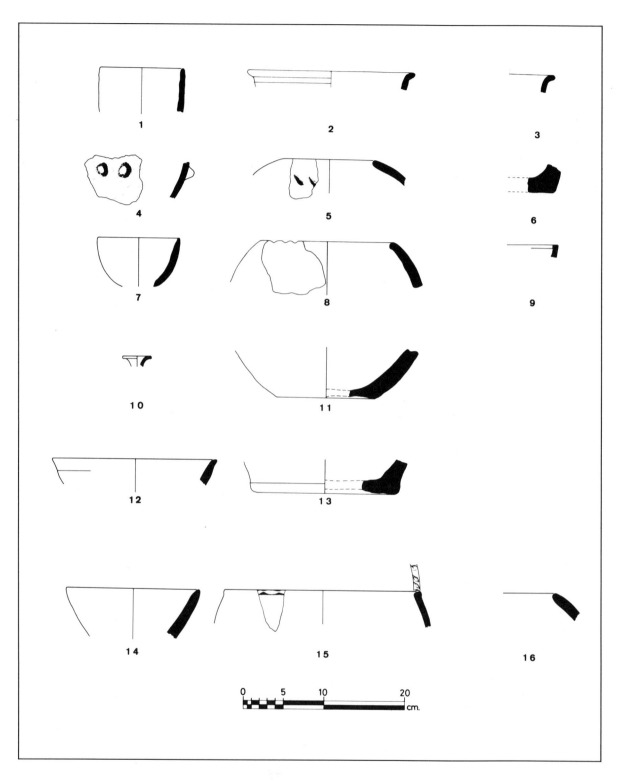

Fig. 4. Field III pottery from Pit 3.003 (nos. 1-6), Pit 3.019, .021 (nos. 7-11, 13), and Installation 5.033 (nos. 12, 14-16). See accompanying legend.

LEGEND FOR FIGURE 4

(Grit frequency chart is given in Chapter VIII, fig. 4)

Vessel No.	Type	Reg. No.	Locus	Pail No.	Description
1	Bowl	70–306	3.003	14	Ext pink (5 YR 7/4), int reddish yellow (5 YR 7/6), ware pink (7.5 YR 8/4), grit freq 4; handmade.
2	Bowl	70–304	3.003	14	Ext pink (7.5 YR 7/4), int reddish yellow (5 YR 6/6), ware light yellowish brown (10 YR 6/4), grit freq 2.
3	Bowl	70–440	3.003	15	Ext light red (2.5 YR 6/6), int and ware reddish yellow (5 YR 7/6), grit freq 2.
4	ud	70–434 70–437	·3.003	15	Ext pink (5 YR 7/4 & 7.5 YR 8/4), int pink (5 YR 7/4), ware reddish yellow (5 YR 7/6), core pink (7.5 YR 7/4), grit freq 5; handmade.
5	Jar	70–303	3.003	14	Ext and int pinkish gray (7.5 YR 7/2), ware reddish yellow (5 YR 6/6), grit freq 5; handmade; two fingernail impressions.
6	Jar Base	70–435	3.003	15	Ext reddish yellow (5 YR 7/6), int light brown (7.5 YR 6/4), ware reddish yellow (5 YR 6/6), core dark grayish brown (10 YR 4/2), grit freq 5.
7	Bowl	71–4997	3.021	48	Ext and int pink (7.5 YR 7/4), ware dark gray (10 YR 4/1), grit freq 3; straw temper; handmade.
8	Jar	71–6847	3.021	54	Ext dark brown (7.5 YR 4/2), int pinkish gray (7.5 YR 7/2), ware brown (7.5 YR 5/2) near ext and pinkish gray (7.5 YR 7/2) near int, core very dark gray (10 YR 3/1), grit freq 2; straw temper.
9	Bowl	71–2374	3.019	44	Ext, int, and ware reddish yellow (5 YR 7/6), grit freq 2; handmade.
10	Juglet	71–2372	3.019	44	Ext, int, and ware reddish yellow (5 YR 7/6), grit freq 2.
11	Jar	71–6846	3.021	57	Ext pink (5 YR 8/3) with traces of red (10 YR 4/6) paint, int pink (7.5 YR 7/4), ware pale brown (10 YR 6/3), core dark grayish brown (10 YR 4/2), grit freq 3; straw temper.
12	Bowl	70–2316	5.029	60	Ext and int pink (5 YR 8/4), ware pink (5 YR 7/4) near ext and pink (7.5 YR 8/4) near int, grit freq 5; handmade.
13	Jar Base	71–5158	3.021	50	Ext light red (2.5 YR 6/6), int pink (5 YR 7/4), ware pink (7.5 YR 7/4), core very dark gray (2.5 YR 3/1), grit freq 6; handmade.
14	Bowl	70–2772	5.033	80	Ext very pale brown (10 YR 7/3) and pink (5 YR 7/4), int pink (5 YR 7/4), ware pale brown (10 YR 6/3), core gray (10 YR 5/1), grit freq 6; straw temper; handmade.
15	Jar	70–2771	5.003	80	Ext and int white (10 YR 8/2), ware very pale brown (10 YR 8/3), core gray (10 YR 5/1), grit freq 5; handmade; irregular impressions on pinched rim.
16	Jar	70–2869	5.033	89	Ext light brown (7.5 YR 6/4), int and ware light red (2.5 YR 6/6), core light yellowish brown (10 YR 6/4), grit freq 8; handmade.

constructed of less permanent materials. Foundations of circular dwellings have been found at Beth Yerah (Stratum I: Maisler, Stekelis, and Avi-Yonah 1952: 167). These "huts" were partly subterranean and had diameters from 3.00 m. to 4.00 m.; in one of them an oven was found, confirming their use as habitations. The foundations of similar structures dated to the fourth millennium have been reported at Beth Shan (Fitzgerald 1934: 124–25), Shechem (Toombs and Wright 1961: 36–37; Bull et al. 1965: 16), Tell el-Farᶜah (N) (de Vaux 1955: 552), Munhata (Perrot 1965: 249; 1967: 63–64), Jericho (Garstang 1935: 149, 153, and pls. 24b and 51a), Tell esh-Sheikh Ahmed el-ᶜAreini (Yeivin 1960: 393; 1975: 96), and Arad (Amiran 1978: 4–6).

The interpretation of all of these installations, including the one at Tell el-Hesi, as dwellings is strengthened by a parallel from predynastic Egypt. At Hemamieh there was a complex of nine well-preserved circular structures. It is unlikely that all of these were dwellings, since the smallest was only about 1.00 m. in diameter; another contained large amounts of sheep or goat dung and may have been used for fuel storage. One of the larger structures, about 2.00 m. in diameter, had a hearth in one corner, suggesting that it and the other larger huts were used for habitation. The foundations of all of the huts consisted of mud walls, partly below the surface, on which the imprints of the reeds which had formed part of the superstructure were occasionally visible; two also had the remains of exterior tamarisk posts which may have been roof supports (Brunton and Caton-Thompson 1928: 82–88).

CONCLUSIONS

The limited extent of these remains and the small corpus of pottery associated with them make any generalizations tentative. It seems clear, however, that the settlement at Tell el-Hesi, which may well have been only brief and seasonal, is to be added to the growing number of Chalcolithic sites in

Fig. 5. The Chalcolithic installation (5.033) during excavation, looking northwest and showing the fill within the structure. Photograph by T. Rosen.

Palestine with connections to the Ghassul-Beersheba culture. The absence of some typical Ghassulian forms and decorations and the circular plan of the dwelling may indicate that the Hesi settlement was on the fringes rather than in the mainstream of that culture and, while contemporary with it, may represent elements derived at least in part from an older, indigenous culture which that of Ghassul-Beersheba absorbed and supplanted.

Given the presence of Chalcolithic material in Areas 3 and 5 of Field III, the absence of Early Bronze Age remains outside the wall complex in those areas as well as in Areas 1, 2, 4, and 7, in which soundings were also made, is significant. That there was an extensive Early Bronze occupation at Hesi is clear from the large proportion of EB III sherds in virtually every locus excavated in Fields I and III, as well as from the excavations of Petrie and Bliss (see Matthers 1989 [Chapter II, above]: table 1) and the more recent work of the Joint Expedition in Fields IV, V, and VI (Fargo

and O'Connell 1978: 171–76, 178–80; O'Connell, Rose, and Toombs 1978: 84–90; Rose, Toombs, and O'Connell 1978: 139–45; Ross 1979). But the approximately 25 acres enclosed by fortifications— the EB "lower city"—were apparently not used exclusively for domestic and public architecture. The lack of EB structures in Field III indicates that part of the "lower city" may also have had an agricultural function.[4]

(Completed July 1978; revised May 1979)

NOTES

1. L. E. Stager was supervisor of Field III in 1970 and 1971; in the preparation of this chapter I have consulted his unpublished field report for 1970. Supervisors were M. D. Coogan in 1970 (Areas 3 and 5) and D. L. Saltz in 1971 (Area 3). — M. D. C.
2. The parenthetic notation following a color description gives the more precise Munsell system color-designation (see Munsell 1975).
3. When a photograph of the structure was first published (Toombs 1974: pl. 5: 8), the caption erroneously referred to a beaten-earth floor. No such floor was found.
4. A complete locus catalogue for Field III will appear in a future Hesi volume on the major Iron II structures in Fields I and III.

Fig. 6. The Chalcolithic installation (5.033) when excavated, looking northwest and showing the walls to their preserved height. The meter stick lies on the basal sand which also surrounds the structure. Photograph by T. Rosen.

BIBLIOGRAPHY FOR CHAPTER IX

Amiran, R.
  1978 *Early Arad: The Chalcolithic Settlement and Early Bronze City. I. First–Fifth Seasons 1962 . 1966.* Jerusalem: Israel Exploration Society.
Brunton, G., and Caton-Thompson, G.
  1928 *The Badarian Civilization and Predynastic Remains Near Badari.* London: British School of Archaeology in Egypt.
Bull, R. J.; Callaway, J. A.; Campbell, E. F., Jr.; Ross, J. F.; and Wright, G. E.
  1965 The Fifth Campaign at Balatah (Shechem). *Bulletin of the American Schools of Oriental Research* 180: 7–41.
Callaway, J. A.
  1972 *The Early Bronze Sanctuary at ᶜAi (et-Tell).* London: Bernard Quaritch.

Contenson, H. de
  1956 La céramique chalcolithique de Beersheba: étude typologique. *Israel Exploration Journal* 6: 163–79, 226–38.
Dever, W. G., *et al.*
  1974 *Gezer II: Report of the 1967–1970 Seasons in Fields I and II.* Jerusalem: Hebrew Union College/Nelson Glueck School of Biblical Archaeology.
Dothan, M.
  1959a Excavations at Meser, 1957: Preliminary Report on the Second Season. *Israel Exploration Journal* 9: 13–29.
  1959b Excavations at Horvat Beter (Beersheba). ᶜ*Atiqot* 2: 1–42.
Fargo, V. M., and O'Connell, K. G., S. J.
  1978 Five Seasons of Excavation at Tell el-Hesi (1970–1977). *Biblical Archeologist* 41: 165–82.

Fitzgerald, G. M.
1934   Excavations at Beth Shan in 1933. *Palestine Exploration Fund Quarterly Statement* 65: 123–34.

Garstang, J.
1935   Jericho: City and Necropolis (Fifth Report). *Annals of Archaeology and Anthropology* (Institute of Archaeology, University of Liverpool) 22: 143–84.

Maisler, B.; Stekelis, M.; and Avi-Yonah, M.
1952   The Excavations at Beth-Yerah (Khirbet el-Kerak) 1944–1946. *Israel Exploration Journal* 2: 165–73.

Mallon, A., S.J.; Koeppel, R., S.J.; Neuville, R.; *et al.*
1934   *Teleilat Ghassul, Compte rendu des fouilles de L'Institut Biblique Pontifical 1929–1932, I.* Rome: Pontifical Biblical Insitute.

Munsell, A. H.
1975   *Munsell Soil Color Charts.* 1975 Edition. Baltimore: Macbeth Division of Kollmorgen Corporation.

O'Connell, K. G., S.J.; Rose, D. G.; and Toombs, L. E.
1978   Tell el-Hesi, 1977. *Palestine Exploration Quarterly* 110: 75–90.

Perrot, J.
1961   Une tombe à ossuaires de IV(e) millénaire à Azor, près de Tel-Aviv, Rapport préliminaire. *cAtiqot* 3: 1–83.

1965   Notes and News: Munhata. *Israel Exploration Journal* 15: 248–49.

1967   Chronique archéologique: Munhata. *Revue Biblique* 74: 63–67.

Pritchard, J. B.
1958   *The Excavation at Herodian Jericho, 1951.* Annual of the American Schools of Oriental Research 32–33. New Haven: American Schools of Oriental Research.

Rose, D. G.; Toombs, L. E.; and O'Connell, K. G., S.J.
1978   Four Seasons of Excavation at Tell el-Hesi: A Preliminary Report. In *Preliminary Excavation Reports: Bâb edh-Dhrâc, Sardis, Meiron, Tell el-Hesi, Carthage (Punic).* Annual of the American Schools of Oriental Research 43, pp. 109–49. Edited by D. N. Freedman. Cambridge, MA: American Schools of Oriental Research.

Ross, J. F.
1979   Early Bronze Age Structures at Tell el-Hesi. *Bulletin of the American Schools of Oriental Research* 236: 11–21.

Toombs, L. E.
1974   Tell el-Hesi, 1970–71. *Palestine Exploration Quarterly* 106: 19–31 and plates 1–6.

Toombs, L. E., and Wright, G. E.
1961   The Third Campaign at Balatah (Shechem). *Bulletin of the American Schools of Oriental Research.* 161: 11–54.

Vaux, R. de
1955   La cinquième campagne de fouilles à Tell el-Fârcah, près Naplouse. Rapport préliminaire. *Revue Biblique* 62: 541–89.

1961   Les fouilles de Tell el-Fârcah. Rapport préliminaire sur les 7e, 8e, 9e campagnes, 1958–60. *Revue Biblique* 68: 557–92.

Wagner, N., and Toombs, L. E.
1971   *A Handbook for Coding Palestinian Pottery.* Waterloo: Waterloo Lutheran (now Wilfrid Laurier) University.

Yeivin, S.
1960   Chronique archéologique: Gath. *Revue Biblique* 67: 391–94.

1975   El-cAreini, Tell esh-Sheikh Ahmed (Tel cErani). In M. Avi-Yonah, ed., *Encyclopedia of Archaeological Excavations in the Holy Land I,* pp. 89–97. Jerusalem: Israel Exploration Society and Masada Press.

Chapter X

A Cemetery from the Persian Period at Tell el-Hesi

by
Michael David Coogan
Stonehill College

Reprinted from
Bulletin of The American Schools of Oriental Research
Number 220 (December 1975): 37-46

During the 1970 and 1971 seasons of the Joint Expedition to Tell el-Hesi more than forty burials were excavated in Field III, which is situated at the base of the tell's southeastern slope (see fig. 1).[1] Dug into all three phases of the massive lower wall complex,[2] this cemetery is the latest major stratigraphic phase in Field III and thus provides a *terminus ante quem* for the walls.

As the plan of the better preserved burials (fig. 2) indicates, the graves were clustered at the eastern edge of the field, and it is likely that a number of burials have washed into the wadi. Evidence for this conjecture is found in 5A.009[3], in which only the lower leg bones were recovered. The location of the cemetery also explains the poor preservation of most of the bones, which lay in shallow graves often just a few centimeters below the modern ground level, and which were thus exposed to considerable water run-off from the upper slopes of the tell. Fig. 3 illustrates one of the better-preserved skeletons; in general, when present at all, the bones were extremely friable. Furthermore, erosion and recent plowing have often obliterated the original contours of the burial cists and have caused some dislocation of their contents; an example of such dislocation is 16.003, where a skull was found upside down in the balk without any associated bones (see fig. 4).

Nearly half of the graves were situated in a large pit dug into the brickwork, which filled most of Area 13 and the eastern half of Area 14. This pit may have been the result of clay mining; the mud bricks of the walls would have been an obvious and accessible source of clay for the inhabitants of the acropolis. Before the burials were dug the pit had filled with over a meter of water-sorted clay and sand, run-off from the slopes above. No sherds in the pit (whose principal locus is 13.018) were later than the Persian Period. The cemetery is thus the latest phase of human activity in Field III during the Persian Period, having been preceded in that era by the construction of and the digging of the pit after the walls had fallen into disuse. The large number of graves in the pit can be attributed to the ease of digging in the relatively soft, water-sorted deposit, as compared with the mud-brick walls.[4]

The remaining graves were dug either into the walls themselves or outside them into the basal sand dune. Apart from some pits (in Area 3) and a circular mud-plaster-lined installation (in Area 5), all from the late Chalcolithic period, there was no evidence of significant occupation south of Zone C. The matrices into which the cemetery was dug—natural sand, mud-brick walls, and water

Fig. 1.   View of Tell el-Hesi (1970), with Field III in the foreground. (Photo by T. Rosen)

deposition—explain the scarcity of artifacts and the consequent chronological uncertainty.

The stratigraphy of the cemetery itself is fairly simple. For the most part the graves do not overlap horizontally. There are, however, at least two examples of one grave lying directly over another: 13.016 is above 13.028, and 13.020 is over 13.022. In addition, the skeleton of 13.014 was above the stones associated with 13.021, and the cist of 2.003 was cut by that of 2.004 (see fig. 5). Thus, the cemetery was in use for some time. The disruption of many of the graves due to the causes mentioned above made the identification of multiple burials difficult; both 5.008 and 13.013 contained fragments of mature and immature skeletons and may be examples of a single grave with more than one occupant.

About 75 percent of the burials were oriented in an east-west direction with the head at the east; this corresponds to the orientation of most of the skeletons in the extensive cemetery at 'Atlīt,[5] as well as of four of the five "Philistine" graves at Gezer[6] and of a double burial from the Persian Period at Lachish.[7] As in these roughly contemporary cemeteries, this orientation was not consistently used at Hesi; 13.013, 13.020, and 13.032 are clear exceptions. Most of the skeletons were extended on their backs (13.032 is again an exception), but instead of the arms being extended at the sides of the body as at 'Atlīt, when observable at Hesi the right (and sometimes the left) elbow was generally slightly flexed with the right hand over the pelvis (see 5.007, 5A.012, 13.021, 13.028, etc.); this is also a characteristic of the Lachish burials. There is no consistent eye direction, although the most frequent is toward the north.

The cists were regularly filled with a relatively loose soil similar in make-up to the surrounding

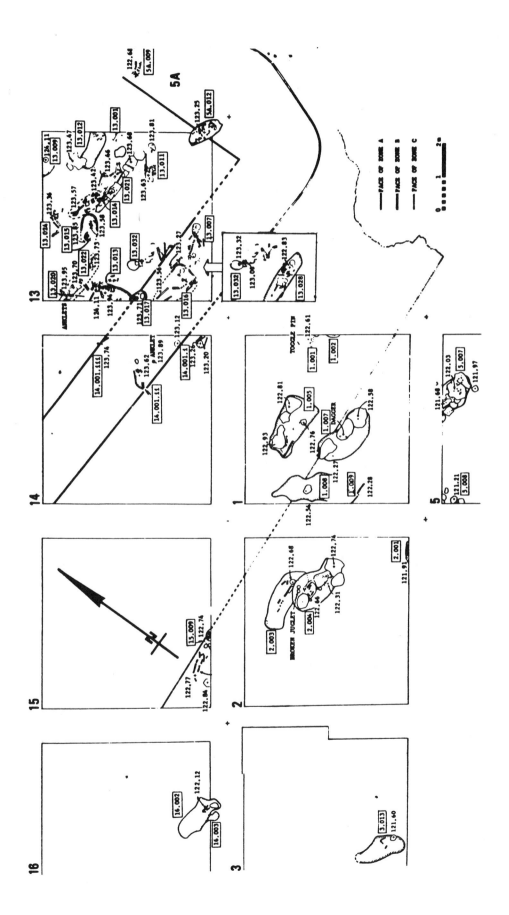

Fig. 2. Top plan of the cemetery.

Fig. 3. Locus 5A.012. (Photo by T. Rosen)

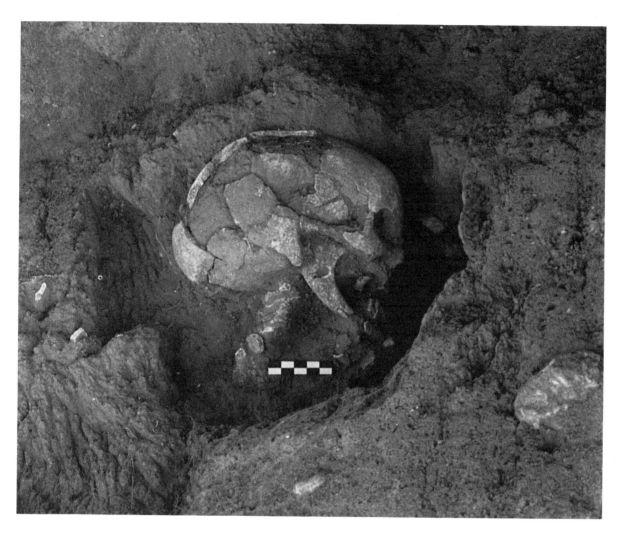

Fig. 4. Locus 16.003, in balk. (Photo by T. Rosen)

dirt; it is thus clear that the soil removed while digging the grave was thrown back after the body had been deposited. Eleven of the graves, in which the skeletons were both male and female, were at least partly covered with stones, generally large, unworked slabs of local limestone (see fig. 5).[8] In 1.005 these stones seem to have been misplaced, for they are adjacent to, rather than directly above, the skeleton; the corpse was covered with soil before the stone covering was added, and the gravediggers may have forgotten the precise location of their client. This may also account for the placement of the slabs in 13.021, though since these are lower on the slope they may simply have slipped after they had been placed.

The population of the excavated portion of the cemetery consisted of thirty-five adults, of which sixteen could be identified as male and seven as female. There were also skeletons of two adolescent females, two infants, and one child. Preliminary anthropological analysis has revealed few abnormalities. In 1.007 and 1.008 the vaults of the skulls (both of males) were thickened, indicating malaria or anemia. The adolescent (female?) in 14.001.ii had unusual and hereditary cupping of the incisors.

Twelve of the burials had objects associated with them. Nearly whole juglets were found with 15.009 and 2.003, and a broken juglet (the lower portion missing) with 1.007. Detailed discussion of these vessels is found below (on fig. 8 they are numbers 1, 2, and 3, respectively). The skeletons in 15.009 and 1.007 have been identified as male, and 2.003 as probably female; the poorly preserved condition of the latter makes firm identification of sex difficult, but if the individual was female we have evidence for the interment of pottery with both sexes.

Fig. 5. The stone covering of locus 2.004 with the excavated cist of locus 2.003 in the background. (Photo by T. Rosen)

Copper anklets, varying in size from 7.7 to 9.2 cm. in diameter, were found in association with five skeletons. The two anklets in 1.005 (reg. number H–70: 19 A–B) and the one in 13.014 (reg. number H–70: 103) were still attached to the lower leg bones of the skeletons, which were both female. In 13.022 the anklets were also in place (reg. number H–70: 128 A–B), and the skeleton was probably male, although the poor state of preservation of the pelvis and skull prevents definitive sexing. In 13.001 and 14.001.iii the sex of the skeletons could not be determined because only the lower leg bones were within the areas excavated; in both cases the anklets had been dislodged from the bones. There were two anklets in 13.001, one of which was broken in half (reg. number H–70: 61 A–B–C), and one in 14.001.iii (reg. number H–70: 23).⁹

A badly corroded iron ring (reg. number H–70: 125) with an inside diameter of ca. 2 cm. was found on the left hand of the male skeleton in 13.016, and a similar ring (reg. number H–70: 102), about half a centimeter smaller, was found in 13.012, where the sex of the skeleton was indeterminable. Locus 1.001 had a copper toggle pin (15 cm. long and 0.5 cm. thick) and a bead (reg. number H–70: 15) associated with it; again, the disruption of the grave prevented sexing.

Associated with the male skeleton in 1.007 were pieces of an iron dagger (reg. number H–70: 32), one of which had three rivets in the tang. The dagger was in two fragments and may have been broken deliberately, but in view of the disruption of the cemetery as a whole this is hypothetical. The two fragments are badly corroded but appear to join, giving a length of ca. 11 cm. from the point

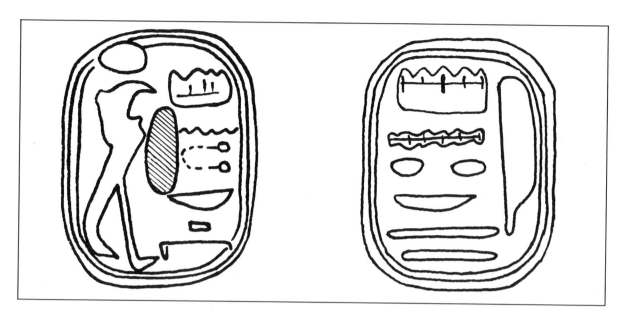

Fig. 6. Drawing of seal found in locus 5A.012.

to the surviving edge of the tang; the width varies from 1.8 cm. just before the point begins to 2.5 cm. at the tang, and the thickness of the blade is ca. 0.2 cm.

A small seal (see fig. 6), 1.15 cm. long and 0.85 cm. wide, was found among the hand bones of the male skeleton in 5 A.012 (see fig. 3). One side has the inscription *Mn[t]w nb pt* "Montu, Lord of Heaven" to the right of a falcon-headed figure surmounted by a sun disk, and the other reads *'Imn-R' nb t zwy* "Amon-Re, Lord of the Two Lands"; the latter has close, if not exact, parallels in two cylinders (?) from Tell Jemmeh.[10]

Finally, we turn to the pottery. The accompanying plate (fig. 8) contains drawings of a selection of the registered sherds from the cemetery which date to the Iron Age and later, as well as those which I have been unable to identify. I have omitted earlier material because it does not aid the dating of the burials and because the sherds represent well-known types. Most frequent, for the reason given above, are Early Bronze sherds, including holemouth jar rims, rims of large burnished bowls, and cooking pot rims and bases. Other common types include Late Bronze cooking pots with collared rims, rims and handles of Late Bronze "milk bowls," and carinated and rounded bowl rims from early Iron II, with the familiar and distinctive red slip and hand burnishing.

Fig. 7. Juglet number 1 *in situ*. (Photo by T. Rosen)

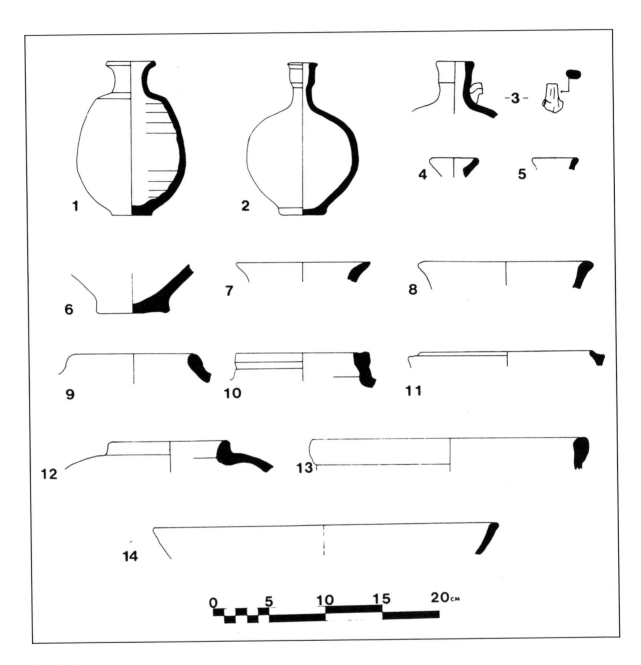

Fig. 8. Pottery.

1. Reg. number H–71: 101; locus 15.009. The ware is reddish brown (Munsell Color 7.5 YR 6/6) with occasional small, white grits, and is evenly fired; there is a pale, whitish slip (2.5 Y 7/2). A photograph of this one-handled juglet *in situ* is given in fig. 7. I am unable to find exact parallels to this vessel. There is a juglet with a similar lower part but with a different rim at Lachish, coming from Level 3, destroyed ca. 598/7 BCE.[11]

2. Reg. number H–70: 1330; locus 2.003. Found broken in two and restored, this one-handled pink (5 YR 7/3) juglet is partially covered by a white (5 YR 8/1) slip. It has close parallels in the later Persian Period from Shiqmona,[12] from Ein-Gedi,[13] and from a tomb at Lachish.[14]

3. Reg. number H–70: 425–426; locus 1.007. This pinkish gray (5 YR 7/2) juglet is similar in form to the preceding, but has a simpler rim. There are parallels from Persian Period strata at Shiqmona,[15] Ramat Rahel,[16] and Megiddo.[17]

4. Reg. number H–71: 152, locus 5 A.012. This pink (5 YR 8/4) vessel has a ware which was evenly fired and which contains very few tiny grits; there is a wash. It is perhaps the rim of an Iron II dipper juglet.

5. Reg. number H–71: 678; locus 15.009. This small sherd is pink (5 YR 7/4) on both sides and has a reddish yellow (5 YR 6/6) core; the ware has a very few microscopic grits. The size of the fragment makes any reading uncertain, but it would fit into the Persian Period, as several parallels from Phase Vb in Field I at Tell el-Hesi suggest.[18]

6. Reg. number H–71: 76; locus 2.004. The sherd is badly corroded, and is reddish yellow (5 YR 7/6) in color with a slightly darker (5 YR 6/6) core; the ware has small red and gray mineral grits in medium frequency. There is a close parallel to this base from Tell en-Nasbeh,[19] but it would be hazardous to assign a definite date.

7. Reg. number H–71: 1019; locus 13.032. Probably the characteristic flare rim of an Iron II carinated bowl,[20] this sherd is very pale brown (10 YR 8/4) on the outside and core, and pink (7.5 YR 8/4) on the inside; there are occasional medium and small, white and gray grits.

8. Reg. number H–71: 42; locus 2.004. This bowl rim has good parallels from Phase V in Field I at Hesi[21] and would fit into the Persian Period. It is pink (7.5 YR 7/4) on the outside, very pale brown (10 YR 7/3) on the inside, and brown (10 YR 5/3) in the core; there are a few tiny, white mineral grits in the ware.

9. Reg. number H–70: 1289; locus 13.011. This rim of an Iron I store jar is pink (5 YR 7/3) and has a close parallel at Beth-Zur.[22]

10. Reg. number H–71: 41; locus 2.004. This is the typical ridged rim of an Iron II store jar, with good parallels at Ashdod,[23] Kadesh-Barnea ('Ain el-Qudeirat),[24] and Lachish.[25] It has a very pale brown (10 YR 8/3) slip, and a light reddish brown (5 YR 6/3) core and is pink to reddish yellow (5 YR between 7/4 and 7/6) on the inside; there are occasional medium to large, white and gray mineral grits in the ware.

11. Reg. number H–71: 45; locus 2.004. This fragment may be the rim of a sixth-century-BCE holemouth jar;[26] it is red (10 R 5/6) on the outside and in the core and has a light red (10 R 6/6) wash on the inside; there are numerous small, black grits in the evenly fired ware.

12. Reg. number H–71: 73; locus 2.004. This is the familiar "sausage jar," discussed in detail by Lapp.[27] The form first appears at the end of Iron II[28] and continues until at least the mid-fourth century.[29] The example illustrated here is from the early Persian Period and is light red (2.5 YR 6/6) with a darker (5 YR 4/2) core, caused by uneven firing; gray grits, both large and small, occur with medium frequency.

13. Reg. number H–71: 156; locus 2.004. This Iron II bowl rim is pink (7.5 YR 7/4) on the inside and outside and reddish yellow (5 YR 6/6) in the core; there are numerous tiny and small, gray and black grits. Parallels are found at Kadesh-Barnea ('Ain el-Qudeirat),[30] and at Tell en-Nasbeth.[31]

14. Reg. number H–70: 1326; locus 2.003. This reddish yellow (5 YR 7/6) bowl rim is probably either late Iron II or early Persian Period.

The limited amount of ceramic evidence prevents absolute dating of the cemetery. Its use followed two other major activities during the Persian Period in Field III: a massive filling operation in the north of the field (probably associated with the similar activity pre-Phase V in Field I) and the construction of the wall system (perhaps to be related to Phase Vb in Field I[32]). The cemetery is thus to be dated toward the end of the Persian Period at Hesi and probably no later, given the absence of Hellenistic sherds.

A fourth century date would connect the cemetery with the construction of the grain-storage pits in Phase Va of Field I. Parallels at other sites to the pottery from the graves and to their orientation and style of interment support this hypothesis. Judging from the austerity of the grave furnishings, the population of which the cemetery contains a sample was not wealthy. If it was in fact this group which built the silos on the acropolis, it was probably not a military garrison (note also the presence of women and children), but is more likely to have been a small agricultural community.[33]

NOTES

1. G. E. Wright was instrumental in beginning the expedition and was its Principal Overseer until his death. During the 1970 and 1971 seasons L. E. Stager was Field Supervisor of Field III, and I have used his preliminary field reports in preparing this article. Supervisors of the areas discussed here were, in 1970, D. Brooks, M. Coogan, R. Doermann, and D. M. Freedman; in 1971, M. Coogan, R. Doermann, and D. Saltz. During January 1974, C.

Redmount was my research assistant and provided invaluable help in the preparation of this report. A complete list of staff is found in Toombs (1974).

2. See Toombs (1974) 28–31, but note that the wall system in its entirety is now tentatively dated to the Persian Period.
3. Graves are identified by areas and locus numbers; thus, 5A.009 is locus 009 in Area 5A.
4. Further excavation of the foundations of the walls is planned. The sherds from the bricks themselves are consistently Early Bronze, indicating merely that the builders of the walls mined the clay for their bricks from the Early Bronze fortifications (not excavated by the present expedition, but see Toombs [1974] 21).
5. Johns (1933) 41–104.
6. Macalister (1912) I, 289–300. On the dating of these richly furnished tombs to the Persian Period, see Iliffe (1935) 185.
7. Tufnell (1953) 225, locus 525. There are three other burials from the Persian Period at Lachish: loci 180 (p. 198), 183, and 184 (p. 199).
8. These are 1.005, 1.007, 2.004, 5.007, 5.008, 13.012, 13.021, 13.025, 13.028, 13.032, and 15.009.
9. For a convenient summary of the use of anklets, see Tufnell (1958) 37–54.
10. See Petrie (1928) pl. 19, nos. 32 and 33. I am grateful to Edward F. Wente of the Oriental Institute of the University of Chicago for the reading of the two sides.
11. Tufnell (1953) pl. 77, no. 10.
12. Elgavish (1968) pl. 33, no. 15.
13. Mazar and Dunayevsky (1967) 33, no. 1.
14. Tufnell (1953) pl. 87, no. 255.
15. Elgavish (1968) pl. 33, no. 16.
16. Aharoni (1964) fig. 14, no. 5.
17. Lamon and Shipton (1939) pl. 1, no. 6.
18. Especially, reg. numbers H–70: 2256 and 3270; H–71: 6627, which will be published in due course. I am grateful to W. J. Bennett, Jr., for having made these and other parallels from Field I available to me.
19. Wampler (1941) 39, fig. 12, no. x53.
20. See, for example, Amiran (1970) pl. 65, no. 8, and pl. 66, no. 9; and Wampler (1941) 29, fig. 4, no. x103.
21. Especially, reg. number H–71: 5040 (Phase Vc), and also H–70: 2841 (Va); H–71: 2873 (Vb-c) and 5872 (pre-Vb).
22. Sellers, et al. (1968) fig. 14, no. 1.
23. Dothan (1971) fig. 48, no. 4.
24. Dothan (1965) 149, no. 7.
25. Tufnell (1953) pl. 96, no. 533.
26. See, for example, Kelso (1968) pl. 66, nos. 5 and 6.
27. Lapp (1970) 182–83; for the type, see fig. 6, nos. 1 and 2, and fig. 3, no. 4.
28. See Amiran (1970) 241–42, and pl. 81, nos. 4–8, and pl. 82, nos. 6–7.
29. In the Persian Period there are many examples. In addition to those listed by Lapp (1970), see especially Elgavish (1968) pl. 59, nos. 139–41.
30. Dothan (1965) 147, no. 2.
31. Wampler (1941) 29, fig. 4, no. x31.
32. More exact correlations of Fields I and III will depend upon excavation of the foundations of the walls and a comparison of their pottery with the Field I corpus.
33. See further Stager (1971) 86–88.

BIBLIOGRAPHY FOR CHAPTER X

Aharoni, Y.
1964 Excavations at Ramat Rahel, Seasons 1961 and 1962. Rome: Centro di studi semitici.

Amiran, R.
1970 Ancient Pottery of the Holy Land. New Brunswick, NJ: Rutgers University.

Dothan, M.
1965 The Fortress at Kadesh-Barnea. Israel Exploration Journal 15: 134–51.
1971 Ashdod II–III: The Second and Third Seasons of Excavations, 1963, 1965. 'Antiqot, English series, 10.

Elgavish, J.
1968 Shiqmona: The Levels of the Persian Period, Seasons 1963.1965. Haifa: City Museum of Ancient Art.

Iliffe, J. H.
1935 A Tell Fāra Tomb Group Reconsidered. Quarterly of the Department of Antiquities of Palestine 4: 182–86.

Johns, C. N.
1933 Excavations at Atlīt (1930–1): The Southeastern Cemetery. Quarterly of the Department of Antiquities of Palestine 2: 41–104.

Kelso, J. L.
1968 The Excavation of Bethel (1934–1960). Annual of the American Schools of Oriental Research 39. Cambridge, MA: American Schools of Oriental Research.

Lamon, R. S., and Shipton, G. M.
1939 Megiddo I: Seasons of 1925–34. Strata I–IV. Oriental Institute Publications 42. Chicago: University of Chicago.

Lapp, P. W.
1970 The Pottery of Palestine in the Persian Period. In Archäologie und Altes Testament (Galling Festschrift), pp. 179-97. Edited by A. Kuschke and E. Kutsch. Tübingen: Mohr.

Macalister, R. A. S.
1912 The Excavations of Gezer I. London: Murray.

Mazar, B. and Dunayevsky, I.
1967 En-gedi: Fourth and Fifth Seasons of Excavations, Preliminary Report. Israel Exploration Journal 17: 133–43.

Petrie, W. M. F.
1928 Gerar. London: British School of Archaeology in Egypt.

Sellers, O. R., et al.
1968 The 1957 Excavation at Beth-Zur. Annual of the American Schools of Oriental Research 38. Cambridge, MA: American Schools of Oriental Research.

Stager, L. E.
1971   Climatic Conditions and Grain Storage in the Persian Period. *Biblical Archaeologist* 34: 86–88.

Toombs, L. E.
1974   Tell el-Hesi, 1970–71. *Palestine Exploration Quarterly* 107: 19–31.

Tufnell, O.
1953   *Lachish III: The Iron Age.* London: Oxford University.

1958   Anklets in Western Asia. *Bulletin of the Institute of Archaeology* (The University of London) 1: 37–54.

Wampler, J. C.
1941   Three Cistern Groups from Tell en-Nasbeh. *Bulletin of the American Schools of Oriental Research* 82: 25–43.

Chapter XI

ARCHEOBOTANIC STUDIES AT TELL EL-HESI

by
Robert B. Stewart
Sam Houston State University

Reprinted from
Economic Botany
Volume 21 (1978), pp. 379-86.

These studies describe the plant inventory and subsistence pattern for occupants of Tell el-Hesi during the Hellenistic occupation period. Attempts are made to interpret the differences seen in the various areas and loci excavated. Statistical analysis has been used to validate these interpretations.

Tell el-Hesi lies on the Wadi el-Hesi about 25 km. from its point of discharge into the Mediterranean. It is well outside the Judean Lowlands (i.e., below 200 m.) and in the transitional zone between the relatively wet Mediterranean zone and the Negev Desert. The annual rainfall is between 300 and 400 mm. This rather low rainfall is much more useful agriculturally than 10–15 inches in the semi-arid areas of the United States, because almost all of it falls between November and April. The soils are loess deposits and quite fertile, as is characteristic of such deposits. It is, then, an area well adapted to small grain culture.

However, this generally favorable agricultural potential is complicated by unpredictability of rainfall (a mean relative variability of 26 percent [Stager, 1971]). This means simply that some years Hesi might well be included in the Negev Desert. Four years of the last 30 had a rainfall of about 200 mm. This unpredictability makes dry farming a precarious undertaking, although not a totally unattractive one in a crowded land.

I am convinced that the agriculturists during the period of occupation represented in these studies probably faced essentially the same climatic conditions described above. Two lines of evidence support this contention. First, the weed seeds from the midden heaps are the same species as those of the wheat field that surrounds Tell el-Hesi today. Second, the palynological studies in the Near East do not suggest a climatic change within our time range (Wright *et al.*, 1967).

MATERIALS AND METHODS

Excavations have been essentially restricted to two so-called "fields," Fields I and III. Field III has concentrated on the walls and fortifications surrounding the acropolis. Although these are architecturally and historically interesting, almost no seeds were recovered.

Field I (the acropolis) has been particularly rewarding. It was studded with pits constructed during the Persian Period of occupation. These pits appear to have been granaries and are usually a meter or two in diameter and about two or three meters deep. Such structures are a common archeological find in the Middle East and excavators are generally agreed about this use. Stager (1971) has discussed their role at Tell el-Hesi and has, I believe, effectively demolished some earlier interest-ing and romantic notions of their purpose. Actu-ally, they can be found in use today in some areas of Ethiopia. After the Persian Period they appear to have fallen into disuse and were filled by kit-chen middens by succeeding occupants. The occu-pants responsible for this fill are labeled Hellenistic on the basis of their pottery, but unfortunately most of the occupation record other than the pits has been destroyed by burials and military trenching in the surface layers.

For these studies, the proximity of these silos to dwellings was most fortuitous, because the oc-cupants had a nearby, convenient disposal for liv-ing area waste. As there were several such pits scattered over the whole acropolis, it appears that they reflect the entire community rather than sim-ply the refuse of a single family unit. Also, the depth of the middens suggests an accumulation for perhaps a generation or longer. Furthermore, such extensive deposits permit application of statistical designs not permitted by more limited deposits and offer a better measure of sampling techniques and perhaps give a degree of confidence that would otherwise not be possible.

A debate has arisen among those interested in bioarcheology about sampling procedure. Some appear to be content with minimal samples of a few seeds or bones taken almost indiscriminately, whereas others insist on "total recovery." It is hoped that these studies at Hesi can help with this question.

Since the size of the pits as well as the excava-tion technique varied, some differences in the num-ber of samples and sampling design occur, but in all cases the pit was divided into several arbitrary levels of 20–50 cm. with random samples taken within the levels. The largest pit (Locus 218 of

Square 31) was divided, and two tiers of samples were taken from top to bottom. As the squares were selected at random (from a botanical point of view, anyway) and well distributed over the acropolis (Field I), an analysis of variance patterned on the classic randomized block concept seemed appro-priate for testing the differences. Only the three or four most common seeds that were represented in each level were used for the analysis of variance.

Samples from dwelling floors, ovens, etc., were taken when such structures were encountered and in as great a quantity as our flotation facilities would permit. The fill selected for botanical study was ex-cavated by the square supervisor, removed from the square in the same manner as all other fill, but, rather than being sieved as was customary, the selected samples of fill were floated.

The flotation scheme used was that of Struever (1968), as modified by Stewart and Robertson (1973). A further refinement on the modification was made during the 1973 field season; a series of three 55-gallon oil drums was substituted for the tank described in the original modification. Also, wom-en's nylon hose were found to be a cheap and con-venient substitution for the expensive and difficult-to-locate carburetor screen suggested by Struever.

Seeds extracted by this method were field-sorted, cleaned, and taken to the laboratory for final study and identification. However, daily tallies and preliminary identifications were communicated to the square supervisor to help guide the sampling process.

RESULTS AND DISCUSSION

Table 1 includes a complete listing of the agri-

Table 1. The plant inventory for Tell el-Hesi during Hellenistic occupation.

Cereals	Pulses	Oil seeds	Other crops	Weeds
Common wheat	Lentils	Flax	Grape	*Bromus* sp.
Six-rowed barley	Chickpea	Olive	Hackberry	*Medicago* sp.
Emmer[a]	Bitter vetch			*Hordeum* sp.
	Pea			*Anchusa* sp.
	Vetchling			Goatface grass
	Horse bean			Wild oats
				Compositae
				Polygonaceae
				Rubiaceae

[a] Emmer here may be considered a weed, although our specimens were cultivated emmer.

cultural plants recovered from the Hellenistic phase of Tell el-Hesi. Considering the range of species and varieties that the occupants might have used, the list is, perhaps, surprisingly short. Furthermore, of the crops found, only common wheat,[1] barley, bitter vetch, lentil, olive, and grape could be said to occur in quantity. The absence of figs, almonds, and dates and the meager representation of most large-seeded pulses and fruits suggest a very limited trade in agricultural products. Most of the crops listed as occurring in quantity could have been, and in all likelihood were, grown in the immediate vicinity. Grapes and olives, particularly olives, were probably brought from nearby areas where moisture was a bit more dependable.

The presence of several pits with substantial deposits of refuse, seeming to represent a discrete provenience, offered a good opportunity to test statistically the uniformity of deposits and to compare individual locations within the settlement and various deposit types. Table 2 shows the mean number of seeds per bucket of fill floated from the indicated squares. All loci from a particular square other than the pits are lumped as a single entry, and buckets without seed from these loci are excluded. Too few flotation samples were taken from

the squares omitted from this table for them to be individually meaningful. Accordingly, they are lumped in table 2 as "All other squares."

The analysis shows that at the 0.01 level there is a significant difference in both the loci and the species tested (table 3). However, the F value for species is much higher than for loci. Table 2 shows that in almost every case the relative numbers of seed are unchanged. There is one prominent exception. In Square 22, Locus 111, the barley count is nearly double that of wheat, while wheat predominates in every other entry, and the "t" test shows that this difference is statistically significant. This uniformity of distribution between loci is more apparent when plotted as shown in fig. 1.

Dennell (1972), in a most significant paper, has properly called attention to error in sampling and interpretation, particularly as practiced in early, albeit otherwise outstanding, contributions. Dennell has emphasized context, and this unquestionably has not been properly considered in every case. The sample size and sampling technique here emphasized is of no less concern. Insofar as the carbonized plant remains represent the economy of the Hellenistic phase of Tell el-Hesi, I think that a valid sample has been taken, and some comments

Table 2. Mean yield per bucket (gufa) of fill.

Deposit type and no.	Barley	Wheat	Lentil	Bitter vetch	Flax[a]	Other crops	Tare	Other weeds	Avg.
Pit 31.218A[b]	39.8	95.6	3.6	25.5	—	1	14.8	3.2	43.5
Pit 31.218B	39.9	85.4	5.0	27.4	—	1	19.7	2.6	
31.other loci	7.3	14.3	1	1	—	2.1	1.4	1.0	6.0
Pit 22.111	50.1	28.0	1	2	—	1.5	21.3	7.8	25.4
22.other loci	4.9	9.4	4	4	—	1.0	2.5	4.0	4.5
Pit 11.258	9.5	19.8	1.4	2.3	3.8	1.0	6.1	1.0	9.4
Pit 11.258.272	16.6	37.6	1.5	1.9	1.0	1.0	16.0	1.3	18.0
Pit 11.265.277	8.9	27.3	2.0	1.8	—	1.5	4.9	1.0	9.4
Pit 11.265.293	8.1	18.8	1.0	1.8	—	1.7	3.8	1.0	
Pit 11.266.297	10.5	26.6	1.3	1.8	—	1.0	10.2	1.0	
Pit 11.266.301	7.1	25.5	11.5	1.0	—	1.0	6.0	1.0	11.2
Pit 11.266.302	8.0	30.6	1.0	1.0	—	1.7	6.6	1.0	
11.other loci	4.1	7.7	1.0	1.0	—	1.0	1.0	1.0	3.6
Pit 12.067	18.4	22.6	1.1	1.0	—	1.4	6.1	1.0	12.0
Pit 12.081	16.3	19.4	1.0	1.0	—	1.0	3.9	1.0	10.0
12.other loci	4.4	7.7	1.0	.0	—	1.0	1.4	1.0	3.8
All other squares	1.4	2.9	1.0	1.0	—	1.0	1.0	4.0	1.6
Average	15.21	23.88		3.3			6.9		

[a]Except in the two instances indicated, flax is included as other crops.
[b]All pit loci are from areas in Field I.

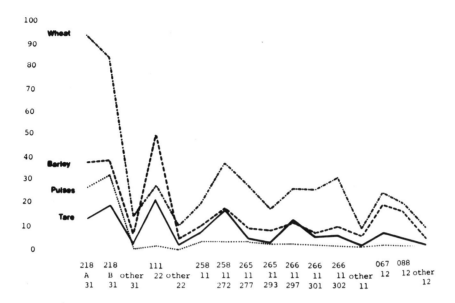

Fig. 1.   Mean number of seeds per bucket for most common seeds, as seen in all loci.

regarding the plant-dependency of the inhabitants during this period are justified.

The agriculture of Hellenistic Tell el-Hesi was a grain economy. Common wheat was the dominant cereal, but barley was widely used and in most loci was at least 50 percent of the wheat count. The diet of the Hellenistic occupant then, while adequate and inclusive of good representation of the three major plant food groups (grains, pulses, oil seeds), particularly as reinforced by animal products, would seem to have offered little variety. Perhaps this might be expected in a city that was, during its most significant period, only a provincial satellite of the border city, Lachish. During the Hellenistic occupation, Tell el-Hesi (Eglon?) is seen as a declining city in its terminal phase. Actually, subsistence patterns in many small towns and villages in today's Middle East would not seem overly favorable in comparison to Hesi. Tare is, of course, a weed and discarded from processed grain. The low percentage of weeds (except tare which, because of its size and specific gravity, is difficult to separate) tells us that we are looking at grain from the final stages of processing.

While perhaps futile, it is interesting to speculate on the source of the error component in our analysis (table 3). The wheat and barley ratio in Locus 111, Square 22, is particularly interesting, as it is the reverse of that in all other loci. Did the occupants using this pit constitute the ghetto of the poor who could not afford the preferred wheat? Or, perhaps, this was "officers' row" and the occupants could afford the luxury of discarding the barley admixture to make a purer wheat bread. Whatever the reason, the individual analysis of this pit suggests this difference to be real. The "t" test for significant differences in mean yields of crops in this pit is 14.91 at the 0.01 level. The difference of 22.13 between wheat and barley is more than that required for significance.

Equally interesting, but perhaps even more perplexing, are the differences between loci. Here the number of seeds required for significance between loci is 11.56 and 15.49 at the 0.01 and 0.05 levels, respectively. Pit 31.218 is significantly richer in seeds than the others, Pit 22.111 being next. Although the difference in the pits of Squares 11 and 12 is not statistically significant, it is interesting to note that Pit 11.258.272, an intrusion into Pit 11.258, according to the square supervisor, contains about twice as many seeds per bucket as the larger pit. There was no significant difference between squares (called "other loci" in table 2). These squares are from Persian Period occupation. The silos were constructed and in use during this period.

The midden material in the individual pits represents an accumulation of some years, perhaps most of the Hellenistic Period. Accordingly, samples were taken at different levels, arbitrarily

Table 3. Analysis of variance for the four most common species (barley, wheat, bitter vetch, and tare) in 12 loci (all pits) shown in Table 2[a].

Variation	Degrees of freedom	Sum of squares	Mean square	F	s
Species	3	3,794.43	1,264.18	19.48[b]	
Loci	11	6,582.39	506.33	7.79[b]	
Error	33	2,337.19	64.92		8.05
Total	47	12,714.01			

[a]Pits divided into separate loci are lumped for this analysis.
[b]Significant at the .01 level.

determined, as it was not practical to link them to stratigraphy more directly.

When the data were arranged in a table for study, it was apparent that level and seed quantity (based on seeds per bucket) were related. This is more easily seen as plotted on a line graph (fig. 2). Although the correlation is less than perfect, it is apparent that seed deposits were heavier near the middle of the accumulation period. Can this be correlated with the rise and fall of the Hellenistic occupation, assuming, of course, that our deposits span the entire occupation? The correlation of the various pits is particularly good near the pit bottoms and less perfect at the top. A partial explanation is that, during the excavation, the beginning of a pit is much more difficult to recog-

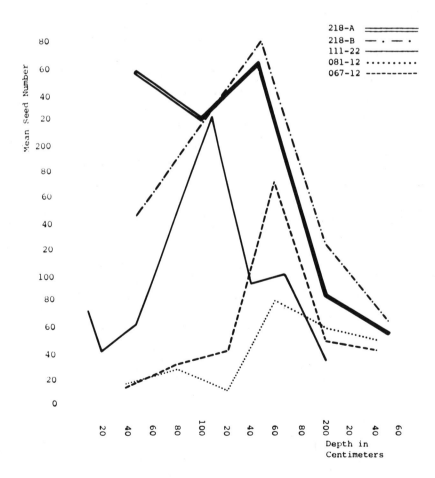

Fig. 2. Mean seed numbers of four loci showing concentration in each level of several pits.

nize than the bottom, which tends to be very discrete. Further archeological evaluation of the deposits may give us some answers to the meaning of these changes.

To put our observations on safer grounds statistically, a 3-factor analysis of variance was made on the three deepest pits. These data are shown in tables 4, 5, and 6.

Pit 218 in Square 31 was divided into halves which were treated separately. An analysis of these data (table 4) shows that in both halves the differences in level, crop, and crop × level interaction are significant, but it is particularly interesting to note the error term in B as compared to A and the corresponding F values. It may also be instructive to look for the source of this error, particularly in light of the rather uniform mean yields, based on seeds per bucket, shown in table 2. The data from which these means are derived show that in the A half of 218 the seeds are quite uniformly distributed, whereas the seeds in the B half are,

to the contrary, quite irregularly distributed. The stratigraphy within Pit 218 does not suggest an explanation for this apparent chance variation. This kind of variation makes a strong argument for statistical treatment. Square 11 contained four pits, three of which were vertically divided, as was Pit 31.218. These pits were all shallow and were not individually analyzed, but the tables suggest greater uniformity within the pits than that seen in Pit 218.

As throughout the entire Hellenistic occupation stratum, Pit 218 suggests a grain economy with common wheat as the dominant grain. The differences in the crop quantities were statistically significant, as were the differences between levels. Assuming the number of people using this pit to be relatively constant, we could interpret this difference to reflect seasonal yields. Of course, the reverse explanation is equally tenable. The significant interaction of crop and level might well have somewhat the same explanation as level

Table 4. Analysis of variance for the four most common seeds per bucket of fill in Pits 31.218A and 31.218B.

Variation due to	Degrees of freedom		Sum of squares		Mean square	F	s
Crop	3	A	96,841.94	A	32,280.64	117.11[a]	
		B	77,934.03	B	25,978.01	19.46[a]	
Level	4	A	49,628.37	A	12,407.09	45.01[a]	
		B	71,573.97	B	17,893.49	13.40[a]	
Crop × Level	12	A	37,463.31	A	3,121.94	11.33[a]	
		B	60,115.30	B	5,009.61	3.75[b]	
Error	80	A	22,051.25	A	275.64		16.60
		B	106,769.45	B	1,334.62		36.53
TOTAL	99	A	205,984.87				
		B	251,972.75				

[a]Significant at .01.
[b]Significant at .05.

Table 5. Analysis of variance for the three most common seeds per bucket of fill in Pit 12.067.

Variation due to	Degrees of freedom	Sum of squares	Mean square	F[a]	s
Crop	2	5,420.93	2,710.46	31.77	
Levels	6	32,752.00	5,458.66	69.98	
Crops × Level	12	15,152.77	1,252.73	14.8	
Error	84	7,166.44	85.31		9.2
Total	104	60,492.14			

[a]Significant at the .01 level.

Table 6. Analysis of variance for the three most common seeds per bucket of fill in Pit 22.111.

Variation due to	Degrees of freedom	Sum of squares	Mean square	F	s
Crop	2	11,371.44	5,685.72	10.96[a]	
Levels	7	35,786.00	5,112.29	9.85[a]	
Crop × Level	14	19,488.94	1,392.07	2.68	
Error	72	37,355.00	518.82		22.76
TOTAL	95	104,001.38			

[a]Significant at the .01 level.

variation, or it might mean that a preferred crop was used, whereas the less preferred was marketed or fed to animals. For example, in level 5 (the bottom of the pit), wheat and barley are about equal, but in level 3 there is about three times as much wheat as barley. Is there a cultural or environmental explanation for this statistically significant variation? Preliminary archeological interpretations offer no explanation.

Pit 067 of Square 12 closely followed the pattern of 31.218, and the F values for crops, levels, and crops × levels were significant (table 5). Also, as with 218A but not 218B, the error (unaccounted-for variations) was very small.

Pit 111, Square 22, was dug as a single unit and has been cited above as an exception to the other loci relative to its wheat and barley ration. Table 6 is an analysis of variance for this locus.

Pit 22.111 was also different in that it did not show a statistical interaction of crop level. In addition, the number of weeds other than tare, as well as pulses such as vetchling, horsebeans, and chickpea, were present in larger numbers although they were of the same type. Unfortunately, the numbers of these pulses were too few to allow for statistical analysis, here as well as elsewhere.

There is no question that total recovery, if possible, would be desirable. However, there is little likelihood of securing the budgets and manpower to recover all the seed in Tell el-Hesi and similar sites. The concept of total recovery is simply impractical for most Palestinian sites. It is apparent, as Dennell has documented, that some very questionable conclusions have been drawn from very small samples treated in a somewhat cavalier manner. We must find ways to improve our sampling methods and statistical treatment of these samples. This paper is an attempt in that direction.

NOTES

1. In order to make bread, emmer must be hulled. This rather laborious processing requirement suggests that a few grains of emmer would be discarded from a common wheat rather than processed and that emmer, therefore, is probably a weed here.

BIBLIOGRAPHY FOR CHAPTER XI

Dennell, R. W.
  1972 The Interpretation of Plant Remains: Bulgaria. In: *Papers in Economic Prehistory*. Edited by E. S. Higgs. Cambridge: Cambridge University Press.

Stager, L. E.
  1971 Climatic Conditions and Grain Storage in the Persian Period. *Harvard Theological Review* 64: 448–50.

Stewart, R. B., and Robertston, W., IV
  1973 Application of the Flotation Technique in Arid Areas. *Economic Botany* 27: 114–16.

Struever, S.
  1968 Flotation Techniques for the Recovery of Small Scale Archeological Remains. *American Antiquity*. 33: 353–62.

Wright, H. E., McAndrews, J. H., and Van Zeist, W.
  1967 Modern Pollen Rain in Western Iran and Its Relation to Plant Geography and Quaternary Vegetational History. *Journal of Ecology* 55: 415–33.

Chapter XII

AN ISRAELITE BULLA FROM TELL EL-HESI

by
Kevin G. O'Connell, S. J.
Le Moyne College

Reprinted from
Israel Exploration Journal
Volume 27 (1977), pp. 197-99 and pl. 26: G-H.

The first piece of Israelite epigraphic material found by the Joint Archaeological Expedition to Tell el-Hesi in five seasons of digging came to light in the sifting of dirt from an Iron Age II surface in Field One (I.11.313).[1] The small lump of charred, black clay, approximately 15 × 14 × 3-5 mm., bears the well-preserved impression of an ovoid seal with a two-line border (fig. 2). Part of the border is missing on the right edge and along the left lower edge of the impression, and a small piece is broken off at the lower left corner. The lump of clay is a bulla, used to seal a document, since on the reverse there is a clear impression of the strings that bound the document (fig. 3). The line of the strings ran perpendicular to the direction of the impression on the front. The complete impression would have measured 14 × 12 mm.

There are two lines of writing within the border, separated by three parallel lines across the centre. One- and two-line dividers are not uncommon on Hebrew seals, but a three-line divider is rare.[2] The script is clearly incised in a good hand dating from the seventh (or perhaps late eighth) to the early sixth century BCE (fig. 1). The top line reads *lmtnyhw*, "belonging to Mattanyahu," while the second line has *yšmᶜ'l*, "[son of] Ishmael." The last two letters are partly broken off, but enough remains to make the reading certain.

The form of the letters is regular for seals and bullae from the period. There is a break obscuring the *alef*, but it appears that the vertical stroke does not extend above the upper cross-stroke. If this is so, then the letter deviates a little from the form known in the Siloam inscription and in many seals. The *yod-he-waw* ligature has a very good parallel in the seal of *ḥlqyhw* recently published by Avigad.[3] There are also examples of the shorter *he-waw* ligature.[4] The slight angle of the lower stroke of the *he*, if it is correctly drawn, may perhaps suggest a later date (in the early sixth century) for the script.[5] The second *lamed* is only partially preserved, but the surviving upper line has the same angle and relative height as the fine initial *lamed* in the top register (not clearly visible in the photograph). The two examples of *mem* and the one *nun* have a well-rounded tail at the lower end of the upright stroke. In the head of the *nun*, the left-hand vertical stroke drops slightly lower than the left end of the horizontal stroke. There is a good parallel in bulla no. 1 of the Lachish cache.[6] The *'ayin* and *taw* need no special comment, but the *shin* has a somewhat unusual feature. The right-hand downward stroke, angled towards the left, extends much farther than usual. The next stroke, turning upward to the left, begins from the halfway point of the first stroke, rather than from the bottom of that stroke, as is common. A somewhat similar *shin* is found in Diringer's collection.[7]

Another may be in Reifenberg's volume, although the photograph is not satisfactory.[8] Better parallels occur in two of the three *'lyšb* seals from Arad published by Aharoni.[9]

The names Mattanyahu (Mattaniah) and Ishmael are both familiar from the Hebrew Bible. They occur most often in late pre-exilic and early post-exilic sources. Mattaniah is the original name of the last king of Judah (2 Kings 24:17), and all other occurrences are in Chronicles, Ezra, and Nehemiah.[10] Ishmael is the name of Abraham's eldest son (Gen. 17:23), of course, but otherwise the name is attested for Gedaliah's assassin (2 Kings 25: 23–25; Jer. 40–41), for several entries in the Chronicler's lists, and once in Ezra.[11] The name *mtnyhw* occurs in the first Lachish ostracon (I.5)[12] and on a Hebrew seal found in the excavations in 1968–69 in the courtyard of the Citadel of Jerusalem.[13] It may also appear on a bulla reproduced by Moscati.[14] Both names were, therefore, in use during the period indicated by the script and by the archaeological context.[15]

Fig. 2. Seal impression on front.

Fig. 3. Marks of string on back.

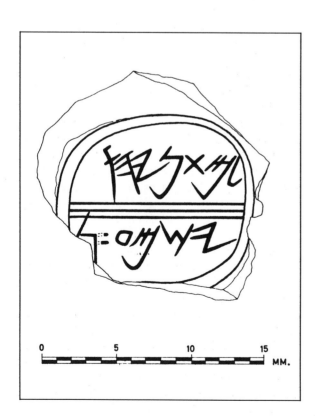

Fig. 1. The bulla (Drawing by B. Zoughbi).

NOTES

1. Locus I. 11.313 is an isolated portion of earth surface, cut off all around by later Persian and Hellenistic pits. It is to be dated either to Stratum VI (just after a major destruction, presumably by the Babylonians) or to Substratum VIIa (prior to the destruction and, hence, probably mid- or late seventh century BCE).

2. There is an example in S. Moscati: *L'Epigraphia Ebraica Antica, 1935–1950*, Rome, 1951, pl. XIV, no. 8. The seal is dated to the eighth-seventh centuries BCE (G.R. Driver: A New Israelite Seal, *PEQ* 77 [1945], p. 5). It contains the sequence *nyhw* written in a form very similar to that found on the present bulla.

3. N. Avigad. New Names on Hebrew Seals, *Eretz-Israel* 12 (1975), pp. 66–71, pl. 14 (Hebrew). The seal in question is no. 2. See also the example cited in note 2, above.

4. E.g., N. Avigad: A Group of Hebrew Seals, *Eretz-Israel* 9 (1969), pp. 1–9, pls. 1–2 (Hebrew). The example is in seal no. 6 on pl. 1.

5. Private communication from F. M. Cross, Jr. When the drawing of the impression was made in the field, the draftsman and I carefully examined the lower stroke of the *he*, and we judged that the slight angle was correctly drawn. It does not appear so pronounced in the photograph, however. If the latter is more exact, Prof. Cross would accept a late seventh or early sixth century date for the *he*.

6. Y. Aharoni: Trial Excavation in the 'Solar Shrine' at Lachish: Preliminary Report, *IEJ* 18 (1968), pp. 165–68, pl. 11. Another good parallel is mentioned above in note 2.

7. D. Diringer: *Le Iscrizioni Antico-Ebraiche Palestinesi*, Florence, 1934, pl. XX, no. 13.

8. A. Reifenberg: *Ancient Hebrew Seals*, London, 1950, p. 33, no. 14. The photograph is printed upside down.

9. Y. Aharoni: Seals of Royal Functionaries from Arad, *Eretz-Israel* 8 (1967), pp. 101–103, pl. 13, nos. 3–4, 5–6 (Hebrew). The photograph of no. 5 is printed upside down.

10. 1 Chron. 9:15 = Neh. 11:17; 1 Chron. 25:4, 16; 2 Chron. 20:14; 29:13; Ezra 10:26, 27, 30, 37; Neh. 11:22, 12:8, 25, 35; 13:13.

11. 1 Chron. 8:38; 2 Chron. 19:11; 23:1; Ezra 10:22.

12. H. Torcziner *et al.*: *Lachish*, I: *The Lachish Letters*, London, 1938, pp. 20–23, 27. I am grateful to M.D. Coogan for calling this to my attention.

13. The seal was found in the fill of a Stratum IV (Herodian) pit, along with many "sherds ranging from Iron IIC to the Herodian period"—Ruth Amiran and A. Eitan: Excavations in the Courtyard of the Citadel, Jerusalem, 1968–1969 (Preliminary Report), *IEJ* 20 (1970), p. 13, pl. 8:C. The published photograph of the seal and its impression shows a script from the seventh or sixth century BCE.

14. Moscati, *op. cit.* (above, note 2), pp. 81–82 (no. 31), pl. 18, no. 10.

15. The fact that Ishmael, the assassin of Gedaliah, was the son of Nethaniah, himself the son of Elishama (Jer. 41:1), raises interesting speculations. Nethaniah is built on the same verbal and nominal roots as Mattanyahu, and Elishama is similarly related to Ishmael. Paponomy, or the naming of grandson for grandfather, was a common practice, and the family of the assassin Ishmael practiced it in a slightly modified fashion (using Ishmael to reflect Elishama). Is it possible that Mattanyahu the son of Ishmael belongs to the same family? He might be Nethaniah (if the alternate forms were interchangeable) or the father of Elishama. It is even possible that he was the son of the assassin Ishmael, although this is the least likely alternative. These identifications remain speculative, of course, but are no less intriguing for all that. This suggestion was first made to a member of the Hesi staff by E. Stern on a visit to the site shortly after the bulla had been found. M. D. Coogan has drawn my attention to a related practice, the use of the same root in the names of father and son; see his brief discussion in *West Semitic Personal Names in the Murasû Documents*, Missoula, 1976, pp. 121–22 and note 4 on p. 127.

CONCLUSION

by
Kevin G. O'Connell, S. J.
Le Moyne College

The reader who has persevered to the end of this volume will have learned much about Tell el-Hesi and the first four seasons of the current excavations there. We hope that the foregoing discussions have stimulated you to learn more about the Hesi project from other volumes in the Hesi series and from the preliminary publications and other studies mentioned in various chapters or listed in the extensive bibliography that concludes this volume. More than that, we hope that those who have participated in the Hesi expedition or in other excavations will have a better appreciation of their experience and that those who have never taken part in an archaeological project will be encouraged to do so when the occasion presents itself.

The Hesi staff is now devoting its resources and energies to the final publication of Phase Two (1977–83) at the site, but we look forward to the eventual start of Phase Three there as well. Then we hope to complete our section through the acropolis in Fields I and III and to arrive at a better understanding of the EB III city through a more extended exploration of the domestic architecture associated with the city wall in Fields V and VI. Perhaps some of you will be with us in the field then, while others will be supporting us in other ways, as we endeavor to make a further contribution to the understanding of peoples and cultures in the ancient Near East. Whatever your participation, it will be most welcome!

BIBLIOGRAPHY OF PUBLICATIONS CONCERNING TELL EL-HESI

Compiled by
Jeffrey A. Blakely
The University of Pennsylvania

The following bibliography lists articles and books that concern Tell el-Hesi known by the compiler to have been published prior to 31 December 1982. It also includes reports on Hesi known to be in press by that time and selected later items. The bibliography is divided into three sections. The first contains references to Hesi that predate excavation there. The second lists primary publications reporting on some aspect of the archaeological investigation of Hesi. The third lists special studies and general works that contain useful reference to Hesi but do not confine themselves to that site. Only those references are cited for which more than a passing note to Tell el-Hesi is made. Encyclopedia references have been kept to a minimum. Works included in the bibliography are for the most part accessible at libraries where archaeological collections are housed, with the exception of the two articles written by Professor Archibald H. Sayce that were published in *The Sunday School Times*. The first, "Mr. Petrie's Excavation in the South of Judah," appeared on 6 September 1890 and is reprinted as Appendix A to the bibliography. The second, "The Latest Discovery in Palestine," appeared on 27 August 1892 and is reprinted as Appendix B.

The compiler wishes to thank Roger W. Anderson, Jr.; Bruce T. Dahlberg; J. Kenneth Eakins; Kevin G. O'Connell, S. J.; James F. Ross; and Miriam D. Ross for their comments, corrections, and additions during the compilation of the bibliography. Special thanks are due Eleaner L. Blakely for locating the aforementioned copies of *The*

Sunday School Times at the Wisconsin State Historical Society in Madison.

Any errors or omissions are fully the responsibility of the compiler.

[Abbreviation: *PEFQS* = *Palestine Exploration Fund Quarterly Statement*]

A. PRE-EXCAVATION SOURCES RELATING TO TELL EL-HESI

Abel, F. M.
    1933   *Géographie de la Palestine.* Vol. I. Paris: Librairie Lecoffre, J. Gabalda et cie.
Beha ed-Din, Ibn Shaddad (Yusuf Ibn Rafi)
    1897   *The Life of Saladin* [ca.1193]. Translated from the French translation of the 1787 Leiden [Schultens] edition, by C. W. Wilson and C. R. Conder. Library of the Palestine Pilgrim Text Society 32. London: Palestine Exploration Fund.
Clermont-Ganneau, C. S.
    1888   *Recueil d'archéologie orientale.* Vol. I. Paris: Ernest Leroux.
Conder, C. R., and Kitchener, H. H.
    1884   *The Survey of Western Palestine.* Vol. 3: *Judaea.* London: Palestine Exploration Fund.
Fabri, F.
    1892,   *The Wanderings of Brother Felix Fabri to*
    1893   *the Holy Land* [ca. A.D. 1480, 1483]. Translated by A. Stewart (The Library

of the Palestine Pilgrims' Text Society, Vols. VII-X). London: Palestine Pilgrims' Text Society.

Guérin, H. V.
1869 *Description géographique, historique, et archéologique de la Palestine*. Vols. 2–3: *Judaea*. Paris: Imprimé par autorisation de l'empereur a l'Impr. imperiale.

Ritter, K.
1866 *The Comparative Geography of Palestine and the Sinaitic Peninsula*. Translated by W. L. Gage. New York: D. Appleton & Co.

Robinson, E.
1841 *Biblical Researches in Palestine, Mount Sinai, and Arabia Petraea*. 3 vols. London: John Murray; Boston: Crocker and Brewster. Reprinted at Salem, NH: Ayer Company, 1977.
1856 *Idem*. Second edition, with new maps and plans.
1867 *Idem*. Third edition, with new maps and plans.

Volney, C.-F. C., comte de
1787 *Voyage en Syrie et en Égypt pendant les années 1783, 1784 et 1785*. Vol. II. Paris: Desenne (English translation: *Travels through Syria and Egypt in the Years 1783, 1784, 1785*. New York: Evert Duykinck, 1798).

Wilken, F.
1826 *Geschichte der Kreuzzüge nach morgenländische und abendländischen Berichten*. Vol. IV. Leipzig: F. C. W. Vogel.

B. PRIMARY ARCHAEOLOGICAL PUBLICATIONS RELATED TO EXCAVATION AT TELL EL-HESI

Amiran, R.
1970 Hesi, Tel. *Encyclopedia of Archaeological Excavations in the Holy Land*. Jerusalem: Israel Exploration Society and Massada, Ltd. (Hebrew). Vol. I, pp. 584-86.

Amiran, R., and Worrell, J. E.
1976 Hesi, Tel. *Encyclopedia of Archaeological Excavations in the Holy Land*. London: Oxford University Press; Englewood Cliffs, NJ: Prentice-Hall. Vol. II, pp. 514-20.

Bennett, M., and Bennett, W. J., Jr.
1976 The Material Culture Registry at Tell el-Hesi. *Journal of Field Archaeology* 3: 97-101.

Bennett, W. J., Jr.
1974 The Field Recording of Ceramic Data. *Journal of Field Archaeology* 1: 209–14.

Bennett, W. J., Jr., and Blakely, J. A.
1989 *Tell el-Hesi: The Persian Period (Stratum V)*. Edited by K. G. O'Connell, S.J., with F. L. Horton, Jr. Excavation Reports of the American Schools of Oriental Research: Tell el-Hesi 3. Winona Lake, IN: Eisenbrauns.

Betlyon, J. W.
1982 The Joint Archaeological Expedition to Tell el-Hesi, 1981. *Biblical Archeologist* 45:124–26.
1986 Coins Excavated between 1970 and 1983 at Tell el-Hesi. *Palestine Exploration Quarterly* 118: 66–69.

Bieber, A. M., Jr.; Brooks, D. W.; Harbottle, G.; and Sayre, E. V.
1976 Compositional Groupings of Some Ancient Aegean and Eastern Mediterranean Pottery. In *Applicazione dei metodi nucleari nel campo delle opere d'arte. Congresso internazionale, Roma-Venezia 24–29 Maggio 1973*, pp. 111–43. Roma: Accademia Nazionale dei Lincei.

Blakely, J. A., and Toombs, L. E.
1980 *The Tell el-Hesi Field Manual*. Edited by K. G. O'Connell, S.J. Excavation Reports of the American Schools of Oriental Research: Tell el-Hesi 1. Cambridge, MA; 2nd printing (1983), Philadelphia, PA: American Schools of Oriental Research.

Bliss, F. J.
1891a Reports from Mr. F. J. Bliss. *PEFQS* 23: 97–98.
1891b Reports from Mr. F. J. Bliss. *PEFQS* 23: 207–11.
1891c Report of Excavations at Tell-el-Hesy during the Spring of 1891. *PEFQS* 23: 282-90.
1891d Excavating from its Picturesque Side. *PEFQS* 23: 291–98.
1892a Notes from Tell el Hesy. *PEFQS* 24: 36–38.
1892b Report of the Excavations at Tell el Hesy for the Autumn Season of the Year 1891. *PEFQS* 24: 95–113.
1892c Notes from Tell el Hesy. *PEFQS* 24: 192–96.

1893a   Report of the Excavations at Tell-el-Hesy, during the Spring Season of the Year 1892. *PEFQS* 25: 9–20.

1893b   Report of the Excavations at Tell el Hesy during the Autumn of 1892. *PEFQS* 25: 103–19.

1894a   *A Mound of Many Cities or Tell el Hesy Excavated.* London: Palestine Exploration Fund; New York: Macmillan.

1894b   Palestine Exploration Fund Quarterly Statement. *Revue Biblique* 3,3: 306–7.

Bliss, F. J., and Macalister, R. A. S.
1902   *Excavations in Palestine During the Years 1898–1900.* London: Palestine Exploration Fund.

Brooks, D. W.
1975   *Persian Period Relationships of Tell el-Hesi as Indicated by Neutron Activation Analysis of Its Imported Ceramics: Implications for Archaeological and Biblical Research.* Hartford, CT: The Hartford Seminary Foundation. Unpublished Ph.D. dissertation.

Brooks, D. W.; Bieber, A. M., Jr.; Harbottle, G.; and Sayre, E. V.
1974   Biblical Studies through Neutron Activation Analysis of Ancient Pottery. In *Archaeological Chemistry*, pp. 48–80. Edited by C. W. Beck. Advances in Chemistry 138. Washington: American Chemical Society.

Budd, D. A.
1976   Pliocene-Pleistocene Sediments of the Southern Coastal Plain of Israel near Tel Hesi. Wooster, OH: College of Wooster. Senior Independent Study.

Coogan, M. D.
1975   A Cemetery from the Persian Period at Tell el-Hesi. *Bulletin of the American Schools of Oriental Research* 220: 37–46. Reprinted in Dahlberg and O'Connell 1989, pp. 177–87.

1989a   Field II. In *Tell el-Hesi: The Site and the Expedition*, pp. 163–68. Edited by B. T. Dahlberg and K. G. O'Connell, S.J. Excavation Reports of the American Schools of Oriental Research: Tell el-Hesi 4. Winona Lake, IN: Eisenbrauns.

1989b   Chalcolithic Remains in Field III. In *Tell el-Hesi: The Site and the Expedition*, pp. 169–76. Edited by B. T. Dahlberg and K. G. O'Connell, S.J. Excavation Reports of the American Schools of Oriental Research: Tell el-Hesi 4. Winona Lake, IN: Eisenbrauns.

Dahlberg, B. T., and O'Connell, K. G., S.J., eds.
1989   *Tell el-Hesi: The Site and the Expedition.* Excavation Reports of the American Schools of Oriental Research: Tell el-Hesi 4. Winona Lake, IN: Eisenbrauns.

Doermann, R. W., and Fargo, V. M.
1985   Tell el-Hesi, 1983. Palestine Exploration Quarterly 117: 1–24.

Fargo, V. M.
1979   Early Bronze Age Pottery at Tell el-Hesi. *Bulletin of the American Schools of Oriental Research.* 236: 23–40.

Fargo, V. M., and O'Connell, K. G., S.J.
1978   Five Seasons of Excavation at Tell el-Hesi (1970–1977). *Biblical Archeologist* 41: 165–82.

Frank, H. T., and Horton, F. L., Jr.
1989   The Volunteer and Educational Program: 1970–1975. In *Tell el-Hesi: The Site and the Expedition*, pp. 88–96. Edited by B. T. Dahlberg and K. G. O'Connell, S. J. Excavation Reports of the American Schools of Oriental Research: Tell el-Hesi 4. Winona Lake, IN: Eisenbrauns.

Hammond, W. M.
1977   *The Raw and the Chipped: An Analysis of Correlations Between Raw Material Tools of a Lithic Industry from Tell el-Hesi, Israel.* New York: Columbia University. Unpublished Ph.D. dissertation.

Havholm, K. G.
1976   Geologic Study of an Archaeological Site at Tel el-Hesi, Israel. Wooster, OH: College of Wooster. Senior Independent Study.

King, K. E.
1975   *Aegean Ware from Tell el-Hesi: The First Three Seasons.* Los Angeles: University of California at Los Angeles. Unpublished M.A. thesis.

Koucky, F. L.
1989   The Present and Past Physical Environment of Tell el-Hesi, Israel. In *Tell el-Hesi: The Site and the Expedition*, pp. 5–36. Edited by B. T. Dahlberg and K. G. O'Connell, S.J. Excavation Reports of the American Schools of Oriental Research: Tell el-Hesi 4. Winona Lake, IN: Eisenbrauns.

Lamdan, M.; Tsippor, D.; Huster, Y.; and Ronen, A.
1977   *A Prehistoric Archaeological Survey in Naḥal Shiqma*. Regional Council of Sha-ar Ha-Negev (Hebrew).

Matthers, J. M.
1974   *A Reassessment of the Early Bronze Age Material Excavated at Tell Hesy, 1890–1892*. London: University of London. Unpublished M.A. thesis.
1975   An Inscribed Sherd from the Palestine Exploration Fund. *Palestine Exploration Quarterly* 107: 151–53.
1989   Excavations by the Palestine Exploration Fund at Tell el-Hesi, 1890–92. In *Tell el-Hesi: The Site and the Expedition*, pp. 37–67. Edited by B. T. Dahlberg and K. G. O'Connell, S. J. Excavation Reports of the American Schools of Oriental Research: Tell el-Hesi 4. Winona Lake, IN: Eisenbrauns.

O'Connell, K. G., S.J.
1977   An Israelite Bulla from Tell el-Hesi. *Israel Exploration Journal* 27: 197–99. Reprinted in Dahlberg and O'Connell 1989, pp. 195–97 (which see, above).

O'Connell, K. G., S. J., and Rose, D. G.
1979   *Report of the Joint Expedition to Tell el-Hesi for the Department of Antiquities of Israel: Season of 1979*. Typescript.
1980a   Tell el-Hesi, 1979. *Biblical Archeologist* 43: 254–56.
1980b   Tell el-Hesi, 1979. *Israel Exploration Journal* 30: 221–23.
1980c   Tell el-Hesi, 1979. *Palestine Exploration Quarterly* 112: 73–91.

O'Connell, K. G., S. J.; Rose, D. G.; and Toombs, L. E.
1977a   *Report of the Joint Expedition to Tell el-Hesi for the Department of Antiquities of Israel: Season of 1977*. Typescript.
1977b   Tell el-Hesi, 1977. *Hadashot Arkheologiyot* 63: 54–55 (Hebrew).
1977c   Tell el-Hesi, 1977. *Israel Exploration Journal* 27: 246–50.
1978a   Tell el-Hesi, 1977. *Palestine Exploration Quarterly* 110: 75–90.
1978b   Tell el-Hesi (1977). *Revue Biblique* 85: 84–89.

Palestine Exploration Fund
1890a   Notes and News. *PEFQS* 22: 59.
1890b   Annual Meeting. *PEFQS* 22: 141–44.

Petrie, W. M. F.
1890a   Mr. Petrie's Egyptian Exhibition. *Illus-trated London News* (London), September 20: 370–71.
1890b   Palestine Exploration Discoveries. *Illustrated London News* (London), September 27: 405–6.
1890c   Summary of the Excavations [included in minutes of the annual meeting of the Palestine Exploration Fund]. *PEFQS* 22: 141–44, 150–56.
1890d   Explorations in Palestine. *PEFQS* 22: 159–66.
1890e   Journals of Mr. W. M. Flinders Petrie. *PEFQS* 22: 219–46.
1890f   Archaeological News: Lachish—Flinders Petrie's Excavations. *American Journal of Archaeology* 6: 335–40 [excerpts portions of Petrie 1890c and 1890d, above].
n.d.   Journals. Unpublished portions archived in the Griffith Institute of the Ashmolean Museum, Oxford.
1891   *Tell el Hesy (Lachish)*. London: Palestine Exploration Fund.
1892a   Notes on the Results at Tell el Hesy. *PEFQS* 24:114–15.
1892b   The Story of a Tell. In *The City and the Land*, pp. 183–207. London: Palestine Exploration Fund.

Pilcher, E. J.
1921   Philistine Coin from Lachish. *PEFQS* 53: 134–41.

Rose, D. G.
1975   Tell el-Hesi. *Newsletter Nos. 3–4 (October–November 1975) of the American Schools of Oriental Research*: 5–7.
1976   Eglon (City). 2. Tell el-Hesi? In *The Interpreter's Dictionary of the Bible Supplementary Volume*, pp. 252–53. Nashville: Abingdon Press.
1977   The 1977 Season at Tell el-Hesi. *Newsletter No. 3 (November 1977) of the American Schools of Oriental Research*: 4–5.
1989   The Methodology of the New Archaeology and Its Influence on the Joint Expedition to Tell el-Hesi. In *Tell el-Hesi: The Site and the Expedition*, pp. 72–87. Edited by B. T. Dahlberg and K. G. O'Connell, S. J. Excavation Reports of the American Schools of Oriental Research: Tell el-Hesi 4. Winona Lake, IN: Eisenbrauns.

Rose, D. G., and Toombs, L. E.
1975a   *Report of the Joint Expedition to Tell el-*

Hesi for the Department of Antiquities of Israel: Season of 1975. Typescript.

1975b Tell el-Hesi, 1975. *Israel Exploration Journal* 25: 172–74.

1976a Tell el-Hesi, 1973 and 1975. *Palestine Exploration Quarterly* 108: 41–54.

1976b Tell el-Hesi, *Hadashot Arkheologiyot* 56: 36 (Hebrew).

Rose, D. G.; Toombs, L. E.; and O'Connell, K. G., S. J.

1978 Four Seasons of Excavation at Tell el-Hesi: A Preliminary Report. In *Preliminary Excavation Reports: Bâb edh-Dhrâ', Sardis, Meiron, Tell el-Hesi, Carthage (Punic)*. Edited by David N. Freedman. Annual of the American Schools of Oriental Research 43, pp. 109–49. Cambridge, MA: American Schools of Oriental Research.

Rosen, S. A.

1982 *Lithics in the Bronze Ages in Israel*. Chicago: University of Chicago. Unpublished Ph.D. dissertation.

Ross, J. F.

1979 Early Bronze Age Structures at Tell el-Hesi. *Bulletin of the American Schools of Oriental Research* 236: 11–21.

Sayce, A. H.

1893 The Cuneiform and Other Inscriptions Found at Lachish and Elsewhere in the South of Palestine. *PEFQS* 25: 25–32.

Stager, L. E.

1971 Climatic Conditions and Grain Storage in the Persian Period. *Biblical Archaeologist* 34: 86–88.

Stewart, R. B.

1978 Archeobotanic Studies at Tell el-Hesi. *Economic Botany* 32: 379–86. Reprinted in Dahlberg and O'Connell 1989 (which see, above).

Stewart, R. B., and Robertson, W., IV.

1973 Applications of the Flotation Technique in Arid Areas. *Economic Botany* 27: 114–16.

Toombs, L. E.

1970a *Report of the Joint Expedition to Tell el-Hesi for the Department of Antiquities of Israel: Season of 1970*. Typescript.

1970b Tell el-Hesi. *Hadashot Arkheologiyot* 36: 19–20 (Hebrew).

1971a *Report of the Joint Expedition to Tell el-Hesi for the Department of Antiquities of Israel: Season of 1971*. Typescript.

1971b Tell el-Hesi. *Hadashot Arkheologiyot* 40: 16–17 (Hebrew).

1971c Tell el-Hesi. *Israel Exploration Journal* 21: 177–78.

1971d Coding Pottery in the Field. In N. E. Wagner, *Coding and Clustering Pottery by Computer*, pp. 25–28. Waterloo, Ontario: Waterloo Lutheran University Press (now Wilfrid Laurier University Press).

1973 *Report of the Joint Expedition to Tell el-Hesi for the Department of Antiquities of Israel: Season of 1973*. Typescript.

1974a Tell el-Hesi, 1970–71. *Palestine Exploration Quarterly* 106: 19–31.

1974b Tell el-Hesi, *Hadashot Arkheologiyot* 48–49: 75–77 (Hebrew).

1982 Tell el-Hesi, 1981. *Israel Exploration Journal* 32: 67–69.

1983 Tell el-Hesi, 1981. *Palestine Exploration Quarterly* 115: 25–46.

1985 *Tell el-Hesi: Modern Military Trenching and Muslim Cemetery in Field I, Strata I–II*. Edited by K. G. O'Connell, S.J. Excavation Reports of the American Schools of Oriental Research: Tell el-Hesi 2. Waterloo, Ontario: Wilfrid Laurier University Press.

1989 The Stratigraphy of the Site. In *Tell el-Hesi: The Site and the Expedition*, pp. 125–62. Edited by B. T. Dahlberg and K. G. O'Connell, S. J. Excavation Reports of the American Schools of Oriental Research: Tell el-Hesi 4. Winona Lake, IN: Eisenbrauns.

Toombs, L. E., and Blakely, J. A.

1981 *Report of the Joint Expedition to Tell el-Hesi for the Department of Antiquities of Israel: Season of 1981*. Typescript.

Toombs, L. E., and Rose, D. G.

1976 Tell el-Hesi. *Revue Biblique* 83: 257–60.

Worrell, J. E.

1970a The Expedition to Tell el-Hesi: A New Joint Project. *Newsletter No. 8* (April 1970) of the American Schools of Oriental Research: 1–4.

1970b Tell el-Hesi: Mound of Many Surprises. *Newsletter Number 5* (December 1970) of the American Schools of Oriental Research: 1–4.

1974 Tell el-Hesi. *Israel Exploration Journal* 24: 139–41.

1975 Tell el-Hesi. *Revue Biblique* 82: 268–70.

1989   The Evolution of a Holistic Investigation: Phase One of the Joint Expedition to Tell el-Hesi. In *Tell el-Hesi: The Site and the Expedition*, pp. 68–71. Edited by B. T. Dahlberg and K. G. O'Connell, S.J. Excavation Reports of the American Schools of Oriental Research: Tell el-Hesi 4. Winona Lake, IN: Eisenbrauns.

Worrell, J. E., and Betlyon, J. W.
1989   Phase One at Tell el-Hesi: A Season-by-Season Account. In *Tell el-Hesi: The Site and the Expedition*, pp. 97–124. Edited by B. T. Dahlberg and K. G. O'Connell, S.J. Excavation Reports of the American Schools of Oriental Research: Tell el-Hesi 4. Winona Lake, IN: Eisenbrauns.

Worrell, J. E., and Toombs, L. E.
1971   Tell el-Hesi. *Israel Exploration Journal* 21: 232–33.
1972   Tell el-Hesi. *Revue Biblique* 79: 585–88.

C. SPECIAL STUDIES AND GENERAL WORKS HAVING USEFUL REFERENCE TO TELL EL-HESI

Albright, W. F.
1924   Researches of the School in Western Judaea. *Bulletin of the American Schools of Oriental Research* 15: 2–11.
1929   The American Excavations at Tell Beit Mirsim. *Zeitschrift für die alttestamentliche Wissenschaft* 47: 1–17.
1942   A Case of Lèse-Majesté in Pre-Israelite Lachish, with Some Remarks on the Israelite Conquest. *Bulletin of the American Schools of Oriental Research* 87: 32–38.

American Institute of Archaeology
1891a   Archaeological News: Tell-el-Hesy = Lachish (or Gath?)--Phoenician Inscription. *American Journal of Archaeology* 7: 129–30.
1891b   Archaeological News: New Excavations. *American Journal of Archaeology* 7: 130.
1893   Probable Excavations. *American Journal of Archaeology* 8: 615.

Anonymous.
1890a   Excavations at Tel-el-Hesy. *The Builder* (London), September 27: 243–45.
1890b   Mr. Flinders Petrie's Discoveries in Egypt. *The Builder* (London), October 4: 263–65.

Ben-Tor, A.
1978   *Cylinder Seals of Third-Millennium Palestine*. Bulletin of the American Schools of Oriental Research, Supplement Series, No. 22. Cambridge, MA: American Schools of Oriental Research.

Bennett, B. M.
1973   The Enviable Life. *Bulletin of the General Theological Seminary* 59: 8–15.

Birch, W. F.
1890   Notes on the Quarterly Statement, July, 1890. *PEFQS* 22: 329–30.

Blakely, J. A.
1981   *Judahite Refortification of the Lachish Frontier*. Waterloo, Ontario: Wilfrid Laurier University. Unpublished M.A. thesis.

Bliss, F. J.
1896   The Mounds of Palestine. In *Recent Research in Bible Lands: Its Progress and Results*, pp. 29–41. Edited by H. V. Hilprecht. Philadelphia: John D. Wattles.
1907   *The Development of Palestine Exploration*. Ely Lectures for 1903. New York: Charles Scribner's Sons.

Clermont-Ganneau, C. S.
1891   Notes on Hebrew and Jewish Inscriptions. *PEFQS* 23: 240.
1892   The Hebrew-Phoenician Inscription of Tell el Hesy. *PEFQS* 24: 126–28.
1896   *Archaeological Researches in Palestine During the Years 1873–74*. Vol. II. London: Committee of the Palestine Exploration Fund.

Cobern, C.
1890   The Work at Tell Hesy, as seen by an American visitor. *PEFQS* 22: 166–70.

Conder, C. R.
1891a   Chronology of Pottery. *PEFQS* 23: 69.
1891b   The Lachish Inscription. *PEFQS* 23: 70.
1891c   The Lachish Pillar. *PEFQS* 23: 71.
1891d   Note on the Lachish Cornice. *PEFQS* 23: 185.
1891e   The Lachish Inscription. *PEFQS* 23: 250–51.
1891f   The Lachish Text. *PEFQS* 23: 311.
1891g   The Lachish Ruins. *PEFQS* 23: 311.
1892a   Notes on Herr Schick's Report, Tell el Hesy Inscriptions, and Dinhabah. *PEFQS* 24: 46.
1892b   The Tell el Hesy Text. *PEFQS* 24: 203–4.

1893   *The Tell Amarna Tablets*. London: Palestine Exploration Fund.

1894   Notes on Tell el Hesy. *PEFQS* 26: 203–5.

Coogan, M. D.

1981   Harry Thomas Frank, In Memoriam, 1933–1980. *Biblical Archeologist* 44: 178.

Dever, W. G.

1980   Archeological Method in Israel: A Continuing Revolution. *Biblical Archeologist* 43: 40–48.

1981   Review of *The Tell el-Hesi Field Manual*, by J. A. Blakely and L. E. Toombs. *Bulletin of the American Schools of Oriental Research* 242: 87.

Doermann, R. W.

1972   Archaeological Excavations. *Lutheran Theological Seminary Bulletin*. Winter.

1973   LTS at Tell el-Hesi. *Lutheran Theological Seminary Bulletin*. Winter.

1979   Trinity Participation at Tell el-Hesi. *Trinity Te Deum*. October.

Drower, M. S.

1985   *Flinders Petrie: A Life in Archaeology*. London: Victor Gollancz.

Duncan, J. G.

1930   *Corpus of Dated Palestinian Pottery*. London: British School of Archaeology in Egypt.

Eakins, J. K.

1980   Human Osteology and Archeology. *Biblical Archeologist* 43: 89–96.

Eakins, J. K., ed.

1978ff. *Trowel and Patish* [Tell el-Hesi Newsletter] Vol. 1 ff. Mill Valley, CA: Golden Gate Baptist Theological Seminary.

Fargo, V. M.

1979   *Settlement in Southern Palestine During Early Bronze III*. Chicago: University of Chicago. Unpublished Ph.D. dissertation.

Fillieres, D.; Harbottle, G.; and Sayre, E. V.

1983   Neutron-Activation Study of Figurines, Pottery, and Workshop Materials from the Athenian Agora, Greece. *Journal of Field Archaeology* 10: 55–69.

Frank, H. T.

1975   *Discovering the Biblical World*. New York: Harper & Row. H. T. Frank, Principal advisor and editorial consultant. See *Reader's Digest*.

Frothingham, A. L., Jr.

1894   Review of *A Mound of Many Cities*, by F. J. Bliss. *American Journal of Archaeology*

9: 227–28.

Glaisher, J.

1892   Excavations in Palestine: To the Editor of the Times. *The Times* (London), July 1: 17. Reprinted in *American Journal of Archaeology* 8: 145–46.

Gressmann, H.

1926   *Altorientalische Texte und Bilder zum Alten Testament*. Berlin and Leipzig: Walter de Gruyter & Co.

Guy, P. L. O.

1931   *New Light from Armageddon. Second Provisional Report (1927–29) on the Excavations at Megiddo in Palestine*. Oriental Institute Communication #9. Chicago: The University of Chicago Press.

Helms, S. W.

1976   *Urban Fortifications of Palestine during the Third Millennium B.C.* London: London Institute of Archaeology. Unpublished Ph.D. dissertation.

1977   Early Bronze Fortification at Tell Dothan. *Levant* 9: 101–14.

Herzog, Z.

1975   The Storehouses. In *Beer-Sheba I*, pp. 23–30. Edited by, Y. Aharoni. Tel Aviv: Institute of Archaeology, Tel Aviv University.

Hilprecht, H. V.

1896   Old Babylonian Inscriptions Chiefly from Nippur. *Transactions of the American Philosophical Society* 18: 221–82.

Holland, T. A.

1975   *A Typological and Archaeological Study of Human and Animal Representations in the Plastic Art of Palestine during the Iron Age*. Oxford: University of Oxford. Unpublished Ph.D. dissertation.

1977   A Study of Palestinian Iron Age Baked Clay Figurines, with Special Reference to Jerusalem: Cave I. *Levant* 9: 121–55.

Iliffe, J. H.

1932   Pre-Hellenistic Greek Pottery in Palestine. *Quarterly of the Department of Antiquities of Palestine* 2: 15–26.

Jankey, T.

1978   The Tell el-Hesi Dig. *Orbit Magazine: The Sunday Oklahoman*, February 12: 10–11.

Kenyon, K. M.

1955   A Crescentic Axehead from Jericho and a Group of Weapons from Tell el-Hesi.

Eleventh Annual Report of the Institute of Archaeology, University of London: 10–18.

1979   *Archaeology in the Holy Land,* 4th edition. New York: W. W. Norton and Co. Inc.

King, P. J.

1979   Through the Ancient Near East with ASOR. *The Bible Today* 103: 2113–20.

1983   *American Archaeology in the Mideast: A History of the American Schools of Oriental Research.* Philadelphia: The American Schools of Oriental Research.

Knudtzon, J. A.

1907–14   *Die el-Amarna-tafeln.* 3 Vols. Leipzig: J. C. Hinrichs. Reprinted as *Die el-Amarna-tafeln, mit Einleitung und Erläuterungen.* Aalen: O. Zeller, 1964.

Lagrange, M.-J.

1894   Chronique. *Revue Biblique* 3: 446–49.

Landay, J. M.

1971   *Silent Cities, Sacred Stones: Archaeological Discovery in Israel.* New York: McCall Books.

Luker, M.

1975   Exploring Ancient Garbage . . . for College Credit. *Emory and Henry Alumnus* 25: 10–12.

May, H. G., ed.

1984   *Oxford Bible Atlas.* 3rd edition. London: Oxford University Press.

Mercer, S. A. B.

1939   *The Tell el-Amarna Tablets.* 2 Vols. Toronto: MacMillan Co. of Canada.

Negev, A., ed.

1972   *Archaeological Encyclopedia of the Holy Land.* New York: G. P. Putnam's Sons.

Neubauer, A.

1891   The Lachish Inscription. *PEFQS* 23: 310.

Newman, T. D.

1969   A Visit to the Jerusalem School–Summer, 1969. *Newsletter Number 1* (August 26, 1969) of the American Schools of Oriental Research: 1–6.

O'Connell, K. G., S.J.

1981   Obituary: Harry Thomas Frank, *Israel Exploration Journal* 31: 134.

1982a   Davis Glenn Rose, In Memoriam 1928–81. *Biblical Archeologist* 45: 54–55.

1982b   Obituary: Davis Glenn Rose. *Israel Exploration Journal* 32: 76.

Palestine Exploration Fund

1890   Notes and News. *PEFQS* 22: 133–34.

1891a   Notes and News. *PEFQS* 23: 3.

1891b   Notes and News. *PEFQS* 23: 88.

1892a   Notes and News. *PEFQS* 24: 1.

1892b   Notes and News. *PEFQS* 24: 175–77.

1892c   Notes and News. *PEFQS* 24: 262.

1892d   Annual Meeting. *PEFQS* 24: 272–82.

1893a   Notes and News. *PEFQS* 25: 93.

1893b   Notes and News. *PEFQS* 25: 181–82.

1893c   Annual Meeting. *PEFQS* 25: 269–81.

1894   Notes and News. *PEFQS* 26: 91–92.

1965   *World of the Bible Centenary Exhibition of the Palestine Exploration Fund in Co-operation with the British School of Archaeology in Jerusalem* [Souvenir Album]. London: Victoria & Albert Museum and Palestine Exploration Fund.

Peiser, F. E.

1899   Die Lachis-Tafel. *Orientalistische Litteratur-Zeitung* 2: 4–7.

Petrie, W. M. F.

1891   Chronology of Pottery. *PEFQS* 23: 68.

1923   *Egypt and Israel.* London: Society for Promoting Christian Knowledge; New York: E. S. Gorham.

1931   *Seventy Years in Archaeology.* London: Sampson & Co.; New York: Henry Holt (1932).

Pritchard, J. B.

1970   The Megiddo Stables: A Reassessment. In *Near Eastern Archaeology in the Twentieth Century,* pp. 268–76. Edited by J. A. Sanders: Garden City: Doubleday & Company.

Reader's Digest

1981   *Atlas of the Bible: An Illustrated Guide to the Holy Land.* Edited by J. L. Gardner, *et al.* Principal advisor and editorial consultant, H.T. Frank. Pleasantville, NY, and Montreal: The Reader's Digest Association, Inc.

Rose, D. G.

1974   Modern Archaeology. *Bethany Guide* 48: 12–15 (April).

1975a   Archaeology & Proof. *Bethany Guide* 49: 11–14 (March).

1975b   Archaeology & the Bible. *Bethany Guide* 49: 11–13 (April).

Rosen, S. A.

1982   Flint Sickle-blades of the Late Protohistoric and Early Historic Periods in Israel. *Tel Aviv* 9: 139–45.

Saunders, T.

1881   *An Introduction to the Survey of Western*

Palestine: Its Waterways, Plains, & Highlands . . . according to the Survey Conducted by Lieutenants Conder & Kitchner, R.E., for The Palestine Exploration Fund. London: Richard Bentley and Son.

Sayce, A. H.
1890a   Mr. Petrie's Excavation in the South of Judah. *The Sunday School Times* (Philadelphia) 32, No. 36 (September 6): 563 (reprinted below as Appendix A).
1890b   Excavations in Judaea. *Contemporary Review* 58: 427–34.
1891   The Lachish Inscription. *PEFQS* 23: 158–59.
1892   The Latest Discovery in Palestine. *The Sunday School Times* (Philadelphia) 34, No. 35 (August 27): 546–47 (reprinted below as Appendix B).
1893   Revue des Revues: Revue anglais de Palestine. *Revue Biblique* 2: 159.

Schaeffer, C. F. A.
1948   *Stratigraphie comparée et chronologie de l'Asie occidentale.* London: Oxford University Press for the Griffith Institute, Ashmolean Museum, Oxford.

Scheil, J. V., O.P.
1893   Une tablette Palestinienne cunéiform. *Recueil des Travaux Relatifs à la Philologie et l'Archéologie Égyptiennes et Assyriennes* 15: 137–38. Reprinted in *PEFQS* 26: 47.
1894   La tablette de Lachis. *Revue Biblique* 3: 433–36.

Silberman, N. A.
1982   *Digging for God and Country: Exploration, Archeology and the Secret Struggle for the Holy Land, 1799–1917.* New York: Alfred A. Knopf.

Stern, E.
1973   *Material Culture of the Land of the Bible in the Persian Period 538–332 B.C.* Jerusalem: Bialik Institute and the Israel Exploration Society (Hebrew). Revised English Edition, Warminster, England: Aris & Phillips Ltd., 1982.
1982   Achaemenid Clay Rhyta from Palestine. *Israel Exploration Journal* 32: 36–43.

Thiersch, H.
1908   Die Neueren Ausgrabungen in Palästina. *Revue Biblique* 17: 634–35.

Toombs, L. E.
1982   David [sic] Glenn Rose (1928–1981). *Newsletter Number 4* (January 1982) of the American Schools of Oriental Research: 1–3.

Trowel and Patish. See Eakins 1978ff.

Tubb, J. N.
1982   A Crescentic Axehead from Amarna (Syria) and an Examination of Similar Axeheads from the Near East. *Iraq* 44: 1–12.

Tufnell, O.
1965   Excavator's Progress: Letters of F. J. Bliss, 1889–1900. *Palestine Exploration Quarterly* 97: 112–27.
1969   The Pottery from the Royal Tombs I–III at Byblos. *Berytus: Archaeological Studies* 18: 5–33.

Vincent, H.
1906   Resumé des fouilles. *Revue Biblique* 15: 42–44.

Watkins, T.
1981   Review of *Preliminary Excavation Reports: Bâb edh-Dhrâ', Sardis, Meiron, Tell el-Hesi, Carthage (Punic).* Edited by D.N. Freedman. *Palestine Exploration Quarterly* 113: 132.

Watson, C. M.
1915   *Fifty Years' Work in the Holy Land: A Record and a Summary, 1865–1915.* London: Committee of the Palestine Exploration Fund.

Winckler, H.
1896   *Die Thontafeln von Tell-el-Amarna.* Keilinschriftliche Bibliothek Vol 5. Berlin: Reuther & Reichard.

Wright, G. E.
1971   A Problem of Ancient Topography: Lachish and Eglon. *Harvard Theological Review* 64: 437–50. Reprinted in *The Biblical Archaeologist* 34 (1971): 76–86.
1974   Annual Report to the Trustees, the Corporation, Members and Friends. *1973–74 Newsletter No. 9* (April 1974) of the American Schools of Oriental Research: 1–12.

Zink, J. H.
1966   Tell el-Hesy. In *The Biblical World.* Edited by C. F. Pfeiffer, pp. 566-69. Grand Rapids: Baker Book House.

APPENDIX A

[Reprinted from *The Sunday School Times* (Philadelphia)
Vol. 32, No. 36 (September 6, 1890): 563.]

MR. PETRIE'S EXCAVATION IN THE SOUTH OF JUDAH

by
Professor A. H. Sayce, LL.D.

At last the spade of the excavator has been driven into the sacred soil of Palestine, and a glimpse has been allowed us, not only into the age of the kings before the Babylonian exile, but even into the older period of the patriarchs which preceded the exodus. After ten years of patient importunity, the Palestine Exploration Fund has persuaded the Turkish Government to grant it permission to excavate in the Holy Land; and the Fund was fortunate enough to secure Mr. Flinders Petrie's services for beginning the work. In spite of Turkish obstruction, illness and bad weather, Mr. Petrie has succeeded, after only two or three weeks of digging, in achieving really marvelous results.

The scene of his excavations has been Tel el-Hesy, about three miles from Umm Lâqis, long supposed to represent the site of biblical Lachish. Umm Lâqis, however, turns out to have been nothing more then [sic] a small village not older than Roman times, and, though it undoubtedly is the Lachish of Jerome, the real Lachish of the Old Testament must be sought elsewhere. Mr. Petrie, in fact, has discovered it at Tel el-Hesy, the name of the ancient city having been transferred to a neighboring village after the return from the exile and the abandonment of the old site.

Tel el-Hesy takes its name from a spring which rises just below its walls. The spring is the only fountain of fresh water for miles around, and accounts, not only for the situation of Lachish, but also for its former importance. At a short distance from the Tel it is joined by a brackish brook, which flows from the adjacent but smaller Tel en-Nejîeh, in which we must now see the site of the original Eglon. The later Eglon of Roman days is at a little distance off, at Khurbet el-Ajlân.

Tel el-Hesy stands on a platform of rock, on which rises an artificial mound two hundred feet square and sixty feet high. The height is formed by the ruins of the towns that have risen, one over the other, upon the spot. At the top come relics of a Greek settlement, which is shown by its pottery to have been earlier than the time of Alexander the Great. The lowest, and therefore the oldest town, was encircled by a brick wall twenty-eight feet eight inches thick, which has been repaired more than once. As Mr. Petrie found black Phoenician pottery of a peculiar type, which has been shown by Egyptian exploration to be of the eleventh century B.C., above the ruins of the wall, it is evident that the city to which the wall belonged must have been the Amorite Lachish which was overthrown by Joshua (Josh. 10 : 32). The huge wall that surrounds it was one of those which caused the Amorite cities to be described as "great and walled up to heaven" (Deut. 1 : 28).

After the destruction of the Amorite fortress came a period of desolation, during which half-civilized nomads built their huts on the mound which covered the remains of the Canaanitish city.

The huts were rudely constructed of mud and rolled pebbles from the valley below, and we must see in them an illustration of the troubled period of the Judges.

With the establishment of the Israelitish monarchy, there arrived a new era of prosperity. A new city arose on the old site, and a new wall, thirteen feet in thickness, was built around it. Towers stood at its corners, one of which still remains. The wall underwent no less than four rebuildings, and possibly more. On the southern side the city was still further fortified, — Mr. Petrie thinks in Manasseh's reign. Here a wall twenty-five feet thick was built over a great *glacis* slope forty feet in height, formed with blocks of stone faced with plaster, and approached by a long flight of steps. The steps started from a building in the valley, the gateway of which is still standing.

The *glacis* slope consists of a layer of earth, ten feet deep, which overlies the ruins of a building eighty-five feet in length. The building itself stands on a bed of soil ten feet thick, beneath which is another large building, which has been burned with fire, but subsequently restored. The walls of the earlier building were of clay brick, the doorways being of fine white limestone. Many of the blocks belonging to it were used a second time when the building was reconstructed. On two or three of them are curious pilasters with volutes which resemble rams' horns. Mr. Petrie suggests that they reveal to us the shape of "the horns of the altar."

The most important fact disclosed by the stones of the earlier building, which is probably as old as the time of Solomon, is that, though drafted, they show no trace of the "claw-tool." Now the "claw-tool" was employed in Greece from the earliest times; and as it was not introduced into Egypt until after the contact of that country with Greece, we may consider it as of Greek invention and

unknown to the East before the age of the exile. At length, therefore, a criterion has been discovered for determining the age of the stone buildings met with in Palestine, and the controversy as to the age of the walls of the Harâm at Jerusalem is finally closed. Since from top to bottom they have been worked with the "claw-tool," we must conclude that they are altogether of Herodian date. On the other hand, the Râmet el-Khalîl near Hebron, in which some scholars have seen the site of Mamre, shows no traces of the tool; and we may accordingly assign it to the pre-exile epoch.

One of the chief results obtained by Mr. Petrie is a determination of the periods to which the various forms of pottery found in Palestine severally belong. We now know what kind of pottery is Amorite, what is early Israelite, what is early and what is late Jewish. The excavator will no longer have to choose his sites at haphazard. A glance at the pottery will henceforth assure him of the age to which a particular site belongs.

Mr. Petrie's excavations have further shown what a rich harvest awaits the scientific explorer in the Holy Land. There, as in Egypt or Assyria, the soil still holds in its bosom the inscriptions and other monuments which are yet to throw floods of light on Old Testament history. Among the Tel el-Amarna tablets are dispatches sent by the governor of Lachish to the Egyptian king in the century before the exodus. Lachish, therefore, must have possessed an archive-chamber, and there is no reason why the clay tablets of the archive-chamber should not yet be found. The short time at Mr. Petrie's disposal last spring prevented him from doing much more than trace the walls of the cities that rose successively on the site of Lachish. It remains for the future excavator to bring to light the monuments that lie buried within them.

Queen's College, Oxford.

APPENDIX B

[Reprinted from *The Sunday School Times* (Philadelphia)
Vol. 34, No. 35 (August 27, 1892): 436-47
Footnotes signed "The Editor"
are by the editor of *The Sunday School Times*.]

THE LATEST DISCOVERY IN PALESTINE

by
Professor A. H. Sayce, D.D., LL.D.

Some time ago I gave the readers of The Sunday School Times an account of the work that had been done in Southern Palestine for the Palestine Exploration Fund by that prince of living excavators, Dr. Flinders Petrie. He had commenced excavations at a lofty *tell* or mound called Tell el-Hesy; and although the time at his disposal had been short, he had succeeded not only in determining the name of the city of which the tell is the last record, but also in founding the science of Palestinian archaeology. He showed that Tell el-Hesy must represent the site of Lachish, one of the most important Jewish fortresses; and he further showed, by means of the pottery he had discovered in his Egyptian excavations, what seem to be the relative ages of the various strata of which the mound was composed.

As at Hissarlik or Troy, the several strata are the remains of the successive cities which rose one above the other on the same site. Each stratum or city was characterized by a particular kind of pottery, and one of the kinds Dr. Petrie had already met with in Egypt in situations where its date could be ascertained. He thus obtained a starting-point for fixing the approximate ages of the different strata of the tell, and for arranging them in chronological order. The lowest stratum, that on the top of which all the later towns had been built, went back to pre-Israelitish days, if his calculations were correct; and in the massive walls of brick by which

it was surrounded he accordingly saw a structure of the Amorite period.

If Tell el-Hesy were Lachish, and if the ruins at the bottom of the mounds were the relics of the Amorite city which had been stormed and taken by the Israelites, it followed that the ruins ought to contain monuments of the age which preceded the Israelitish invasion of Canaan. Now, it so happened that, when Dr. Petrie began his work at Tell el-Hesy, the cuneiform tablets found at Tell el-Amarna in Egypt, and now preserved in the museums of Gizeh and Berlin, had just been published. Among them were letters sent to the Egyptian Pharaohs, in the closing years of the eighteenth dynasty, by the vassal kings and governors of Southern Palestine. These letters give us a good deal of information about Lachish. Two of them, in fact, were written by governors of that city, one of whom was named Zimridi, or Zimrida, and the other Yabni-el. The latter name is substantially the same as the biblical Jabin.[1]

A letter from the king of Jerusalem informs us that Zimrida was murdered at Lachish by "the servants of the [Egyptian] king." It is therefore possible, if not probable, that Yabni-el was his successor. It is, however, with Zimrida, and not with Yabni-el, that we are at present engaged.

Dr. Petrie left Tell el-Hesy at the beginning of the summer of 1890, and did not return to it again. The committee of the Palestine Exploration Fund was therefore disinclined at first to continue the excavations there. I pleaded, however, on behalf of their continuance, and promised that, when the "Amorite" stratum was reached, cuneiform tablets would be found in it. The committee allowed itself to be persuaded; and Mr. Bliss, the son of the well-known principal of the American college at Beyrout, undertook to carry on the work of excavating.

My promise may seem to have been a rash one. But Dr. Petrie had made it clear that he had discovered the site of Lachish, and that considerable remains of the pre-Israelitish city still existed on the spot. Moreover, the letters sent to Egypt by the governors of Lachish showed that an official correspondence was kept up between them and the Egyptian court. There must therefore have been an archive-chamber in the palace of Lachish, in which that correspondence was preserved. As the letters were written upon imperishable clay, I felt confident that sooner or later they would be found. I had long believed that libraries of clay tablets, similar to those of Babylonia and Assyria, once existed in Palestine,—Kirjath-Sepher or "Booktown,"[2] for example, being one of the places where they were established; and the discovery of the Tell el-Amarna tablets raised my belief almost to a certainty. Hence my anxiety that the excavations begun at Lachish should not be allowed to lapse.

But for a long while the persevering labors of Mr. Bliss bore no fruit. A considerable amount of money and time was spent, with little or no result. The committee of the fund began to despair. But just at the last moment, when the work was being suspended for the summer season of 1892, and Mr. Bliss's health was demanding his instant return to Beyrout, the workmen found their way to the remains of the Amorite Lachish. First of all, Egyptian beads and scarabs and Babylonian seal-cylinders were disinterred, and then came the crowning discovery of all. Unfortunately, it came on the very morning when the workmen were being dismissed, and their tools stored away, and so afforded but a Pisgah glance into the promised land.

The scarabs and beads belong to the age of the eighteenth Egyptian dynasty; and on one of the beads is the name and royal title of Queen Teie, the wife of Amenophis III., and the mother of Amenophis IV., to whom most of the Tell el-Amarna correspondence is addressed. The discovery proves the correctness of Dr. Petrie's arrangement of the pottery found in the tell. Among the beads, it may be mentioned, are two of amber,

which testify to trade with the Baltic as far back as the century before the exodus.

Some of the cylinders came from Babylonia, and their style indicates that they belong to the period B.C. 2000–1500. One of them is of Egyptian porcelain, and must have been manufactured in Egypt in imitation of some Babylonian original, thus affording a fresh testimony to the intercourse which existed between the valleys of the Euphrates and the Nile. Others, again, are rude copies of Babylonian cylinders, many examples of which have already been found in the prehistoric tombs of Cyprus, as well as Phoenicia. Hitherto, it has been impossible to assign a date to them and the various objects with which they were associated; the discoveries at Lachish now tell us to which age they must be referred. The fact is a striking illustration of the way in which one archaeological discovery throws light on another, as well as of the closeness of the ties which bound together the nations of the ancient Oriental world.

I have said that the last morning of work at Tell el-Hesy was productive of a crowning discovery. A clay tablet covered with cuneiform characters was brought to light. As it was claimed by the Turkish government under the firman which permitted excavations to be made, casts only of it could be sent to England. The arrival of these casts I awaited with considerable anxiety. Cuneiform inscriptions on large slabs of stone have been forged, of recent years, in Palestine, and the telegram which announced the discovery of the tablet left me in doubt as to whether it might not be one of these slabs of stone. When the casts arrived, however, a glance at them was sufficient to dispel all doubts. Not only was the tablet like the larger part of the Tell el-Amarna tablets in size and shape, but the forms of the characters inscribed upon it resembled those of the Tell el-Amarna letters, which had been sent from Southern Palestine.

When I began to copy the text, I found that the grammar and formula were also those to which the correspondence of the kings and governors of Southern Palestine found in Egypt had already accustomed us. But this was not all. The name of Zimrida twice occurred in the text, thus proving that Dr. Petrie had been right in identifying Tell el-Hesy with the ancient Lachish.

No cast, however good, can be as clear as the original, and consequently there are one or two characters about which I am not certain. Moreover, some words occur in the letter, for such it is, the meaning of which I do not know. The following translation of the tablet, accordingly, is offered only tentatively, doubtful words being marked by a query: "[To] the governor Bal. . . , I. . . abi prostrate myself at thy feet. Verily thou knowest that Baya and Zimrida have *brought the spoil* [?] of the city; and Dan-Hadad says to Zimrida my father, The city of Yarami has sent to me [and has] given me 3 pieces of. . . wood and 3 slings and 3 falchions, since I am appointed over the country of the king; but it has acted against me; but unto my death do I remain. As regards thy *mul* which I have *brought* [?] from the enemy, I. . . , and I have dispatched Bel[?]-banilu; and. . . rabi-ilu-yu-ma[khir] has sent his brother to this country to [defend it]."

The city of Yarami may be the biblical Jarmuth, since the latter word is merely a plural of which Yarami would be singular.[3]

It is difficult at first to realize the full importance of the discovery which Mr. Bliss has made; but the romantic side of it cannot fail to strike everyone. The archaeological world has hardly as yet recovered from the astonishment caused by the discovery at Tell el-Amarna, in Upper Egypt, of cuneiform tablets which contain the correspondence carried on between Asia and Egypt more than three thousand years ago. Among them is a letter from a certain Zimrida, the governor of Lachish, in the south of Canaan. Scarcely have the letters been published and read, when excavations carried on in Southern Palestine, on a site ingeniously identified by Dr. Petrie with that of Lachish, bring to light a cuneiform tablet similar to those found in Egypt, and belonging to the same age. When it is copied and deciphered, it turns out to contain the name of the very Zimrida whose acquaintance we had just made. Since the days of Moses, the letter sent by Zimrida to the Pharaoh, and the letter which had been stored in the archive chamber of his own Canaanitish city, had been lying buried beneath the ground. But scarcely has the one been disinterred from its long resting-place, before the other also is discovered, and the two halves of a correspondence which was already past in the time of the exodus are again joined together.

The importance of the discovery is far reaching. It is clear that Mr. Bliss has at length made his way to the governor's palace in the Amorite city of Lachish, and is already at the entrance to its ancient archive chamber. The discovery of one tablet is a guarantee for the discovery of others. Doubtless the majority of them will be letters; but the analogy of the Tell el-Amarna collection leads us to believe that letters will not be the only form of literature which we shall find. The readers of The Sunday School Times have learned from Dr. Zimmern's article on "An Old Babylonian Legend from Egypt" that mythological texts were also included among the archives of the Egyptian Pharaohs; and the fact that one of the cities of southern Canaan was called Kirjath-Sepher indicates that the libraries of Canaan, like the libraries of Babylonia, were stocked with veritable books. Who knows what is in store for us, during the next few years, if only sufficient funds can be provided for carrying on the costly work of excavation? Histories of the patriarchs, records of Melchizedek and his dynasty, old hymns and religious legends, may be among the archaeological treasures that are about to be exhibited to the wondering eyes of the present generation. A few years ago such a possibility could not have been dreamed of by the wildest imagination; now it is not only a possibility, but even a probability. To dig up the sources of Genesis is a better occupation than to spin theories and dissect the scriptural narrative in the name of the "high criticism." A single blow of the excavator's pick has before now shattered the most ingenious conclusions of the Western critic; if the Palestine Exploration Fund is sufficiently supported by the public to enable it to continue the work it has begun, we doubt not that theory will soon be replaced by fact, and that the stories of the Old Testament which we are now being told are but myths and fictions will prove to be based on a solid foundation of truth.

University of Oxford.

NOTES

1. Professor Dr. Hilprecht regards these two names as substantially different,—*Yabni-el* meaning "God creates"; the biblical Jabin meaning "He [that is, the child] is intelligent." —The Editor.
2. While this interpretation of Kirjath-Sepher is the ordinary one, there are Semitic scholars who deem it an improbable, or indeed an impossible, one. —The Editor.
3. Professor Sayce apparently reads the Hebrew consonants as *Jarmôth* (plural), not, as commonly read, *Jarmûth* (singular). —The Editor.